THE
TEIGN VALLEY
LINE

THE
TEIGN VALLEY
LINE

PETER KAY

WILD SWAN PUBLICATIONS LTD.

ENTRANCE TO CHUDLEIGH.

CONTENTS

Continued overleaf

ISBN 1 874103 28 3

FOR
JIM SERCOMBE
A proper Teign Valley man

Designed by Paul Karau
Printed by Amadeus Press, Huddersfield

Published by
WILD SWAN PUBLICATIONS LIMITED
1-3 Hagbourne Road, Didcot, Oxon, OX11 8DP

CONTENTS *continued*

PREFACE AND ACKNOWLEDGEMENTS

An enormous amount of material is preserved from most of the 24 Parliamentary applications that brought the line to birth, and in order to make Chapters 1–11 readable it has been necessary to skate comparatively briefly over some of those aspects which did not in the outcome lead anywhere. Even so, this part of the book is inevitably complex and requires a higher-than-normal level of concentration from the reader! It might be noted that, in discussing the 1850s–60s period, the term 'narrow gauge' is used in the contemporary Devonian sense, i.e. 4ft 8½in. From Chapter 4 onwards, the term 'standard gauge' is used in lieu.

The book does not deal with those matters which are more properly a part of the history of the railways of the city of Exeter. Therefore the GWR's City Basin branch is only covered insofar as the Teign Valley branch is concerned, and the history of Alphington Road Goods Depot (and Exeter Cattle Market sidings) post-1905 is not covered. Similarly, events on the branch's Exeter stump post-1958 (the Marsh Barton sidings, and the second City Basin signal box) are excluded. Also, Heathfield is only dealt with insofar as the Teign Valley trains are concerned, and there is no discussion of the station's own goods traffics, or of the line between Heathfield and Newton Abbot which was at certain times used by Teign Valley trains but which is properly part of the Moretonhampstead branch.

Thirty-four years after the passenger closure, time has taken its toll of the line's former staff, and scattered most of those who are still with us to other corners of the county where they are only locatable with some detective work. 'Staff interviews' are always one of the most pleasant parts of researching a book of this kind, and my thanks are due to

Ossie Biddiscombe	Porter, Heathfield
Josie Bissett	Porter, Trusham 1943–4
Stan Dart	Signalman, Trusham 1944
Peter Davies	Signalman, Longdown 1958
Frank Edworthy	Signalman, Longdown 1944–9
Alf Haywood	Signalman, Longdown 1925–8, Christow 1928–36
Bob Legg	Travelling Shunter 1966–8
Dennis Luxton	Fireman 1944
Jim Sercombe	Porter, Chudleigh 1937–8, Ashton 1946–59
Alf Stonelake	Christow Permanent Way Gang 1952–8
John Court	Son of Fred Court, Signalman Trusham 1927–58
Cynthia Edworthy	Daughter of Wilf Cox, Signalman Christow 1922–c.1952
Freda Yandell	Wife of Bernard Yandell, Stationmaster Christow 1954–8

It might be noted that, as the branch's heyday was over by 1935, the account of its operation in its busy years is largely dependent on the recollections of Alf Haywood who was 91 at the time of the interview. Fortunately Alf has a better memory than anyone else I have ever interviewed. He was moved to liken the conversation to 'the Spanish Inquisition'. I do not suppose that, when he applied to join the GWR's service in May 1914, he ever suspected that his daily life would become the subject of such interest!

The valley's industrial past brought a need to seek out former mine and quarry workers and on this front I am grateful to Arthur Ball of Christow, formerly of Great Rock Mine; Ernie Beer of Dunsford, formerly of Bridford Barytes Mine; Leroy George of Newton Abbot, formerly of Bridford Barytes Mine; Peter Hughes, the present Manager of ARC's Trusham Quarry; Tubby Hodge of Teign Village, formerly of Great Rock Mine, Scatter Rock Quarry, and Crockham Quarry; and Janny Bradford of Teign Village, who started work as a farmer's boy in 1912, and accosted Mr Bathurst, the Manager of Crockham and Whetcombe Quarries, in the street in 1914 to ask him for a job. I found myself adopting the same technique as I had to walk through Janny's front door quite unexpected and accost him sitting there in his armchair!

Other local help was given by Mrs Margaret Howard, of W.S. Howard & Sons, Coal Merchants, Ashton; Mr E. Lee, Town Clerk of Chudleigh; and Mr and Mrs Smale of Christow, who started the trail which led me on to Frank & Cynthia Edworthy in Rockbeare, John Court in Stoke Canon, and finally to Freda Yandell in Saltash.

J.S. Yorke of Forthampton Court, Gloucester, sent me a very lengthy letter on the career of his grandfather V.W. Yorke, Chairman of the Exeter Railway 1904–23 (who would otherwise have been but a name). Lord Brabourne assisted me in obtaining the portrait of his grandfather C.M. Knatchbull-Hugessen, the previous Chairman of the Exeter Railway 1895–1904. Mrs E.A. Eden of Culver House provided information on, and the photographs of, Edward Byrom who had much influence on the Exeter Railway's construction. C.J. Schmitz of the University of St Andrews allowed me to purloin information from his published works on the Teign Valley lead industry (the existence of which saved me having to research this aspect from scratch myself). Les Folkard provided information on the Devon General bus services which did so much to seal the fate of the line. John Morris and Tony Cooke were subjected as ever to lengthy correspondence concerning the branch's signalling arrangements and track layouts respectively. (As is inevitable, the further research carried out by Tony and myself, since the publication of the last edition of Section 14 of his GWR Track Diagrams in 1984, has revealed a number of errors therein; there is no disagreement between us and the revised details will be incorporated in a future edition of Section 14). Dick Lystor lent material, gathered over the years from odd corners of the Teign Valley Granite Co's offices at Crockham, which has greatly improved the accounts of the quarries' rail traffic. Other help on railway historical matters was provided by

Peter Gray, Michael Messenger, Peter Mitchelmore, John Owen, Bob Palmer, Lawrence Popplewell, Tom Reardon, Peter Rowledge, Frank D. Smith, and Chris Turner. On the illustrative front we must all be grateful (as always in any work on Devon) to the Chapmans of Dawlish, whose negatives are now preserved in the Devon County Record Office and whose Edwardian postcards are lovingly sought after by many collectors (of whom I am grateful particularly to Steven Court). Also to the late G.N. Southerden whose 1920s & 1930s views of the line are all the more valuable for the fact that hardly anybody else seems to have paid the line photographic attention at that time. Of latterday photographers, pride of place must go to Peter Gray without whose contributions things would be very much the poorer.

Research was carried out primarily at the Public Record Office, the Devon County Record Office, the West Country Studies Library, Exeter, and Torquay Library. I am also grateful to Torquay Museum and the Dartington Rural Archive.

The manuscript was read through by Colin Burges who made many suggestions both factual and presentational, and who has shown the greatest enthusiasm for the project.

It is an author's privilege, in works of this kind, to be able to preserve for future generations much that would otherwise perish with the years. There is not too much left to see on the ground today, and I am told that there are now people living in the valley who do not even realise that it ever had a railway. Only through the memories of the older generation can we now hurry down to Ashton station on a winter's morning to find Guard Jack Harvey waiting

P. J. Garland

for us on the end of the platform, climb through flower-strewn cuttings to Longdown on a summer's afternoon, or return merry from St Thomas through oil-lit darkness on the Saturday night late train. Many of the photographs in these pages were taken from old family albums and show us those who worked or travelled on the line doing their ordinary jobs on 'just another day'. They were the Teign Valley line, just as much as the 517s, the Motors, and the 14XXs were, and it is my pleasure that they should be remembered here.

✣ POSTSCRIPT ✣

Since the completion of the manuscript in 1992, I have been able to make contact with further people who have assisted in improving some aspects of the account. Cecil Edwards (son of Louisa Edwards and brother of Eva Joiner, both crossing keepers at Chudleigh Knighton) and his brother Tom Edwards, whose wife Emily was the last keeper at Bovey Lane, have given a full picture of life at those two locations, on which I previously had little information. Mavis Piller, formerly of Ide, was able to call on the memories of the older generation there, and also loaned several photographs from her extensive collection of Teign Valley views. I must also thank Chips Barber for introducing me to her. Derek Turner, now of Exeter S&T, recalled the start of his career as a 'probationer' on the Teign Valley in 1956. Jim Kelly lent a valuable collection of old press cuttings on the line, and contemporary GWR material relating to diversions in the interwar years, including the 1930 timetable now reproduced in Chapter 15. Lewis Baycock pursued photographs in Chagford.

Further research was done at the Railway Studies Library, Newton Abbot, with the assistance of its ever-helpful librarian and creator Don Steggles. Michael Cook and others made available their research into the difficult subject of the contractor's locos used on the building of the Exeter Railway, on which I might otherwise have fallen into error.

Four years on, the Teign Valley has slipped still further from its railway past. The Newton Abbot–Heathfield Railway has just closed, and unpleasant suburbanisation quite undreamed of even as recently as 1992 has been inflicted in the very heart of the valley, its National Park status counting for nothing. On the other hand, a new pleasant place has been given to us by Colin Burges at Christow goods yard, where 'the sound of the locomotive' is once again heard on the branch after 25 years absence.

Peter Kay
Teignmouth
May 1996

INTRODUCTION

It took 43 years, two railway companies, and eighteen Acts of Parliament (and six more failed Bills) to make the 15¾ miles of railway from Exeter to Heathfield that became known latterly as the Teign Valley Branch. Even in a country whose railway system at large had a distressing tendency to benefit the pockets of lawyers at the shareholders' expense, this was some achievement.

The first of the two companies involved, the Teign Valley Railway, was the rump of a much more grandiose scheme of 1860, the Devon Central Railways. Its promoters had hopes of becoming part of the LSWR system, but never succeeded in obtaining that company's active support, although they did succeed very well in gaining the hostility of the Broad Gauge camp! The TVR as built was authorised in 1863 and, on and off through the '60s and

'70s, the promoters kept trying, with few friends and little money, to get this essentially unjustifiable rump line completed from the 'heath' at Chudleigh Road (Heathfield) to the 'ploughed field' at Teign House (Christow), and to secure an extension to Exeter which might turn it into a useful piece of railway. For long periods the half-completed earthworks were left to nature. When the rump finally opened in 1882 (with all hopes of extensions given up), it was as a 'narrow' (standard) gauge line worked by the GWR and quite isolated from the rest of the national standard gauge system — a situation which somehow encapsulated the TVR's unhappy inability to find a home in either the Broad Gauge or the Narrow Gauge camps. The traffic results of this isolated concern were predictably disappointing, and were not helped by the fact that the val-

517 class 0–4–2T No. 831 leaving Christow for Heathfield with a Wednesday & Saturday Only train in September 1924. The auto-trailers being propelled were Nos. 44 and 42 (leading). *G. N. Southerden*

ley's lead mining industry, which had been the prime inspiration for the railway, had collapsed shortly before its long-delayed opening.

The Teign Valley company was financially and spiritually exhausted by 1882, and an entirely separate company, the Exeter Teign Valley & Chagford Railway, had to be formed in 1883 by Exeter interests to secure the desired extension to Exeter. This was to prove as long in the making as the original line, and by the time it was completed in 1903 had become simply the Exeter Railway, having been obliged to give up the Chagford branch. Its Chairman, C.M. Knatchbull-Hugessen, had not even been born at the time the Teign Valley schemes had first been mooted! So far as its hapless shareholders were concerned, the Exeter Railway was another disaster. People had been enticed into investing on the basis of a large revenue accruing from GWR through traffic diverted this way to avoid congestion on the coast line at Dawlish, but the GWR had never actually promised to send any through trains this way in normal working, and never did. For the first two or three years after 1903 the extended branch therefore remained almost as sleepy as it had been before. The GWR had no desire to take over the unprofitable Teign Valley and Exeter companies, and they remained independent until 1923.

On the passenger front, the branch was never to be a great success, for the simple reason that not many people lived near it. But on the freight front it suddenly found itself, in the late 1900s, becoming a busy railway, as several large roadstone quarries were established in the valley. The rise of the motor car saw demand for roadstone booming, and by 1913 Trusham had the sixth highest goods traffic figures in the Exeter Division. The line's roadstone heyday lasted some 25 years, fading in the 1930s as the quarries became exhausted. The branch also acquired a new (if occasional) purpose as an emergency diversionary route when the main line was blocked by cliff falls or sea wall breaches, as happened all too often in the interwar years. In the Second World War major improvements were carried out on the branch as an insurance against trouble on the main line. Alas, this could not save the line. The already-small passenger traffic had been badly eaten into by the new bus services in the 1920s and '30s, and with the decline of the quarry traffic the writing was on the wall by 1950. Passenger closure came in 1958, one of the first in the West Country, and the whole of the goods-only residue left from Heathfield to Christow was itself gone by 1968, leaving only another half-mile stub at the Exeter end which still clings tenuously to life in the 1990s.

Cottages at Higher Ashton in 1912.   *Chapman collection, cty. Steven Court*

CHAPTER ONE

THE ROUT OF THE DEVON CENTRAL
1860–1862

IN the 1840s the Teign Valley might have found itself on the Exeter–Plymouth main line; there were many advocates of a Teign Valley route, right up to the Parliamentary hearings on the South Devon Railway Bill in 1844. But Brunel's coastal route won the day.

The railway map of Central and South Devon saw no change for a decade after the opening of the SDR main line through to Plymouth in 1849. The SDR's impoverishment, in the wake of the Atmospheric, exacerbated the general post-mania apathy. Of the small number of schemes proposed in the 1850s, only the Plymouth–Tavistock line and the Torquay–Paignton extension came to fruition in that decade (both opening in 1859, and both of course broad gauge). But by 1860 times were becoming favourable to railway promotion again — the years 1861–66 were to see the greatest bout of promotion nationally since the 1840s — and in Devon the completion in 1860 of the London & South Western Railway (LSWR) narrow-gauge link from London to Exeter provided additional inspiration for new schemes. West of Exeter, a vast area of Devon still lay open and unplanned for, waiting for local initiatives or for whichever of the Broad or Narrow Gauge camps stepped in. In addition to those places which still had no railway at all, there were others already served by the SDR which now wanted a narrow gauge link too, to benefit from competition just as Exeter was benefiting.

Although the rail-less area of Central Devon was vast, it was not for the most part heavily populated — indeed much of it was moorland. The largest places unserved were:

1861 populations

Okehampton	1,929
Chagford	1,379
Moretonhampstead	1,468
Chudleigh	2,108
Bovey Tracey	2,080
Ashburton	3,062
Buckfastleigh	2,544

In retrospect none of these places — except perhaps Ashburton and Buckfastleigh, where there was still a large woollen trade — were likely to be able to support a profitable rail link, unless a through traffic to places further west were to be carried also. But in the 1860s even the smallest towns were coming to see a railway connection as a necessity to avoid decline; and most of these towns also had historical reasons for seeing themselves as more important than they really were. In particular, Chudleigh and Ashburton had been coaching towns on the Exeter–Plymouth road up to the 1840s, and had thus enjoyed excellent long-distance transport facilities which had now ceased; they therefore particularly resented being rail-less.

As far as the Broad Gauge camp was concerned, these towns could only be served by dead-end branches. The SDR was, however, still in no financial position to build branches itself; it needed local initiatives and it could only offer them moral and administrative support, not large-scale financial contributions. The SDR, as the occupying company in South Devon, also suffered from local criticisms of its services and policies, although it was only in Torquay (because of its 'branch line' situation) that there was a really strong element of public hostility to the SDR. The great attraction that an SDR connection held to would-be local promoters was that the SDR's established position meant easier planning for any SDR-linked scheme.

The LSWR, in contrast, was known to be looking to extend its main line westwards to Plymouth and Cornwall, with the Okehampton corridor the most likely choice for this new through route. Torquay was also a temptation to Waterloo but a lesser priority. The LSWR had little interest in the smaller towns, but this did not stop local promoters, who saw the LSW as the new and progressive company offering national connections on the narrow gauge, pushing schemes which they hoped the LSW might work. Local promoters were in fact obliged to lean to either the Broad Gauge or the Narrow Gauge camp, for assistance in promotion and for a Working Agreement when completed. In some cases the local promoters might nevertheless have the upper hand; it was a well-known ploy by this date to push 'auction lines' in the hope of forcing one of two rival established companies to buy them up merely to prevent the other from doing so. But in other cases the established companies could collaborate despite their rivalry, to the cost of local parties, as indeed the LSWR and the Broad Gauge companies were to do on many occasions.

On top of the dilemma of whether to associate with the Broad Gauge camp or the Narrow, the promotion of railways in Central Devon was made complicated by the fact that all the rail-less towns had badly split traffic desires. This meant that there was no one obvious choice of route for a branch to any of these places; whichever routes were proposed, there was bound to be debate, dissension, and delay as the local notables discussed the merits of alternatives. In some cases, the local geography also made rail links on desirable corridors impossible. In particular:

Moretonhampstead and Chagford looked to both Exeter and Newton Abbot/South Devon, but clearly could not support rail links from both. Exeter offered the best links to the national system, yet a direct Exeter–Moretonhampstead route was all but impossible owing to the hills east of the town; the best that could be done was a station three miles from the town at Sandypark on an

Exeter–Teign Gorge–Chagford route. In contrast, Newton Abbot–Moretonhampstead–Chagford was a comparatively easy line to build, and would serve Bovey on the way. Indeed, a 'Newton and Moretonhampstead Railway' Committee had been set up in August 1858 to promote such a line, although they had not got anywhere beyond a preliminary survey and the securing of the support of Lord Courtenay.

Chudleigh had traditional connections with Exeter as well as the nearer market at Newton, but the Haldon Hills meant that any rail link to Exeter would have to be an indirect one via the Teign Valley and a Perridge tunnel. Again, Newton–Chudleigh was in contrast easy territory (although nobody, in the event, ever proposed a simple dead-end branch of this kind, all Chudleigh proposals being for through routes).

Ashburton and Buckfastleigh had a four-way split, having traditional links with Exeter, Newton, Totnes, and Plymouth. They could, however, only support one rail link. Newton was probably the most sensible compromise, and indeed such a line was authorised in 1846 and might have been built but for the post-mania depression. Totnes was probably the cheapest route.

All in all, the stage was set for controversy. It was no surprise that extensive rival schemes were to come before Parliament in 1861.

THE PROMOTION OF THE DEVON CENTRAL RAILWAYS (1860–61)

During the course of 1860, an ambitious series of railway schemes evolved in the minds of two men, Sir Lawrence Palk, the leading landowner in the Teign Valley and Torquay, and William Toogood a Parliamentary Agent with interests in railway promotion nationally. They brought the Earl of Devon into their camp, and several other local notables. The various people involved had differing interests, and the need to ensure that everybody's interests were catered for was indeed one of the reasons why the proposals became so extensive.

The Provisional Committee of the Devon Central Railways Company comprised Palk, the Earl of Devon, William Kitson, Baldwin Fulford, the Revd Hayter Hames of Chagford, and Henry Tootal. Toogood was the company's solicitor. The positions and motives of these protagonists (except Tootal, who disappeared from sight immediately and need not concern us) must now be considered at greater length:

Sir Lawrence Palk (1818–1883), 4th Baronet Palk from 1860, elevated to the peerage 1880 as the 1st Lord Haldon, was Conservative MP for South Devon 1854–1866 and East Devon 1866–1880. Palk lived in Haldon House, a large mansion situated on the Haldon Hills to the west of the Chudleigh–Exeter road, and also had residences in Torquay (the Manor House) and London.

The Palks had established themselves in the area in the 1770s, and had acquired large estates in the Teign Valley

Sir Lawrence Palk in 1878.

and Torquay, the latter originally a place of no significance but which the Palks had ideas of turning into a port to rival Dartmouth. This never really came to be to the extent hoped for; instead Torquay began to develop in the early nineteenth century as a seaside resort, and this was enhanced in the 1850s and '60s after the SDR provided a rail link in 1848. This development brought much income to the Palks. In 1864 Torquay was described as 'the most opulent, the handsomest, and the most fashionable watering place in the British Isles'.

The 3rd Baronet, Sir Lawrence Vaughan Palk, who succeeded in 1813 at the age of 20, was an 'incapable spendthrift' who devoted much of his time to pleasure on the continent (in part compulsorily, as he was under threat of imprisonment for debt had he stayed in England). He died in May 1860. Sir Lawrence, the 4th Baronet, was determined to manage the estates in a very different vein, and by the 1870s he was enjoying a notional annual income of over £100,000 from his lands in Devon.

The fact that Palk succeeded to the Baronetcy in May 1860 was very significant so far as the promotion of the Devon Central Railways is concerned, as it meant that he was put in a position to implement his ideas at the very time when the national financial climate and the arrival of the LSWR in Exeter also conspired to make railway promotion in the area seem much more practicable than it had been previously. Palk had never been involved in railway promotion before 1860[1] but he had a number of strong reasons for getting involved now, and he was very much the leading figure in the Devon Central Railways and its successor the Teign Valley Railway (he was Chairman of the companies through to his death in 1883). As he said to the Parliamentary Committee in 1864, 'I

Built in the 1730s, Haldon House was bought by Robert Palk, the 1st Baronet Palk, in 1772, after he had made a fortune in India with the East India Company and latterly as Paymaster to the Army and Governor of Madras. He had formed a close friendship in India with Major-General Stringers Lawrence, who died in 1775, leaving Palk £50,000, as a result of which the eldest son of the Palk line always received the name 'Lawrence' subsequently. In 1788 the grateful Palk built the Belvedere Tower (also known as Lawrence Castle) on the summit of Haldon as a memorial to his friend. *Chapman collection, cty. Devon County Record Office*

have always promoted the line, I am the person who has promoted the thing from its commencement'.

Firstly, Palk wanted a railway link to the Palk lands in the Teign Valley, to enhance their agricultural and mineral value, and most particularly to encourage the lead mines (some of them on Palk land) which were enjoying a boom period in the 1850s (see Chapter 2).

Secondly, he wanted to improve Torquay harbour and give it a railway link, both to improve the harbour's trade at large and in particular with notions of a much-increased output from the Teign Valley lead mines being exported via Torquay instead of Teignmouth. In this respect the Palks were, however, in conflict with an influential section of public opinion in Torquay, for the town's development as a resort had brought an 'amenity lobby' against any ideas of developing the port commercially, and in particular against ideas of railway lines along the front. Back in 1852/3 when the SDR had let it be known that it would support any good scheme to extend the Torquay branch to the harbour, there had been as much opposition from the town as support, and nothing had come of it. When the Dartmouth & Torbay Railway succeeded in getting an Act for a Torquay (Torre)–Dartmouth line in 1857, no Torquay harbour branch was included; so the map was still open for any harbour scheme, either as a short branch from the SDR line or (better, in Palk's eyes) in connection with a new narrow gauge line from Exeter.

(The Harbour at Torquay was in due course improved by Palk in 1867–70 when a large outer breakwater was added at a cost of £70,000. But the desired railway link never materialised.)

Thirdly, Palk more than anybody else had reason to dislike the poor train service that the SDR was giving Torquay. He saw it as a handicap to the town's growth — although the town was in truth growing fast enough as it was — and thereby to the Palk estates' income. As an MP he was the natural focus of public complaints at large, and most particularly he was a very regular traveller himself. The 1850s were the SDR's worst period and the whole train service west of Exeter was indeed inconvenient, infrequent, slow, unpunctual, expensive, and regarded as dangerous because of the frequency of cliff falls at Dawlish. In 1860 one still had to leave Paddington at 11am to reach Torquay the same day, and there was a particular dislike in Torquay of the inconvenient station at Newton and missed connections there. Palk was forever firing off letters at the SDR Chairman Thomas Woollcombe. The SDR further damaged its cause in Torquay in August 1859 when the first section of the Dartmouth line was opened from Torre (previously 'Torquay') to Paignton, and many of the better trains had their Torre stops cut out, only calling at the new Torquay (Livermead) station which was inconveniently situated for much of the town and was a very third-rate structure in terms of the station facilities provided.[2] There was much protest, and on 27th August Palk found himself Chairman of a public meeting in the Town Hall. He brought laughter in the hall when he commented that the hours he had wasted at Newton waiting for trains 'if put

Haldon House has been largely demolished, and the Palk baronetcy has been extinguished following the failure of the line. However, the Belvedere Tower still stands today as a conspicuous feature of the area.   *Chapman Collection, cty. Devon County Record Office*

together would make many years', and that 'if Newton were made a Borough Town he would be entitled to a vote there on the score of residence'. If the SDR would not provide a decent service, he believed that the South Western Company (hear! hear!) might seriously consider the making of a line — the first known reference to Palk having this hope in mind. The meeting appointed a committee to present a deputation to the SDR Board, but they did not really get any joy (which, of course, strengthened Palk's hand in seeding ideas of a new line). In October 1859 the *Torquay Directory* reported rumours that the LSWR was wanting to extend to Plymouth, either via Okehampton or via Chudleigh, Buckfastleigh, and Brent; the latter idea was to be very much pushed by Palk, as we shall see.

The SDR was in fact very conscious of the poor service it provided at this time, and in its 1860 Act it secured powers for the doubling of the line from Exeter to Dawlish and Teignmouth Old Quay to Newton to improve punctuality, and for the rebuilding of Newton station. By 1861 the Exeter–Starcross doubling and the new station at Newton were completed, and the SDR's reputation began to improve. But in 1859/60 these improvements were of course still in the indefinite future so far as the Torquay public was concerned.

From Palk's personal viewpoint, therefore, everything fell into place during 1860. What was needed was a narrow

William Reginald, 11th Earl of Devon, an 1874 portrait.   *Cty. Powderham Estates*

gauge line from Exeter Queen St to Torquay, and the only available route for such a line was via the Teign Valley.

The Earl of Devon. William Reginald Courtenay (1807–1888), Lord Courtenay in the 1840s and '50s and 11th Earl of Devon from 1859, was an unlikely figure to find in the Palk camp. Although active Conservatives politically like Palk, the Courtenays were leading figures in the Broad Gauge camp, and the 11th Earl had himself been an active SDR Director for many years and (although no longer a Director) was still 'in very friendly relations with the South Devon company' in 1860. His temporary flirtation with the Narrow Gauge camp in 1860/61 was due to his frustration at the SDR's inability for financial reasons to promote a rail link to the Moretonhampstead/Chagford area where he had large estates, followed by the failure of the 'Newton and Moretonhampstead' scheme of 1858. A line to the Moreton/Chagford area could easily be tagged on to Palk's Exeter–Teign Valley–Torquay ideas, and this attracted the Earl. He had no wish to fall out with the Broad Gauge camp and therefore found himself rather embarrassed in public when he became seen as a leading promoter of the Devon Central. At a public meeting in Exeter in December 1860, John Drew, the Earl's agent,[3] was obliged to explain somewhat two-facedly that, whilst the Earl was giving his 'general support' to the Devon Central, he could not be regarded as committed to the whole of it! As the Earl was one of the Directors this did not sound too good. Later the Earl was to say that the link to Moreton and Chagford was his only reason for getting involved with the Devon Central in 1860.

William Kitson (1800–1883), Solicitor, was known as 'the maker of Torquay' and long exercised a ruling control over the town's affairs.

He had studied law in the Ashburton office of his uncle Robert Abraham, and set up in practice in Torquay in 1826. In 1833 he founded the Torquay Bank in partnership with Edward Vivian, and in 1835 he became Chairman of the newly-established Local Board.

Abraham had been steward of the Palk Estates in Torquay, and when he died in 1833 Kitson took over, in practice in sole control, as Trustee, thanks to the 3rd Baronet spending so much of his time on the Continent. It was really Kitson who set about the development of the resort with such success (he was of course in a position to ensure that no difficulties arose on the Local Government front!). Kitson was not known as 'Penny Bun Kitson' and 'Darning Needle Kitson' for nothing, and he controlled the Palk revenues tightly. This brought conflict in the 1850s with Sir Lawrence Palk who was, as heir, in practice under Kitson's thumb and only allowed a fixed annuity for himself. In a town where he was both the leading landowner and the MP, it was natural for Palk to resent the way in which Kitson could control his affairs. In 1858 Palk tried to get his father declared a lunatic so that he could take control of the estates himself, but Kitson had contrived to prevent this!

Kitson naturally attended the Torquay protest meeting in August 1859, and it was indeed he who (as Chairman of the Local Board) headed the subsequent Deputation to the SDR Board. Despite the animosity between the two, Palk needed Kitson's support for any railway scheme, and Kitson was in fact to continue as a Teign Valley Railway Director until a few months before his death, even though any hopes of the TVR reaching Torquay had long been given up by then. He was never very active in the com-

William Kitson at the height of his power in Torquay.

pany's affairs but his position was ensured by the TVR's indebtedness to his bank.

Kitson was removed as Chairman of the Torquay Local Board in 1860, but he never lost his influence in the town and always headed the poll at Local Board elections. He continued in charge of the Palk Estates in Torquay until retiring in 1874.

Baldwin Fulford (1801–1871) of 'Great Fulford' two miles north west of Dunsford (where the Fulfords had lived since the time of Richard I), was a large landowner in the Dunsford area, Chairman of the Devon Quarter Sessions, and a leading figure in the Devon county gentry. He seems to have had a straightforward landowner's interest in improved communications. He was quite heavily involved with Palk in organising things in 1860, and became a Teign Valley Railway Director in 1863, but was more on the sidelines after this. His nephew and successor Francis Drummond Fulford (1831–1907) was, however, to be active in supporting rail links to the area in later decades.

The Revd Hayter George Hayter Hames, Rector of Chagford from 1852 until his death in 1886, was a tireless advocate of everything Chagford. Amongst his achievements were the formation of a gas company in 1869 and the promotion of an electricity company which in 1889 resulted in Chagford becoming the 'first place west of London' to have electric lighting in the streets. He created the Chagford tourist industry; 'resolved on pushing the place, he invited down magazine editors and professional litterateurs, entertained them, drove them about, and was rewarded by articles appearing in journals and serials, belauding Chagford . . .'.[4] Hayter Hames naturally wanted a rail link to Chagford, and this was his first serious chance of getting one. From Palk's viewpoint, Hayter Hames was a useful figure to parade to show that the Devon Central schemes had genuine local support in the Chagford area.

Hayter Hames never gave up his attempts (destined to failure) to get a railway to Chagford, by whatever route, but after 1861 he was always a voice from outside.

William Toogood was the dark horse in the promotion of the Devon Central. His interests in railway promotion were particularly centred on the Somerset & Dorset, starting with the Somerset Central and the Dorset Central in the mid-1850s. He was in effect Parliamentary Agent to Charles Waring, the well-known contractor, who was the centre-pivot of the scheming to get the S&D completed as a through line. However Toogood was also cultivating interests elsewhere. In 1854 he was involved in the promotion of the Border Counties Railway (Hexham to Falstone, extended by an 1859 Act to Riccarton Junction) whose engineer was J.F. Tone. Toogood's introduction to the Devon Central was either through Tone (see below), or through his relative Dr Isaac Baruch Toogood who was a surgeon in Torquay and who attended the August 1859 public meeting. (Dr I.B. Toogood later became a Teign Valley Railway Director, no doubt to give William Toogood, who never became a Director himself, a face on the Board.)

William Toogood was the DCR's and TVR's solicitor and Parliamentary Agent from 1860 to 1880, but up to 1864, and again from 1872 to 1877, he was also de facto Secretary and Manager of the company and ran the show on a day-to-day basis. At times in the 1870s Toogood *was* the company. The local press in Devon were quite aware of Toogood's habits and regularly referred to the DCR/TVR in denigratory terms as 'Toogood's Line', suggesting that Palk was only Toogood's puppet, although this was an exaggeration. Toogood no doubt saw the many-tentacled DCR as an 'auction line' which could be sold for personal profit to the highest bidder of the SDR or LSWR.

Toogood gradually drifted apart from the TVR after 1877 and was eventually dismissed as solicitor in highly strained circumstances in 1880.

Having assembled this somewhat loosely-tied body of support, Palk was able to commission the engineer John Furness Tone to prepare plans for the 1861 Parliamentary session. Tone lived in Newcastle, with an office at 10 Market St, Newcastle, and was the Engineer to the Blyth & Tyne Railway and also to the Border Counties (as noted above) and the Wansbeck Railways. He had been sent to Devon in 1860 by the Duke of Northumberland (who lived at Alnwick Castle and had clearly had local contact with Tone) to survey a Tavistock–Launceston line for himself and the Duke of Bedford who were the largest landowners in West Devon. This did not in itself come to anything, as the two Dukes soon decided to support the Mid-Devon & Cornwall Railway instead (see below). But it brought Tone to the attention of Palk who asked him to survey the Devon Central, which he did in good time for the depositing of plans in November 1860, much of the work being done in fact by Tone's assistants William John Browne and J.J. MacDonnell. Tone and Browne were to remain the DCR/TVR's Engineers until the TVR's collapse in 1867.[5]

Details of the DCR plans are shown at *Fig. 1*. It will be seen that the Chagford line was to be extended through to Okehampton and Lidford. The DCR had no particular supporters in this area and one must assume that this was done in the hope of making the line look more attractive to the LSWR, which still had no definite route in mind for a thrust west from Exeter. The DCR was somewhat at a loss to explain what the trains were supposed to do when they reached the end of its line in the middle of a field at Lidford! Clearly there were hopes of Tavistock and Launceston lines to connect, but the DCR had no such plans ready for the 1861 session, probably because the Duke of Northumberland (at whose expense Tone had just surveyed these corridors) was not a DCR supporter and so would have objected to Tone including them in the DCR scheme. The DCR's Crediton line was added with ideas of minerals from the Teign Valley being shipped to South Wales from North Devon ports, although the junctions at Lea Cross and Crediton would have required two reversals for this traffic. The Torquay line, surprisingly, did not include a link to Torquay Harbour.

The DCR's grand system would have fulfilled the following purposes:

Exeter to 'Moretonhampstead' (Sandypark), Chagford, and Okehampton
Exeter to the Teign Valley and Chudleigh
Teign Valley to North Devon
Teign Valley and Chudleigh to Newton Abbot and Torquay
Narrow Gauge route from London to (eventually) Cornwall
Narrow Gauge route from London and Exeter to Torquay
Inland route between Exeter and Newton avoiding the sea wall section

The DCR promoters soon set about holding the conventional public meetings — at the New London Inn, Exeter, on 11th December 1860 with Palk in the chair; at the White Hart Inn, Moretonhampstead, on 29th January 1861 with Fulford in the chair; and at the Globe Hotel, Newton Abbot, on 30th January with the Earl of Devon presiding. These produced the usual unanimous resolutions in favour, despite the great potential for subsequent disagreement. An anti-SDR 'remonstrance' was also arranged in Torquay in December, and anonymous letters were printed in the *Torquay Directory* criticising the SDR, one of them just happening to make the point 'surely with such treatment as this, the inhabitants should not lose sight of the efforts being made by the South Western Co. (*sic*) to give us another line?'

A later public meeting was held at the Clifford Arms, Chudleigh, on 8th April 1861. With a parliamentary contest pending, Palk was now keen to play down the DCR's anti-SDR origins, and present it rather as a line which the local gentry were promoting to give facilities which the SDR could not afford to provide, so that the SDR's hostility (it was claimed) was hardly reasonable.

THE MID DEVON & CORNWALL RAILWAY

Even if they had experienced no trouble from rival schemes, the DCR would have had a hard job getting their grandiose plans through Parliament, in the face of the inevitable opposition of the Broad Gauge camp and the lack of any evident source for the necessary finances. But in fact there was a rival narrow gauge scheme in the 1861 session — the Mid Devon & Cornwall Railway (also shown in *Fig. 1*). The MD&C was another attempt to latch on to the LSWR's arrival in Exeter, but some of its supporters had been involved in earlier schemes in the same corridor, notably the 'Plymouth, Tavistock, Okehampton, North Devon & Exeter Railway' of 1853. The opening of the SDR's Plymouth–Tavistock branch in 1859 now effectively prevented the MD&C from trying for a line through to Plymouth, so their scheme was instead for a line from Coleford Junction on the North Devon line — which the LSWR was about to convert from broad to narrow gauge — to Tavistock and Launceston. The MD&C was basically a local landowners' promotion; the Duke of Northumberland and the Duke of Bedford, both large

landowners in west Devon, were the most influential backers, but the Chairman of the Provisional Committee and the main activist was S.C. Hamlyn of Colebrooke who had been dreaming of a railway on this corridor since the day he saw the Liverpool & Manchester opened. The LSWR was, of course, there in the background, a point emphasized by the fact that the LSWR's Engineers, J.E. Errington and W.R. Galbraith,[6] were also the MD&C's Engineers.

THE DEVON CENTRAL AND THE MD&C IN PARLIAMENT (1861)

The Devon Central's collapse began even before its Bill was presented in Parliament. In January 1861 it was decided to abandon the Newton–Torquay and Crediton–Dunsford sections, probably because of pressure from the

Fig. 1. Railways in South Devon as at November 1860.

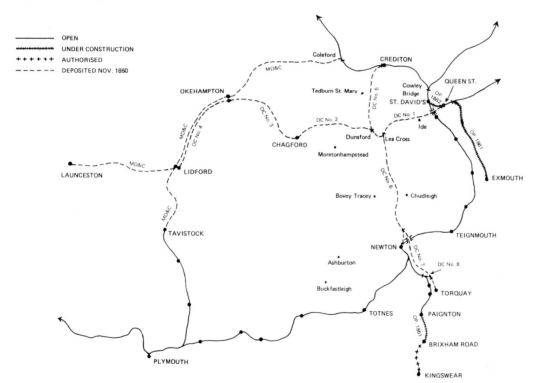

The Devon Central Bill sought powers to make their line either Broad or Narrow Gauge, a sensible piece of bet-hedging. The MD&C Bill specified that the line was to be Narrow Gauge. No running powers were sought by either company, beyond the use of the stations at the ends of the lines.

DEVON CENTRAL RAILWAYS — November 1860

		Miles
Rly. No. 1	Exeter (LSW station) to Dunsford (Lea Cross)	7¼
Rly. No. 2	Dunsford (Lea Cross) to Chagford	10¼
Rly. No. 3†	Chagford to Okehampton	9½
Rly. No. 4†	Okehampton to Lidford	9¼
Rly. No. 5*	Crediton to Dunsford (nr. Reedy Bridge)	7½
Rly. No. 6	Dunsford (Lea Cross) to Newton (Jn. with SDR)	11
Rly. No. 7*	Newton (Jn. with No. 6) to Torquay	6½
Rly. No. 8*	Connection to SDR line at Torquay	¼
	Total	61½

ESTIMATE: £470,000

* Abandoned before Bill promoted.
† Abandoned in Committee.

Earl of Devon who must have found the blatantly anti-SDR Torquay line the most embarrassing part of the scheme, and also perhaps in order to reduce the SDR's opposition. These abandonments must, however, have been a bitter pill for Palk.

The SDR was naturally wholly against both the DCR and the MD&C. Thomas Woollcombe, the SDR Chairman, discovered the MD&C's intentions and reported them to his Board in July 1860, but the SDR does not seem to have known what the DCR were planning until the public notices appeared in November. On 20th November the SDR Board's attentions were directed to the two applications 'for the construction of various lines of railway to connect the narrow gauge system with Torquay, Okehampton, Tavistock and Launceston' — a good expression of how the SDR saw the DCR as an entirely hostile scheme from the start. The SDR Engineer, P.J. Margary,[7] was directed to study the DC and MD&C schemes in detail, and the SDR's Surveyor Dymond was instructed 'to endeavour to organise an opposition (to the DC) on the part of the landowners' — an unusually frank entry for the Minutes! Petitions were lodged against both schemes, and arrangements made for John Fowler to appear as an independent engineering witness for the SDR, for a fee of 100 guineas. (Fowler was to work regularly for the SDR, from this time on, as Consulting Engineer.) The Bristol & Exeter was persuaded to petition against the Bills too, and they agreed to pay half the costs of a jointly-organised Parliamentary opposition.

The LSWR's opposition to the Devon Central seems to have taken the DCR by surprise. With the LSWR in expansive mood in 1860, the DCR seem to have assumed their support; there is no reference to Palk ever having actually consulted the LSWR. But in reality the DCR had little to offer the LSWR. The MD&C gave a much better route into Cornwall, having better gradients and curvature than the DC's line via Chagford, as well as being shorter in terms of the new construction needed, thanks to its commencement much further west at Coleford Junction. Such potential interest as the LSWR had in Torquay was, of course, removed when the DCR abandoned its Torquay line in January. Worse, the LSWR took a dislike to the DC's proposed junction at the west end of Queen Street station, which was right at the end of the platforms and at the top of the 1 in 36 bank up from St David's. (The St David's–Queen St connecting line was under construction at this date, opening in 1862.) Errington — who of course had personal reasons for wanting to see his MD&C defeat the DCR! — recommended against this junction, and, acting on his advice, the LSWR Board resolved on 31st January 1861 'that every opposition be given to that part of the projected line which interferes with the construction and working of the Exeter Junction line'. Some time after this an agreement was come to between the DCR and the LSWR, under which the DCR undertook to withdraw the first 1½ miles of its line at the Exeter end from the Bill, with the intention that there would then be further talks

between the two companies to decide on an alternative junction arrangement at Exeter for inclusion in a further Bill next session.

The DCR Bill sought powers to enable both the SDR and the LSWR to subscribe to the DCR and to make Working Agreements with it. Neither company had been consulted by the DCR on this, and both took a dislike to the clauses. The SDR considered them 'calculated to mislead the public' by creating the impression that the SDR was favourable to the DCR, and Woollcombe accordingly wrote to the LSWR asking for a joint objection to the clauses. The LSWR happily agreed, probably seeing it as a chance to make a show of being nice to the SDR in respect of something which they would have done anyway. The LSWR Secretary was told to add to the reply 'a hope on the part of the Board that this evidence on their part of a desire to maintain friendly relations with the South Devon Co, will induce them to reciprocate a further extension of privileges as regards traffic'. This was a little dishonest given the LSWR's intentions regarding the MD&C!

The MD&C and DCR Bills were taken together by the same House of Commons Committee, beginning on 9th May 1861. The MD&C was considered first. The outstanding objectors were the SDR, the Bristol & Exeter, and the 'inhabitants of South Tawton' who just happened to have William Toogood as their Agent. The DCR and MD&C were also mutually opposed, except that the MD&C did not oppose the DCR's Newton line. A few days before the Committee began, Archibald Scott, the LSWR's Manager, had made a definite promise to Hamlyn that the LSWR would work the MD&C line, and Scott repeated this publicly to the Committee. Buller, the B&E Chairman, also now made approaches to Hamlyn — 'I have not gone a-begging to the Broad Gauge, but they have made approaches to us', Hamlyn told the Committee — suggesting that the line might be mixed gauge.

On 14th May, when the Committee considered the rival merits of the DC and MD&C as routes to West Devon, it became clear that the DC scheme, with its unexplained terminus at Lidford, was not going to stand much chance. Accordingly, Calvert, the DC Counsel, announced that he was abandoning the DC line west of Chagford and would restrict himself to advocating 'a line between Exeter and Newton which would afford the means of communication with Torquay and Dartmouth (*sic*) . . . and a line from Chagford to Lea Cross which would give considerable local accommodation, the necessity for which he should establish before the Committee'. The Devon Central had shrunk again (*Fig. 2*).

For some days the MD&C seemed likely to be successful, but the Committee was much impressed by Margary's and Fowler's evidence heard on 15th & 16th May, mainly attacking the MD&C's estimates of construction costs. Eventually, on 28th May, the MD&C Bill was rejected.

The DCR was considered on the same day (28th May 1861). After the various abandonments, all that was left was a line from a point 1½ miles from Exeter to Chagford and Newton. The DC asked for an adjournment of several days to reconsider their case in the light of the Committee's rejection of the MD&C — meaning in particular that they might now wish to reactivate the section west of Chagford. But this was refused; the DC case had to proceed immediately. Counsel for the LSWR made it clear that he would·resist the passing of the Bill on any terms other than those of the DCR/LSWR agreement (i.e. with the first 1½ miles omitted), but other opponents then objected that without this section to give a connection at Exeter, the proposals would not agree with the preamble of the Bill! This put the DCR in a cleft stick, worsened by the fact that the Committee expressed a dislike of agreements of this sort being 'made behind the back of Parliament', and of the idea of a further Bill being presented next session for the missing 1½ miles, leaving Parliament unable to consider it properly, with the rest of the line already authorised as a gun at their necks.

As a result, the Committee rejected the whole DCR Bill straight away on 28th May, without hearing any witnesses as to the merits of the proposals. As with the MD&C, the high cost of the schemes and the promoters' inability to explain where the money might come from, had no small influence on the Committee.

REGROUPING (1861–2)

The collapse of all existing plans for lines west of Exeter led to everyone having to reconsider their positions. In the course of the summer of 1861, the greater part of the future railway map of central Devon was fixed. The SDR succeeded in splitting the Devon Central alliance, enticing the Earl of Devon back to his natural place in the Broad Gauge camp, and leaving Palk out in the cold through

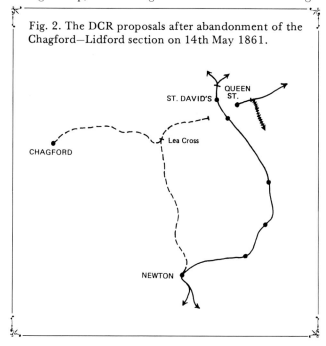

Fig. 2. The DCR proposals after abandonment of the Chagford—Lidford section on 14th May 1861.

being over-ambitious in sticking to an independent line when others were carving the map up successfully between them.

Immediately after 28th May, Woollcombe had the first of many lengthy conferences with Fowler and others as to what course the SDR should pursue for the Central Devon area. The Broad Gauge camp had had no scheme on offer in the 1861 session, and were lucky not to have lost out badly as a result; it was therefore now clear to them that they would have to promote lines to fill in the vacant areas of the map, to forestall further narrow gauge plans so far as possible. Woollcombe also had at this time the first of several meetings with Lord Devon. Simultaneously, Palk wrote to Woollcombe on 3rd June 'enquiring whether it was likely that the Co. would do anything to provide for the extensive country unprovided with railway communications'.

The SDR's financial situation was still such that any new lines would have to be promoted by nominally independent companies, although the SDR could offer favourable Working Agreements (Fowler proposed that they should work such lines for 50% of the receipts and also give a 25% rebate on through traffic). On 4th June Woollcombe told the SDR Board that they would have to secure the promotion of a Tavistock–Lidford–Launceston line, and another line 'to communicate with the district north of Newton'; but it was not yet certain whether a Newton–Moreton line, or a Newton–Dunsford line via the Teign Valley, was most appropriate. Palk was told that the SDR was willing to talk to the landowners (of whom he was, of course, a major one) as to the best way of 'giving effect to any well matured scheme'. Late in June there was a Woollcombe–Palk–Lord Devon–Fowler meeting in London. Palk may still have had hopes of agreement at this stage, but further investigations carried out by Fowler and Margary in July led Fowler to conclude that a Newton–Moreton line had the best potential. Woollcombe and the SDR Board fell behind Fowler's recommendation.

The die was now cast. After giving up the Torquay line, Palk's greatest personal interest was in getting a rail link to his Teign Valley estates, and, now that the SDR had gone against a Teign Valley route, the possibility of agreement between him and the SDR evaporated. Palk therefore fixed a meeting in London with former DCR and MD&C interests, and agreed with them on the promotion of a 'Devon & Cornwall Railway' (not to be confused with the later company of that name) from Exeter via Tedburn St Mary to Okehampton, Tavistock, and Launceston, with a branch from Crediton to Tedburn and another from Tedburn to Newton via the Teign Valley. On 12th August 1861 Palk held a hastily-convened 'public' meeting in Plymouth, attended largely by 'persons favourable to his views'. Fulford and Hayter Hames were present from the DCR camp, and Cornish interests included John Ching of Launceston, a Director of the West Cornwall Railway. Woollcombe was able to get there and was allowed to speak at length, but, not surprisingly in the circumstances, there was a large majority in favour of the 'Devon & Cornwall' scheme. A Committee was set up to form a company to promote this line, and Tone was engaged to do such new surveys as were necessary. The Committee had definite intentions at one point of a Bill in the 1862 session for the Crediton–Tedburn–Teign Valley–Newton section, but, as the weeks went by, they found all doors closing against them. Initial approaches to the LSWR got nowhere, as that company was falling behind the rival 'Okehampton Railway' scheme. The B&E was then approached, also without result. By January 1862 Palk's Committee had been forced to accept that they were not going to get anywhere, and they issued a public statement on 6th January conceding this, but insisting that 'the Committee will not relax their efforts to secure that railway accommodation which the best interests of the two counties require'. Palk and Toogood had been outmanoeuvred, and their camp (such as it now was) was left with nothing for the 1862 session.

The Earl of Devon's position was quite the opposite. The SDR's Newton–Moreton proposal served his main personal aim — rail access to his estates in the Moreton area — admirably, and he agreed to become Chairman of the Provisional Committee of the SDR-backed Moretonhampstead & South Devon Railway (of which Woollcombe was also a director). The M&SDR was presented as, and regarded by some of those involved as, a continuation of the former (but dormant) 'Newton & Moretonhampstead' Committee of 1858, and indeed used the same Minute Book. The name was formally changed by a resolution of 7th October 1861; several of the former N&M Committee attended the first M&SD meetings in the autumn of 1861, and one of them, Thomas Wills of Lustleigh, became an M&SD Director. Public meetings to gain support for the M&SD were held in Newton, Bovey, Moreton, and Chagford in October 1861, and Margary was appointed as Engineer and prepared plans which were deposited in November in time for the 1862 session. The line was to terminate at Moreton, but there was talk of an extension to Chagford in the near future as soon as finances allowed. The Palk camp was always to begrudge the Moretonhampstead line as a 'Block Line' pushed by the SDR to obstruct their own plans for accommodating the area, which in a sense it was. But, as we have seen, such a line had in fact been proposed by local interests in 1858 before the DCR's schemes had been evolved, and all in all it was a sensible scheme.

(The Earl of Devon was regularly to oppose Teign Valley schemes in Parliament from 1863 on. His position in the Broad Gauge camp was reaffirmed in 1865 when he became Chairman of the Bristol & Exeter on the death of Buller, a post which he held until the GWR takeover. He also acquired a great interest in railway directorships at large; by 1867 he was also Chairman of the Metropolitan District, the South Wales and Great Western Direct Railway, and the Rathkeale & Newcastle Junction; and a director of the Kingsbridge Railway and the Tiverton & North Devon. Others added to the list later included the Listowel & Ballybunion!)

In August 1861 Woollcombe also had talks with the Chairmen of the B&E and the LSWR to see if some common front could be come to regarding schemes west of Exeter, and after this date the SDR seems to have accepted that the Exeter–Okehampton corridor would fall to the narrow gauge.

In the new atmosphere of agreement, the 1862 session of Parliament therefore saw Acts passed for three major schemes to fill in the main gaps in the map (see *Fig. 5*):

1. The SDR-sponsored, Broad Gauge, Launceston & South Devon Railway for a Launceston–Lidford–Tavistock line.
2. The SDR-sponsored, Broad Gauge, Moretonhampstead & South Devon Railway for a Moretonhampstead–Newton line.
3. The LSWR-sponsored, Narrow Gauge, Okehampton Railway for a Coleford Junction–Okehampton line very similar to the MD&C's.

These three lines opened in 1865–7.

October 1862 saw a formal agreement on spheres of influence drawn up between the LSWR and the Broad Gauge interests, under which the LSWR was to suppress (temporarily!) its desires to extend west of Okehampton. Accordingly, when an Act for an Okehampton–Lidford line was obtained in 1863, the LSWR protested disassociation; but few believed them. By the mid-'60s it was in fact clear that the LSWR *was* going to secure a link to West Devon and Cornwall via Okehampton; and there was no longer the slightest prospect of the narrow gauge link to the west following the Exeter–Lea Cross–Chagford corridor that the DCR had hoped for in 1861.

1. Palk had turned the first sod of the Dartmouth & Torbay Railway on 21st January 1858, but this was in his capacity as MP.

2. After much pressure the 1859 station was eventually replaced in 1878 by the present Torquay station, a very generous structure, on the same site.

3. John and Henry Drew, Surveyors and Estate Agents, 15 Queen St Exeter, were the Earl of Devon's Agents.

4. See J. Hayter-Hames, *A History of Chagford*, Phillimore 1981.

5. Tone also became involved in Toogood's Somerset & Dorset schemings. In November 1860 plans (prepared by Tone) were also deposited by Toogood for a North Somerset Railway from the Somerset Central at Wells to the Midland at Bristol. This failed to get off the ground, but the later Bristol & North Somerset Railway which got its Act in 1863 was another Tone/Toogood line.

6. John Edward Errington (1806–1862), worked under Rastrick and then with Joseph Locke, and was appointed Engineer to the LSWR after Locke experienced difficulties with the Directors. In charge of the Yeovil–Exeter line. In the Parliamentary Committee on the MD&C Bill, Errington stated openly 'Mr Locke and myself have been engaged in this county for twenty years in promoting the extension of the narrow gauge system up to and beyond Exeter', and indeed they had been the Engineers to the failed 1853 Exeter–Plymouth scheme.
    William Robert Galbraith (1829–1914), articled to Errington 1846, heavily involved with LSWR work from 1855 and Resident Engineer of the Yeovil–Exeter and Exeter–Exmouth lines. Appointed as LSWR New Works Engineer on the death of Errington in 1862, and in charge of most new LSWR lines until the 1900s.
    Errington and Galbraith were always Consulting Engineers, not LSWR employees, and they also did some work for other companies. But they were both so closely associated with the LSWR that any 'independent' line they worked for in the West of England was bound to be seen by all as approved by Waterloo.

7. Peter John Margary (1820–1896). Articled to Brunel's office, SDR Resident Engineer from c.1849, appointed Engineer on Brunel's death in 1859. Also became Engineer to several SDR-backed branches including Moretonhampstead and Ashburton. On the GWR takeover in 1876, appointed Divisional Engineer Plymouth. Retired 1891. Margary was therefore involved with the SDR's opposition to, and negotiations with, the DCR and TVR throughout; and became directly responsible for the Teign Valley line after its belated opening in 1882.

CHAPTER TWO

THE TEIGN VALLEY RAILWAY AND ITS INITIAL EXTENSION SCHEMES
1862–1866

As we will from this point on be concerned primarily with the Teign Valley itself, rather than the wider areas of Central Devon that had exercised the DCR's hopes in 1860/1, this is perhaps the appropriate place to consider in greater detail the valley's economic situation at the time the railway was being promoted.

The River Teign's course from its rising on Dartmoor (as the North and South Teign rivers, meeting at Chagford) can be divided into four very distinct sections.

1. The heavily-wooded 'Teign gorge' section from east of Chagford to Dunsford, where the river flows west-east through confined but 'romantic' gorge scenery that was to become popular for day trips in later decades.
2. The agricultural section of the valley from Dunsford to Chudleigh Knighton, where the river flows north-south in a wider but still picturesque valley. It is this section — through which the Teign Valley branch line was to run — that is generally referred to as 'the Teign Valley', and is our main subject in this book.
3. The flatter lower section from Chudleigh Knighton to Newton Abbot, where the landscape is scarred by the Ball Clay industry. Being located so close to the navigable section of the river and served also by the Stover and Hackney canals, the Ball Clay industry had adequate transport links before the railways arrived. As a result, neither the clay industry, nor this section of the valley at large, had any real impact on the themes of this book.
4. The navigable tidal estuary from Newton Abbot to the sea at Teignmouth, where the river runs west-east again.

As Palk's detractors were forever pointing out, the Teign Valley was not a heavily populated area. There was only one town, Chudleigh, and most of the villages were on the small side. (Moreover, all the settlements, except for the hamlets of Lower Ashton and Chudleigh Knighton, were situated on the valley slopes a mile or more uphill from any possible station sites.) The real inspiration for the railway schemes was the fact that in 1860 the Teign Valley was in the middle of a mining boom, which was bringing extra income to the landowners (Palk and Lord Exmouth) and which there was reason to believe would boom further if only the mines could reduce their transport costs.[1] Mining had begun in the valley in the 1810s but only became a large-scale enterprise in the 1850s. Lead was the primary product, but silver found in the same lodes was a useful by-product, and there were also certain amounts of zinc, iron, barytes, and manganese. The River Teign above Newton was not navigable, and the output of the mines had to be taken by road to the Stover Canal at Ventiford, or to Newton itself, for transfer to river barges to take it to sea-going ships at Teignmouth Harbour. The coal needed for the mine engines had to be brought in by the same route. Now that rival mines elsewhere were getting railway links, this expensive road cartage was becoming seen as a threat to the Teign Valley mines' future, and it was perfectly logical for the mine interests to press for a railway to the valley.

(The dilemma which they and Palk evaded, though, was that whilst the mines needed a railway to reduce their transport costs, their total output was not and was never likely to be high enough to make a railway economic.)

The lead production figures in the table show how Palk was moved into his railway promotions at the height of the boom. In the event, the boom was to prove very shortlived. The difficulties brought by transport costs were soon swamped by the simple limited extent of the Teign Valley deposits, which saw each mine close after a few years, and then by a disastrous collapse in the price of lead in 1878 when largescale supplies from overseas became available at much lower prices than the British mines could offer (a factor which, admittedly, nobody could have anticipated in 1860). The last lead mine in the valley closed in 1880, two years before Palk's long-gestating railway was completed. However, the Bridford Barytes Mine (for details see Chapter 18), the Great Rock Iron Mine, and the Shuttamoor Iron Mine all survived into the twentieth century. The mining had brought an additional population to the valley, and its collapse brought population decline (as the 1901 figures here show) which further reduced the potential traffic for a railway.

The Teign Valley also had known granite and basalt reserves which had been little exploited up to this date, mainly because of transport costs. These were another factor in the promotion of the railway, but a minor one compared to the faith that was put in the future of the lead mines. In the event it was the stone quarrying that actually benefited from the railway's construction more than any other industry, bringing an enormous stone traffic to the line from the 1900s to the 1930s.

The small spoil-heaps on the western slopes of the valley did not hide the fact that it was fundamentally an agricultural area with picturesque scenery, and there were hopes of enhancing the agricultural rents by rail access to the growing population of Torquay (served by the Newton Abbot market), and also of attracting residential development.

POPULATION FIGURES		
	1861	*1901*
Chudleigh	2108	1820
Hennock (incl. Chudleigh Knighton)	1004	711
Trusham	223	165
Ashton	347	168
Christow	941	520
Doddiscombsleigh	343	210
Bridford	576	404
Dunsford	921	633

Fig. 3. The Teign Valley mines and transport links in 1862
(only major roads are shown)

The four lead mines shown on the map are those which were open in 1862. Other mines had been opened at various dates in the 1840s and 1850s, but found little or no workable ore and quickly closed.

Wheal Adams, Wheal Exmouth, Frank Mills, and South Exmouth mines were all run by the same interests — primarily Exeter people, which was one of the reasons why there was such interest in a rail link to Exeter as well as to Newton Abbot. They paid dues on the production to the landowners (Palk in the case of South Exmouth mine, Lord Exmouth in the case of the others). Details of these four mines are:

Wheal Adams — Opened c.1839, extended south 1853 to join with Wheal Exmouth and thereafter regarded as the same mine.

Wheal Exmouth — Opened 1828 but large-scale workings only began 1851-1853 when a new shaft was built. The mine's best period was 1854-9; 265 were employed in 1859. After that it was largely exhausted but there was some production until final closure in 1874. (Referred to as 'Old Exmouth' during periods of closure in the 1860s).

Frank Mills — (Francis Mills, a banker, was the largest shareholder in Wheal Exmouth.) Commenced 1854, production began 1857. At its peak in the late 1860s, declined in the '70s and closed 1880. The most successful of the mines.

South Exmouth — Worked 1862-1867 and employed 122 at its peak, but always less important than Wheal Exmouth and Frank Mills. (The same lodes had been worked from a different shaft, Wheal Hennock, in the 1812-1840s period, intermittently; this was the first lead mine in the valley.)

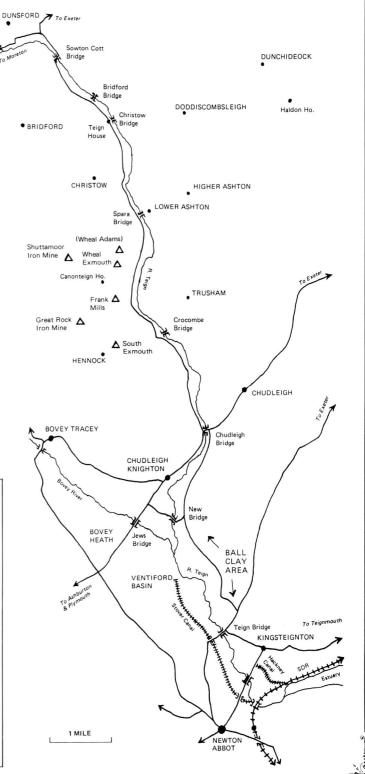

LEAD PRODUCTION IN THE TEIGN VALLEY

	Tons		Tons
1845	59	1865	1500
6	33	6	460
7	250	7	569
8	56	8	1520
9	382	9	1058
1850	395	1870	1008
1	460	1	828
2	705	2	654
3	755	3	516
4	1153	4	323
5	1297	5	250
6	1447	6	376
7	1600	7	333
8	1662	8	220
9	2082	9	120
1860	1414	1880	15
1	1514		
2	1246	NIL thereafter	
3	1008		
4	1261		

Source: Mineral Statistics of the United Kingdom, quoted by Schmitz. There are no figures before 1845, but production was very low previously. The figures are for tonnage of lead ore, the actual lead content was about two-thirds of this.

Views of the lead mines in their active days seem unobtainable, but this 1905 photograph of Shutta-moor Iron Mine gives a glimpse into the valley's mining past. The machinery is a four-head 'Californian' stamp set used to crush the mined ore.

Chapman collection cty. Devon C.R.O.

Great Rock Mine was opened in the early nineteenth century, abandoned, re-opened from 1849 to 1889 as Hennock Iron and Tin Mine, abandoned again, and finally worked from 1902 to 1969 by the Ferrubron Manufacturing Co. Ltd. It produced haematite used for iron oxide pigment in paint and was known locally as the 'Shiny Ore Mine'. With 30 tons of waste for every ton of the finished product, output was never more than 600-800 tons per annum. After the 1902 re-opening, the ore was packed in wooden barrels and carted to Trusham station for despatch by rail, much of it going to the London or Bristol docks for export to Australia and New Zealand. Although a regular traffic (until much of it was transferred to BRS latterly), it was not, of course, a large traffic from the Trusham station staff's viewpoint, being quite swamped by the stone traffic there. In this 1905 view we see the outdoor dressing plant at the mine. When closed in 1969, Great Rock was the last active metal mine in Devon. *Chapman collection, cty. Devon C.R.O.*

No book on the Teign Valley would be complete without a view of Canonteign Barton, the old Canonteign house which was let off to the tenant farmers after the new house was built. Farmer George Grant was the occupier from 1853; he gave evidence for the TVR in Parliament in 1863 and was in charge of the Ashton Committee organising the opening celebrations in October 1882. By the time this photograph was taken in the 1890s, the whole house was most romantically ivy-covered. It got into a poor state in the twentieth century but was restored in the 1970s. Adjacent to the house is the Wheal Exmouth Engine House, which still stands today as one of the few reminders of the valley's industrial past.   *Chapman collection, cty. Steven Court*

Canonteign House, home of the Viscounts Exmouth who, as landowners, profited from the lead mines in the 1850s-70s. This elegant Grecian mansion was built c.1820 by the 1st Lord Exmouth who had received his title for his part in the sack of Algiers. The house turned out to be situated above the main lead lodes, and a mine ventilation shaft was built on the lawn! Edward Pellew, the 3rd Viscount (succeeded 1833, died 1876), and Edward Fleetwood John Pellew, the 4th Viscount (born 1861, succeeded 1876, died 1899), were both always favourable to Palk's railway schemes, although they never took a really active role in the promotion of the line. The 4th Viscount did take a conspicuous role in the opening celebrations in October 1882, and became a director of the Exeter, Teign Valley & Chagford Railway for a time in the 1890s.   *Chapman collection, cty. Steven Court*

Chudleigh town centre in the railway heyday, with not a road vehicle in sight! After 1919 the population would soon be reminded again that this was the main road from London to Plymouth.

The former coaching town of Chudleigh did not share in the valley's 1850s/60s boom. If the grass was not quite growing in the streets, the population was declining badly after 1846 and was to continue to do so for several decades to come. As Palk was to say at the DCR's April 1861 public meeting in the town:

> 'There was a time when Chudleigh was the most lively town in this part of the country; being on the high road to Newton and Ashburton, it had coaches continually passing through it. He remembered when it was in its prosperity, but now he thought it looked as though it was asleep.'

It was said that 150 horses had been kept in the town for the coaches alone. Now the stables were empty, and the hands had moved elsewhere. In place of frequent coaches, the town now had no transport beyond market day carriers' carts to Exeter, Newton Abbot, and Dawlish. Such was the power of progress, and Chudleigh now looked to a railway of its own to restore its name to the map.

THE DEVON CENTRAL'S TEIGN VALLEY TRAMWAY SCHEMES (SPRING 1862)

The realisation by Palk and Toogood in the winter of 1861/2 that their grander ideas were not going to get anywhere, served to concentrate their minds for the moment on more readily-achievable schemes for securing improved communications to the Teign Valley itself.

Tone was naturally familiar with the practice in the North East of building mineral lines on a 'wayleave' basis, without an Act of Parliament, in cases where all the landowners were agreeable. Knowing that Lord Exmouth, and Lord Clifford of Ugbrooke House (who together with Palk owned most of the land in the valley) were favourable to Palk's ideas, Tone suggested that the DCR might try to get a line built in the Teign Valley on this basis. Although nowhere specifically stated, it is to be assumed that a goods-only line was intended. In February 1862 Toogood sought Counsel's opinion on the legal aspects:

'Several Gentlemen connected with the South of Devon have lately entertained the project of a tramway or railway to be constructed along a portion of the valley of the River Teign from Teignmouth or its vicinity to a point inland from whence the produce of the district consisting principally of minerals pottery wares and granite might be brought down to the coast . . .' If this were done by forming a Limited Liability partnership, and with wayleaves for land not owned by the promoters themselves, how could the crossings of public roads be arranged and would it be possible for the tramway to be used as a public highway by any willing to pay tolls for such use?

The response from Counsel was, in the way of such things, less than definitive, but the promoters pressed on with the idea. There were notions of having hinged rails at level crossings that would only be moved out over the road

The public house which gave its name to a GWR branch line terminus. The Teign House Inn is seen here in 1952.
Chapman collection cty. Devon C.R.O.

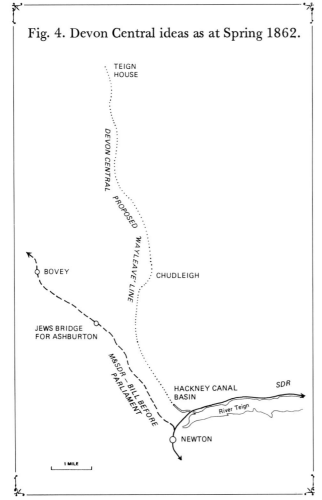

Fig. 4. Devon Central ideas as at Spring 1862.

TEIGN HOUSE

DEVON CENTRAL PROPOSED 'WAYLEAVE' LINE

BOVEY

CHUDLEIGH

JEWS BRIDGE FOR ASHBURTON

M&SDR — BILL BEFORE PARLIAMENT

HACKNEY CANAL BASIN

SDR

River Teign

NEWTON

1 MILE

when a train had to cross. Tone now drew up a definite scheme for a tramway from the Hackney Canal at Kingsteignton to the Teign House Inn at Christow — the first time that a Teign House terminus to a Teign Valley railway had been suggested. On 2nd April 1862 Toogood offered to pay Tone £60 for a fuller survey and estimate of this line.

Unfortunately, it became clear in the weeks after this that the legal difficulties in the way of getting such a tramway built by wayleaves were likely to be insurmountable, and that the expense of another application to Parliament would therefore have to be faced after all.

EXETER, ASHBURTON, BUCKFASTLEIGH, AND PLYMOUTH

Grander ideas had never been forgotten. In the autumn of 1861 the Palk camp had started taking an interest in Ashburton and Buckfastleigh, for which there had been no schemes in the 1861 session, probably because neither Palk nor the Earl of Devon had any personal property interests there. There were, however, two good reasons for taking an interest now. Firstly, the SDR/LSWR carve-up of the map in Summer 1861 had still produced no schemes for these towns (the SDR probably feeling unable to support a third new line in the same session as Moretonhampstead and Launceston) so there was still a chance for the DCR to get a wedge in here. And secondly, as Palk became forced to admit defeat on the Okehampton axis, he began to dream up ideas of a further narrow gauge route (in the long term) from Exeter to Plymouth by the Teign Valley, Ashburton, Buckfastleigh, and Brent. Indeed, in September 1861 Tone did an outline survey of this corridor as far as Brent. Palk was always fond of making remarks at public meetings about inland routes from Portsmouth to Plymouth and said

Fig. 5. Railways in South Devon as at Summer 1862.

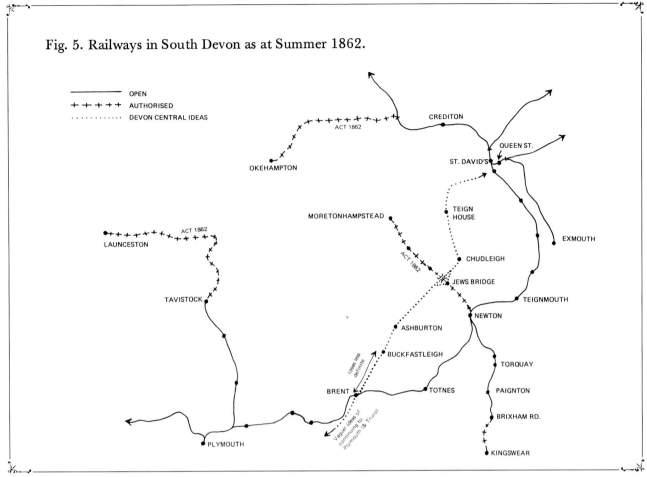

seriously that he would be happy to see three or four such routes built!

A Newton or Exeter to Ashburton and Buckfastleigh line would be an easy and innocent-looking preliminary stage to such vaguer long-term hopes, and in October 1861 Palk made himself conspicuous at a public meeting held in Ashburton by the Portreeve to discuss the general question of rail links to Ashburton. At this stage the best the town had on offer was a proposed 'Jews Bridge for Ashburton' station (on the site of the later Heathfield station) on the M&SDR line, but, as this was six miles off, it was not held in any great favour. Attempts were also being made to float a broad gauge Totnes–Ashburton line. But the feeling of the meeting was very encouraging to the Devon Central camp — most people wanted direct links to Newton or Exeter and not the Totnes scheme.

Ashburton and Buckfastleigh ideas were put on the backburner whilst the Tramway scheme was investigated, but returned to the fore when that collapsed. May 1862 saw Tone's assistant Browne going over the ground again to choose a rough Teign Valley–Ashburton–Buckfastleigh line.

Another factor which now came into play was the M&SDR getting its Act (as had been expected) on 7th July 1862. This offered the DCR the chance of saving some construction costs on a Teign Valley to Newton route, by joining the M&SD line somewhere along its route instead of having to build an independent line all the way into Newton (albeit with the difficulty that the M&SD was to be a broad gauge line). If the DCR had had no ulterior motives, it would have been most sensible to join the M&SD north of Teigngrace, about 2½ miles out of Newton. But the DCR camp were now getting ambitious again, and decided on joining the M&SD at Jews Bridge 3¾ miles out of Newton. This was illogical in itself; it meant higher mileage payments to the M&SDR for running trains over their line, and a rather circuitous route for Teign Valley–Newton journeys, whilst not actually saving anything in the cost of building the line in the Teign Valley. But Jews Bridge was exactly where the DCR needed to go for a direct Exeter–Ashburton–Buckfastleigh line. Thus it was that the eventual junction point of the TVR with the M&SDR was decided.

In the summer of 1862 Tone and Browne did full surveys for an Exeter–Teign Valley–Jews Bridge–Ashburton–Buckfastleigh line (not going beyond Buckfastleigh — the route beyond to Plymouth was always to remain a vague dream). This scheme was a neat one insofar as it would

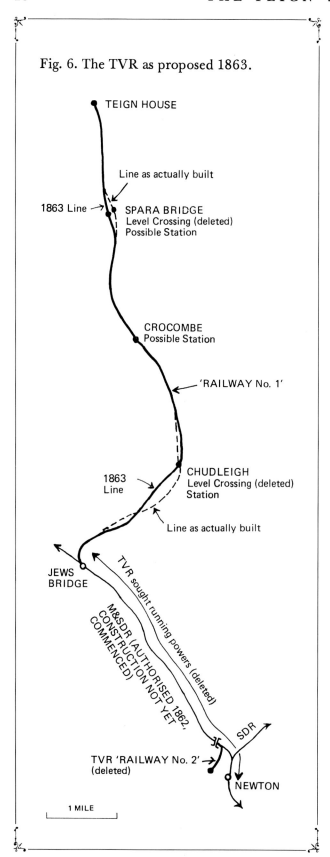

Fig. 6. The TVR as proposed 1863.

TEIGN HOUSE

Line as actually built

1863 Line →

SPARA BRIDGE
Level Crossing (deleted)
Possible Station

CROCOMBE
Possible Station

'RAILWAY No. 1'

1863
Line

CHUDLEIGH
Level Crossing (deleted)
Station

Line as actually built

JEWS
BRIDGE

TVR sought running powers (deleted)

M&SDR (AUTHORISED 1862,
CONSTRUCTION NOT YET
COMMENCED)

SDR

TVR 'RAILWAY No. 2' →
(deleted)

NEWTON

1 MILE

have enabled the DCR to run a reasonably direct Newton–Ashburton–Buckfastleigh service, in addition to providing the desired Exeter–Teign Valley, Teign Valley–Newton, and Exeter–Ashburton/Buckfastleigh facilities. However, when it came to the depositing of plans in the autumn, Palk and his friends got cold feet. As an 1866 document puts it: 'it was however at that time found that the cost of such a line coupled with the hostility with which it was certain to be met by the South Devon Co, rendered it inexpedient to proceed with it.' If there had been any hopes of an LSWR interest, these were quashed when that company made its pact with the GWR in October 1862.

Instead, it was decided to go to Parliament for a Teign House–Jews Bridge line only, so that a pretence could be made that this was nothing more than a local feeder line to the M&SDR. This ploy worked in so far as it enabled Palk and friends to get an Act, but at the end of the day it backfired, for the always-intended extensions were never gained in the event, and the company ended up with this unremunerative rump to Teign House as its only piece of railway.

THE TEIGN VALLEY RAILWAY (1863)

With the new emphasis on the 'local' nature of the proposals, it was decided in November 1862 to change the company's name, and the plans that Browne put on a train at Newcastle station for despatch to Toogood on the evening of 25th November 1862, bore the new name 'Teign Valley Railway'.

The plans envisaged a main route (Railway No. 1) from the M&SDR at Jews Bridge to a terminus at Teign House, or, as the Act put it, 'from Bovey Tracey to the town of Chudleigh, and thence to Doddiscombsleigh.'[2] Additionally, a short branch (Railway No. 2) was proposed from the M&SDR to an independent TVR station in Newton. There were no difficult works on the line, beyond a number of bridges over the River Teign and one over the Bovey River. The estimate for the line was only £29,126 plus £4,000-6,000 for stations and £4,200 for land (much of the land was owned by Palk himself, and would not have to be paid for). In detail the route of Railway No. 1 as planned in 1862 and authorised in the 1863 Act was rather different from the railway as actually built, most notably insofar as it would have been on the west bank of the river on the Chudleigh Knighton-Chudleigh section, and also on the west side of the river through Ashton (see *Fig. 6*; the reasons for the changes at these points are explained later in this section). Stations were intended at Jews Bridge, Chudleigh, Crocombe Bridge and/or Spara Bridge, and Teign House[3] (only later in 1863/4 was it definitely decided to have stations at both Crocombe Bridge and Spara Bridge, so providing stations by all the river bridges in this section of the valley).

Given that it was now only to connect into the broad gauge system, the TVR was now proposed to be a broad gauge line itself (the 1863 Act specified that it must be so). Palk cannot have liked this, but may have been anticipating that the TVR would be able to get another Act authorising an Exeter extension and change of gauge before the time came to actually lay the track. The Bill sought running powers over the M&SDR from Jews Bridge to the SDR junction at Newton, and over the SDR from the junction to Newton station, plus the use of the SDR's Newton station. It also sought powers to make Working Agreements with the M&SDR or the SDR — in reality, as it was known that the M&SDR was itself to be worked by the SDR, this meant with the SDR.

'Railway No. 2' in Newton was not a very serious proposal; it was, as the TVR Counsel's brief put it, a throwaway 'proposed in order to assist the promoters negotiate with the SDR'. (The TVR's public front was that Railway No. 2 was necessary in case the M&SDR agreed running powers but the SDR did not; the SDR suspected, probably wrongly, that it was the start of a line to Plymouth.) The running powers and SDR agreement were seriously sought, but the SDR, which had resolved to oppose 'Mr. Toogood's project', was almost implacably hostile, and negotiations got nowhere. The TVR then decided to withdraw both Railway No. 2 and the applications for running powers and Agreements from the Bill. The TVR had tried separate negotiations with the M&SDR, putting forward various suggestions to them — that the TVR might pay half the cost of building the Jews Bridge–Newton Abbot section, or build the whole of that section of the M&SD line, or have running powers over it for a rent of half the annual upkeep costs — but the M&SDR, whilst it no doubt found any idea that would help reduce its own costs interesting, and had local supporters who resented having to toe the SDR's anti-TVR line, was nevertheless too much a child of the SDR to be able to consider entering into agreements that the SDR was hostile to. Having therefore given up ideas of getting any Working Agreement, the TVR began talking to rolling stock manufacturers as to the acquisition of stock to enable them to run the line themselves, and Tone went into some details of this in Parliament.

In Parliament, the TVR found itself faced with opposition from the SDR and M&SDR (the latter's case actually, of course, organised by the SDR); the Earl of Devon (largely at the SDR's bidding); Robert Pulsford, the owner of 'Pitt House' and the fields on the west side of the river south of Chudleigh; and 'Merchants & landowners of Newton Abbot'. Pulsford was placated by a promise to get the line diverted away from his land in a subsequent session, or pay him £1,000 an acre if this were to prove impossible (in the event, a deviation was later secured). The Merchants of Newton were not anti-TVR as such, but disliked some of the local effects of 'Railway No. 2', and when that was withdrawn they were happy. So in effect there was only the SDR opposition to deal with by the time the TVR came to Committee.

The TVR had a quick and easy time before the Commons Committee on 4th May 1863, as the

Committee ruled that the SDR and M&SDR had no locus standi now that the applications for running powers and agreements had been withdrawn. The Commons Committee did, however, insist on the deletion of the two remaining level crossings (several others had been withdrawn voluntarily by the TVR after talks with the Board of Trade) at Chudleigh Bridge and Spara Bridge. Tone had been reluctant to give up these two, as they were both located at station sites, and so close to the road bridges over the river that wholly new road bridges would have been needed over the river if the roads were to be elevated over the railway. When they were deleted, it inevitably meant that considerable changes had to be made to the line at these points (although nothing was said about this at the time). At Ashton the line was moved over 100yds eastwards to the east bank of the river.[4] At Chudleigh the problems of crossing the road, coupled with the need to avoid Pulsford's land if possible, threw the whole route back into the melting pot from summer 1863 on, and the situation was not resolved until 1872 (and was a major factor in preventing the TVR being completed and opened in the 1860s).

After the Bill's passage in the Commons, Fowler advised the SDR to seek a Working Agreement with the TVR, presumably on the grounds that the TVR now seemed likely to get its Act and it was desirable to prevent any other company securing an agreement with them. Fowler was authorised to meet the TVR promoters, but for some reason he was unable to, and the opposition continued.

The Lords took a more charitable view towards the Broad Gauge camp, and allowed the M&SDR to appear, which effectively enabled the SDR to make all the objections it wished. The Committee hearings were on 29th and 30th June. Palk, the TVR's main witness, stressed the claim that this was a local line that would benefit the M&SD by bringing extra traffic to it. (However, under cross-examination, reminded of his past statements about Portsmouth–Plymouth routes and the like, he blurted out more realistically 'At present it is nothing but a local line — I have no means of making any other — if I had I would make it tomorrow, I tell you!') The Moreton line was of no use to the population of the Teign Valley because the hills between the two valleys would make it inaccessible in practice. Palk had necessarily to overemphasize the Teign Valley's connections with Newton and underplay its connections with Exeter. The choice of Teign House as a terminus was another difficult point — 'a weak point in the case,' noted the Counsel's brief — both because Teign House was in itself clearly not a location offering much traffic potential and because this then added to the likelihood of people believing the SDR's claims that the TVR did not really intend Teign House to be the terminus at all. Palk spoke of the Teign House Inn as 'the centre where all the business of the neighbourhood is transacted', but few were likely to find the idea of a rural pub producing enough traffic to justify a railway line too credible! Palk defended the TVR from the suggestion that it was a 'contractor's line' (correctly, but hardly anyone had made that accusation — there were rather more suspicions of it being an 'auction line', of which Palk had less to say!). He 'had no doubt that the whole of the capital for the line will be forthcoming from residents in the neighbourhood'.

Baldwin Fulford, the second witness, got into difficulties under cross-examination as a result of his claim that the line would serve a population of 11,000 people. This was a gross exaggeration — Fulford, it transpired, had included all sorts of places miles from the line — although perhaps no worse than Palk's amazingly ignorant estimate of the population of Chudleigh as 'about 800'. An interesting point mentioned by Fulford was that it had of late become the practice to cart coal for the Dunsford area from the North Devon line at Yeoford, rather than from Newton.

Other TVR witnesses were Tone, several persons connected with the mines, and the usual array of local traders and farmers. There were petitions in favour from 'Inhabitants of Newton Abbot and Newton Bushel', 'Inhabitants of Bovey Tracey, Hennock, Kingsteignton, Trusham, Christow, Ashton, and Doddiscombsleigh', and 'Inhabitants of Chudleigh'; and, to the SDR's annoyance, a petition of 10th June 1863 from those M&SDR shareholders in favour of the TVR.

The SDR's public case was angled mainly at the lack of traffic potential in the Teign Valley — the TVR was already being mocked as the line that 'commenced on a heath and ended in a field'. Margary also attacked the estimates, producing a counter-estimate of £67,000. But the real cause of the SDR's hostility was, of course, that they knew that the TVR had every intention of coming back to Parliament in subsequent sessions for extensions to make an anti-SDR rival route from Exeter; and these ulterior motives of the TVR were stressed by the SDR in the Lords.

The SDR's arguments were not enough to persuade Parliament to reject the line, and the Teign Valley Railway Act 1863 received the Royal Assent on 13th July 1863. 'Sir Lawrence Palk Baronet, Baldwin Fulford, William Kitson (and) Thomas Eales Rogers' were to be the first directors of the TVR Company.[5] The share capital was to be £45,000 (2,250 £20 shares) and £15,000 could be borrowed in addition. The line was to be built within five years.

EXTENSIONS FOILED: THE 1864 BILL
The TVR was able to start construction work in 1864 and, although clearly short of money, gave a credible impression through 1864 and 1865 that the line might be completed and·opened to traffic in the near future. Details of the building of the line are given in Chapter 3. For the moment it is sufficient to note that this enabled the company to be optimistic enough to proceed with extension schemes.

Those who had insisted in the summer of 1863 that the TVR's facade of a local line was a mere ploy, and that they would soon come back for extensions, had a mere five months to wait before proof of their words appeared. The

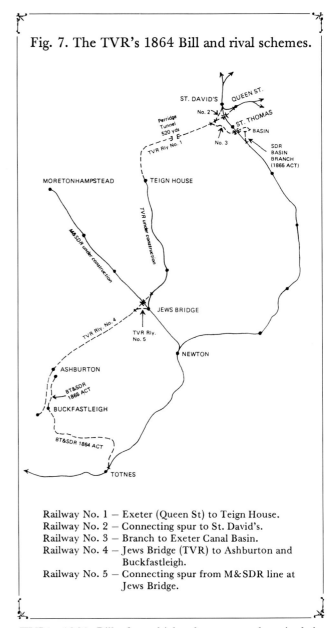

Fig. 7. The TVR's 1864 Bill and rival schemes.

Railway No. 1 — Exeter (Queen St) to Teign House.
Railway No. 2 — Connecting spur to St. David's.
Railway No. 3 — Branch to Exeter Canal Basin.
Railway No. 4 — Jews Bridge (TVR) to Ashburton and Buckfastleigh.
Railway No. 5 — Connecting spur from M&SDR line at Jews Bridge.

TVR's 1864 Bill, for which plans were deposited in November 1863, was certainly not designed to placate the SDR, for it involved the promotion of the whole scheme of summer 1862 which had been largely held back from Parliament in 1863, plus a line to the Exeter Canal Basin. Details are given in *Fig. 7.* Power was sought to make all these lines, and the 1863 Act Jews Bridge–Teign House line, mixed gauge. Tone stated that he proposed to construct the system broad-gauge-only initially, except for the Queen St–Railway No. 3 Junction–Canal Basin section, which would be mixed from the start to give LSWR trains access to the Basin. But he argued that in five or ten years time the whole national railway system would be converting to the narrow gauge, so it was prudent for any company to seek to have powers to convert — a point which it was difficult to argue against. Powers were also sought to make Working Agreements with the SDR or the LSWR.

The SDR, of course, had no hesitation in opposing the Bill, and at a meeting held at Paddington on 27th January 1864 to consider the schemes of the current session, discussion was especially directed to the TVR plans. The M&SDR had to follow the SDR line. Unfortunately for the TVR, the LSWR (as in 1863) also concluded that the balance of circumstances brought no reason to get involved with the TVR, and in February the LSWR Secretary sent a friendly missive to Paddington stating that the LSWR had no intention of making an Agreement with the TVR. The Agreement clauses were in due course withdrawn from the Bill. The TVR, however, was not without friends altogether. Chudleigh was pro-TVR, as it was throughout, no other company having ever sought to serve the town. At Ashburton the public view was very much in favour of the TVR plans, and against a rival scheme being promoted by the Buckfastleigh, Totnes & South Devon Railway (an SDR offshoot) for a broad gauge Totnes–Buckfastleigh 'Great Way Round' line similar to that which had been in the air in 1861.[6] The Portreeve of Ashburton held another public meeting in May 1864 which resulted in a unanimous resolution for the TVR scheme. There was also support from Exeter Corporation, who were anxious to get a rail link to the Canal Basin and therefore came down in January in favour of the TVR, although not without suppressing some doubts about the TVR promoters' real motives and their financial ability to actually build the line! As ancient enemies of the Earl of Devon, the Exeter Corporation were always that bit more prepared to come down in favour of anything that the Earl and the Broad Gauge camp were known to be against. The St. Thomas Local Board also approved the TVR plans, provided that the TVR built a station in St. Thomas.

The Parliamentary Committee hearings were protracted — five days in the Commons in May/June, three days in the Lords in July. The S&D/M&SDR case was backed up by Lord Devon, who had instigated a Petition of Owners and Occupiers. (The force of this was somewhat dampened by the fact that the scheme which the Earl was now finding property objections to was all but identical to that which he had been actively promoting himself in 1861! — he responded that he did not object as a landowner, but because he saw no traffic need for the line.) The SDR's attack concentrated on the TVR's bad faith in having tried to convince Parliament the previous year that their line was a mere local branch — 'We object to the Bill as being only another instalment towards the establishment of a competing line of railway between Exeter and Plymouth' — and on the TVR's poor financial situation, which was beginning to become all too clear by this date. Back in January, an anti-TVR *Western Morning News* article had focused on this:

'The question is, whether the Teign Valley Railway is a myth . . . anything but a name? . . . the promoter who pulls the strings [Toogood]

and causes so many agreeable and graceful movements of the landed and automatol figures around him, should state the financial condition . . . Is there one shareholder in the company?'

(Palk was asked in Parliament how many shareholders there were, and refused to reply!)

The fact that the TVR was promoting expensive extensions at a time when it could not raise enough money for its existing line was, said the SDR, even clearer proof that the TVR was just an 'auction line' meant for selling to one of the existing companies.

There was also much debate over the details of the Canal Basin branch, with its level crosssings over the busy Cowick Street and Alphington Road, and street running in parts of Water Lane. The Bill ended up containing clauses prohibiting locomotive power or 'atmospheric agency', and prohibiting trains of more than six wagons, or at less than ten minute intervals, over the level crossings. There was then argument over the ability of horses to haul the traffic, if locomotives were barred.

The Bill was passed in the Commons, but failed in the Lords at the end of July 1864, primarily due to the hostility of Lord Devon and Lord Churston (who had lands at Dean Prior south of Buckfastleigh, through which any extension to Brent and Plymouth would have to pass).

The TVR's allies expressed their regrets. The Portreeve of Ashburton wrote 'lamenting the loss of the TVR Bill'; but the fact was that the rival BT&SDR had got its Act, and another part of the map had thereby been shut off to the TVR camp. (In 1865 the BT&SDR received powers for a Buckfastleigh–Ashburton extension; the line opened in 1872.) After 1864 there was no further talk of westward extensions from Jews Bridge. Eighty-seven inhabitants of Chudleigh signed a petition, forwarded by Lord Clifford, urging the TVR not to give up its Exeter extension ideas. But the Exeter Corporation lost interest in a TVR Basin link. Woollcombe had promised in May that the SDR would build a mixed-gauge Canal Basin branch if the TVR scheme failed, and the House of Lords in July recommended that this should be done. On 26th October 1864, at an Exeter Corporation committee meeting, Toogood conceded defeat regarding the Basin. The SDR Basin line was approved by Parliament in 1865 and opened in 1867.

After the disaster of the loss of the Bill, the TVR made attempts to rally a show of support at public meetings. There was grand talk of going back to Parliament next year for Exeter and Torquay lines. A first meeting at Torquay in August did result in a 29–19 show for a pro-TVR resolution, but only because the hall was 'packed' with members of the Toogood and Kitson clans (and only after a 'great disturbance' led by an SDR faction under Woollcombe). The SDR got itself better organised for the second meeting at Newton on 23rd August. Public opinion in Newton was generally fairly pro-SDR anyway, but Woollcombe made sure of things by packing the meeting with dozens of SDR employees who gave a big cheer when he and the other directors entered the hall! Palk was not present, but Toogood was and he received a rough ride. Most speakers attacked the TVR, and one speaker from Torquay expressed his objections to 'bubble schemes to serve the purposes of private individuals' and said that Torquay did not want a new railway in the centre of the town to carry Palk's mineral traffic! The resolution went against the TVR and the organisers could only mutter complaints over the 'packing'. Plans for further meetings in Exeter, Ashburton, and Buckfastleigh had to be given up.

SDR NEGOTIATIONS (AUTUMN 1864)

The loss of the 1864 Bill, the lack of any signs of interest from the LSWR, and the poor results of the public meetings, combined with the fact that the TVR was at this date still entertaining hopes of opening its line in 1865, really left the TVR with little choice but to go begging for a Working Agreement with the SDR. (Ideas of the TVR working the line itself seem to have been forgotten, probably because it did not have the finances to buy rolling stock.) The SDR for its part, now that it had succeeded in knocking the TVR's ambitious ideas on the head, was willing in principle to work the TVR, although it was another matter whether agreement could be reached on details, given the SDR's and TVR's differing views on the traffic potential in the valley.

Palk must have written to Woollcombe immediately after the Bill was lost, as his letter was considered by the SDR Board on 9th August. The TVR shareholders' meeting on 31st August was told that negotiations were in progress with the SDR. The SDR sent the TVR a draft agreement, probably in standard terms as for the other lines to be worked by them, but the TVR rejected this and drew up proposals of their own, which were discussed by Palk and Toogood in attendance on the SDR Board on 18th October. The TVR was rather demanding, insisting that they must be free to extend to Exeter, Crediton, and Chagford. (Crediton had been rather on the back burner since 1861, but up to 1880 the possibility of a Crediton line was always there in the TVR's thoughts.) As an alternative to a Working Agreement, they would be willing to sell the TVR to the SDR for £90,000. The SDR, not surprisingly, rejected both proposals.

In November 1864 the SDR put forward another proposal:

1. The TVR to complete the line to Teign House, to the satisfaction of the SDR Engineer, the line to be transferred to the SDR on completion.
2. The TVR not to undertake any further extensions.
3. The SDR to work the line.
4. The SDR to pay a perpetual rent of £2,900 p.a.

Woollcombe and Palk had some talks on this, but from December 1864 everything went dead. The SDR were to claim later that they assumed that this was because the TVR had accepted the scheme! But in reality the TVR could not find it acceptable because, as the February 1865 TVR shareholders' meeting was told: 'it would have entirely put an end to the extension of the line to Exeter and Crediton, and made it merely a branch line of the SDR'.

The TVR had recovered a little from the shock of July 1864 by this date, and was also concerned that the securities in which the SDR was proposing to pay the rent charge might not be realisable for as much as the SDR implied.

THE 1865 ACT

Despite the collapse of the negotiations in the winter of 1864/5, the TVR included powers for an SDR Agreement in its 1865 Bill, and with the SDR now in favour of an Agreement (in principle) and not objecting, these powers were secured in the Teign Valley Railway Act 1865 which received the Royal Assent on 29th June 1865. A proposed clause empowering the TVR to sell the line to the SDR was, however, left out.

The 1865 Bill was promoted for a number of unconnected reasons and had the new luxury, for the TVR, of being unopposed in its later stages. It was, however, to turn out of little practical value to the TVR. The immediate interest in an SDR Agreement was, as we have seen, gone before the Act was passed. The other major powers in the Act, for the creation of additional share capital, were in the event never exercised. And the clause in the Bill for a deviation line to resolve the pressing route problems at Chudleigh had to be withdrawn.

THE EXETER EXTENSION FAILS AGAIN: THE 1866 BILL

The 1866 Bill marked the TVR's last effort at extensions in the initial period, before their own financial situation, combined with a generally depressed national situation, forced them to give up all extension ideas for a decade.

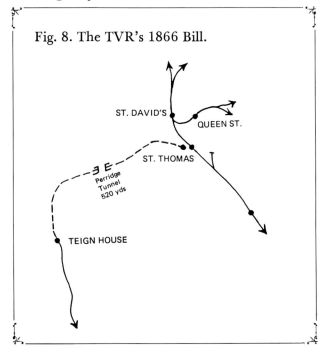

Fig. 8. The TVR's 1866 Bill.

After 1864 people in Torquay and Ashburton soon came to realise that they were not going to get anything out of the TVR. But Chudleigh people still had great hopes of the line and of an extension to Exeter, and this gave a visible public support to the TVR Directors' own strategic desires to see such an extension. (Unfortunately, there was almost no population on the line between Teign House and Exeter, so there was no local support in that area to speak of.)

In July 1865 the TVR Board 'considered the expediency' of applying for an extension to Exeter again, and, at the shareholders' meeting on 31st August, Charles Langley of Chudleigh,[7] who was both a leading figure in the town and possessed of influence with the TVR, secured cheers when he spoke keenly in favour, saying that the line would be 'of very little value to Chudleigh' without an Exeter extension. A resolution was passed (as the Directors no doubt wished) that powers should be sought in the next session.

It was decided to promote a simple line to a terminus 'in a garden at the back of the Moreton Inn' (100 yds north of Cowick St.) near St Thomas station. This was primarily a ploy to prevent the SDR having any *locus standi* in Parliament, in which respect it was successful; the SDR made a petition but it was disallowed. However, one suspects also that the TVR must have been a little uncertain at this date which railway they might best seek a junction with at Exeter, so a non-committal line which could be amended at a later date had other advantages too.

The 1864 plans were re-used, avoiding the expense of a new survey. The terminus was on the line of the 1864 Canal Basin branch. The Engineer's estimate was £140,000. The 1866 Bill also sought powers to raise further share capital to finance the extension, and (as in 1864) powers to make the 1863 line and the Extension mixed gauge instead of broad gauge.

Things were set up for another Parliamentary contest, with a petition from Lord Devon and others (complaining of 'repeated and unwarrantable attacks' on their property) giving the SDR an opening, and petitions in favour from Exeter Corporation, St Thomas Local Board, Lord Exmouth, Lord Clifford, and 'inhabitants' of most places in the vicinity. But after the Bill's second reading in the Commons on 21st February 1866, it was withdrawn by the promoters. The reason will become clear in Chapter 3 — the TVR had by this date sunk into such a desperate financial crisis that any extensions were now quite out of the question.

1. For full details of the Teign Valley mines see C.J. Schmitz, 'The Teign Valley Silver-Lead Mines 1806-1880,' *British Mining No. 15*, Northern Mine Research Society, 2nd edn. 1980; also A.K.H. Jenkin, *Mines of Devon — North and East of Dartmoor*, Devon Library Services, Exeter, 1981.
2. The terminus station was to be on the east bank of the river and was therefore in Doddiscombsleigh parish; the Teign House Inn itself was on the other side of the river in Christow parish, and the passenger station eventually opened in 1903 was to be called 'Christow'.
3. *Jews Bridge*. As noted previously, the M&SDR had been intending to have a station here anyway. They did not, in the event, build it until 1874 when it opened as 'Chudleigh Road' (see Chapter 4), being renamed 'Heathfield' in 1882. There was no habitation at this point, but it was on the main Exeter–Plymouth road (A38) and the closest point on the M&SDR line to Chudleigh.

    Chudleigh. Sometimes referred to as 'Chudleigh Bridge' pre-1882.

    Crocombe Bridge. This is the established spelling now, various other spellings in use formerly. The TVR in the 1860s/70s usually referred to this station as 'Crocombe' (or Crowcombe, or Crocomb, or Crockham). It took the name 'Trusham' when opened in 1882 but had never been so called previously. The railway bridge over the river south of the station became known as Crockham Bridge, and the nearby quarry as Crockham quarry.

    Spara Bridge. Alias 'Sparrow Bridge.' Already often referred to as 'Ashton' in the 1860s/70s, and so called on opening in 1882.

    Teign House. Sometimes referred to as 'Doddiscombsleigh' in 1863, but always called 'Teign House' after this date.
4. No deviation powers were ever obtained at the relevant time, even though the section through Ashton station was outside the 1863 Act's limits of deviation. The actual line was authorised retrospectively by the TVR's 1872 Act. Perversely, the new line still had a level crossing over the same road; powers were sought for this in the 1872 Bill without succes, and not obtained until the 1878 Act.
5. The Devon Central company had not of course got to the stage of being statutorily incorporated. The TVR directors regarded the TVR as the *same* company as the DCR. Thomas Rogers was a leading figure in Ashburton. Various further directors were appointed from 1864 on, but none were to have any significant influence on the company.
6. The TVR did manage to get some of its share capital taken up by local people in 1864/5, and looking down the list of these small shareholders one sees that a very large proportion of them were in only three places — Chudleigh, Ashburton, and Torquay. These were the places where the TVR had active local support. Very few shares were taken in Exeter, or outside the area.
7. Charles Langley (1805-1892). Set up as an Attorney in Chudleigh in 1832 and acquired a near monopoly of legal work in the town. He was very concerned by the slump in property values after 1846 and always a keen supporter of any railway to the town. On the Newton & Moretonhampstead Railway Committee 1858–1861 (when that seemed Chudleigh's best chance), but not involved with the M&SDR after 1861, as the TVR began to offer Chudleigh a better option. Langley did much legal work for the TVR in the 1860s and gave evidence in Parliament in 1863. He became an Auditor of the TVR company and then a Director in 1868 for a time.

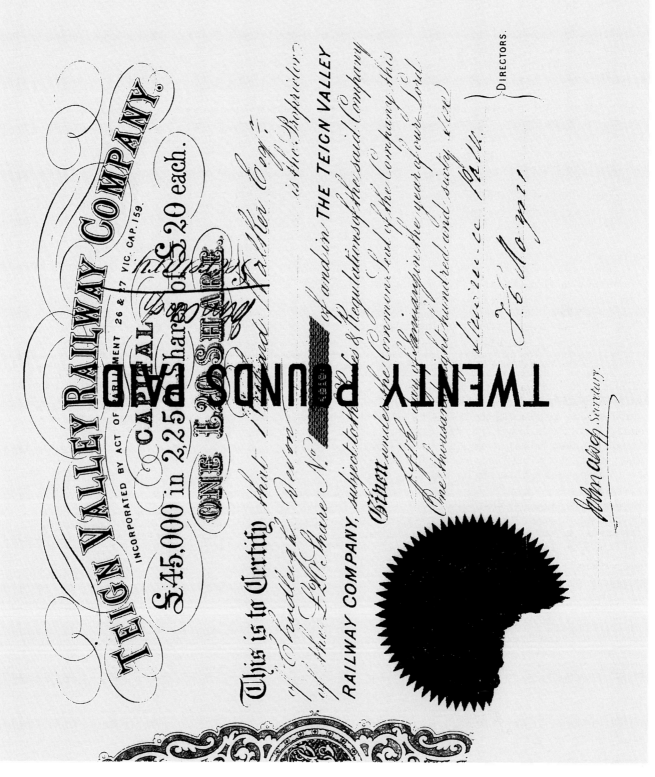

CHAPTER THREE
BUILDING THE TEIGN VALLEY RAILWAY (1)
1864-1870

THE Teign Valley Railway from Jews Bridge to Teign House should have been an easy line to build (as Tone said in Parliament in 1863). But things did not turn out so. Recurring financial crises led to construction being carried out in five distinct bursts over no less than 18 years (1864–6, 1869–70, 1877–8, 1879–80, 1881–2) with long periods of inactivity in between, during which the works were left to decay, sometimes, people began to think, left for good.

WALKER'S CONTRACT (1864–6)

Tone had made it clear in 1863 that the TVR did not intend to let a contractor 'take' the line (i.e., take the whole share capital and be responsible for everything including land purchase), but would buy the land themselves and give a straightforward construction contract.

The contract, dated 23rd February 1864, was given to Richard Walker, a small contractor whose route of introduction to the TVR is not known. He was then living in Ware, completing the loose ends of the Ware Hadham & Buntingford Railway on which he had been active since 1859 (and which was already open to traffic). The TVR contract price was £44,000, to be paid £39,000 in cash and £5,000 in paid-up shares. The completion date (provided that the TVR had delivered the land — which it did not) was 31st May 1865, soon changed to 31st June (*sic*), a reasonable enough anticipation for such an easy line. There were only the river bridges, and some lengths of low embankment and shallow cutting, in the way of significant works. It was specified that the stations were not to cost more than £2,000 each including signals, turntables, points and crossings; and that the bridges and other structures were not to be of timber but brick or good stone or iron (which, like most of the things anticipated in this contract, did not come to pass!).

At the same time as the contract was let, the TVR appointed Norman F.G. Uniacke as its first Secretary, to relieve Toogood of the day-to-day administrative work. Uniacke lived in Torquay and was also Secretary of Palk's Torquay Hotel Co. (He resigned in 1865, finding his lack of experience in railway work a disadvantage — although it did not stop him from becoming a TVR Director for a time afterwards. James Hutt, who replaced Uniacke in 1865, himself resigned in 1867 to be replaced by John Alsop.)

Walker began work immediately in February/March 1864.[1] In early March people in Chudleigh were expecting a 'First Sod' ceremony any day, but it is not clear that any such ceremony actually materialised. Because of the problems over the route at Chudleigh Bridge, and problems

over land acquisition (mainly from the Duke of Somerset) on the Jews Bridge–Chudleigh section, Walker was not able to do anything at this end of the line, and had to restrict his activities to the section between a point just north of Chudleigh Bridge and Teign House. Most of the land on this section was owned by Palk or Lord Exmouth, both of whom put the TVR in possession immediately without any definite arrangements on recompense. The initial public reports of Walker's work naturally concentrated on the bright side. A shareholders' meeting on 28th March 1864 was told by Walker (surely with some exaggeration!) that 1½ miles of line (i.e. earthworks) should be completed by the end of the next week. One hundred and fifty men were reported at work in May, and the next meeting on 18th June heard that 'four miles of the line had already been completed (again, earthworks were meant) and the contractors only wanted possession of more land to go on with the work, and if the land could be obtained the whole of the line might be finished within six months'.

The Moretonhampstead line had been commenced in August 1863, only six months ahead of the TVR, and was a more difficult job (in theory), so it was reasonable enough for the TVR Board to think initially that they might have their line ready for traffic by the time the M&SDR opened in, say, the summer of 1865. Indeed, Palk was claiming in summer 1864 that the TVR was holding back its operations to avoid finishing pointlessly soon, before the M&SDR. Good progress on the northern half of the line led to ideas of an initial Chudleigh–Teign House opening; the TVR Board on 25th February 1865 (having by then given up hopes of having the whole line open that year) asked Browne 'to direct the contractor so that the portion of the line between Teign House and Chudleigh Bridge may be ready for traffic during the autumn', and 'to construct a temporary station (north of Chudleigh Bridge) on such land as he may see fit'. What traffic such a truncated railway might have attracted is very doubtful, but it could obviously have been a useful public relations exercise to get something opened.

In contrast, the situation on the Jews Bridge–Chudleigh section had still hardly progressed at all at summer 1865. (It was claimed at the August 1865 shareholders' meeting that 'operations had commenced' on this section, but in reality hardly anything was done by Walker.) The Duke of Somerset's land, and Pulsford's land, had still not been obtained. Amongst the reasons for this was the fact that the TVR had no money to pay for it! (and no powers of compulsory purchase, because its share capital was not fully taken). Hopes were still being expressed in August 1865 that the whole line would be finished at the same time as

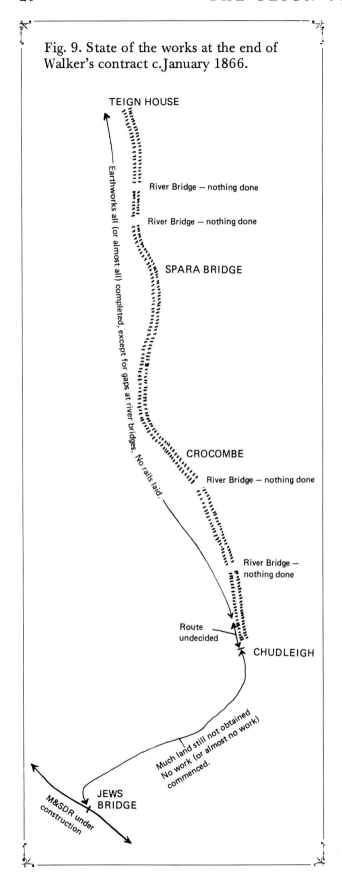

Fig. 9. State of the works at the end of Walker's contract c.January 1866.

TEIGN HOUSE

River Bridge – nothing done

River Bridge – nothing done

SPARA BRIDGE

Earthworks all (or almost all) completed, except for gaps at river bridges. No rails laid.

CROCOMBE

River Bridge – nothing done

River Bridge – nothing done

Route undecided

CHUDLEIGH

Much land still not obtained
No work (or almost no work) commenced.

M&SDR under construction

JEWS BRIDGE

the M&SDR (the latter itself now delayed), but this was beginning to look a little far-fetched to outside observers.

THE TVR'S FIRST CRISIS (1866–7)

Despite various ruses, such as not publishing the accounts on the grounds that this or that Secretary had only just been appointed, or that it saved printing costs, the TVR's failure to raise any significant sum of money could not be suppressed for ever. At the start of 1866 only 879 of the 2,250 £20 shares had been taken up, and 250 of those had been issued to Walker fully-paid and so did not represent real income. As calls of the full £20 had not been considered practical, the sum actually raised was only £11,037. This hardly covered what had been spent on Parliamentary expenses. A fifth call of £3 per share in January 1866 did not produce encouraging results. (By September 1867, when the issuing of further shares ceased, 1,037 shares had been taken and £18,456 paid up.)

The TVR had fudged the situation for two years by the usual expedient of not paying those to whom it owed money — primarily its own contractor and servants. Walker had done £19,244 of certified work at January 1866, for which he had been paid only £2,700 in cash (which he had foolishly lent to Toogood to pay Parliamentary costs — there is no evidence that he ever got it back), and £5,000 in shares, so that £11,544 was outstanding. He had been given Lloyd's Bonds for this — effectively only a 'promise to pay' that the TVR could not in practice fulfil. Other debts (at 1867) were £12,720 to Toogood (although this was to be the subject of dispute!), £3,420 to Tone, £509 to Browne (who seems to have become a TVR employee in 1864), £290 to Uniacke, £219 to Hutt, £8,965 to landowners, and finally £74 miscellaneous.

The situation was pushing Walker into financial problems of his own,[2] and with £25,000 of work still to be done and no evidence that there would be any means of payment, he decided that enough was enough. On 18th and 29th January 1866 he wrote two letters to the TVR Board, the content of which was too embarrassing to be recorded in the Minutes, but which led the Board to decide to look for another contractor who would not demand to be paid in cash. Walker ceased work, no other contractor came into view, and in February the Board gave Browne three week's notice (although he was to be commissioned again in the autumn of 1867 to prepare the plans for the 1868 Bill). The SDR's petition against the TVR's 1866 Bill, prepared at this time, noted that the TVR had 'ceased to make any material effort to complete their railway'. The February 1866 TVR shareholders' meeting heard a pack of fairy tales from Palk about the works having been relinquished in bad weather because there was no point finishing before the M&SDR, and that they 'could be completed at short notice'; but soon after this the truth became clear to all. The M&SDR line opened on 4th July 1866 with the TVR works abandoned.

For a full year after the spring of 1866, the TVR floundered hopeless, the poor state of ther national money market discouraging any attempt to raise further funds. The February 1867 Meeting could not get a quorum. However, efforts were being made behind the scenes. It was decided to apply for a 'Scheme of Arrangement' in the Court of Chancery, as was newly permitted by the Railway Companies Act 1867. This required the agreement of the company's creditors and shareholders, Walker being the largest in both categories. The Scheme was approved by the Court on 29th October 1867. It cancelled the unexercised powers of borrowing in the 1863 and 1865 Acts, and the 1865 Act's powers to issue extra share capital; and authorised instead the issuing of £79,000 in debenture stocks,[3] an initial purpose of which could be the payment of the sums due to Walker (who now agreed to take payment for past work in debentures instead of cash). In fact, though, these stocks were not issued until 1869–71 and even then only £27,650 was issued (mostly in payment to a new contractor) and Walker was not paid.

THE CHUDLEIGH DEVIATION

The other problem which had to be resolved before there was any chance of completing the line, was the route at Chudleigh. It will be recalled that this had been thrown back into the melting pot in summer 1863 by the deletion of the powers to cross the turnpike road (A38) at Chudleigh Bridge on the level, which rendered the intended route unviable, and by the promise made to Robert Pulsford of Pitt House that a new route would be evolved to avoid his lands. Initially it seems to have been hoped to resolve these problems quickly; on 12th August 1863 Tone (in Newcastle) wrote to Browne (in Devon) to say that he was coming down on about the 25th and wanted plans of 'the deviation to avoid Pulsford's property' ready for him when he arrived. In the event, it was to take nine years to resolve the situation.

Nothing was included in the 1864 Bill. A Chudleigh deviation was included in the 1865 Bill, but unsuccessfully. This proposed to run the railway further east and then under the turnpike road by elevating the road 16ft on embankment. The Revd Frederick Ensor, owner of the 'Rocklands' property north of the road, a small and unimportant part of which had to be acquired, objected, probably because the newly-elevated road would have overlooked his grounds (although the TVR suspected that he had been got at by the SDR!). The TVR then decided it was best to withdraw the deviation from the Bill. Nothing was included in the 1866 Bill, either.

Eventually, the matter was taken in hand in October 1867, at the same time as the company's financial problems were being sorted out. This new line in the 1868 Bill reverted to a level crossing option and (at the expense of introducing a considerable curvature in the line, and abandoning some 15 ch. of line already constructed) avoided the Rocklands grounds altogether. It also avoided Pulsford's lands. The TVR managed to get up a petition locally asking for a level crossing instead of an 'unsightly embankment', but to no avail — Parliament, whilst autho-

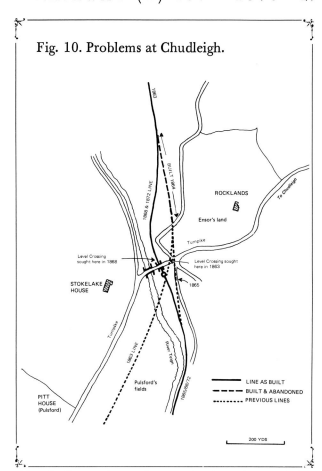

Fig. 10. Problems at Chudleigh.

ROCKLANDS

Ensor's land

To Chudleigh

Turnpike

Level Crossing sought here in 1868

Level Crossing sought here in 1863

STOKELAKE HOUSE

1865

Turnpike

1863 LINE

River Teign

Pulsford's fields

PITT HOUSE (Pulsford)

LINE AS BUILT
BUILT & ABANDONED
PREVIOUS LINES

200 YDS

rising the line, again struck out the level crossing, rendering it unbuildable as such. It was back to square one.

Finally, the TVR's 1872 Act authorised a bad compromise solution under which the line was to be built more or less on the 1868 route, but lower than originally intended so that it could pass under the turnpike road without the latter having to be raised more than 7ft. The TVR was very reluctant to be pushed into this solution because it left the railway running beside the river below the normal flood level, as was to be demonstrated on many occasions after the line opened, although fortunately with no worse effects than temporary closures until the waters subsided. But Parliament's implacable opposition to a level crossing forced the situation.

The Teign Valley Railway Act 1868 also authorised an extension of time for the whole railway (the 1863 Act powers expiring on 13th July 1868, the very day on which the new Act was passed). The new powers now ran until July 1870.

HUMPHREYS' CONTRACT (1869–70)

After the restoration of its affairs in 1867/8 to a position where it might possibly proceed to complete the line, the TVR's initial thoughts were directed towards getting Walker to resume the works. In February 1868 it was estimated that £28-30,000 was needed to complete the line.

Fig. 11. State of the works at the end of Humphreys' work, July 1870.

Source: Myers' report of September 1870 in RAIL 1057/208.

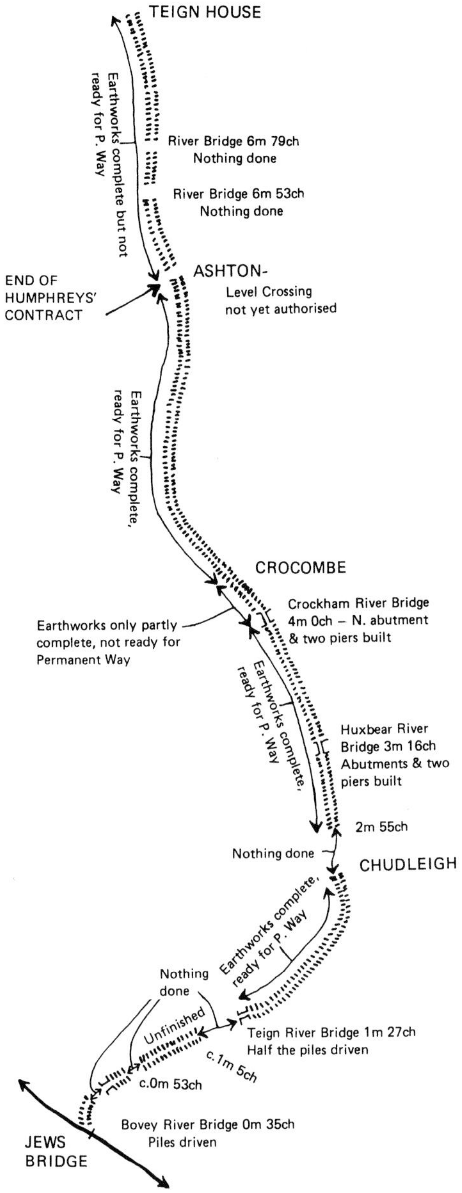

TEIGN HOUSE

Earthworks complete but not ready for P. Way

River Bridge 6m 79ch
Nothing done

River Bridge 6m 53ch
Nothing done

END OF HUMPHREYS' CONTRACT

ASHTON-
Level Crossing not yet authorised

Earthworks complete, ready for P. Way

CROCOMBE

Crockham River Bridge 4m 0ch – N. abutment & two piers built

Earthworks only partly complete, not ready for Permanent Way

Earthworks complete, ready for P. Way

Huxbear River Bridge 3m 16ch Abutments & two piers built

2m 55ch

Nothing done

CHUDLEIGH

Earthworks complete, ready for P. Way

Nothing done

Unfinished

c.1m 5ch

Teign River Bridge 1m 27ch Half the piles driven

c.0m 53ch

Bovey River Bridge 0m 35ch Piles driven

JEWS BRIDGE

Summary of situation:
5 miles — ready for P. Way
2 miles — earthworks partly or nearly complete
¾ mile — nothing done at all.
None of the river bridges completed.
No work done on stations or buildings.
No rails delivered (but 2,000 sleepers delivered).
The great majority of the work south of Chudleigh Bridge had been done by Humphreys, the great majority of that north of Chudleigh Bridge by Walker.

Walker's contract still stood; the problem lay in persuading Walker to accept non-cash payment instead of the cash payment to which he was entitled. (He had only agreed to accept debentures for the past work.) Palk saw Walker in April 1868 to 'ascertain upon what terms he will undertake the completion of the line', and in July Walker, 'being desirous of assisting you in making an arrangement for completing the works', made a detailed proposal to the TVR Board. Things then dragged on until February 1869 when Walker was told firmly that the TVR could pay in debentures but had no cash, and that if he did not reply immediately accepting payment in debentures 'it will be considered a refusal on his part to execute the works'. Walker's answer must have been negative as there is no further reference.

The TVR Board's pressure on Walker in February 1869 was partly due to the fact that they had received offers from two other contractors, John Morton and Alfred Davis. But in fact nothing came of these two. Only in the late summer of 1869 did the TVR succeed in finding a new contractor. Edward Humphreys of London wrote on 16th August 1869 offering to complete the line, from Jews Bridge to Ashton only, for £50,000 to be paid in 1867 Scheme debenture stock (£45,000) and ordinary stock (£5,000). The idea of omitting for the present the last 1½ miles from Ashton to Teign House was presumably the TVR's rather than Humphreys'; it does not seem to have signified more than that, if the TVR had to omit any section to cut initial costs, then it obviously had to be at that end of the line. This decision in 1869 was, however, the cause of the eventual failure to run passenger trains beyond Ashton in the 1882-1903 period. Humphreys wished to reserve to himself the right to complete the line on to Teign House, and to build any future extensions.

Kitson was able to tell the 28th August 1869 shareholders' meeting that the works were about to resume. Humphreys communicated with Walker who agreed to give up his contract, and on 21st September the Board sealed Humphreys' contract and appointed Thomas Myers — who had been over the line with Humphreys prior to his offer — as their Engineer to supervise the work. (Tone and Browne seem to have decided that they had had enough of the TVR in 1867.) The completion date was set at 20th June 1870, a rather optimistic date given that some land still had to be acquired and that most of the work would have to be done in the winter. The Duke of Somerset's land was eventually acquired at this time.

With opening now seeming possible again, the TVR made approaches to the SDR (who they had ignored since 1865, except for some talks in 1866) in January 1870, asking if they would be prepared to work the line on completion. At the same time, the TVR's 1870 Bill included a new application for running powers between Jews Bridge and Newton Abbot, in case the TVR ended up working its line itself. The Broad Gauge camp was in fact now much less anti-TVR; with the TVR seemingly having given up grand ideas, and the M&SDR not enjoying the traffic levels it had hoped for, the extra traffic that would be brought to the Moreton line was not unwelcome, and at the February 1870 M&SDR shareholders' meeting the Earl of Devon expressed the hope that the TVR would manage 'a speedy completion of their line'. (Nevertheless no company liked to concede running powers to another for no extra return, and the SDR and M&SDR petitioned against this aspect of the TVR Bill, forcing the withdrawal of the offending clauses.)

Humphreys seems to have made a good start, particularly on the Chudleigh Knighton–Chudleigh section (previously uncommenced), and to a lesser extent on the earthworks of the Jews Bridge–Chudleigh Knighton section and on the river bridges throughout the line (on which Walker had done little or no work). The shareholders heard from Palk in February 1870 that the works were progressing quickly and that 'the contractor had every reason to hope that the line would be finished before the expiry of the present Act'(in July). By Myers' 5th Certificate of 3rd July 1870, £19,290 of work had been done, and 138 tons of rails for the line had arrived at Teignmouth (with another 220 tons ready in the works at Stockton).[4] Humphreys was asked on 8th July to have the rails at Teignmouth delivered to the line within 14 days. But they never arrived. During July Humphreys fell into financial difficulties and all work ceased. The plant in his works yard at Chudleigh Bridge was handed over into the possession of the West of England and South Wales Bank for £400, and on 27th August they had it auctioned off (see advertisement reproduced here). Amongst the timber sold was that prepared for the river bridges.

The auction itself was successful, but, as the *Flying Post* reported:

'On Monday morning the purchasers of the plant arrived at the depot to remove their bargains, but found the yard barricaded by more than a hundred navvies . . . the men refusing to allow the plant to be removed until they had been paid their wages. The poor fellows are in great distress, and subscriptions were made at Chudleigh on their behalf. The police did not interfere on Monday and yesterday the navvies were still on defiance bent.'

The TVR's half-yearly meeting was held on the same day as the auction but had a distinctly poorer attendance. Meanwhile the Teign Valley Railway Act 1870 had been passed unopposed, authorising a further one-year extension of time for building the line (until July 1871) and the making of Agreements with the SDR and M&SDR for a junction station at Jews Bridge (for which see Chapter 4).

In September the TVR asked Myers to report on the current state of the line and what needed to be done to complete it. He estimated that £9,000 was needed to complete the works — a gross underestimate! — but could not discover Humphreys' current situation. He could only say to the TVR that:

'The non-fulfilment of their engagement has caused me as much regret and surprise as it has to yourselves, as soon as I perceived their defalcations I wrote from Chudleigh and complained to them individually . . . I insisted on their fulfilling the terms of their contract by

delivering the rails without further delay, my urgent applications up to this hour have remained unanswered by them, and I can only explain their unjustifiable conduct by the unhappy complications and embarrassment of their affairs.'

In fact Humphreys was bankrupt (and died soon afterwards). His Trustees in Bankruptcy followed the Bank by selling off his property. An auction of timber fencing posts and sleepers was held at Crockham Bridge on 3rd July 1871. This process brought the TVR's first court cases, regarding whether items removed for sale had belonged to Humphreys or the TVR.

Humphreys' acceptance of payment in debenture stock had, of course, been on the assumption that he would sell these stocks to others for cash, and this he was able to do, albeit at prices less than the nominal value. Of the £22,050 1867 debenture stock issued to him (the TVR had for some reason given more than the value of the work completed), he disposed of £17,800 to H.R. Taylor, a London solicitor, and £1,000 to Uriah Miller, a London stockbroker, leaving £3,250 to pass to his assignees after his bankruptcy. Taylor was destined to cause the TVR Board problems at a later date.

After Humphreys' collapse in July 1870, it was to be a full seven years before the sound of construction work was again heard in the Teign Valley. Most local people lost any interest they had had in the railway, and began to treat it as a joke, fit only for showing to visitors as a folly.

1. The *Weekly Express* noted on 17.2.1864 that the staking out of the line was in progress. Browne told a TVR Meeting on 12.3.1864 that the contractor 'had his plant on the ground, and will forthwith commence proceedings'.
2. Walker was bankrupted in March 1866, but this was common enough amongst contractors; he was discharged on 25th May 1866.
3. For full details of the TVR's share capital and borrowing powers throughout, see Chapter 7.
4. Had the rails actually been laid at this date, they would of course have been laid as Broad Gauge.

Chapman collection, cty. Steven Court

Trusham, in 1905, looking south-east over the village.

CHAPTER FOUR

THE TEIGN VALLEY RAILWAY IN LIMBO
1870-1877

IN the seven years after 1870, the Teign Valley Railway company hardly existed except in the persons of Palk and, most particularly, Toogood. Alsop, the Company Secretary, was disposed of in 1871 and administration was left in the hands of Toogood, as 'Manager'. Unfortunately, Toogood had little interest in running the company's affairs in a normal way. The Minute Books were not kept between October 1871 and May 1877, although there were some Board and Company meetings in this period. The cash books were not kept either, with the result that the accounts for the period from 1st January 1872 were not published until 1878 when a new Secretary was obliged to cobble something together out of Toogood's straws. Toogood's neglect naturally makes it that much more difficult to give a good account of the period; but essentially these years were spent in despondency, interspersed by several attempts by Toogood or Palk to concoct yet another scheme for getting the line off the ground again, all of them unsuccessful.

NEGOTIATIONS 1871-2

The first serious chance of reviving things came in July 1871 when Toogood persuaded Waring, one of the leading contractors of the day (and heavily involved with Toogood in the machinations for the Somerset & Dorset), to take an interest in the TVR. Waring went to see Woollcombe with ideas of an arrangement under which Waring would complete the TVR, and it would then be transferred to the SDR for a rent charge of £3,000 p.a. — essentially the same as had been suggested in 1864 by the SDR itself. However the SDR did not want to go along with this particular scheme, and Waring withdrew.

The SDR was, however, willing in principle to come to an agreement on this 'rent charge' basis, and the TVR were for the present in a humble mood and became inured to it themselves. Serious negotiations were in progress with the SDR from November 1871 on, and it began to seem that an agreement might be possible at a sum of £2,600 p.a. In May/June 1872 a group of GWR and SDR officers went over the line, and Margary and the new TVR Engineer Edward Appleton[1] prepared a joint statement on the estimated costs of completion. There was also a Chairmen's Conference in London between Gooch, Woollcombe, and Palk. After this the surviving records unfortunately become too incoherent; it is obvious that no agreement was actually come to, but SDR/TVR relations seem nevertheless to have been positive up to 1877 (when the TVR started getting grand ideas again).

THE DEVON & CORNWALL INITIATIVE (1873)

With the TVR company seemingly moribund, all sorts of ideas began to be floated for railway schemes in South Devon. November 1872 saw the Exeter Chamber of Commerce moved to propose a 'County Committee' to give more considered thought to the extension of railway communications in Devon.

One idea which might have come to something was an alliance forged in the autumn of 1873 between the Devon & Cornwall Railway and certain interests in Torquay who were raising anti-SDR talk again. The Devon & Cornwall, a renaming of the Okehampton Company of 1862, was by this date under the control of a syndicate, known as the 'Imperial Credit Co. Ltd.', which also controlled the Belfast Central, the Neath & Brecon, and the Hoylake & Birkenhead Railway and Tramway Co. They were in expansive mood and in the D&C 1873 Bill they had just been seeking (largely unsuccessfully) powers for extensions deep into Cornwall. The Torquay activists had given up hope of getting a new line from the LSWR which, as they correctly perceived, 'appeared to be under some compact with the South Devon'; but the D&C, although recognised as an LSWR protégé, was free to extend where it wished, and C.N. Luxmoore, the leader of the Torquay interests, gained promises from the syndicate that if people in Torquay would raise £30,000, the D&C would 'come to Torquay'. It was promised that the D&C Engineer (i.e., Galbraith, the LSWR Engineer) would prepare the necessary plans, and a public meeting was held in Torquay on 1st November 1873 to raise an initial £1,000 to fund this. Amongst the speakers in favour was Edward Appleton, the TVR Engineer (although he did not appear under that hat), who made very clear references to the fact that the D&C intended to 'use the Teign Valley line' to achieve this purpose. (Presumably a connecting line from Crediton to Teign House was anticipated?) A committee was set up to further the scheme, but as nothing came of it we can assume that little money was actually promised in Torquay and that the D&C lost interest as a result. In April 1874 the D&C was formally absorbed by the LSWR and there was no longer any 'independent' force for dissatisfied Devonians to turn to.

THE TVR IN PARLIAMENT 1872-1874

The TVR's inability to turn a sod in these years did not dampen its already-all-too-evident enthusiasm for wasting money on Parliamentary Bills — a characteristic due no doubt to Toogood's presence at the helm, for there was little to stop him from increasing his own income by engaging in as much work as he wished on the company's behalf. Toogood's control over the company was enhanced from 1873 by his taking the company to court for the large sum of money which was (or was alleged to be) due to him, and gaining a judgement against them (unopposed, thanks of course to Toogood, the company's only officer and lawyer, having failed to appear in court against himself on the company's behalf!). This judgement could not be enforced for the present becase the TVR had no money to pay, but Toogood was able to hold it as a sword at the company's neck. Despite this situation, Toogood continued to act as the company's lawyer for another seven years after 1873.

Bills were promoted every year in 1872-5. The Teign Valley Railway Act 1872, the most useful piece of TVR legislation in this period, authorised, amongst other things:

(a) the building of the line as standard gauge or mixed gauge, instead of the 1863 Act's obligation to be broad gauge only. This time there was no objection from the SDR, no doubt because they, too, had to recognise that the days of the broad gauge were passing.

(b) an extension of time for the building of the line (the powers had lapsed in July 1871) until February 1874.

(c) the raising of an additional £ 72,000 share capital (with the intention of converting the 1867 scheme debenture stock into share capital, if the owners could be so persuaded), and £ 24,000 by borrowing. In the event these powers were not exercised until after 1877.

(d) the building of two mineral branches, never built (see below).

In 1873 the TVR promoted a Bill to enable the making of Working Agreements with, the leasing of the TVR to, or the selling of the company to, any of the SDR, GWR, or B&E. This Bill was presumably a result of the negotiations referred to above. However, it was withdrawn by the promoters, for reasons unknown, during its passage through Parliament.

The Teign Valley Railway Act 1874 authorised a further extension of time for the line, until August 1877. (The application to Parliament in November 1873 had sought powers to abandon the line and the company, or to build the line to 2 ft 6 in gauge — an interesting reflection of the TVR's desperate state — but these clauses were dropped.)

THE MINERAL BRANCHES (1872)

The Teign Valley lead mining interests were obviously not happy at the TVR's failure to make more progress. In the c1870 period the fact that the industry was in terminal decline was not yet apparent, and there was not only a desire to get the TVR opened, but also ideas of building short branches to the mines in order to cut out expensive cartage to the TVR stations. In 1869 Palk had become involved in the floating of a new company, the Tram-Railway Company of Great Britain Ltd. (of which Thomas Myers was Manager, and William Toogood, Solicitor), whose prospectus referred to the fact that the company had made 'provisional arrangements for the formation of tram lines' in connection with the TVR, and these we can assume were to have been mine branches. Powers for branches to the Frank Mills and South Exmouth mines were obtained in the TVR's 1872 Act (see *Fig. 12*). Unfortunately the Tram-Railway company seems

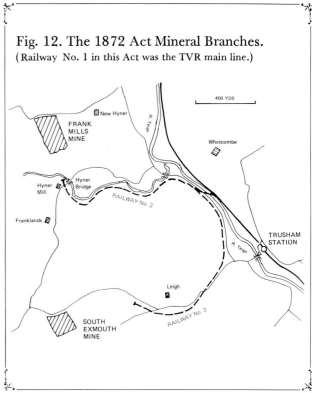

Fig. 12. The 1872 Act Mineral Branches.
(Railway No. 1 in this Act was the TVR main line.)

to have given up its endeavours in 1872. The powers for the mineral branches were revived by the TVR in its 1874 and 1878 Acts, but the TVR was preoccupied enough with building its main line and the lead mines were declining year by year. In 1881 it was noted that these branches were 'considered abandoned'.

THE OPENING OF CHUDLEIGH ROAD STATION (1874)

As noted in Chapter 2, the M&SDR had intended originally to have a station on its line at 'Jews Bridge for Ashburton', which would also serve Chudleigh if there were no Teign Valley line. After the TVR was promoted in 1863, the M&SDR no longer needed to serve Chudleigh, but it was still assumed that there would be a station here for junction purposes. However, no definite arrangements were come to in 1863 as to who would now pay for the station — in normal practice the TVR would have been expected to pay a large share of the costs — and the TVR, unable as they were to get any work started on this end of their line, never made any approaches to the M&SDR on this subject in 1864/5. This left the M&SDR feeling unable to do anything themselves, and, with the authorising of the BT&SDR line to Ashburton promising to take away any Ashburton traffic that might have come this way, they lost immediate interest in providing a station here, and the line opened in 1866 without one (although the land for a station had been bought).

In the autumn of 1867 the M&SDR had an additional small station built on their line at Teigngrace, and this seems to have encouraged the inhabitants of Chudleigh (who had by this date no doubt given up hopes of the TVR getting anywhere in the foreseeable future) into presenting a memorial to the M&SDR Board asking that the station at Jews Bridge should now be built. Although three miles from Chudleigh town, it would be better than nothing. The leading figure in this petition was G.B. Ellicombe, the new occupier of the 'Rocklands' property. The M&SDR were not unfavourable but were concerned about the cost and responded initially that they could do nothing at present; but in December 1868 they agreed to build the station if Ellicombe and his friends would take £700 of M&SDR shares to finance it.

However, no sooner was this being agreed than the TVR sprang back into active life again, throwing uncertainty into the picture and preventing immediate action. In the autumn of 1869, after Humphreys' contract was settled, the M&SDR was at last able to get the TVR to discuss matters in detail. Myers, the TVR Engineer, met Margary on site on 1st November 1869 and agreed to draw up a plan and send it to the M&SDR for approval. Meanwhile, powers were (as noted briefly earlier) being obtained in the TVR's 1870 Act for them to enter into agreements with the M&SDR and SDR regarding 'the construction, use, management, and maintenance of a joint station at or near the junction of the Teign Valley Railway, with all proper and necessary approaches, works, and conveniences connected therewith, and the appointment of a Joint Committee, with all usual and necessary powers for the regulation control and management of such a station'. An agreement was in fact drawn up under which the TVR were to build and own the station and the M&SDR pay an annual rent charge for their use of it.

After this, of course, nothing happened, due to the TVR falling back into inactivity again. Margary and Myers had never actually produced any agreed plan, so the situation was really left quite open again.

The station was eventually built in 1874 by the SDR (which had taken over the M&SDR in July 1872) without the TVR being involved at all. G.B. Ellicombe approached the SDR again in March 1873 and received a positive response; plans were approved by the SDR Board in December 1873 and construction work began early in 1874. In April 1874 it was decided to call the station 'Chudleigh Road' instead of 'Jews Bridge', and also, following a memorial from local farmers and traders, to provide a siding for goods traffic. The passenger station opened on 1st July 1874 and the goods siding shortly afterwards.

From 1874 to 1882 Chudleigh Road station was the railhead for Chudleigh and the southern end of the Teign Valley. A bus service was run between the station and Chudleigh town.

When the TVR eventually reached Chudleigh Road, it was a different gauge to the SDR line, and so no arguments about the junction layout were necessary, the TVR effectively building a separate station, as described later.

THE CREDITON EXTENSION AND THE 1875 ACT

As will be recalled from Chapter 1, the idea of a connecting line from Crediton to the Teign Valley went back to the TVR's origins as the DCR in 1860/1. In 1874 the idea was revived as the latest hope of getting the TVR off the ground again. It was an extraordinary move, at a time when the TVR was all but totally moribund, to borrow large sums of money to finance yet another Parliamentary application, for a line that would cost an estimated £96,000 to build, a sum which there was no obvious prospect of raising. But the most extraordinary thing about the Crediton extension was that, unlike all the other TVR extension plans, it was actually authorised by Parliament!

The Crediton extension does not seem to have been proposed as an easy backdoor way of getting into Exeter, but rather owed its origins to the TVR's exaggerated notions of the mineral traffic that might be exported from the Teign Valley through the North Devon ports if such a direct link existed. These hopes were typified by an anonymous letter in the *Torquay Directory* in December 1875 which referred to '2000 tons per day of iron, barytes and lead' being shipped from Bideford if this line were built; this figure was more than the Teign Valley's annual output!

The route was very similar to that of 1861. The plans were drawn up in the autumn of 1874 by W. John Ashdown, who had been brought into the area shortly before this by Palk to act as an adviser on the mining potential of his Teign Valley lands, and who now became the TVR Engineer also (until his death in 1878). The line was 9 m 42 ch long, and powers were obtained for an extra capital of £150,000, and £50,000 borrowing, to finance it. Running powers were sought over the North Devon Railway, the Exeter and Crediton Railway, the B&E from Cowley Bridge to St. Davids, and the LSWR up to Queen Street. The LSWR had not been consulted in advance about this and was very unhappy about it; as a result, these applications for running powers were withdrawn from the Bill. The LSWR also disliked the proposed junction at Crediton which was located at a point where they might wish to provide additional sidings in future. The SDR seem to have been largely unconcerned by the Bill — surprisingly so.

The Teign Valley Railway (Extension) Act 1875 was passed on 2nd August 1875. It also authorised the TVR to make Working Agreements with the GWR, the B&E, or the LSWR, as well as with the SDR (for which powers already existed under the 1865 Act).

Nothing whatsoever was ever done to bring the Crediton Extension to reality. It did, however, become intertwined with various schemes for Exeter extensions in 1877–9, to be described in the next chapter, before eventually being abandoned in 1880-2.

---

1. Edward Appleton F.I.B.A., Architect and Civil Engineer, lived at Cotswold, Warren Road, Torquay and also had an office at Queen St. Chambers, Exeter. Myers had severed his connections with the TVR in 1870, and Appleton (along with J.H. Tolmé) was chosen to prepare the TVR's deposited plans in November 1871 for its 1872 Bill. He then did such other work as was needed by the TVR until 1873.

Fig. 13.
The Crediton Extension 1875
The Exeter & Chagford Railway proposals 1877/8
The TVR 1878 Bill proposals

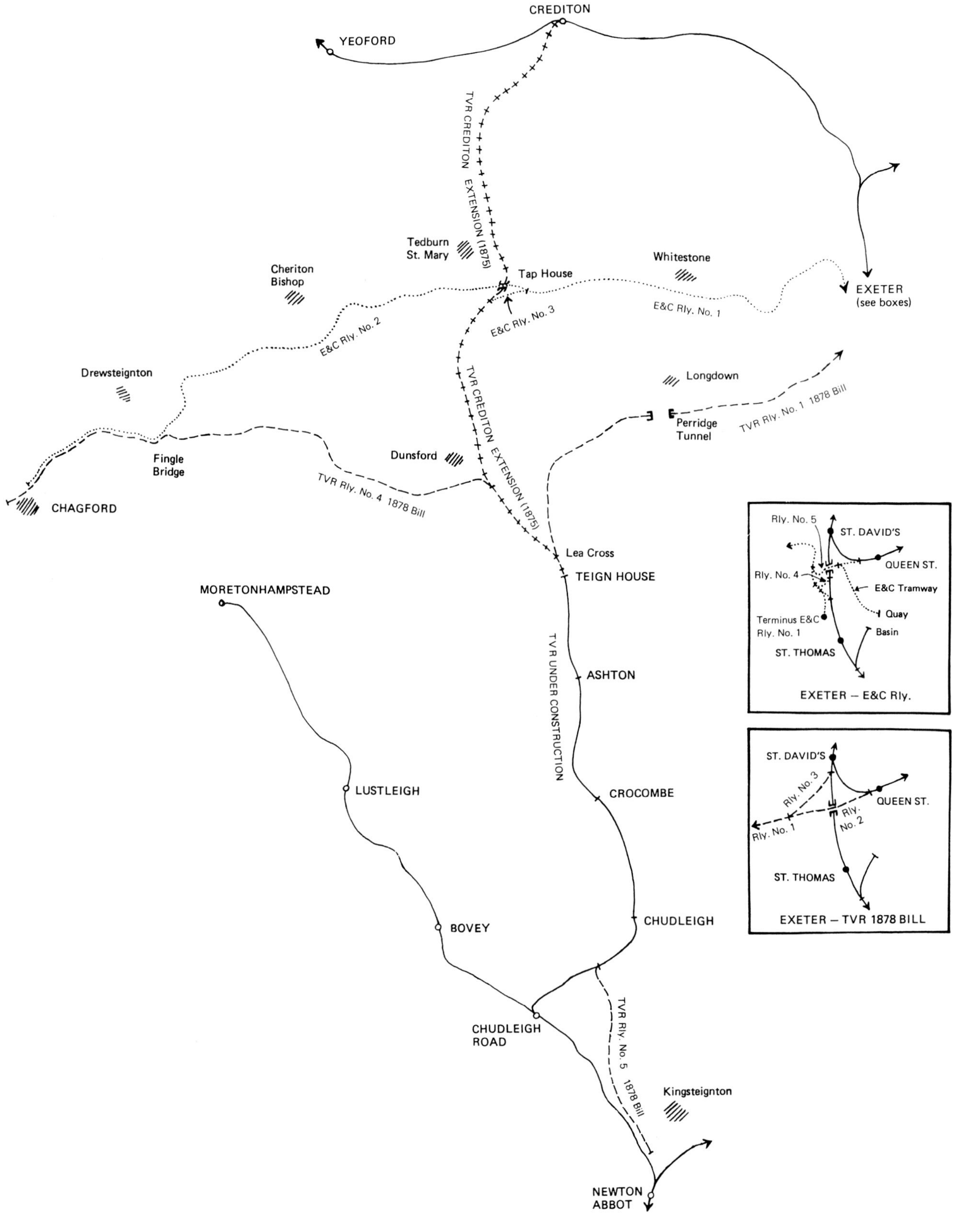

CREDITON

YEOFORD

TVR CREDITON EXTENSION (1875)

Tedburn
St. Mary

Tap House

Whitestone

Cheriton
Bishop

E&C Rly. No. 3

E&C Rly. No. 1

EXETER
(see boxes)

E&C Rly. No. 2

Drewsteignton

Longdown

Perridge
Tunnel

TVR Rly. No. 1 1878 Bill

Fingle
Bridge

Dunsford

TVR CREDITON EXTENSION (1875)

TVR Rly. No. 4 1878 Bill

CHAGFORD

Lea Cross

TEIGN HOUSE

TVR UNDER CONSTRUCTION

MORETONHAMPSTEAD

ASHTON

LUSTLEIGH

CROCOMBE

BOVEY

CHUDLEIGH

CHUDLEIGH
ROAD

TVR Rly. No. 5 1878 Bill

Kingsteignton

NEWTON
ABBOT

Rly. No. 5

ST. DAVID'S

QUEEN ST.

Rly. No. 4

E&C Tramway

Terminus E&C
Rly. No. 1

Quay

Basin

ST. THOMAS

EXETER — E&C Rly.

ST. DAVID'S

Rly. No. 3

QUEEN ST.

Rly. No. 1

Rly.
No. 2

ST. THOMAS

EXETER — TVR 1878 BILL

CHAPTER FIVE

THE TEIGN VALLEY RAILWAY REVIVED:
NEW CONFLICT AND PERMANENT AGREEMENT, 1877–1882

IN the spring of 1877, the long-dormant TVR staged a miraculous recovery. A new 'Scheme' was effected to set financial affairs on a workable footing again, and Walker (after eleven years away from the line) was persuaded to take on a new contract to complete the works — now as a standard gauge line, for the days of the broad gauge were over. A Board Meeting on 9th May 1877 — the first recorded since 1871 — approved the new contract with Walker, the appointment of John H. Thomson as Company Secretary so that Toogood was no longer in sole control, and the appointment of Henry St John as Resident Engineer. In 1877 it was thought that the line might be opened in a matter of months, but in the event it took another 5½ years, with two further crises intervening. Details of the company's financial situation in these years, and of the construction work and eventual opening of the line in 1882, are given in Chapter 6.

1877 also saw the commercial interests in Exeter awakening to what they saw as the need to get lines built from the city to the Teign Valley and Chagford. Up to this date Exeter people (except the mining interests) had given little or no practical support to the TVR, but they now began to see a greater need for it from their own point, whilst at the same time beginning to suspect that the TVR company would never now manage to construct a Teign House–Exeter extension themselves, and that Exeter would therefore have to take the initiative. In this suspicion they were to be proved correct. In 1877, though, the TVR was not yet prepared to admit this, and the first Exeter-sponsored scheme promulgated in that year, the Exeter & Chagford Railway, was subjected to a hostile blocking counter-scheme from the TVR, resulting in much wasted energy and the collapse of both schemes.

THE EXETER & CHAGFORD RAILWAY (1877/8)

On 5th February 1877, there was a 'large and influential' public meeting held at Exeter Guildhall by the Mayor, William Cuthbertson, to rouse the citizens to the need to do something to get a railway connection from the city to the Teign Valley. The primary inspiration was the fact that the M&SDR line had diverted trade from the Moretonhampstead/Chagford area to Newton Abbot instead of Exeter, a process which the opening of the TVR to Teign House would exacerbate. (In retrospect the Exeter interests seem to have attached a rather exaggerated importance to this diversion of trade, which was hardly very significant by comparison with the total Exeter market!) There was also hostility in Exeter to the Crediton Extension — it would be 'a disgrace to Exeter' if the TVR

extended to Crediton instead of Exeter, said the Mayor. And there were hopes of improving the fortunes of the Ship Canal — a perennial theme in Exeter — by getting the railway to produce a revival in the production of Teign Valley minerals and exporting them through the Canal Basin (rather than North Devon ports as the Crediton extension foresaw). This would give shippers a backfreight which was currently lacking, so much so that ships were currently often refusing to come to Exeter at all. In retrospect this idea, too, was hopelessly over-angled; it should have been clear to all by 1877 that the lead mines were in terminal decline. But people in Exeter were desperate to do something about the Canal's financial problems, and were prepared to put faith in anything that had a facade of credibility.

In addition to the interest in an Exeter–Teign House link, there was now a revival of interest in an Exeter–Chagford line, due to the SDR's failure to construct a Moretonhampstead–Chagford line as had been anticipated in the years after 1862.[1] One speaker at the meeting looked forward to the day when 'Chagford would become the Malvern of the west, and Fingle, Chudleigh and Dunsford beautiful suburbs of Exeter'.

Palk was at the meeting and spoke in supportive terms, although he would not agree to give up the Crediton extension. The general tone of the meeting was in favour of getting an Exeter–Teign House line built initially, with the link to Chagford following on. A Committee was set up to raise money for preliminary expenses and to arrange a survey.

Unfortunately, the Committee was destined to create dissension. It is clear that the majority were possessed of ideas of getting a Working Agreement with the LSWR — no surprise in a city that had always been pro-LSWR — and an approach to that company was made only a few days after the meeting (although without positive results). They also chose the LSWR Engineers, Galbraith & Church, to do their survey. Instead of drawing up an Exeter–Teign House Line as authorised by the meeting, the Committee became distracted to a direct Exeter–Chagford route which only served the Teign Valley by means of a connecting curve to the TVR Crediton extension at 'Tap House' (Tedburn St Mary), a very indirect route. Several members of the Committee resigned over this, Capt. Halford Thompson insisted on producing a minority report, and a number of those who had paid towards the survey expenses were alienated.

Another public meeting was held on 30th October 1877. In the circumstances this did not, of course, produce unanimity, but the Committee determined nevertheless to deposit plans for the 1878 session, under the name 'Exeter & Chagford Railway'. The Provisional Directors of the company were:

William Cotton (Manager of the National Provincial Bank, Exeter)
Henry Drew (the Earl of Devon's Agent)
Charles J. Follett (Exeter Solicitor, Mayor 1872-4)
Thomas P. Varwell (Coal Merchant, Exeter)
William Hood Walrond (of New Court, Topsham, owner of much of the parish of Holcombe Burnell [Longdown area]).

The curving contour-following line was costed at £199,985 — an enormous sum for a line to serve one town with a population of 1,400 and nowhere at all of significance en route! The scheme included an elaborate series of links at Exeter to give access to St. David's, Queen St., the Canal Basin, the Exeter Quay via a new tramway along Commercial Road, and an independent terminal station. Running powers were sought over the TVR from Tap House to Chudleigh Road, plus powers to make Working Agreements with the GWR, SDR, TVR, or LSWR (all bets thereby being hedged on that front). In fact the E&C were still hoping to get an Agreement with the LSWR, and further approaches were made to that company in October 1877. The LSWR was again unenthusiastic, and finally in January 1878 discussed the question at their 'Committee of Consultation with the GWR', after which they gave the E&C a definite no. In December the E&C had approached the GWR for an Agreement, with similarly negative results.

To make matters worse for the E&C, the TVR had decided to turn hostile and had deposited plans for a rival scheme (see next section). The E&C's Bill was faced with petitions against from the SDR, the GWR, and the TVR, as well as the usual opposition from landowners, the latter partly stirred up by the TVR. Faced with this almost universal hostility, the E&C promoters lost heart and in March 1878 they withdrew their Bill after its second reading. This first effort from Exeter was therefore an utter failure.

THE TVR's 1878 BILL, EXETER AND CHAGFORD LINES

The TVR was in confident (overconfident) mood again by summer 1877, with the works under way and hopes of opening by the year end. When the Exeter Committee went for the Exeter–Tap House–Chagford route instead of a direct Exeter–Teign House link, the TVR's potential interest in its activities as a way of getting the TVR its Exeter link faded; in the autumn of 1877 the TVR decided at the last minute to submit a rival scheme to Parliament for the 1878 session to defeat the E&C. The main motive, one imagines, was a realisation that if an Exeter–Tap House line were to be built, there could never be a direct Exeter–Teign House link.

The TVR's Engineer, Ashdown, and his assistants, Henry St John and Thomas Large, were thrown into frenzied activity in November 1877 in order to get the plans completed by the 30th November deadline. They were helped by the fact that the 1864 Bill and 1866 Bill plans

could be re-used for the Exeter–Teign House section. However, it was only on 30th November itself that St John was able to hurry around the Parish Clerks depositing copies of the plans. He was delayed somewhat at Alphington where there was no clerk and the rector himself had to be seen; he was 'over 80 and in his dotage and I could not make him understand'!

The TVR was now in an aggressive mood and the plans (*Fig. 13*) included much to upset the SDR as well as being intended to block the E&C. In addition to the Exeter line (Railways 1, 2, and 3) and the Chagford line (Railway 4), there was an independent line from Chudleigh Knighton to Newton Abbot (Railway 5). The total estimate was no less than £316,003 — a sum which the TVR really stood no chance of raising. But much of it was just politicking. Railway No. 4 had been put in purely to defeat the E&C, the TVR having no serious interest in building a line to Chagford at this stage, and it was withdrawn from the Bill immediately when the E&C conceded defeat in March. Railway No. 5 seems to have been meant as a throwaway to help in the inevitable negotiations with the SDR, as the Bill was also seeking running powers from Chudleigh Road to Newton Abbot and power to make the SDR lay a third rail over this section — a new need now that the TVR was being built standard gauge. (In the event, the TVR had to withdraw all these clauses from the Bill, and withdraw Railway No. 5 also.) Running powers were also sought into St Davids and Queen St, and power to make the SDR lay a third rail on the up line from St Davids to the Canal Basin branch.[2]

After several unopposed Bills, the TVR seems to have almost been keen for a big Parliamentary contest, and they got one! Once again they seem to have assumed that the LSWR would be in favour of the scheme, given that it offered 'a chance to get to Torquay'; but once again they actually found them hostile, on account of the proposed junction at Queen St (as in 1864) and the fact that the LSWR did not want any further trains congesting the station there. But the primary opposition was, of course, from the GWR and the SDR. Fowler and Margary made very successful criticisms of the traffic need for the Crediton and Exeter lines (showing how inflated were the TVR's hopes for the now-nearly-dead mineral traffic) and the TVR's ability to finance these grandiose schemes when it was having such difficulties funding its original line. (The TVR replied that Walker had agreed to take one-third of the capital for the new lines in shares, but it was not evident where the other two-thirds might come from.) The TVR had also tried to present their line as a useful 'relief line' to the SDR route — this, of course, would only apply after the SDR trains were converted to the standard gauge — but Fowler responded that it was of little use for this purpose due to the gradients, that no relief was needed in traffic terms at the present time, and that troubles on the sea wall had ceased since the works carried out after the bad winter of 1872/3 had been completed. Fowler — by this date a figure of some status — was very anti-TVR before the Parliamentary Committee, attacking them as an 'annoying company' that had wasted everybody's time for far too long:

'They come every year, year after year, promoting some enormous schemes and some small schemes, generally of a tentative character, a little bit, getting the thin end of the wedge in . . . I never in all my experience have seen so expensive a line proposed for so small an object'

On 12th April 1878 the Commons Committee decided that they agreed with Fowler, and rejected all the new lines ('there is really no capital to justify their going on with so expensive a part of the Bill').

However, there were other less contentious matters in the Bill, which was proceeded with (minus the new lines and running powers) and passed as the Teign Valley Railway Act 1878. Most notably, the lapsed powers for the Chudleigh Road–Teign House section were extended again to 10th December 1878, and those for the Crediton Extension from 1880 to 1883.

THE EXETER EXTENSION FAILS A FOURTH TIME; THE TVR's 1879 BILL

What happened next was almost an exact repeat of what had happened in 1866 following the failure of the 1864 Bill. The TVR came back in the 1879 Session with another Bill for an Exeter extension which involved no connections with any other line in Exeter, as a ploy to deprive other companies of any *locus standi* in Parliament. This time, however, a 'Tap House' route was adopted, very similar to the E&C's 1878 line on this stretch although without the latter's curving contour-following. (Why the TVR should have chosen such a route now, when they had objected to it in 1877/8, is not clear.) This enabled an estimate of only £94,672 for 6m 27ch of new line, although this, of course, excluded the cost of the Teign House–Tap House section of the Crediton line.

The ploy worked as such, the GWR's petition being disallowed. But, just as in 1866, the TVR lapsed into a financial crisis after the Bill had been introduced. The LSWR and GWR also consulted with each other again, discussing the TVR at one of their regular 'Consultation Committee' meetings in December 1878, to ensure that the TVR was not trying to play them off against each other; and both undertook not to support the extension. The Bill had to be withdrawn by the TVR.

THE 1879 GWR AGREEMENT

The failure of the 1879 Bill was to be the last nail in the coffin for Palk and Toogood's ideas of an Exeter extension. The LSWR's continuing refusal to be interested, and the company's new financial problems (combined with the fact that their line nevertheless seemed near completion), pushed the TVR in March 1879 into seeking serious negotiations with the GWR for a Working Agreement. Seeing the chance to bring this longstanding thorn in the side under control at last, the GWR, too, was in a mood to negotiate positively, and everything was now agreed very quickly. (The GWR had taken over the SDR in 1876/8,

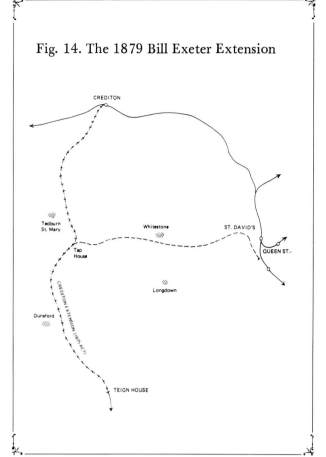

Fig. 14. The 1879 Bill Exeter Extension

and this probably made things easier on this front, as Paddington had always been one step removed from the TVR and there were not the personal antipathies that there had been, as a result of such protracted hostility, in SDR days.) The GWR Board approved the proposed terms on 19th June 1879, and the TVR Board on 5th July. In summary, they were:

- The GWR to work and maintain the line from Chudleigh Road to Teign House, and any portion of the Crediton Extension constructed.
- Rates and fares to be fixed by the GWR.
- 'The Gross Receipts of the line to be apportioned as to 55% thereof to the Great Western Co. as an allowance for the expenses of working and maintenance . . . the remaining 45% to be paid to the Teign Valley Co. subject to Article 4.'
- 'The sum of £1,200 a year to be a first charge on the gross receipts of the line and paid to the Teign Valley Co. in half yearly amounts.' (These two clauses were to cause much trouble later! — see Chapter 7.)
- The Teign Valley Co. to complete the line to Teign House within 12 months.
- The Teign Valley Co. to maintain the line for 12 months after opening.
- The Great Western Co. to commence to work the line when passed by the Board of Trade.
- The Teign Valley Co. to withdraw the current (1879) Bill for an extension to Exeter.
- The Teign Valley Co. to apply in the next session of Parliament for the abandonment of the Crediton Extension, except that if asked to do so by the GWR, the TVR shall construct 'one or two miles' of the Extension, the cost of this to be met by the GWR with the TVR paying 4% interest on it.

The GWR had kept the LSWR Chairman informed of what was being proposed.

The TVR/GWR Agreement was not actually formalised in a legal document until March 1882. Although the TVR had on previous occasions sought Parliamentary authority to make an Agreement with the GWR, the relevant Bills had been unsuccessful, so powers to make the Agreement had to be obtained in the TVR's 1880 Act. Nevertheless, it was in practice known to all from the summer of 1879 that the TVR was destined to open as a GWR branch line and not as the rival route that had once been dreamed of.

THE DUNSFORD EXTENSION

For a while after 1879 there were, however, ideas of a short extension to a terminus at Dunsford using the 1875 Act line (hence the references to building part of the Crediton Extension in the 1879 Agreement above). These ideas probably emerged for the simple reason that it would at least give a terminus for the (now dead-end) branch in a vil-

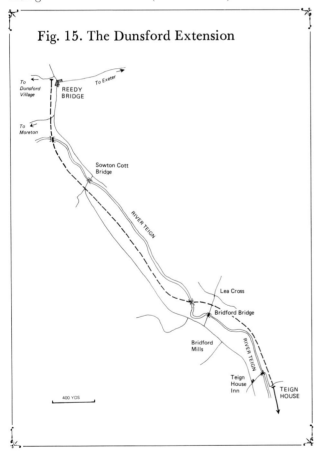

Fig. 15. The Dunsford Extension

lage, rather than in the middle of nowhere at Teign House. It was estimated initially that such an extension to Dunsford, 2m 20ch long, could be built cheaply for £7,000–£8,000.

However, when Margary and Owen, the GWR Engineer, went into the matter more deeply in the autumn of 1879, they found that the cost was likely to be nearer £13,000. The GWR Board now became less keen, and in November 1879 they decided 'not to call upon the Teign Valley Co. to make the line at the present time'. Nevertheless, the Teign Valley Railway Act 1880, promoted mainly to authorise the abandoning of the Crediton Extension in accordance with the Agreement, kept the powers for the southernmost 2m 20ch alive.

After this the TVR made several attempts to persuade the GWR to approve the extension to Dunsford; but in each case the answer was that they did not at present wish to do so. The powers for compulsory purchase expired in August 1881 without any land having been bought, and finally in October 1881 the GWR sent the TVR a letter stating formally that they did not intend to authorise the extension. The Teign Valley Railway Act 1882 was therefore obtained to secure the abandonment of this last section of the 1875 line (the primary benefit of this to the TVR being to gain the release of the Parliamentary Deposits paid in 1875 and 1880). The 1882 Act formally defined the undertaking of the Teign Valley Railway Company as being a line from Chudleigh Road to Doddiscombsleigh.

From May 1882, therefore, there were no current ideas at all for extensions northwards from Teign House. The TVR, which now really was about to open its line, was stuck with what it had obtained in 1863, and the vast sums which had been expended in Parliament in promoting repeated extensions had, at the end of the day, proved a complete waste of money.

However, just six months later, another company, the Exeter Teign Valley & Chagford Railway, was to successfully apply for powers for an Exeter–Teign House line, and the saga was to begin all over again — as described in Chapters 8 and 9.

---

1. In 1864 the M&SDR had actually deposited plans for a Moretonhampstead–Chagford line, but they had not promoted the Bill. By the 1870s there was a regular connecting bus service between Moretonhampstead and Chagford, supplemented from 1875 by an LSWR Yeoford–Chagford bus. But the tireless Revd Hayter Hames was still calling for a railway. In July 1875 he secured a promise from the SDR that if the local landowners gave the land free of charge, the SDR would probably be induced to make and work the line; but nothing came of this, and by 1877 the Chagford interests were beginning to give up on the SDR.

2. There was already a third rail on the down line, for the mixed gauge Basin branch goods trains, but not on the up line.

CHAPTER SIX

BUILDING THE TEIGN VALLEY RAILWAY (2)
1877–1882

THE 'Scheme' of 26th February 1877 which sorted out the TVR's financial problems involved the issuing of the £72,000 (preference) share capital authorised by the 1872 Act, and £10,000 (only) in debentures — less than the 1872 Act's £24,000 authorisation as it was thought at this date that no more than £10,000 could possibly be needed. The £72,000 share capital now issued did not, however, represent a genuine increase of anywhere near this sum in the money available to the company, as much of it went to the 'buying out' of the 1867 Scheme debenture stock holders (as had been intended in 1872, but was only now done), and to the settlement of the company's past debts (in lieu of paying the creditors in cash). Palk did, however, take £15,000 of the new share capital himself paying in cash, and this, as real income, was a vital factor in getting things moving again. The £10,000 debentures were not issued until 1879 (see below).

The TVR had not been allowed to forget Richard Walker after 1869 because he had still been pressing for proper payment for his 1864–6 work. He petitioned against the TVR's 1872 Bill in Parliament, and this resulted in the TVR agreeing to pay him £5,625 so that he would withdraw the petition. Exactly how he was satisfied is unclear due to the absence of any TVR records for this period, but clearly any remaining differences between Walker and the TVR were patched up as part of the negotiations under which Walker agreed to return to take a new contract in 1877. Since leaving the valley in 1866 he had (*inter alia*) built the Thetford & Watton and Watton & Swaffham lines; on the Thetford & Watton he had had six miles of permanent way laid within nine months of starting work, which shows that he was quite capable of getting on with the job for any company which paid properly.

The new contract with Walker, approved by the TVR Board on 9th May 1877, was for £30,000, of which £13,000 was to be paid in cash (Palk's £15,000 subscription effectively guaranteed Walker that sufficient cash would be available) and £17,000 in the new preference shares. It required Walker to finish the line all the way to Teign House so that it could be 'open for public traffic on or before 25th December 1877'. The main works still to be done were:

- Completion of the earthworks, notably on the Chudleigh Road–Chudleigh Knighton section.
- Provision and laying of the Permanent Way, standard gauge, for the whole length of the line, there being no track of any kind laid to date.
- Completion of the five barely-begun river bridges between Chudleigh Road and Ashton, and building from scratch the two river bridges between Ashton and Teign House.
- Erection of station buildings and platforms etc. (nothing having been done yet on this front).
- Making and metalling the road bridge and level crossing approaches.[1]
- Provision of signalling.

Vincent James Barton of St Clements Lane, London, Iron Merchant, was to act as 'surety' to perform the contract in case of Walker becoming bankrupt. Barton was an old acquaintance of Walker and had been involved on the Thetford & Watton where he had undertaken to work the line on completion — an undertaking which he had failed to carry out! He was also to supply Walker with the ironwork for the new TVR contract.

Walker began work immediately in May 1877, under John Ashdown as Engineer and Henry St John and Thomas Large as Resident Engineers, and proceeded to good effect. The (as ever) over-optimistic completion date was not met, but there was at least a railway in existence by the end of 1877, the track having been laid from 0 m. 10 ch. at Chudleigh Road to Ashton Station (6 m. 17 ch.).[2] The shareholders were told in February 1878 that Chudleigh station buildings were nearly complete, and by July 1878 Crocombe and Ashton were also nearing completion. Walker had now done £24,051 of work, and been paid £10,716 in cash and £13,335 in shares.

The Parliamentary powers for building the line had in fact expired in August 1877, and it was being built illegally after this date until the passage of the TVR's 1878 Act on 8th August 1878, which retrospectively approved the previous work and approved a further extension of time to 10th December 1878. (Such unauthorised construction work after powers had expired was nothing unusual; a railway company could get away with it providing there was nobody with a grudge against the company who might challenge in the courts.)

The decision to build the line standard gauge, taken finally in 1877, was probably intended more as a simple inevitability in changing times than as the act of hostility to the broad gauge camp that the TVR's enthusiasm for the 'narrow' gauge had been in the 1860s. The B&E had laid the third rail to Exeter in 1876, and the SDR had obtained powers in 1875 to change its gauge, and might well have done so had it remained independent. It was quite reasonable to think in 1877 that the railways of the West of England would all be standard gauge within a short time, and one cannot blame the TVR for failing to anticipate that the authorities at Paddington were in fact going to cling on to Brunel's gauge for another fifteen years. In an attempt to ensure that transhipment (with its bad economics) would not be needed for the main local goods traffics, the TVR sought powers in their 1878 Bill to compel the GWR to lay a third rail between Newton Abbot and Chudleigh Road. Although these powers were not obtained, the TVR does not seem to have worried too much about the gauge problem, for even if the broad gauge did linger on at Chudleigh Road for a few years,

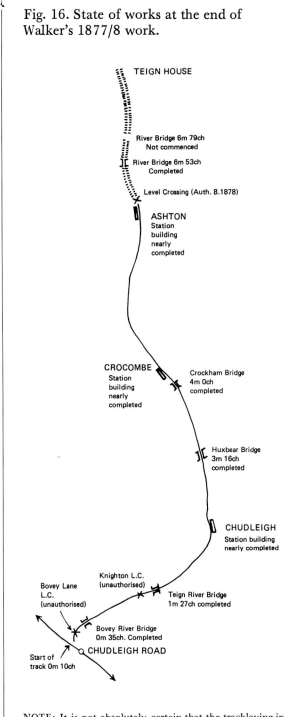

Fig. 16. State of works at the end of Walker's 1877/8 work.

NOTE: It is not absolutely certain that the tracklaying in 1877/8 ended at Ashton station, rather than some way beyond. There is no specific reference to when the track was laid between Ashton station and 6m 70ch; this was most likely done during Walker's 1879/80 work. Certainly it was laid up to 6m 70ch prior to 1881.

they still had connections planned with the standard gauge system at Exeter or Crediton.

IDEAS OF OPENING (1878)

By 1878 the TVR Engineers were starting to consider the practicalities of opening. Although there was always the possibility of a Working Agreement being made with the GWR (as actually transpired in 1879), the TVR was in an anti-GWR mood in 1878 and started to think of working the line itself initially, or entering into a contract with Walker (it was quite common for small lines of this kind to be worked by the contractor initially, and Walker was prepared to do so).[3]

Whatever the future held, there could be no doubt that there would initially be a break of gauge at Chudleigh Road, and no physical junction could be made there. There was, nevertheless, still a need for negotiations with the GWR over the station at Chudleigh Road (it will be recalled that the previous 1870 discussions had never produced a result). These were not conducted with any alacrity — Margary noted in April 1878 that nothing had yet been broached on this front — and in fact Walker did nothing on the ground at Chudleigh Road station in 1877/8. This was obviously likely to delay opening, at least to passenger traffic (the line as laid from 0 m. 10 ch in 1877 was close enough to the Moretonhampstead branch siding to enable transhipping of goods).

There were three other factors of doubt to be borne in mind in 1878 when considering the opening of the line:

(a) The comparative lack of progress on the Ashton–Teign House section, thanks to nothing having been done here in 1869/70, to the delay in authorising the level crossing at Ashton (which prevented tracklaying north of here in 1877/8), and to the delay in starting the two river bridges on this stretch (the bridge at 6 m 79 ch was not started until 1879, in the event). All this naturally brought ideas of an initial 'Stage 1' opening to Ashton only, for a short period, in order to get some revenue in as soon as possible.

(b) The track as laid in 1877 was very rough and (although this is nowhere mentioned as a factor in contemporary statements) there must have been some doubt whether it would have been passed by the Board of Trade for passenger trains. Therefore there were ideas of the 'Stage 1' opening being for goods traffic (which did not require outside approval) only.

(c) There was at all times up to 1881 the probability or possibility of a northward extension from Teign House (to Crediton, Exeter, or Dunsford) following on soon. This led to doubts about whether it was worth spending money on a shortlived 'stage 2' terminus station at Teign House (and Walker did nothing here in 1877/8). It was also felt by some that Lea Cross was a better site for a station in traffic terms than Teign House, whether as an intermediate station on an extended line, or as a permanent terminus if the extensions failed; there were, of course, already powers to build to Lea Cross under the 1875 Act. All this uncertainty over the northern end of the line was a further reason to adopt the doubt-free Ashton station as the 'Stage 1' terminus.

PARTIAL OPENING TO GOODS TRAFFIC (1878)

On 6th August 1878, Large, the resident engineer, accordingly wrote to Ashdown: 'In my opinion the railway could be open for goods traffic in the space of one month . . . to Ashton, and I think such a course would be a judicious one as it would establish a confidence, and may induce persons in the locality to come forward and assist (i.e. financially) to extend the line from Ashton to Lea Cross.'

(Large also recommended Lea Cross for a 'Stage 2' opening to the Shareholders' Meeting on 28th August; by this date he was *de facto* Engineer, as Ashdown had died suddenly on the 26th. The Lea Cross idea seems to have faded after the 1879 GWR Agreement, which specifically referred to Teign House.)

In the autumn of 1878 the line was opened for public goods traffic from Chudleigh Road (0 m 10 ch) to Ashton, worked by Walker for 40% of the receipts, with the trucks hauled by Walker's horses.[4] This was a very low-key opening and usage was probably restricted to local minerals customers with (one imagines) 're-booking' at Chudleigh Road.

This positive step was, unfortunately, counteracted by a cessation of the works at the same time. The company had run out of money again.

THE 1878/9 CRISIS

This 1878/9 crisis was the least serious of the TVR's four crises, and the stoppage of the works seems to have lasted only for some eight months (autumn 1878–summer 1879). In April 1879 a prospectus was issued for the £10,000 of debentures authorised by the 1877 scheme — it had presumably been felt in 1878 that the general economic situation did not allow this to be done then — and in June 1879 there was a further 'Scheme' agreed, which postponed problems with creditors for a while and also authorised the issuing of a further £14,000 of debentures,[5] for which another prospectus was issued in September. The combined £24,000 of debentures was successfully taken up at various dates between May 1879 and August 1880, mostly by genuine outside parties representing real income to the company (although £6,000 went to pay creditors).

At the same time the GWR Agreement gave the company a definite future. After the works resumed in summer 1879, the TVR had ideas of improving the goods service — which seems to have carried on running through the 1878/9 crisis — by introducing locomotive power. This really needed the GWR's agreement, and in November 1879 the TVR wrote to Paddington asking 'whether the Directors are prepared to put on a small engine and a few trucks to run over the portion already completed, with a view to facilitating the mineral traffic'.

Unfortunately the response was that 'the Directors do not see their way themselves to provide an engine', although they were willing 'to supply some trucks'.

How long the goods service actually lasted is not clear. It did not last through to the full opening of the line in 1882 and, as Walker's August 1880 letter refers to it as something in the past, one suspects it came to an end about May 1880 when (as noted below) the TVR's situation took a turn for the worse again.

WALKER'S 1879/80 WORK

The summer of 1879 saw the TVR back on its feet again — for a time. A new Engineer was appointed in June 1879 to replace Large and the late Ashdown. S.W. Jenkin[6] of Liskeard had long experience of railway work and had in fact prepared the deposited plans for the TVR's 1879 Bill in the autumn of 1878. He brought in William Lidstone as his assistant. He agreed to take the post of Engineer 'on being informed that the company would have no difficulty in finding the money required for completion, and that the work would probably be in hand in about three months'.

Unfortunately Jenkin soon discovered that the TVR was not as 'complete' as it seemed. As a result of the protracted and much-interrupted building of the line under different Engineers and contractors, much paperwork had been lost, and the company now had no plan of the line and gradients, no plans of the stations, and no drawings of any of the bridges or other structures. Even if Jenkin had been prepared to fudge this situation himself, the new GWR Agreement required the line to be completed to the satisfaction of the GWR Engineer, and therefore meant that full station plans would have to be submitted to the GWR for approval[7] and full drawings submitted of the major works, notably of all underbridges. Jenkin and Lidstone had therefore to begin by inspecting the works in detail in order to prepare new plans and drawings on the ground. But as soon as they began this job, it became clear that the works had been 'scamped throughout', and that much that was purportedly completed stood no chance of being approved by the GWR and would have to be rebuilt.

Jenkin was particularly concerned at the wooden underbridges on the line. Contrary to the contracts (but no doubt with official approval, to save money), all the underbridges, except the Teign River bridges at 3 m 16 ch and 4 m 0 ch, were wholly timber-built. The situation was not fully revealed until April 1880 when Jenkin removed the superstructure of the bridge at 6 m 53 ch to examine the piling, and reported (in good topical style!) to the Board that:

'the piles have not been driven more than a few inches into the bottom of the river, as they came to rock — Mr Margary naturally declines to accept — there is nothing to prevent the whole bridge from turning over in case of being heavily loaded, like the Tay Bridge . . . Mr. Walker must have been aware.'

Further investigation revealed that *all* the wooden underbridges were too weak and would have to be rebuilt.

As he found more problems, Jenkin's estimate of the cost of completing the line increased, from £3,440 in November 1879 to £4,885 in March 1880, excluding signals in both cases. The TVR Board did not like this and in August 1880 they asked the GWR to do an independent estimate; this resulted in an inspection of the works on 11th August 1880 by Margary and Sir Daniel Gooch. Margary's estimate was £10,000.

From around August 1879 to the spring of 1880, Walker did a certain amount of work on a rather fitful basis. A start was made on rebuilding several small underbridges, the previously-unstarted river bridge at 6 m 79 ch was built, and much of the track was realigned and reballasted to render it fit for passenger trains. Some £4,242 of work was certified in this period.

By March 1880 Walker was experiencing cashflow problems himself, and the TVR had to resort to buying materials for him in order to keep the works going. But Walker's financial problems were really insignificant compared with the TVR's. Jenkin complained at being obliged to do everything 'bit by bit, at intervals', which doubled the cost, and at the 'continual discharge and taking on of men'. It became clear that the 1879 scheme had not really resolved the TVR's problems at all, and by the summer of 1880 all work had come to a halt again, Jenkin writing to the TVR Secretary Thomson on 1st July 1880, 'You are no doubt aware that at present the works are suspended altogether and Mr. Walker's establishment broken up'.

'A STATE OF APPARENTLY HOPELESS INSOLVENCY': THE TVR's FINAL CRISIS (1880/1)

The TVR's 'Schemes' of 1867, 1877, and 1879 had only patched up its problems. The list of creditors had been growing all the time, and many of them began to lose patience. This resulted in a rash of court cases in 1879/80, all of which the TVR lost. By the end of 1880 the company's situation had become quite desperate, with sums due under the judgements but no money to pay them. Further actions were being threatened, and in addition to those who might be seen as 'hostile', there were large sums due to those still connected with the company who needed to be repaid by some means.

The most important of the court actions were those brought by:

William Toogood, the TVR's promoter. Although still acting as the company's Solicitor and Parliamentary Agent, Toogood seems to have gradually drifted apart from the TVR Board after 1877, as new faces came in. Large sums of money were due to him, and one suspects also that he had little interest in the line now that it was turning into a mere GWR branch line incapable of fulfilling the grand ideas of 1861. As noted in Chapter 4, Toogood had back in 1873 secured a judgment against the company for the sums due to him up to that date, but had not sought enforcement as he was well aware that the TVR could not then pay. In the autumn of 1879, however, when the TVR

had money coming in through the placing of debentures, Toogood decided to activate his judgment, and on 20th December 1879 he obtained an 'attachment' of the money held in the TVR's account by the bankers, Sanders & Co., in Exeter. The TVR responded by opening a new account with the London & Westminster Bank and transferring most of their money there! This dispute was temporarily patched up in March 1880 when the TVR promised to pay Toogood in cash and debentures, and he undertook 'to cooperate in every way with the Directors'. However, the TVR only paid in part, and in November 1880 Toogood served a writ on the TVR for £20,000 (a sum which there was no chance of them being able to pay). This was too much for the Board and Toogood was immediately dismissed from his position of solicitor. From this time he had no further connection with the company which he had promoted. In the TVR's view it was not impossible, given the sums that had been paid over to Toogood and the uncertainty of the company's accounts under his management, that it might not be Toogood that owed *them* money rather than vice-versa.

Edward Ellis, Civil Engineer and Surveyor of Exeter, who had given Parliamentary evidence for the TVR on a number of occasions, and been engaged in 1877/8 and 1878/9 to assist in the preparation of plans for the Exeter extensions. He had not been paid, and in August 1880 he issued a writ for £1,488. In December 1880 he obtained a court warrant to 'distrain on the company's line', and under this he seized £577 of TVR property from the works, mostly timber, as an initial attempt at recovery. From this and other such orders the company was at risk of having the rails of its line removed, and the situation was regarded very seriously.

The West of England Bank, in respect of Bellamarsh Mill near Chudleigh Knighton. The Mill Leet had been illegally diverted by the TVR when the line was built, and the Bank had now secured a judgment requiring the completed railway line at this point to be removed, and diverted so that the leet could be restored.

V.J. Barton, the 'surety' of the 1877 contract. Barton had been supplying girders but some were held up in Antwerp when the port was frozen up, and Jenkin had to arrange to obtain from another supplier. When Barton eventually delivered, the TVR refused to pay, and Barton went to court. (The TVR paid him in 1882.)

R.J. Jenkins, who had lent money to Walker and also for the costs of the 1878 Bill, and not been repaid. Jenkins took action against Walker who responded that he was himself owed a larger sum by the TVR, as a result of which the court awarded Jenkins a 'garnishee order' against the TVR in January 1880 for £568. (Jenkins — for whom see Chapter 7 — was bought off by being made a Director, and became a very active supporter of the TVR and later of the Exeter Railway also.)

S.A. Gurney was Walker's banker in Kings Lynn. By an agreement of July 1879 Gurney had lent Walker £1,000, which was to be repaid by £1,000 in TVR debentures. However, the TVR did not give Walker the debentures when due and he could not pay Gurney, who took legal action and obtained judgment against the TVR in June 1880. (The TVR had paid him by the end of the year.)

The TVR's troubles were exacerbated by the fact that it was impossible for the Board to discover exactly what the state of the company's affairs was. The majority of the company's documents — everything except the Minute Books and the Share and Debenture Registers — were held by Toogood, who refused to hand anything over until his own claim was settled. Thomson, the Company Secretary, knew almost nothing of what had happened before his own appointment in 1877. The one person who did have a good idea of the company's situation from the start, Palk — who was granted the title of Lord Haldon in 1880 and will be so referred to henceforth — was dangerously ill through most of the winter of 1880/1 and could not attend Board meetings.

On the dismissal of Toogood, Lord Haldon's private solicitor, Benjamin Lake (of the firm of Lake, Beaumont, & Lake), was appointed the TVR's Solicitor, and it fell to him to try to produce a report on the company's position. This he did with promptitude, in November 1880. Lake really wanted the company to be abandoned and a new Act obtained 'incorporating a new company for construction of the line, which could (buy) up the property of the present undertaking and (start) clear of all the existing embarrassment'. But the Directors did not wish to proceed along these lines, and Lake accordingly recommended:

- A new survey of the present condition of the works.
- A new contract 'from a responsible contractor' to complete the line to the GWR's satisfaction, the contractor taking payment in debentures which Lord Haldon undertook to take from the contractor for cash. (Lord Haldon was agreeable to making £10,000 available to complete the line providing that this could be arranged in such a way that the creditors could not get their hands on this money.)
- Purchasing the Bellamarsh Mill property, as the easiest way out of the difficulties there, to avoid having to divert the line. (This purchase was effected in 1881.)
- The drawing up of a 'Registered Bill of Sale' passing over to the new contractor all the company's effects capable of being seized, in order to prevent creditors such as Ellis seizing them. (In the event, such a Bill of Sale over the company's movable property, plus a mortgage of all the company's lands, was made out on 24th December 1880 to Lord Haldon, not the contractor. In return for this Lord Haldon paid Ellis — although only by dint of borrowing the money from the Torquay Bank!)
- The drawing up of a new 'scheme' to deal with the company's debts, and in particular to reduce the rate of interest on the debentures from 5% to 4%.
- Formalising the GWR Agreement in a proper Deed. (This was done in March 1882.)

In January 1881 Lake drew up as best he could a list of the TVR's debts. The total was £44,000 or so, but much uncertainty attached to some of the items and there could be no guarantee that the list was complete. Unless all the creditors and all the shareholders agreed to a new Scheme, the company would have to be abandoned. In the search for a solution to these problems, the Board, which had been used to only the most infrequent meetings, found itself having to meet every 2–4 weeks during 1881.

'It is difficult to conceive of worse management than has been the lot of this unfortunate company', wrote Lake of Toogood's management of the company in past years.

Obtaining reports on the current state of the works was probably the easiest part of the route out of the jungle. Jenkin's report of 7th February 1881, which naturally concentrated on the progress made since 1879, estimated the cost of completion at £8,240. Jenkin also offered to draw up a detailed specification of the works needed for a new contract for 50 guineas, which was agreed. An independent report was also obtained (in December 1880) from John Fowler; this largely agreed with Jenkin's views and suggested that £9,000 was required. As if two reports were not enough, Lawrence Hesketh Palk (Lord Haldon's eldest son and heir), on behalf of his sick father, commissioned a third privately, from Walrond Smith. This was written in more scathing language, commenting *inter alia* that 'the present condition of the works is deplorable' (as a result of the long times that had elapsed without attention). Walrond Smith's estimate was £11,000.

The Shareholders' Meeting of 30th March 1881 was given a detailed report on the situation. It was stated that Walker was prepared to sign a new contract (if Lake had wanted someone other than Walker he was overruled) and that the line could open to traffic within six months of a resumption of work. But £15,000 had to be raised and this was dependent on all agreeing to the 'Scheme', which had now been prepared. If the Scheme were not agreed, the Board could see no way of completing the line and would propose that the undertaking be abandoned. The Scheme was considered at a special meeting on 6th April but it was found impossible to persuade H.R. Taylor (the solicitor who had taken most of Humphreys' stock) to agree to it. This meeting did, therefore, pass a resolution for abandonment, but the application to the Board of Trade to autho-

---

CLAIMS AGAINST THE TVR AS AT JANUARY 1881

Land Owners	Lord Clifford	£3,000
	Others	3,005
Traders	F. Hill & Co, Rails ordered but not delivered	438
	Gabriel & Sons, Timber delivered and seized by Ellis	323
	GWR, Carriage of Timber	134
	Panteg Iron Co, switches ordered but not delivered	31
	Morning Post, advertising	30
Loans	Lord Haldon's Advances	2,684
	Torquay Bank	1665
	E.C. Nicholls	58
Former & Current Engineers and Officers &c.		
	Richard Walker	7,376
	J. Thomson, Secretary, ½ year's salary	100
	S.W. Jenkin	293
	R. Read, for arranging terms of GWR Agreement	110
	Mr Baker (had acted as Arbitrator)	75
	Mrs Ashdown, residue of larger claim	448
	Edward Ellis	500
	William Toogood	claim of 20,000
	R.J. Jenkins, re action against Walker	382
	Gurney, interest due on debt now paid	160

plus others which Lake was unable to establish clearly at this date

TOTAL   Approx.   £44,000

SUMMARY OF WORK ON THE STATIONS AND
RIVER BRIDGES

The 1877 contract required that the 'station buildings, platforms, gates, and wrought fencing are to be constructed at stations the exact counterpart in all respects as to size and quality of materials as the Chudleigh Road station on the Moretonhampstead Branch Railway'. This was at least a convenient way for the TVR to avoid any design costs! However, only the first station to be built, Chudleigh (started in Autumn 1877), was in fact given a station building and goods shed to the same design as those at Chudleigh Road. The station buildings at Crocombe and Ashton, both started a few months after Chudleigh in Winter 1877/8, were built of brick to a very plain design, and no goods sheds were built at these locations. This change must have been approved by the TVR, presumably in order to save money. Although not identical to Teigngrace, these two stations seem to have been modelled on Teigngrace, and the subsequent 1881 contract required them to be 'fitted up in all respects similar to Teign Grace station'.

Chudleigh Road
(The TVR line laid 1877 began at 0m10ch and therefore excluded the station area; this was no doubt due to the continued lack of any agreement with the SDR/GWR on the station arrangements. The TVR did some work at Chudleigh Road in 1879/80, including the building of part of the TVR platform; but in April 1880 work was stopped on the GWR's orders, until a May 1880 meeting between the GWR and TVR officers resulted in an agreed plan. As a result, most of the work at Chudleigh Road was only done in 1881/2.)
35ft extension to (1874) Goods Shed built 1881.
(1874) Broad Gauge siding extended 1881 to act as BG Transhipment siding in addition to handling station goods traffic. (Work done by GWR and recharged to TVR.)
TVR platform lengthened to c270ft and completed 1881.
TVR line and sidings in station area laid 1882.
Signal box built 1882.

Bovey Lane Crossing
Cottage largely built 1880, completed 1881.

Knighton Crossing
Cottage built 1881.

Chudleigh
Main line laid 1877.
Station building erected 1877/8, fitted out 1881/2.
Platform built 1877/8 (incomplete), lengthened 20ft at south end and completed 1881.
Goods shed built 1877/8.
Loading Bank built 1879/80, completed 1881.
Steps to road built 1881.
Crane 1882.
Signal Box built 1882.
Siding and connections laid 1882.

Crocombe (Trusham)
Main line laid 1877.
Station building erected 1878, fitted out 1881.
Platform built 1878 (incomplete), lengthened 24ft at south end (to 160ft) and completed 1881.
Road diversions completed 1877/8.
Loading Bank built 1879/80, completed 1881.
Coal and Lamp House 1882 (on request of GWR).
Signal Box built 1882.
Sidings and connections laid 1882.

Ashton
Main line (up to LC) laid 1877.
Station building erected 1878, finished and fitted out 1881.
Platform built 1878 (incomplete), lengthened (to 160ft) and completed 1881.
Loading Bank built 1879/80, completed 1881.

'Goods Shed' (Extension of main building) 1882 (on request of GWR).
Porters' Room, and Coal and Lamp House, 1882 (on request of GWR).
Crane 1882.
Engine Shed 1881/2.
Carriage Shed 1881/2.
Signal Box built 1882.
Sidings and connections laid 1882.

Teign House
Main line laid 1881 (? up to stops ?).
Second siding and connection laid 1882.
Office hut erected 1881/2.
Crane 1882? (no ref. at the time).

BRIDGES

Bovey Marsh Bridge 0m 27ch (Later quoted as 0m 25½ch)
Built as timber bridge 1877/8.
Major strengthening 1880, some minor work not done until 1881. (Still an all-timber bridge).

Bovey River Bridge 0m 35ch (Later quoted as 0m 33½ch)
Piles driven 1869/70 but timber for rest of bridge seized by Bank before being taken to site.
Completed 1877/8 as timber bridge.
Superstructure removed 1881 and piles tested. Masonry abutments built and strengthened timber superstructure reinstalled thereon.

Teign River Bridge 1m 27ch (Later quoted as 1m 24½ch)
Half the piles driven 1869/70 but timber for rest of bridge seized by Bank before being taken to site.
Completed 1877/8 as timber bridge with eleven 17ft spans.
Superstructure removed 1881 and piles tested, strengthened timber superstructure reinstalled (i.e. still an all-timber bridge).

Bellamarsh Mill Leet 2m 00ch
Built 1869/70 (?) as timber bridge.
Existing bridge removed altogether 1881, and new bridge built with masonry abutments and timber superstructure.

Teign River Bridge (Huxbear Bridge) 3m 16ch (Later quoted as 3m 13½ch)
Abutments and two piers built 1869/70.
Completed 1877/8 as girder bridge.
Superstructure removed 1881 and girders replaced in different fashion.

Teign River Bridge (Crockham Bridge) 4m 00ch (Later quoted as 3m 77½ch)
North abutment and two piers built 1869/70.
Completed 1877/8 as girder bridge.
Superstructure removed 1881 and girders replaced in different fashion.

Ashton Mill Leet 6m 40ch
Built as timber bridge.
Existing bridge removed altogether 1881, and masonry culvert built instead.

Teign River Bridge (Ashton Bridge) 6m 53ch (Later quoted as 6m 53½ch)
Built 1877/8 as timber bridge.
When inspected April 1880, piles found defective. Existing bridge removed altogether 1881 and new bridge built of 32ft girders on masonry abutments.

Teign River Bridge (Christow Bridge) 6m 79ch (Later quoted as 6m 75¼ch)
Built 1879/80 as girder bridge on masonry abutments.

rise this was unsuccessful. In May it was decided instead to apply to Parliament for leave to introduce a Bill to approve the Scheme despite Taylor's opposition to it. This was granted but Taylor then petitioned against the Bill. The matter was only resolved by Lord Haldon agreeing to purchase Taylor's shareholding himself. The Teign Valley Railway Act 1881 was then passed on 11th August 1881, authorising the paying off of the existing 5% debentures (which was done in 1881/2) and their replacement by £59,000 of new 4% debenture stock. Lord Haldon himself took the whole £15,000 of the new 'B' debentures intended to finance the completion of the line.

Meanwhile, Toogood had agreed in June to accept £5,500 in an out-of-court settlement of his £20,000 claim, giving up all his actions against the company and handing over all the papers held by him.

By the end of July 1881 it was therefore clear that the obstacles had been successfully overcome — although this had once again only been possible because of Lord Haldon's willingness to dip into his own pocket when other sources failed. The way was clear for the fifth, and, thankfully, final phase in the construction of the line.

WALKER'S 1881 CONTRACT AND HIS 1881/2 WORK

On 3rd August 1881 a new contract was signed with Richard Walker, with his relatives John and William Walker, farmers of Terrington St Clement, near Kings Lynn, as 'sureties'. Walker was required to, and did, put the works in hand within a week of this. The line was to be completed for opening by 28th February 1882 and the contract price of £9,000 included the usual maintenance for 12 months after opening.

Some time in the late spring of 1881 it had been definitely decided that the Ashton–Teign House section would be opened for goods traffic only and that no passenger station would be built at Teign House. Jenkin's report in February 1881 had still spoken of the need to build a station here and we do not know what prompted the subsequent change of plan, although it did, of course, save £1,000 or so in construction costs.

The major works carried out by Walker under this contract were:

- Making good slips in the earthworks, including a 175 ft slip of the bank at 2 m 6 ch south of Chudleigh caused by river flooding.
- Ballasting and laying the track from 0 m 0 ch to 0 m 10 ch, and 6 m 70 ch to the end of the line.
- Slewing and reballasting of the line from 0 m 10 ch to 0 m 20 ch (between Chudleigh Road and Bovey Lane).
- Lowering of the rock cutting and relaying of the track from 4 m 52 ch to 4 m 62 ch north of Trusham.
- Replacing many of the sleepers which, although only put down in 1877, were very decayed and rotten. 3000 new sleepers were ordered in November 1881. The original sleepers were to prove a very bad lot and many more had to be replaced shortly after the line opened.
- Completion of the main station buildings (already largely done) and provision of other structures and fittings at the stations.
- Laying of all sidings at the stations (only the main line had been laid in 1877).

- Reconstruction in whole or part of most of the river bridges (see Table for details).
- Improvement of the fencing, as many of the posts were now rotten.
- Erection of signal boxes and provision of signals and telegraph.
- Metalling of the approach roads at the three level crossings, completion of the crossing keeper's house at Bovey Lane, and building of a crossing keeper's house at Chudleigh Knighton.
- Erection of an Engine Shed and Carriage Shed at Ashton. (Nothing had been done about such facilities prior to this, due no doubt to the uncertainty over where the line's terminus was to be).

This time Walker seems to have been able to proceed as fast as possible without being constrained by financial difficulties. Nevertheless the deadline could not be met, for reasons outside Walker's control. The points and crossings needed for the stations, which had already been made[8] by the Panteg Engineering Co. before Walker began work, were not delivered because that company went bankrupt. A new order had to be placed with the Isca Foundry Co., and they only delivered from March, so that the station sidings could not be laid until March–May 1882. Secondly, Margary and C.E. Compton, the GWR Divisional Superintendent, made an inspection of the line in December 1881 which produced a further list of facilities that the GWR required; and then the GWR delayed giving its agreement to the signalling plans, so that the signal boxes could not be commenced until March 1882 and the signalling was not completed until June, this being the last item left.

On 8th June 1882, J. Luxmore, the Divisional Locomotive Superintendent at Newton Abbot, visited the Teign Valley line to check on the state of completion and the locomotive facilities in particular. He reported to William Dean:

'The line is complete throughout but the signals and points are not all connected up in the Signal Boxes. This work it is considered will be

---

AUGUST 1881 CONTRACT — SPECIFICATION FOR ENGINE SHED AND CARRIAGE SHED AT ASHTON

'An engine shed 60ft by 20ft to take two engines to be provided with a small store room and engineman's room with a fireplace in the latter, also a window in each room and a door connecting with the shed. A pit is to be made in the engine house the full length of the house and properly drained, a stop block to be fixed at the end of the siding, roof to be ventilated, proper doors to be fixed at the ends of the house and to be provided with a bar and padlock, &c. Water to be laid on into the shed and a hydrant fixed for washing out the engines. A hose pipe with nozzle elbow and union to be provided. The floor of the Engine House and pit to be bricked. A work bench and vice to be fixed on the side of the house. A circular water tank and crane to be fixed outside the Engine House as shown to hold at least 3000 gallons with proper foundations and a dripping place under the crane properly drained, the water is to be pumped into this tank from the stream running through the station yard by a pump so constructed that it can be worked by the steam from the engine while standing in the shed at night. A proper coal platform must be erected near the Engine House as shown, to be 30ft long by 7ft wide. A proper ash-pit to be made between the rails by the side of the coal platform with a brick bottom the length of an engine and 18in deep, and to be properly drained.

'A carriage shed 140ft long by 18ft wide as shown on plan. This may be made of corrugated iron as by drawing to be hereafter supplied.'

Source: RAIL 1057/240

done in about 10 days' time when the line will be ready for inspection. Before the Board of Trade Inspector comes, however, an Engine will be required to work over the line and give it a good trial.[9]

'A brick Engine House has been erected at Ashton . . . capable of holding two tank engines. The roof is corrugated iron[10] with not much allowance for ventilation . . . The pit in it is far too deep (3 ft) and will certainly have to be made shallower. No water has been laid on as yet but arrangements for the purpose are being made.

'The shed is fixed in my opinion the wrong side of the line, and it would have been much better, if it had been erected on the siding side of the line. (See O.S. map in Chapter 18.)

Fig. 17. The Teign Valley Railway 1882.

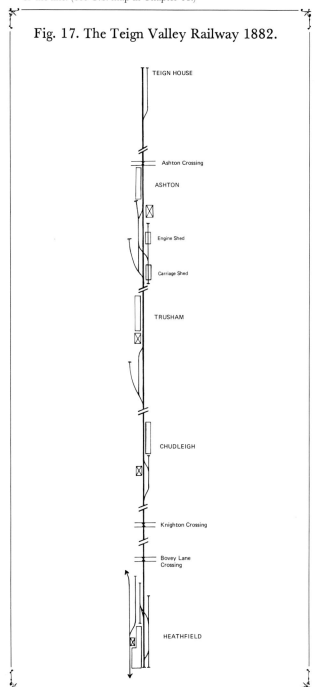

'A coal stage has been put up and the foundations for a water tank is (sic) being erected . . . these are placed at the wrong end of the shed, and the engine will have to run through the shed, which is provided with large doors at each end, every time it has to take water or coal. This will be very inconvenient . . .

'A carriage shed has been erected and it would have been better if the Engine Shed had been where the carriage shed is and vice-versa.

'No provision has been made at Chudleigh station for water which will be necessary. A good deal of shunting will undoubtedly be necessary at Chudleigh Road, but no water can be obtained there.

'At Chudleigh the river is close in front of the station, and a water tank should be put up and a supply obtained. At Chudleigh Road there should be an ash pit made so that the Engineman can get under his engine there and examine it.'

This shows the exacting standards that were always demanded when another company was building a line — the GWR's own branch lines did not have such frequent water facilities as Luxmore was demanding! In fact, the water supplies demanded at Chudleigh Road and Chudleigh were never provided. The pit at Chudleigh Road was provided, although it is not known for sure that this was done at this date.

Some time in the latter half of June 1882, two standard gauge tank locomotives must have been brought down for the line on broad gauge trucks from Exeter.

It was decided in the summer of 1882 that Chudleigh Road station should be renamed 'Heathfield' to avoid confusion with the new Chudleigh station. (Jenkin had pointed out the need for a renaming back in February, but he had suggested 'Chudleigh Knighton' as the new name, which was hardly very suitable!) The new name was adopted as from 1st October 1882. There was no such place as 'Heathfield', the name referring to Bovey Heathfield the surrounding heath.

It was also decided that Crocombe station should be known instead as 'Trusham'. This one imagines was done at the GWR's insistence to avoid confusion with Crowcombe Heathfield on the Minehead line (which was confusing enough as it was!).

INSPECTION

Lidstone had written to the Board of Trade in March 1882 to say that the works were nearly completed, and asking for the necessary paperwork to be forwarded. His next letters were on 13th and 17th June, when he sent the formal 'Second Notice' of opening and asked if an Inspecting Officer could come on or about 24th June as it was desired to open the line on 1st July.

In the event, the inspection process was to hold up opening for a further three months. It was perhaps predictable that faults would be found in a line built in the way that the TVR had been.

Col. Yolland came on 30th June[11] to make what turned out to be the first of four inspections. The line was put up for inspection only as far as Ashton Station (6 m 17 ch), the goods-only line beyond to Teign House being outside the Board of Trade's purview. Accompanying Yolland in the Inspection Saloon, hauled by the two locos on the line, were Margary, Compton, W.H. Avery (Divisional Goods Superintendent), Lucas (the GWR Permanent Way Inspector), and Jenkin. Yolland objected to the two unauthorised level crossings at Bovey Lane and Chudleigh Knighton (as well he might!); to the absence of starting signals in some cases and a few other signalling details (see Chapter 17); the absence of clocks at the stations; the position of the guard rails and baulks under the rails on the viaducts, which might be hit by the locomotive; and the layout of the station sidings. This was enough for the Board of Trade to require postponement of opening, and the TVR was so notified on 3rd July.

The TVR was lucky regarding the level crossings; the Board of Trade decided to allow the line to open with them provided they were only there temporarily. The signalling matters and the clocks were easily dealt with. The details of the viaducts were resolvable but were to prove the factor that held up the opening, as noted further below. The views expressed by Yolland on the layout of the station sidings were somewhat eccentric. They had been built as double-ended sidings simply because that was easier for shunting than a dead-end siding, and there was no intention of using them as passing loops, but Yolland wrote:

'A peculiar arrangement has been adopted at all the stations on the line. There are loops or loop sidings which are not placed opposite the single line platforms, so that if these loops are maintained it will be requisite to have an undertaking from the company that no passenger train shall be stopped on these loops at the stations where there is no platform alongside for the passengers to get out, or that the loops should have one or other of the facing points taken out and their being thus converted into regular sidings with only one connection with the running line.'

The civil servants at the Board of Trade seem to have been mystified by Yolland's ideas on this and ignored the point in their correspondence with the TVR; the sidings stayed as they were.

On 25th August Lidstone was able to write to the Board of Trade asking for a second inspection on 2nd September, and it was indeed on 2nd September that Col. Rich (not Yolland) came down for this purpose. However, this second inspection was something of a waste of time; Rich found that the guard rails on the viaducts were still too close to the engines. It was now decided to resolve the problem by making alterations to the brake gear of the two locomotives on the line, instead of altering the viaducts themselves. As this was apparently regarded as an easy job, hopes were now entertained of opening on 2nd October, and indeed the new GWR 'Service Book' for October included the TVR service with a note that the line would 'probably' open on 2nd October. On 22nd September the GWR told the TVR that one of the engines had already been altered and another would be 'sent down in a day or two'. However, as the formal authority of the GWR Board was needed before the line could be opened, and there was no Board Meeting until 4th October, it would now be necessary to change the opening date to 9th October. The TVR forwarded the GWR's letter to the Board of Trade and asked for permission to open.

Rich returned, for the third inspection, on 27th September. Unfortunately, the second engine had still not arrived and Rich refused to allow opening until it did, on the grounds that if there was only one engine able to work the line the service could not be run if it should break down. The second engine duly appeared shortly afterwards, but difficulties now arose over the TVR's 'single line working' undertaking, as told in Chapter 17. Only after a rush of correspondence with the Board of Trade on Friday 6th and Saturday 7th October was it possible for Lake, the TVR Solicitor, to inform everybody that the proposed opening on the 9th could actually go ahead.

Trial runs were made on the line under Luxmore's supervision on the 7th as a final check that all was well, and by that evening it was known that, after 22 years, the line really was going to open on Monday morning.

'The town of Chudleigh is very jubilant over the approaching event', it was reported.

OPENING (9th OCTOBER 1882)[12]

The normal timetabled service was run on the opening day, Monday 9th October, although, as is often the way on such occasions, timekeeping was to become badly disrupted by the celebrations before the day was out. All six coaches allocated to the line were used on the trains, and the loco, driven by Driver Mark Sutton, was decorated with the conventional flags and evergreens.

There is no record of any organised celebrations for the first train, the 7.15 am from Ashton, this being a little early for the gentlefolk! The 8.45 am from Heathfield carried a full load including the local GWR officers who were to take charge of the day — Luxmore, Assistant District Engineer Luke, Chief Inspector Northcott, and Inspectors Millman and Hockaday — plus Jenkin and Walker.

The main ceremonies were reserved for the 12.20 pm from Heathfield, in order to give those from far afield time to get to the scene, and because it accorded conveniently with the lunch following. The higher GWR officials, including P.J. Margary and Burlinson, the Assistant Superintendent of the Line, travelled on this train. Unfortunately, two of the carriages of this train were derailed as it was run into the station! They were rerailed with reasonable promptitude but the train nevertheless left half an hour late and with only four carriages (it being impossible, of course, to procure any extra standard gauge coaches). As a result the dignitaries were somewhat packed into the compartments. It was reported that 'the scenery along the slopes of the valley was much admired' by those many who were strangers to the neighbourhood.

When the train arrived at Chudleigh, the members of the Town Committee, set up two weeks earlier to organise the opening celebrations, were waiting on the platform distinguished by white rosettes. With them were Lord Haldon and the other TVR Directors, a detachment of the Chudleigh Rifle Volunteers in full dress, and the Chudleigh Brass Band which played 'an appropriate tune'. The station and approaches were decorated in the usual way with flags and evergreens, and a cheering crowd looked on from the overbridge and the station yard. Lord Haldon and others then boarded the train to participate in the ceremonies at Ashton.

Ashton was reached just before 2 pm, 1¼ hours late. A Reception Committee had been organised here by the notables of the surrounding villages, and the Moreton Brass Band had been booked to play 'See The Conquering Hero Comes' as the train drew in. An address of welcome had been prepared by Farmer George Grant of Canonteign Barton, to be read by the 21-year-old Viscount Exmouth (who had spent much of the morning looking around the station and expressing his admiration of the 'completeness of the signalling system'). However the original intention of reading this address on the platform had to be abandoned due to the large crowd there, and an adjournment was made to the road outside in order to get the proceedings over before the train's 2.10 pm departure time. The address was fortunately short:

'The Committee, on behalf of the inhabitants of Ashton, Christow, Doddiscombsleigh, and neighbourhood, beg to welcome the Directors of the Teign Valley Railway, trusting it may be the means of more fully developing the mineral and other resources of this neighbourhood, and that the returns will be satisfactory to the promoters as well as a great accommodation to the public. We have no doubt that the Railway Company will render every assistance to promote the working of the line. We beg to heartily welcome you on this occasion, and to specially thank Lord Haldon for so actively and energetically promoting this railway.'

After the cheers died down, Lord Haldon made a similarly brief reply in which he 'observed that the work of making the line had been long in hand, and supposed that there must have been some excellent reason why it should have taken such a time to bring it to a successful conclusion'.

Lord Haldon, the GWR officials, and others, then rejoined the train to return to Chudleigh for the celebratory luncheon there. A procession was formed up at Chudleigh Station, with the Volunteers and the Band, for the mile-long journey to the Clifford Arms in the town centre where the 'collation' was waiting. The entrance to the station yard was spanned by a banner reading 'Success to the Teign Valley Railway', and the whole of the main street decorated with foliage, flags, and mottoes, one of which read (in reference to the celebrated 'Chudleigh Rock' south of the town):

'Like our rock which have for ages stood
May our railway prove a lasting good.'

The church bells were rung throughout the proceedings.

Lord Haldon took the chair at the luncheon, with G.B. Ellicombe of 'Rocklands' as Vice-Chairman. Ellicombe initiated the proceedings with a toast to Lord Haldon, and the latter replied with a speech in which the opposition which the TVR had faced over the years was referred to only in polite and amusing terms. Burlinson, as the senior GWR official present, replied just as politely on the GWR's behalf.

Meanwhile the Ashton Reception Committee and friends had walked the short distance across the fields to the Old Mill for their own luncheon, presided over by Viscount Exmouth. The room was decorated with a large motto 'GWR Welcome to Ashton 1882' over the chair, and another 'Unity is Strength' at the far end. Whatever the precise significance of this was meant to be, some of the speakers started drifting into religious controversy until F.D. Fulford (heir of the late Baldwin Fulford who had been one of the original Devon Central promoters) re-established concord with a toast to the success of the railway.

Outside, 300 workmen were entertained to the traditional bread, beef and beer, and later took part in some athletic sports. In the evening a public dance was held. The later trains all continued to run crowded.

Everything (apart from the embarrassing derailment at Heathfield) had gone off with proper convention and decorum. Yet there must have been many there who knew full well that the confident talk of a revival of the mines, and profits for the railway shareholders, was all pie in the sky. The Editor of the *Devon Evening Express* wondered more realistically whether Lord Haldon should really be 'congratulated' on the opening of a line which had such limited traffic potential. 'Let us hope it will struggle on to Exeter some fine day' he concluded.

---

1. None of the three level crossings had been authorised by Parliament. That at Ashton was authorised in 1878, before the track was laid; but those at Bovey Lane and Chudleigh Knighton were built illegally and only authorised retrospectively in 1884.

2. The track was laid with 75 lb Vignoles rail in 18, 21 and 24 ft lengths, on half-round uncreosoted yellow pine sleepers and with ballast taken from the River Teign. The evidence for the 0 m 10 ch commencement point is the 1881 Contract.

3. The 1878 Bill Counsel's brief states "Until the Company have constructed the extension to join the LSWR at Crediton, or made an agreement with the Great Western Co., it is the intention of the company to work the line themselves or through the contractor, and for this purpose rolling stock will have to be hired".

4. This opening is very badly documented. However, there is an irrefutable reference by Walker in an 18.6.1880 letter in Devon C.R.O. 7259M/B17: 'The line was open for public goods traffic two years since by horse . . .' The April 1879 TVR prospectus, reprinted September 1879, also contains the statement: 'The railway, now complete, is already used for the carriage of goods . . .' There is no actual reference to Ashton being the terminus of this service, but Large had proposed Ashton shortly beforehand and nowhere else is at all likely.

5. Thus bringing the figure back up to the £24,000 limit originally authorised in the 1872 Act, but reduced to £10,000 in 1877. For the complete picture see Table in Chapter 7.

6. Silvanus William Jenkin (1821–1911). Assisted Robert Coad in surveying the Liskeard and Caradon Rly in 1842, and soon afterwards succeeded him as L&C Engineer, a post which he held (responsible for the Liskeard & Looe also from 1878) until 1901. Assisted Brunel in surveying sections of the Cornwall Rly; later Engineer of the Lostwithiel & Fowey (opened 1869), Newquay & Cornwall Jn (op. 1869), and Helston (op. 1887) lines. Long in partnership as a Consulting Engineer in Liskeard ('Jenkin & Trathan') with James Trathan, but the partnership broke up in acrimony in 1874. County Surveyor of Cornwall 1856–1911, and involved in many Harbour, Mine, and Water works in Cornwall. Mayor of Liskeard 1877 and 1878, and a Director of the Liskeard Temperance Hotel.

7. This was eventually given in June 1880 for all stations except Teign House.

8. Except for 5 of the 6 needed for Ashton, where the layout was altered in 1881 as a result of the decision to place the Engine shed here.

9. It seems clear from this and other references that Walker had only used horses.

10. It was slated in later years.

11. According to the TVR Minutes. The *Flying Post* account says 1st July. Yolland's report is dated 3rd July but (as usual) does not state when the inspection itself took place.

12. Goods traffic (including, it appears, traffic to Teign House) also began 9.10.1882. For details of the train services see Chapter 12.

CHAPTER SEVEN

THE TEIGN VALLEY RAILWAY COMPANY
1882–1923

WHEN the TVR opened, there were still a number of points that the GWR and the Board of Trade were unhappy about. Rich, who seems to have been concerned about the line at large, insisted on making a fourth inspection on or about 16th October 1882, after which he reported that the permanent way was so weak that he could not countenance the running of the trains at more than 12 mph. The TVR was obliged to accept this (at least in theory) and the trains had to be decelerated as a result (see Timetables in Chapter 12). Rich also made further comment on the two unauthorised level crossings at Bovey Lane and Chudleigh Knighton. On 28th October the Board of Trade wrote formally to the TVR demanding a signed undertaking that the speed of trains suggested by Col. Rich would be complied with, and that the level crossings would be replaced by bridges within 12 months. However there is no evidence that any such undertaking was actually given.

The TVR was obliged (as was normal) to maintain the line for 12 months after opening, and had provided for this by including a requirement in Walker's 1881 contract that he do this. Jenkin's services were also retained for this period. When the end of the 12 months was approaching, Margary did a survey of the state of the works, and wrote to the TVR on 4th October 1883 stating that before the GWR would take over the works they required the TVR to:

- provide a further 4,500 new sleepers to replace most of the remaining 1877 sleepers (only the worst ones had been replaced in 1881/2 and most of the rest were now rotten too).
- resolve the situation regarding the level crossings (the TVR had done nothing).
- repaint all the signal arms 'the red having completely washed off'.
- repair the buffer stops at Teign House which had been 'knocked back', presumably during overenthusiastic shunting.

Jenkin estimated the cost of Margary's requirements at £2,217 (of which no less than £1,800 was for the sleepers). This was considered by the Board on 23rd October 1883 and it was noted that, far from having any money to pay for these works, the company at present had further liabilities of £1,321 outstanding!

It was decided to promote a Bill in the 1884 Session to authorise a further £6,000 of debenture stock, and also to authorise retrospectively the two level crossings to avoid the cost of having to build bridges. This became the Teign Valley Railway Act 1884 and was the company's twelfth (and final!) Act. The new stock had to be issued primarily to creditors but a sum was kept back for paying the GWR. In the meantime it had been agreed that the GWR would carry out the necessary works, and be repaid by the TVR, the second Lord Haldon giving an understanding to pay personally if the TVR funds proved inadequate; and on this basis the GWR took over maintenance of the line (some months later than it should have done) early in 1884.[1] The GWR was probably not really surprised when in 1885 it was discovered that the TVR did not now have the funds necessary to pay for the work. In accordance with the guarantee, Nelson, the GWR Solicitor, called upon the second Lord Haldon to pay the sum of £1,760 plus interest. Lord Haldon was himself in financial difficulties and asked to pay £800 immediately and the rest six months later; with the resignation needed for financial dealings with the aristocracy, the GWR Board asked Nelson to 'make the best possible arrangements'!

CHANGES IN THE BOARD

Small companies like the TVR generally showed two noticeable trends in their development. Firstly, the original Board of local interests would become diluted over the years by the death or removal of the originators of the scheme (and the unwillingness of other local people to become involved), and the increasing influence of 'London' or other outside financial holdings as the issuing of large shareholdings and debenture holdings to those involved in the building of the line (or their nominees) brought new faces on to the Board. Secondly, if the line when opened was worked by a larger company, the local company would generally lapse into a kind of half-life within a couple of years of the line being opened, with little work for the Directors to do on the rare occasions they met, and the users of the line gradually forgetting that the local company existed at all, until in due course the formal takeover by the larger company was a non-event.

The TVR showed both these trends to some extent, although (thanks to the heavy Palk commitment) it retained a strong 'local' interest on the Board to the end, and it was also unusual in continuing to exist through to the 1923 Grouping.

When the TVR revived itself in 1877, it was still under the same Palk/Kitson/Toogood control as in the 1860s. But in the six years after this, deaths, disputes, and new faces brought a complete changeover in the directorate, the only continuity being the retention of a strong Palk family interest. We have already seen how William Toogood ceased to be involved with the company after 1880, and his representative on the Board, Dr. I.B. Toogood, resigned at the same time. Kitson resigned in 1882, probably simply from age (he died in 1883). In contrast to Toogood's drifting out from the centre of things after 1877, Palk (Lord Haldon) strengthened his already-dominant position in the company in these years thanks mainly to the very large sums of his personal wealth that he was prepared to put into the company in 1877 and 1881, to enable work to continue when it might otherwise have ceased. Lord Haldon ended up with £6,280 of ordinary stock, £34,400 of 1877 preference stocks, and £25,373 in debenture stocks, all this totalling £66,053 and representing 45% of the company's total capital. When he became ill in November 1880, his younger son, the Hon. E.A. Palk, was added to the Board to give another active Palk representative in the direction, and also probably because Lord Haldon knew he would not have long to live and wanted his son to get some experience now. In 1879–81 three further new faces, J.H. Hiley, Capt. Gerald F. Talbot, and the strongly GWR-connected R.J. Jenkins, were brought on to the Board, and (unlike many previous TVR directors) they were all to take an active interest.

The not-unexpected death of Lord Haldon in March 1883 saw E.A. Palk elected as the new Chairman; he retained the office until 1923 so that the Chairmanship was in Palk hands throughout the TVR's 60 years. The second Lord Haldon, Lawrence Hesketh Palk (E.A. Palk's older brother), does not seem to have shown any wish to be actively involved in the company. He found on succeeding to the title that much of the Palk estates had been mort-

gaged to realise the sums that his father had poured into the TVR (and the Torquay Harbour works), so he probably had good reason to regret the whole enterprise. From this time onwards the Palk family fortunes were in decline (there were large auctions of the leaseholds of the Torquay properties in 1885, followed by the sale of the remaining freeholds and the manorial privileges in 1894) and there is alas little doubt that the 1st Lord Haldon's commitment to the TVR had been a major factor in bringing about this situation. S.E. Maskell, the second Lord Haldon's Torquay estates solicitor, was put on the TVR Board in 1883 as Deputy Chairman to further enhance the Palk control of the company, but he did not make much of a mark and resigned in 1886, upon which J.H. Hiley became Deputy Chairman.

The new Board of E.A. Palk, Hiley, Talbot, and Jenkins which ran the company from the 1880s to the 1900s was a very much more businesslike organisation than the old

---

THE TEIGN VALLEY RAILWAY COMPANY
including the Devon Central Railways

Chairman	1860–1883	Sir Lawrence Palk (became 1st Lord Haldon 1880) (*deceased*)
	1883–1923	The Hon. Edward A. Palk
Secretary	(1860–1864)	(Toogood acted as Secretary)
	1864–1865	Norman F.G. Uniacke (*resigned*)
	1865–1867	James Hutt (*resigned*)
	1867–1872	John Alsop
	(1872–1877)	(Toogood acted as Secretary)
	1877–1884	John H(ugh) Thomson
	1884–1900	W. Daniel
	1900–1923	H.R. Cox
Solicitor	1860–1880	William Toogood (*dismissed*)
	1880–1923	Benjamin Lake of Lake Beaumont & Lake followed by others in same firm and its successors.
Engineers	1860–1867	John F(urness) Tone, and William J(ohn) Browne (Resident Engineer)
	1869–1870	Thomas Myers
	1871–1872	J.H. Tolmé amd Edward Appleton
	1874–1878	W. John Ashdown (*deceased*)
	1877	Henry St. John (Resident Engineer)
	1877–1878	Thomas W. Large (Resident Engineer)
	1879–1882	John Fowler (Consulting Engineer)
	1879–1883	Silvanus W. Jenkin (Engineer)
	1879–1882	William Lidstone (Resident Engineer)

Board Members from 1878 only (due to poor records pre-1878 those who had ceased to be Board Members before 1878 are omitted)

	1860–1883	Sir Lawrence Palk [Chairman] (*deceased*)
	1860–1882	William Kitson (*retired*)
	1869–1880	Dr Isaac Baruch Toogood (*resigned*)
	187x–1879	Sir G. Bowyer (*resigned*)
	187x–1881	Edward Byrom (*resigned*)
	1879–1909	J(ames) H(enry) Hiley
	1879–1894	Capt. Gerald F. Talbot (*resigned*)
	1880–1923	The Hon. E.A. Palk [Chairman from 1883]
	1881–1922	R(ichard) J(onathan) Jenkins (*deceased*)
	1883–1886	Stuart E(aton) Maskell (*resigned*)
1901–1902, 1922–1923		George M. Shaw-Mackenzie* (*resigned*)
	1909–1923	H.F. Bassett
	1909–1915	A. Middleton
	1915–1916	Thomas E. Button
	1916–1922	G.W. Claridge

*The then TVR Solicitor

R.J. JENKINS

Richard Jonathan Jenkins was born on 11th December 1839 in Tredegar, eldest son of Richard Jenkins, a leading figure in the area.

Educated at Cowbridge Grammar School, he studied for the Royal Engineers but decided on a civil career and became articled to Daniel Gooch at Swindon Works. Here he was active in promoting the Workmen's Schools and also became Captain of the local Volunteers.

He left Swindon in 1864 to superintend the alterations to the *Great Eastern* for laying the Atlantic Cable. When Gooch left the GWR in 1865 to carry out the laying of the Cable, he appointed Jenkins as his Private Secretary to transact his public and private affairs in England in his absence. This included getting Gooch elected as Conservative member for Cricklade whilst he was away. Jenkins was retained as Gooch's Private Secretary for many years after his return.

In 1866 Jenkins went into partnership with Gooch's son-in-law F. Newton, trading as Newton & Jenkins, dealing in engineering supplies for railways, water and gas works, etc. This firm was active until 1901 when Jenkins retired and moved to Bexhill. Over the years Jenkins acquired directorships of W. T. Henley's Telegraph Works Ltd., a water company, and several mining companies.

A staunch Conservative, Jenkins was to have been candidate for Monmouth and on another occasion for Criccieth, but was prevented from proceeding by illness in both cases. He was an active Freemason and a founder of the Gooch Lodge in Swindon.

Jenkins' railway directorships included the Staines & West Drayton Railway (of which he was Chairman 1881-2) and the London, Hendon & Harrow Railway. He was made a director of the TVR in 1881 as a result of his court case referred to in Chapter 6, but became one of the company's most loyal advocates. He was still attending Board Meetings in his 80s and actually died at a TVR Board Meeting on 18th July 1922. From 1909 he had been Deputy Chairman.

From 1895 to 1902 Jenkins was also an active director of the Exeter Railway — the only director to be involved with both companies. His role there is described in Chapter 9.

TVR of the Toogood period. They had no interest in getting involved in any grand extension schemes, recognising that they had enough to do to keep the company afloat at all.

Once the GWR took over the works in 1884 and there was no longer a contractor and engineer to be dealt with, the Board was able to cut its meetings down to half-yearly, holding them on the same dates as the half-yearly shareholders' meetings (the latter of course hardly attended by anyone except the Board themselves). All Board and shareholders' meetings had been held in London from the 1870s. Lake, the Solicitor, was now the central pivot of the company's running, dealing with the GWR as necessary.

In 1894, when the Exeter Teign Valley & Chagford Railway was in confident mood, an agreement was made under which they were to take over the TVR; this was kept alive for some years but the ETV&C were unable to find the funds. Details are given in Chapter 9.

FINANCES

When the accounts were made up to the end of 1882, it was recorded that the TVR had spent £169,907 on its 7¾ miles of railway instead of the £44,000 once anticipated. It must have been obvious to any realistic person long before the line opened that the ordinary and preference shareholders were never going to get a penny for their investment (although the Board did not of course wish to mention this, and over-optimistic expectations rarely faded before the first period's traffic returns were produced). It was, however, reasonable to think up to 1881 that the company would earn enough to pay the interest on the debentures; the clause in the 1879 GWR Agreement requiring the first £1,200 of the line's annual receipts to be paid over wholly to the TVR was so worded because £1,200 was the sum needed to pay the annual interest due on the then debentures (5% of £24,000). But in 1881 the debenture stock was increased to £59,000, and in 1884 to £65,000, and that put a very different complexion on things; an annual income of £2,600 or so was now needed just to pay the debenture interest. Right from the start it was clear that this was not going to be achieved and that the company was therefore destined to insolvency.

The first directors' report after opening, for the second half of 1882, noted, in words familiar to railway shareholders all over the country, 'The Directors regret to say that the amount of traffic receipts from the railway has, so far, disappointed their expectations . . .'

The figures for the first full year, 1883, showed gross receipts of only £997. Thanks to the terms of the Agreement the GWR had to pay the whole of this over to the TVR. Throughout the 1880s the receipts continued to hover unhappily around the £1,000 mark. This was just enough to pay the £960 interest on the 'A' debentures, the priority stock, and this was done regularly. But there was nothing for the other debenture holders, and the unpaid interest had to be put down as a liability in the accounts. In

1891 the Board considered the possibility of applying for a Receiver, but nothing was done on this front.

In addition to the increasing sums due to the debenture holders in back interest, the TVR was also amassing an ever-increasing debt to the GWR. Thanks to the obligation to pay over the entire earnings to the TVR so long as they were less than £1,200 p.a., the GWR never received a penny from the line prior to 1894 (see Table). But the GWR was nevertheless entitled in the long term to its full 55% of the receipts of these years, so this sum, although being paid over to the TVR at the time, was put down in the accounts as an advance by the GWR to the TVR which would have to be repaid one fine day and on which

	Gross Receipts of line £	TVR Co's income £	
1882	191	191	
3	997	997	
4	1005	1005	
5	986	986	
6	967	967	
7	1009	1009	
8	1110	1110	
9	1047	1047	
1890	1030	1030	
1	1140	1140	
2	1194	1194	
3	1175	1175	
4	1229	1200	
5	1346	1200	
6	1583	1200	
7	1474	1200	
8	1632	1200	
9	2057	1200	
1900	1936	1200	
1	2022	1200	
2	1893	1200	
3	2436	1200	
4	3086	1200	
5	2900	1200	
6	3999	1200	
7	4841	1200	
8	5257	1200	
9	5644	1200	
1910	6154	1200	
1	7386	1200	
2	7349	1200	
3	9383	1200	
4	8973	4048	
5	9373	4231	
6	9395	4253	Government
7	9628	4488	Control
8	9487	4342	Period — 1913
9	9559	4412	figures used as
1920	9368	4228	basis of payment
1	9591	4401	
1922	nk	nk	

TEIGN VALLEY RAILWAY COMPANY : GROSS RECEIPTS OF LINE AND TVR Co's INCOME 1882–1922

Source: 1882–1906 figures from RAIL 1057/229. These are believed to exclude the company's small income from non-GWR sources.
1907–1921 figures from TVR half yearly reports.

The 'Gross Receipts' figures are (one assumes) the receipts for the portions of journeys (whether booked at TVR stations or elsewhere) on TVR metals; therefore they are less than the actual takings at TVR stations (for which see Table in Chapter 14).

interest at 5% was charged. By 1895 this 'advance' had reached £7,171 and the interest a further large sum.[2]

Eventually, in the 1900s, the line's gross receipts began to increase very markedly thanks to the expansion of the roadstone traffic from the new quarries in the area. But, due to the need to repay to the GWR the large sums 'advanced' in past years, this increase in the gross receipts did not now produce any extra income for the TVR company; although from 1904 the line was earning enough for the TVR's 45% share to exceed the minimum £1,200 for the first time, the GWR (quite properly) held the annual payment to the TVR at £1,200 and took the rest of the TVR's 45% for itself to start recouping the past advances.

After 1904, therefore, the TVR's debt to the GWR was decreasing every year as more was paid off, and with the stone traffic seemingly destined to continue increasing yearly, the TVR Board could see by the late 1900s that they would within a few years have repaid the whole GWR debt and be able to start receiving their full 45% of each year's income for the benefit of the long-suffering debenture holders (whose turn had to wait until the GWR was fully paid off). In 1914 E.A. Palk decided to accelerate this by taking an 'assignment' of the GWR debt himself. Palk paid the GWR the £12,136 then still due,[3] so fully clearing the TVR's slate with the GWR, and the TVR undertook to pay Palk off at £1,000 pa henceforth; so that the TVR's annual income shot up from £1,200 pa to over £4,000 pa (or over £3,000 pa if one allows for the payments now to be made to Palk).

By this date (1914) the enormous sum of £44,940 was owed in back interest to the debenture holders. It was never likely that the whole of this could be paid off, but a serious start could now be made. The '1884 stock', the second priority, had in fact received occasional interest since 1894; it now received its proper interest regularly and the back interest on it was fully paid off by 1922. But the main beneficiaries of the new arrangements were E.A. Palk himself and his relatives (hence, of course, his wanting to take the initiative in the matter). They owned the whole of the £15,000 'B' debenture stock, the third priority, on which nothing had been paid prior to 1914 but which now received significant sums of back interest each year as the company's current income permitted (even so, £12,700 was still due on this stock at 1922). The 'C' debenture holders never did receive anything.

ABSORPTION (1923)

When the Government assumed control of the railway system through the Railway Executive Committee in 1914, the main effect so far as 'worked companies' like the TVR were concerned was that their income was frozen at the 1913 level for the duration of the war and (in the event) until 1921. It so happened that 1913 was the TVR's best year ever, so it did unusually well from this arrangement.

After a lot of talk of nationalisation, the future of the railways was sorted out by the Railways Act 1921, under which all small companies in the area were to be absorbed into the GWR. At the end of 1921 the TVR joined the 'Association of Smaller Railway Companies' which had been set up in 1919 to assist the small companies in their negotiations with the Government and the larger companies.[4] But in fact the TVR's absorption into the GWR was done without difficulties arising. An initial meeting was held at Paddington on 16th January 1922 with one representative of each of the companies to be absorbed, and F.J.C. Lake, the TVR Solicitor, attended this. In April 1922 the TVR told Paddington that it was agreeable to the terms proposed, as set out in the Table. As was usual with the arrangements made at grouping, the debenture stock holders received full or almost full payment in GWR stock (the 'B' and 'C' debenture holders benefiting from the fact that they would now receive guaranteed regular interest at last), but the preference and ordinary shareholders at the bottom of the pile got next to nothing for having supported the company in its first years. (By 1922 most of the orig-

TEIGN VALLEY RAILWAY CAPITAL				
	Authorised		Actually Issued	
	Share Capital	*Borrowing*	*Share Capital*	*Borrowing*
1863 Act	£45,000	£15,000	£20,740	Nil
Under 1867 Scheme, Authorised Capital reduced to 31,000 and borrowing powers annulled. No further stock actually issued after 1867. Stock issued figure later quoted as £15,140.				
1865 Act	30,000	10,000	Nil	Nil
Powers annulled (unused) under 1867 Scheme				
1867 Scheme	–	79,000	–	27,650
'A', 'B', and 'C' Deb Stocks				
Extinguished 1877, holders issued with 1877 Pref. Shares				
1872 Act	72,000	24,000	(Nil)	(Nil)
Not exercised until 1877 Scheme (under which £24,000 borrowing powers reduced to £10,000) — see below.				
1875 Act	150,000	50,000	Nil	Nil
To have been a separate capital for Crediton extension. Powers annulled 1880				
1877 Scheme				
(No.1 Prefs 5%)	40,000	10,000	40,000	10,000
(No.2 Prefs 5%)	22,000		22,000	5%
(No.3 Prefs 5%)	10,000		10,000	Debentures issued 1879/80 paid off 1881
1879 Scheme (Restored full 1872 Act borrowing powers)	–	14,000	–	14,000 5% Debentures issued 1879/80 paid off 1881
1880 Act Intended for Dunsford extension. Not exercised	40,000	13,300	Nil	Nil
1881 Scheme/Act (Extinguished the 1877 and 1879 Debentures).	–	24,000 15,000 20,000	–	24,000 'A' 4% Deb Stock 15,000 'B' 4% Deb Stock 19,250 'C' 4% Deb Stock
1884 Act	–	6,000	–	6,000 '1884 Stock' 4% Deb Stock

TEIGN VALLEY RAILWAY.

Secretary:
HERBERT R. COX.

Telephone:
GERRARD 3242.

CRAVEN HOUSE,

KINGSWAY, W.C. 2.

15th Novr 1921

Arrd 16/11/21

W. J. Calder Esq,
        Secretary
        Exeter Railway Coy.
            43 Shoe Lane. E.C.

        Dear Sir,

                I have received a letter from the Great
        Western Coy suggesting that this Company should continue to
        receive its Revenue, on the basis of the 3 half years arranged with
        H.M. Government during the War, until such time as the Railway is
        taken over under the Railways Act 1921. The suggestion is of
        course in accordance with the power given them under clause 76
        of the Act.   In reply to a letter from me the Great Western
        Company have promised to send a statement shewing the number of
        Passengers and weight of Merchandize Traffic each Month but
        evidently intend to omit the amount of Revenue arising therefrom.

                I have also received a letter from the
        Railway Companies' Association in connection with Section 12 and
        the sub-sections thereto. and a letter from the Secretary of
        the Association of smaller Railways (althoughthis Company has not
        joined the Association) on the same subject.

                As our Companies are in exactly similar
        positions in connection with the points raised in the correspon-
        dence referred to (I am assuming that you have received similar
        letters) do you mind exchanging confidences on these matters as
        we may probably be able to help each other ?.

                If you are agreeable I shall be pleased to
        hear from you.

                                and remain,
                                Yours faithfully

                                Herbk Cox.
                                    Secretary.

Correspondence between the TVR and the Exeter Railway Company was infrequent, despite their owning the two halves of the same branch line; such problems as arose were normally handled by the GWR dealing with both companies itself. However, in the instant case here, the motive for direct communication is obvious! Few people by 1921 would have known that the independent Teign Valley Company still existed. Indeed, even back in 1900, letters from John Campfield, the GWR Exeter Divisional Superintendent, reveal that he was not really sure whether the TVR Company still existed. Even less did the average user of a worked line perceive the existence of anything other than the GWR.   *Public Record Office*

CAPITAL OF TVR
as at 1922 (representing post-1884 situation), in order of preference for interest/dividend

'A' Debentures	£24,000	— Full 4% interest paid regularly
'1887 Stock'	6,000	— Some interest paid from 1894. Fully paid by 1922
'B' Debentures	15,000	— Some interest paid from 1914, arrears in interest of £12,700 at 1922.
'C' Debentures	19,250	— Arrears in interest of £30,100 at 1922.
No.1 Pref Shares	40,000	
No.2 Pref Shares	22,000	
No.3 Pref Shares	10,000	No dividends ever paid.
Ordinary Shares	15,140*	
TOTAL CAPITAL ISSUED	£151,390	

* Originally quoted at £20,740, but this lower figure is always quoted from the mid-1880s on.

inal shareholders in the company were, of course, dead, and their heirs had probably become used to the fact that their stock in the TVR was near-worthless.) A Special General Meeting of the TVR on 13th December 1922 officially approved the arrangements, and the absorption of the TVR into the GWR, under the 'GWR (Western Group) Absorption Scheme No. 3' of 19th January 1923, took effect as from 1st July 1923. The unhappy life of the Teign Valley Railway Company was at an end.

1. The tripartite (GWR/TVR/Lord Haldon) legal agreement under which this was done was dated 24.4.84. It required 6,000 sleepers to be replaced and a large number of minor works, primarily fencing and painting jobs.
2. Additionally, the GWR was 'advancing' further sums for capital works on the line since 1884, which the TVR should have paid for but could not afford to. Fortunately there was little need for expensive capital works on the line prior to the 1900s.
3. £8,913 on the revenue account and £3,223 on the capital account (there had been increased capital expenditure on the line in the 1900s, notably on the new work at Trusham).
4. Membership as at autumn 1920 comprised the B&M, Bridgwater, DN&S, East & West Yorks Union, Festiniog, FY&N, Harborne, Isle of Wight Central, Mansfield, Mawddy, Mold & Denbigh, North Lindsey, North Sunderland, Sheffield District, South Yorks Jn., and SMJ companies.

PAYMENT MADE BY GWR
on takeover of TVR Company in 1923

		Sum Paid
'A' Debentures	£100 GWR 4% Deb. stock for each £100	£24,000
'1884 Stock'	£100 GWR 4% Deb. stock for each £100	6,000
'B' Debentures	£80 GWR 5% Consol. Pref. stock for each £100	12,000
	plus £50 cash in lieu of arrears of interest	7,500*
'C' Debentures	£80 GWR 5% Consol. Pref. stock for each £100 (arrears of interest not paid)	15,400
No.1 Pref Shares	14s cash per £5 share	5,600
No.2 Pref Shares	9s cash per £5 share	1,980
No.3 Pref Shares	6s cash per £5 share	600
Ordinary Shares	21s cash per £20 share	795

TOTAL SUM PAID BY GWR   £76,175
(30,000 in 4% Deb. Stock; 27,400 in
5% Consol. Pref. stock: 18,775 in cash)

* Income Tax was due to be paid on this; the GWR appear to have allocated £2,300 cash for this which, when added to the figures here, gives the total of £76,175 quoted in the original documents.

CHAPTER EIGHT

THE EXETER, TEIGN VALLEY & CHAGFORD RAILWAY
1882–1893

AFTER the dissension and failures of 1877/8, the Exeter commercial interests lost the urge for promoting Teign Valley railway connections for some years. But when in 1881/2 the TVR started to look like it really was about to open its line at last, Exeter began to reawaken; and immediately after the TVR's opening in October 1882 there was a flurry of activity in the city which, within the year, saw a new company obtaining almost without difficulty an Act for the Exeter extension for which the TVR had tried five times without success. There were a number of reasons why the new promotion was able to succeed where the TVR had failed:

- As interests quite independent of the TVR, they did not have to counter the automatic hostility which the TVR, thanks to its anti-broad gauge origins, had always received from the SDR and the GWR.
- The 'gauge war' was now largely over anyway, and, with the TVR now firmly under GWR control, any company promoting an Exeter extension was also all but obliged to look for a GWR Agreement; so there was no real likelihood of LSWR involvement.
- The TVR was now an exhausted company and had no wish to engage in blocking counter-schemes as it had done in 1877/8; indeed it was probably pleased to see another company doing the job.

Even so, the new initiative nearly collapsed in the same dissension over routes that had afflicted the 1877/8 initiative. And the quick success in obtaining an Act was not to be followed by any similar success in raising money to get the line built.

THE PROMOTION OF THE EXETER TEIGN VALLEY & CHAGFORD RAILWAY (1882/3)

On Thursday, 19th October 1882, a semi-public meeting was held at the offices of the Exeter Chamber of Commerce to discuss the question of turning the reawakened interest into a practical scheme for the next session of Parliament. The first and principal speaker was William Cotton who had been a leading figure in the Exeter & Chagford scheme in 1877/8, so it was no surprise that Cotton should once again have advocated that the Tap House route be adopted. Apart from the fact that he no doubt still genuinely believed a Tap House route the easiest (he admitted that it was not the most direct), there was the question of the £3,000 which he and the other E&C promoters had spent in 1877/8 and which they might now be able to recover in part if a line were now to be built using their old plans. Others, just as predictably, spoke in favour of an Ide–Perridge route along the lines of the TVR's 1861, 1864, 1866, and 1878 Bills. Discussion was kept amicable and a Committee appointed with John Oak Harris[1] as Secretary; he had appeared for the TVR in

Parliament in 1878, so perhaps an attempt was being made to avoid any one faction dominating the Committee.

Quick action was needed in order to get Parliamentary plans deposited by 30th November. The Committee consulted Francis Fox, the former B&E Engineer, who had set himself up as a Consulting Engineer after the GWR takeover in 1876 but still had strong GWR links (he was at this time acting as Engineer to the Weston-super-Mare loop, and the Exe Valley line, for the GWR). Fox recommended an Ide–Perridge route and the Committee accepted this (although not unanimously) on the basis that one of the main reasons for adopting a Tap House route in 1877/8 had been that the TVR's Crediton Extension was then intended to be built anyway, which made Exeter–Tap House the shortest link to the TVR; whereas with the Crediton Extension now given up for good, the Tap House route now involved a greater new construction mileage than the Perridge route. Fox, who was very much on the look-out at this period for new schemes which he might associate himself with, also stated that he would be able to assist with the costs of obtaining an Act if he could be convinced that the scheme had enough support in Exeter to go ahead (see below for more on this front).

The Committee reported back to a more widely-advertised public meeting held at the Exeter Guildhall on Friday 3rd November 1882 uner the auspices of the Mayor, Samuel Jones. This time there were a number of influential figures from Chagford, Drewsteignton, and Dunsford present, so dissension over whether and how to serve Chagford was added to the existing conflict over the best route from Exeter to the TVR. Henry Drew, the Earl of Devon's Agent, another 'E&C' man in 1877/8, was at this meeting, and provided a further voice in favour of the now-fading Tap House idea (the Earl disliked the Perridge route as it passed through his estates in Alphington). Jones became very concerned that the whole thing would collapse in disagreement, and expressed this view to the meeting. Another Committee was then appointed (with Harris as Secretary again).

The new Committee seems to have succeeded in suppressing the Tap House camp, and also succeeded in finding sufficient funds for the Parliamentary deposit, and in depositing plans in due time under the name of the Exeter Teign Valley & Chagford Railway. A Chagford branch was added to placate the Chagford interests; this was a seriously-intended scheme although Chagford people always suspected (correctly) that the Exeter–TVR link had priority in the eyes of most of those involved. Most of the survey work was done by William Lidstone who had also been associated with Fox elsewhere (see below). The legal work was done by Bartholomew Gidley who was one of the leading promoters of the company and now became its solicitor.

The portion of Railway No. 1 between Teign House and a point east of Perridge Tunnel was very much along the established corridor of the DCR/TVR 1861, 1864, 1866, and 1878 Bills; indeed some of this length was directly on the original 1861 Bill line. But the Exeter end of the route, which passed south of Ide, was rather different from anything seen before. As it was no longer intended to have a connection to the LSWR at Queen St., the line was able to follow this more southerly route to a GWR junction south of St Thomas and a better connection with the GWR's Canal Basin branch than had been possible in 1864 when there had been so much debate over the proposed level crossings. With ideas of reviving the canal by exporting Teign Valley minerals brought in by the new railway still very much to the fore, the ETV&C's Canal Branch link was seen as an important part of the scheme. The exact role seen for the Alphington Road terminus at this stage is not clear; it was later to be built as a purely goods station to serve an industrial part of the city remote from St David's, but it may originally have been meant as one of those independent termini that promoters of small railways so often included as a backstop in case running powers over another company proved difficult to obtain. Nothing definite was said about intermediate station sites, but it seems that Lea Cross South Junction and Ide were the intended sites.

The Chagford branch (for details of which see the 6in maps at p. 283) was much as the TVR's 1878 route, the geography of the gorge preventing any real variation. The terminus was near Rushford Bridge, ½ mile east of the town, a reasonably convenient site. Railway No. 5, the north curve at Lea Cross which allowed direct Exeter–Chagford running, was a new idea which was no doubt intended to placate the 'Exeter & Chagford' lobby; but (as was usually the case with railway promotions!) no real thought seems to have been given to the question of what pattern of train service might actually be run over the new lines, given the small total number of trains that was likely to be possible.

Some of the Exeter interests, including Bartholomew Gidley, Samuel Jones, Walter Pring (later a leading director — see Chapter 9), and William Easton (the owner of Westcott and Blackingstone quarries, west of Bridford, then the only active quarries in the valley area), did make contributions to the Parliamentary costs. But the greater part of the costs were funded by a syndicate associated with Francis Fox who were very active in railway promotion in the 1880–83 period.

Edwin Fox, John Walker, a retired Colonel of Broomhill, Colchester, and John Norton, a London architect, had first become involved together in railway promotion in 1879/80 when they funded an Act to revive the Freshwater, Yarmouth and Newport Railway. Edwin Fox

then appointed himself as 'Managing Director' of this company at the not insignificant salary of £500 a year, although it is doubtful if he ever received anything as it proved impossible to raise any cash at this date and the company was dormant until 1886.

The next venture was in 1881/2 when Edwin Fox and John Walker helped fund the revival of the Kingsbridge & Salcombe Railways (amongst their fellow directors were the Earl of Devon and Benjamin Lake, the TVR's solicitor). This time Francis Fox (who had not been involved with the FY&N) was involved as Engineer, with William Lidstone under him. Once again, however, it proved impossible to raise enough funds to start work on the line. (Eventually, in 1888, the Act was sold to the GWR and Edwin Fox and Walker resigned as directors; the line was then built to Kingsbridge in 1890–93 with William Clarke and not Francis Fox as Engineer).

In the autumn of 1882 Francis Fox made a bid to purchase the Liskeard & Looe and Liskeard & Caradon Railways on behalf of 'an unnamed syndicate' whose identities we can now guess; however, this bid proved unsuccessful.

Thus when the full team of Edwin Fox, Walker, and Norton as financiers, and Francis Fox and William Lidstone as Engineers, came together again to help the ETV&C off the ground, they were fully experienced at the game. One is tempted to imagine that it was they (alerted by Lidstone's local presence) who made approaches to the Exeter Committee, rather than vice-versa. Unfortunately the ETV&C was to prove a third case of their being unable to raise funds after getting an Act! It might be recorded here, though, that they did succeed in getting the Freshwater, Yarmouth & Newport line built in 1886–9, with William Lidstone again as their Engineer.

THE GWR AGREEMENT AND THE 1883 ACT

The ETV&C made a point of approaching the GWR before they went to Parliament. J.O. Harris wrote to Paddington on 16th November 1882 asking to send a deputation to the Board, and this took place on 29th November. Led by Mayor Jones and Willey the Sheriff, this deputation wore the civic hat, but was obviously intended to support the ETV&C and seek a Working Agreement from the GWR. The GWR promised to consider the scheme, and replied early in January that they would be prepared to enter into an Agreement to work the Exeter–Teign House line but not the Chagford line. (This decision was to prove fatal to the Chagford line's chances, although it was to be fifteen years before it was finally abandoned.) R.J. Palmer, who had taken over from Harris as Secretary now that the company was becoming established, [2] drafted an Agreement under which receipts would be divided 50/50 and the ETV&C receive rebates on all journeys booked to/from the GWR. This was perhaps optimistic, and the GWR responded with an offer of a 55% GWR and 45% ETV&C split, the same as the TVR's

Fig. 18. The Exeter Teign Valley & Chagford Railway Lines authorised by 1883 Act.
(also showing diversions of line as built, authorised by 1898 Act.)

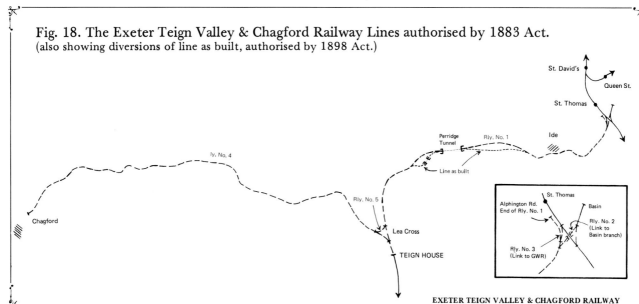

EXETER TEIGN VALLEY & CHAGFORD RAILWAY
November 1882

	Length	Estimate
Railway No. 1		
Exeter (Alphington Road Terminus) to TVR at Teign House	8m 20ch*	£159,631
Railway No. 2		
Connection to GWR Basin Branch	0m 22ch	3,621
Railway No. 3		
Connection to GWR Main Line	0m 20 ch	1,856
Railway No. 4		
Lea Cross (Junction with No. 1) to Chagford	9m 65ch†	71,796
Railway No. 5		
North curve at Lea Cross	0m 23ch	5,562
	18m 70ch	£242,466

*Compare the 8m 07ch of the line as built. The stops at Alphington Road were 6½ch further from Teign House than the junction points at City Basin Jn. from which the later mileage was taken, but the 1898 Act diversions added 2ch to the length of the line to balance against this; so the 8m 20ch figure still seems erroneously high.

†After the decision in 1895 to move the junction further south, Railway No. 4 was 10m 19ch long.

The ETV&C normally used the spelling 'Lea Cross'; the name was also spelt 'Leigh Cross' and this is the established twentieth-century spelling.

Agreement. But after the Mayor attended again with another deputation on 24th May, the GWR agreed to accept a 50/50 Agreement, provided it was written into the Act that the GWR were to work the line. This was accepted and the Agreement was formally made on 3rd July 1883.

The GWR's refusal to have anything to do with the Chagford line was, however, still a concern to the ETV&C promoters. There was public agitation over this at another public meeting held in Exeter on 22nd June 1883, notably from the ubiquitous Revd Hayter Hames who insisted that 'the line would develop a traffic between Exeter and Chagford such as would astonish everyone'. The 5th July, therefore, saw Mayor Jones (this time on his own) troubling the GWR Board yet again on this front. He extracted a promise from them that the GWR 'while retaining the opinion that it would not be desirable to construct the Chagford section of the line at all events for the present . . . would be prepared to work it if constructed, at cost price'. Whatever this meant, it was enough to encourage the promoters to keep the Chagford line in the Bill, even though it was still to be excluded from the Agreement.

When the ETV&C Bill was introduced in Parliament, it had attracted objections from the GWR, the TVR, the LSWR, the Ecclesiastical Commissioners (as the major landowners in Ide), and the Earl of Devon (as the major landowner in Alphington). The GWR, TVR, and LSWR petitions were directed at the ETV&C's applications for running powers (to St David's, to City Basin via the GWR Basin Branch, to Queen St., and over the whole TVR) and did not indicate any general hostility. When it became clear that a GWR Agreement was going to be made, these clauses were withdrawn as there was no longer any need for running powers. (Oddly, the Act failed to say anything about the fact that the ETV&C line was going to be a dif-

ferent gauge to the GWR line at the junction at Exeter!) The Ecclesiastical Commissioners and the Earl of Devon were also not out to stop the line, but only to protect their interests. Drew, the Earl of Devon's Agent, suspected that Exeter people would not be so keen to put their hands in their pockets as they were to make fine speeches in favour of the line (this was to prove all too true!) and therefore foresaw that the line might be commenced at the Exeter end and then expire half way, leaving abandoned earthworks through the Earl's fields in Alphington. To prevent such a scenario, an Agreement was made with the Earl of Devon dated 8th March 1883 (and included in the Act) requiring the line to be commenced at the Teign House end, and no land to be taken in the parish of Alphington until the railway was complete to formation level up to the western mouth of Perridge tunnel. A similar Agreement was made with the Ecclesiastical Commissioners with respect to their lands in Ide. Necessary though they were at the time, these two Agreements were to prove a serious delaying factor when the line was being built.

The various opponents having thereby been placated, the ETV&C Bill was able to proceed as an Unopposed Bill, and the Exeter Teign Valley and Chagford Railway Act 1883 received the Royal Assent on 20th August 1883. The company was authorised to raise £240,000 in £20 shares, and £80,000 by borrowing. Five years were allowed for building the line. The first directors were to be Edwin Fox, John Walker, John Norton and three others to be decided.

AN INABILITY TO RAISE CAPITAL: THE ETV&C 1883–6

The 22nd June 1883 public meeting already referred to heard J.O. Harris reporting on what had happened since November and making it clear that it was now necessary for Exeter people to come forward and take up shares. The meeting gave its support to the Committee's plans to make arrangements for canvassing the area.

The results, unfortunately, were anything but encouraging, and it was decided to make no serious effort to raise capital for the present. The value of the shares was altered from £20 to £10 in 1884 (this was done by a section in the GWR's 1884 Act) to encourage small investors. Meanwhile Fox had put the line to various contractors who were said to be agreeable to take a contract as soon as £20–30,000 was raised. In February 1885 the Board decided that the

---

**SYNOPSIS OF THE GWR/ETV&CR AGREEMENT
of 3.7.1883 as set out in the 1883 Act**

1. The ETV&CR to construct railways 1, 2, and 3.
2. To be a single line with land and bridges for a double line.
3. The ETV&CR to maintain the railway for 12 months after opening, thereafter the GWR to maintain.
4. The GWR to work the line in perpetuity, and provide all requisite staff, locomotive power, rolling stock, etc.
5. The ETV&CR to pay all tithes, etc, usually paid by landowners.
6. The GWR to pay all wages, except those of the Directors, Secretary, and Auditors of the ETV&C Company.
7. The ETV&CR to 'make and satisfy all expenditure and liability chargeable against capital'.
8. The ETV&CR to pay any rent payable to the Teign Valley company for the use of their Ashton station.
9. The GWR to accommodate the ETV&CR's traffic in their Exeter station free of charge, until such time as the ETV&CR can pay a 5% dividend (N.B. There is no specific reference to the use of St. Thomas station also).
10. The gross revenue to be divided 50% to the GWR and 50% to the ETV&CR.
11. (Deductions to be made for Government duty, cartage, collection & delivery, etc, before the division of the gross receipts).
12. The ETV&CR to receive rebates of 10% of the GWR portion of all takings on journeys booked at/to stations Plymouth to Bristol to/from the new line, and 5% ditto stations elsewhere on the GWR.
13. Any differences to be settled by arbitration.

---

time had come to seek support, but again nothing was achieved.

The company just kept alive — six Board meetings and three shareholders' meetings were held between 1884–1888.

The compulsory purchase powers expired in August 1886 and to keep things alive the Exeter Teign Valley & Chagford Railway (Extension of Time) Act 1886 was obtained; this extended the compulsory purchase powers until August 1888 and the time for completion of the line to August 1891.

ELECTRIC TRAINS TO CHAGFORD? (1887–8)

In the summer of 1887 negotiations were entered into with the contractors, Naylor Bros. of Denby Dale, who agreed to build the line for $7/8$ shares and $1/8$ cash payment if the ETV&C could raise the requisite £30,000 cash portion. Additionally, talks were held with the Electric Motor Co. to equip the Chagford branch as an electric railway with the River Teign providing the power supply, one imagines on the model of the Giants Causeway line which was in many ways similar to the Chagford line in traffic terms.

These possibilities brought a revival of enthusiasm and in October 1887 a further public meeting was held in the Exeter Guildhall by the Mayor at the ETV&C's request. Lidstone was the main speaker for the company and found himself subjected to a lot of detailed questions from people whose interest clearly depended on how immediately useful the line would be to them. Some wanted a station at Alphington, which Lidstone could not promise, as it was too close to Ide. Lidstone postulated that the contractors might build the Chagford line first as it was an easy job and could be finished 'in about 10 months' whereas the main line would be held up by the building of the tunnel at Perridge. He also considered that the GWR would soon be under pressure to put in a third rail between Heathfield, Newton, and Torquay.

After a unanimous resolution in favour of the line, a Committee was set up in Exeter to canvass for the raising of funds. Similar meetings were held in Chagford and Chudleigh, and Committees set up there also. Gidley drew up a prospectus and in December the contract with Naylor Bros. was sealed, conditional on the required capital being raised by 1st March 1888. In March the deadline was extended. But it was once again found that the money could not be raised.

In March 1888 the three vacant places on the Board were filled by the election of three local Directors — Viscount Exmouth, F.D. Fulford, and Walter Pring, an Exeter Alderman and owner of the City Brewery who was to be the company's keenest supporter in the city in the 1890s and remained a director until 1904. These appointments were no doubt meant to make a better local impression for fund-raising. But in the event there were to be no further Board meetings for them to attend, and the appointments lapsed in practice.

NO PROGRESS: 1888–1893

After the failure to get the Naylor Bros. contract off the ground in 1888, the ETV&C slept for five years, without a single Board meeting being held.

In 1890 Gidley made representations to the GWR that they might 'purchase the Act', or alternatively give the ETV&C financial assistance, but Paddington rejected both ideas.

In the 1891 session the ETV&C promoted two Bills, one for the abandonment of the line and the other for a further extension of time. The two were obviously meant as alternatives, and in the event the latter was proceeded with. It became The Exeter Teign Valley & Chagford Railway (Extension of Time) Act 1891 and extended the compulsory purchase powers until August 1893 and the powers to build the line until August 1894.

---

1. John Oak Harris, Accountant Auditor Stock and Share Broker, Exeter, was Purser of the Frank Mills Mining Co. and Secretary of the Bridford Barytes Mine which particularly stood to benefit from the new line.
2. Richard John Palmer was also Secretary of the Kingsbridge & Salcombe and (from 1886) the Freshwater Yarmouth & Newport.

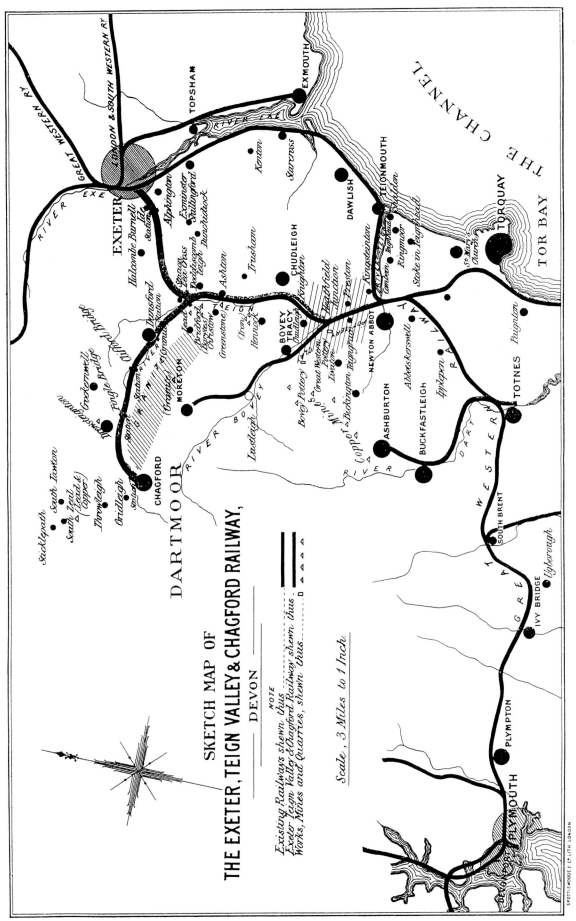

SKETCH MAP OF
THE EXETER, TEIGN VALLEY & CHAGFORD RAILWAY,
— DEVON —

NOTE

Existing Railways shewn thus ————
Exeter Teign Valley &Chagford Railway shewn thus ·····
Works, Mines and Quarries, shewn thus □ △ △ △

Scale, 3 Miles to 1 Inch.

SPOTTISWOODE & C? LITH. LONDON.

This map actually comes from the 1896 prospectus but it illustrates the railway that the ETV&C was trying to 'sell' in 1894. The warning *caveat emptor* might apply! Dunsford and Drewsteignton are shown the same size as Teignmouth and Dawlish, and Chagford the same size as Newton Abbot! The ETV&C line is shown extending through to Heathfield, reflecting the intention to purchase the TVR. Lea Cross station is shown instead of the later Christow station. There are rather a lot of spelling mistakes.   *Public Record Office*

CHAPTER NINE

THE REACTIVATION OF THE EXETER, TEIGN VALLEY & CHAGFORD RAILWAY

IN summer 1893 a new syndicate of financiers was formed to take over the moribund ETV&C company and build the line. This appears to have been done with the support of the existing Board of Walker and Norton (Edwin Fox had died in February 1893) and the Exeter interests, no doubt because they were pleased to support any attempt to get things moving and also hopefully recover the money they had laid out in 1882/3 on Parliamentary costs.

A limited company, the Railway & Industrial Syndicate Ltd, was set up to assist in the financing of the ETV&C by acting as a 'dealer company' using City contacts on the ETV&C's behalf. The subscribers of this company, registered on 5th August 1893, were:

> G.F.S. Warne (Chairman) — India Rubber Manufacturer, Gresham St., London EC; later an ETV&C director.
>
> D.F. Carmichael — 'Gentleman', 16 Grenville Place, London SW. Chairman of the ETV&C 1894–5 and Director 1894–7; also a Director of the Madras Railway Co.
>
> The Hon. C.M. Knatchbull-Hugessen, 10 Ashley Place, London SW. Cecil Marcus Knatchbull-Hugessen (1863–1933) was the son of Sir Edward Knatchbull-Hugessen, the 1st Lord Brabourne (who took a great interest in railway directorships in his last years; he was Deputy Chairman of the South Eastern, Chairman of the London & Greenwich, and a director of the Metropolitan and the Cranbrook & Paddock Wood). Cecil Marcus was a barrister by profession but it was perhaps no surprise when he, too, became involved in a railway scheme. He was to be an ETV&C director from 1894–1914 and was Chairman from 1895 to 1904, a leading figure in the direction at the time the line was under construction. In 1915 he succeeded to the title (unexpectedly) as the 4th Lord Brabourne. Perhaps finding the ETV&C's difficulties enough, he never became involved with any other railway company.
>
> F.W. Tuppan, R.H.P. Hutchinson, William Tuke— These three never had any active role, and all forfeited their shares in 1896.
>
> James Dickson and John Dickson, who were to be the ETV&C's contractors (see below).
>
> William Lidstone — the ETV&C's Engineer, who no doubt took shares on the basis that it might turn his nominal post as the company's Engineer into a real source of income.

The R&IS Ltd's involvement with the ETV&C was openly admitted to, the July 1894 ETV&C prospectus referring particularly to the fact that Knatchbull-Hugessen and Carmichael were directors of both companies.

On the basis of the R&IS Ltd being able to raise the necessary finance, the ETV&C on 2nd October 1893 gave a contract to John and James Dickson for the building of the line — to be precise of Railways 1, 3, and 4 only, i.e. omitting the Canal Branch and the Lea Cross north curve. The Dicksons were brothers, sons of the perhaps better known John Dickson (1819–1892) who had been active as a railway contractor in the 1840s–1880s period and had lived since the 1860s in Swansea where he had promoted the Neath & Brecon as a 'contractor's line' and bought up the Oystermouth Railway which he ran himself as the

Cecil Marcus Knatchbull-Hugessen, in a portrait dated 1922 by De Laszlo. *The Knatchbull family portrait collection, photograph Courtald Institute of Art, reproduced by permission of Lord Brabourne*

'Swansea & Mumbles Railway Ltd'. Later he had become involved in promoting the Mersey Railway and the Whitby, Redcar & Middlesbrough Union Railway.

John Dickson (Junior) had qualified as an engineer and had been Engineer to his father's Swansea & Mumbles Railway. By the 1890s he had moved to North Yorkshire where he had taken the Glaisdale Ironworks. James Dickson lived at Townsend, St. Albans, and was manager of the Holborn Wire & Cage Works at 48 Grays Inn Road, London. He was also active as a contractor, primarily on sewerage/drainage/waterworks schemes in the 1880s–1910s period, but also engaging in railway contracts when he could, notably for the Sutton & Willoughby Railway in 1885/6 and its extension to Mablethorpe in 1886–8, and later the GWR's Garnant to Gwaun-cae-Gurwen line in 1904–8. The ETV&CR was the only contract that James and John are known to have taken on together. They were introduced to the ETV&C by Hurrell & Mayo the R&IS Ltd's solicitors, who had been on the lookout for a contractor willing to 'take' the line for shares rather than payment in cash. John Dickson was destined to become a leading figure in the ETV&C company, and an important influence on the development of stone quarrying in the valley.

The contract required the works to be completed in 24 months from the start of work, and required the Dicksons

Fig. 19. Diagram of ETV & CR as anticipated by the 1893 Contract (sidings omitted)

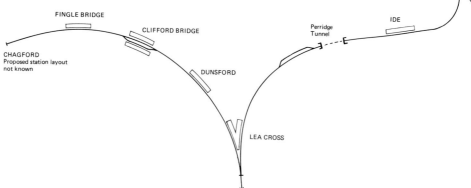

Railways 1 and 3 (Exeter—Teign House) to be built as a 'first class branch of the GWR' with 76lb bullhead rail. To be single line with land and overbridges for double line.

Railway 4 (Chagford branch) to be built as a Light Railway with 65lb flat-bottom rails. To be single line with land and overbridges for single line.

Junction with GWR near St. Thomas — Double junction, double line to be extended one furlong beyond the junction.

Formation of Goods Yard at Alphington Road including Loading Dock with 5 ton crane, carriage shoot, weighing machine.

Ide — Passenger Station — ('Building to be of simple design').
    Ticket office cum cloakroom cum parcels office
    Booking Hall cum General Waiting Room
    Ladies Room & WCs
    Porters' Room
    Gents WCs
    Coal Shed
    240ft platform excluding ramps
    Goods Yard including Loading Dock

Siding or passing place, at or near the west end of the tunnel.

Lea Cross — Station and Goods Yard. Similar to Ide, but platform to be placed in the fork of the lines and needs two faces.

Junction with TVR — No points & crossings needed but TV line will need to be slewed.

Dunsford — small passenger station.
    Ticket Office
    Ladies Room & WCs
    Covered shelter or alcove
    Gents WCs
    Shed for lamps and coals
    Platform 180ft long
    Goods Yard as at Ide

Clifford Bridge station — As Dunsford, but small Station Master's house must be built. Also additional platform for the passing place, 200ft long with shelter.

Fingle Bridge Station — As Dunsford, but small Station Master's House must be built.

Chagford Terminus — Station (as at Ide)
    Ticket Office cum Cloakroom cum Parcels Office
    Booking Hall
    General Waiting Room
    Refreshment Room
    Ladies Room & Wcs
    Porters' Room
    Gents WCs
    Coal Shed
    Platforms 240ft long
    Goods Shed 24ft by 16ft
    Engine Shed 60ft by 20ft
    Carriage Shed 140ft by 16ft
    Coal Stage 30ft by 10ft
    Water Tank 2000 gallons
    Small store room and enginemen's room (all to be of simplest design)
    Carriage Shoot
    5 Ton Crane
    Engine Turntable 30ft
    Loading Dock

Total cost of stations etc. including signals not to exceed £6,100.
Erect telegraph.

NOTE: It is clear that Ide, Lea Cross, and Chagford were to have 'proper' station buildings, but Dunsford, Clifford Bridge, and Fingle Bridge were to have 'Light Railway' type buildings. All stations were to have goods yards. Ideas of electric operation of the Chagford line had clearly been given up.

Very imprecise ideas of crossing places on the 'main line' — one wonders where the next crossing place south of the west end of Perridge tunnel loop was anticipated as being — unless an additional facility were provided by the TVR there would be no crossing place at all between Perridge Tunnel and Heathfield. The ETV & C made suggestions to the TVR regarding the payment of rent for the use of Ashton station; it may be that the Chagford branch trains were anticipated as running to/from Ashton where there were convenient run-round and locomotive facilities.

Fingle Bridge c.1902, looking up the gorge. This shows the easy route available for the railway despite the restricted valley. Fingle Bridge station would have been off-picture to the left here. *Chapman collection, cty. Devon C.R.O.*

to accept payment in 'fully paid' shares and debentures, the contract price of £320,000 in fact comprising the entire authorised stock of the company at the time. This was a very common arrangement in the case of small railway companies; the expectation was that the contractors would sell the shares and debentures to others for cash. (The contract specifically freed the contractors from the 24 month deadline if they were unable to sell enough shares.) However, the contract also provided for the ETV&C to make a public share issue in the 'normal' way, in which case the contractors were obliged (and of course pleased!) to accept part payment in the cash thereby raised instead of in shares. As was always the case, all payment to the contractors was only to be made as the works proceeded, on receipt of the Engineer's monthly certificates.

The 1893 contract was arranged with the old ETV&C Board of Walker and Norton (though obviously with the involvement of the R&IS Ltd) and it was not until the summer of 1894 that the 'takeover' of the ETV&C company was carried out. At a two-day Board meeting on 10th and 11th July 1894, Walker and Norton resigned and a new Board was elected, consisting of:

D.F. Carmichael (Chairman) ⎫ representing the R&IS Ltd
C.M. Knatchbull-Hugessen ⎭
Lord Norreys

Thomas Cory of Swansea	(who was also on the Rhondda & Swansea Bay Board)
Walter Pring	⎫ representing local interests — as
Viscount Exmouth	⎭ noted in Chapter 8, they had in fact been elected to the Board before in 1888.

(Norreys, Cory, and Lord Exmouth never took any really active role in the event.)

The same Board meeting also authorised the issuing of the company's prospectus. This was done under various agreements made between the ETV&C, the R&IS Ltd, and the Dicksons, under which the R&IS Ltd were to arrange underwriting contracts to ensure a minimum subscription of 5,500 shares (£55,000). The prospectus was issued on 31st July 1894 in both London and Exeter (the arrangements at the Exeter end being handled by the brokers W. Mortimer & Son of 14 Bedford Circus). Emblazoned in large red letters at the head were the words 'NEW ALTERNATIVE ROUTE TO PART OF GREAT WESTERN MAIN LINE', and the prospectus continued:

'The Exeter, Teign Valley & Chagford Railway Company has been incorporated by Act of Parliament for the purpose of connecting the city and Port of Exeter with the Teign Valley Railway, already opened, and the rich mineral and agricultural district which lies in and around the valley of the Teign — a connection which has for many years past been an acknowledged necessity — and affording direct railway com-

The Teign Gorge area grew in popularity as a daytrip destination at this time. Here we see Drewsteignton village centre on a sleepy summer's afternoon around 1902.
Chapman collection, cty. Devon C.R.O.

munication with Chagford, Fingal (*sic*) Bridge, and the romantic scenery of the District, which is rapidly coming into popularity as an important health and pleasure resort . . .

'The first section of the railway, taken in connection with the Teign Valley Railway, affords an alternative route[1] to the Great Western Main Line between Exeter and Newton Abbot, upon which the traffic is very heavy and is occasionally interrupted by the falling of the cliffs or a breach of the sea wall. The line, moreover, is only single in parts between Dawlish and Teignmouth, and there can be no doubt that the Great Western Co. will be glad to avail themselves of this alternative route, in the case of interruption to or great pressure of traffic, and send their trains via the Teign Valley, the distance being somewhat shorter.[2] This alone would secure considerable traffic over the first 8 miles of the proposed undertaking.

'The connection with the existing Teign Valley line will have the effect of placing Chagford within easy reach of Torquay and other South Devon watering places, and there can be no doubt that Chagford, with its mild bracing moorland air, its abundant natural attractions, with direct access by Railway from the south and east, will rapidly increase in importance, and develop a considerable traffic . . .

'The valley of the Teign has long been famed for its mineral deposits. Large mines of lead ore lying close to the projected line, 'Old Exmouth' and 'Frank Mills' in particular, have, in years gone by, returned an immense quantity of mineral, and afforded regular employment to a large number of persons. Spathose Iron Ore of the highest quality is found there in abundance. Sulphate of Baryta of exceptionally good quality is raised in large quantities, and Manganese, a mineral now much used, has been extensively worked. Owing to the cost of carriage by road, the works are closed, but no doubt will be worked again under the very favourable conditions of

carriage which the railway will supply. The Co. has already been promised by (amongst others) Messrs. William Easton & Co., and the Teign Valley Barytes Mining Co., the carriage of large quantities of granite, Macadam stone, and Barytes.

'The district is abundantly supplied with both Granite and Limestone. The Drewsteignton lime[3] is noted for its agricultural and building purposes, for which it is consigned to distant places. Green stone, a peculiarly tough stone for road making, and one not common in this country, is also found in immediate proximity to the proposed railway, and where it can be easily worked.

'At Exeter there is a large import coal trade through the Ship Canal. At present the great majority of the colliers return in ballast; but it is confidently anticipated that the construction of the proposed railway will afford them a return freight, the Northern and Welsh ports taking the Iron Ore, and the Welsh the lead for the smelting works, while the Sulphate of Baryta and the Timber which are at present hauled into Exeter at a great cost by road will be carried thither on the railway, and taken by the existing siding direct to the port.

'The projected line will open up for building purposes the beautiful Ide Valley, which, although distant only 2 miles from Exeter, is at present difficult of access, by reason of the range of steep hills which shuts it off from the city.

'Fingal Bridge is now resorted to by great numbers of holiday makers in the summer time, and the traffic in this season to this spot when the line is open will doubtless be greatly increased.'

The prospectus concluded by referring to the 'exceptionally favourable' GWR Agreement, and in particular the arrangements for rebates.

This was as overoptimistic a prospectus as was ever produced — not least because the GWR had never undertaken to route any of its trains via the Teign Valley, and, as we shall see, never did for scheduled purposes.

The national subscription lists were held open from 2nd to 7th August, and on the 8th it was reported to the Board that 6,372 shares had been allotted, this presumably including those taken by underwriters. To encourage the take-up of shares locally, a public meeting was held in the Exeter Guildhall at the ETV&C's request on 17th August. Although the national take-up was regarded as comparatively satisfactory, the company wished to see £20,000 raised in the Exeter area. A committee was therefore formed to canvass, under Matthew J. Dunsford, the Manager of the Bridford Barytes Mine, who had agreed to act as the company's Local Secretary in Exeter *pro tem*; similar committees were set up in Chudleigh and Chagford (as in 1887). However, there is no evidence that these committees succeeded in raising any very great amount of hard support. By November the number of shares issued was stated to be 7,061, and a call of £2 per share was made to enable £15,000 to be raised before work was started.

In connection with the R&IS Ltd 'takeover', most of the ETV&C's officers were also changed. A.W. Hurrell and C.R. Mayo of Hurrell & Mayo, the R&IS Ltd's solicitors, now became the ETV&C's solicitors also (the firm became 'Mayo & Co.' in 1896). They were asked to arrange offices and a Company Secretary in London, and as from January 1895 Frank Faulkner became Secretary of both the R&IS Ltd. and the ETV&CR. However, it was thought desirable to have an office in Exeter also, and Walter J. Pring, the solicitor son of Walter Pring the director, was appointed Local Secretary in place of Dunsford in January 1895, at a salary of £60 pa., using an office at 19 Bedford Circus. Relations began badly with Pring junior complaining, even before he took up office, of the 'incourteous' behaviour of the company in not letting him have proper details of what was required! (The Exeter office was given up for financial reasons in the autumn of 1896, after which Pring senior had to act as the company's Exeter voice at his own expense.)

Lidstone as Engineer was to be in charge of the works, but it was necessary to appoint a new Consulting Engineer to replace Francis Fox who had recently retired from active

An Edwardian pleasure party starting off from the Druids Arms at Drewsteignton, quite possibly in a carriage hired from landlord Alfred Mudge. *Chapman collection, cty. Devon C.R.O.*

work at the age of 75. The choice fell upon Robert Elliott-Cooper.[4] He retained the post until after completion of the line but was not often called upon for advice.

By the end of all these changes, therefore, the only people left from the company's 1882 origins were Pring in Exeter and Lidstone as Engineer; and Lidstone was himself only to last until 1896.

By the Exeter, Teign Valley & Chagford Railway (Extension of Time) Act 1894 (the third such Act) the compulsory purchase powers were extended until August 1896 and the time for completion until August 1897. With the two-year construction period expected, this would have given plenty of time. The Act also authorised an additional share capital of £24,000 (taking the total up to £264,000) and additional borrowing of £8,000 (total now £88,000).

BUYING THE TVR

The ETV&C's 1894 prospectus announced confidently that the company had entered into a provisional agreement to purchase the TVR. This was a logical enough move — had the ETV&C actually had the money! The formal agreement was dated 30th December 1893 and required the purchase to be done by the 1896 Parliamentary session at the latest, for £45,000.

In April 1896 the TVR agreed to extend this limit to the 1898 session, and in 1898 to the 1900 session. But the TVR put up the price to £50,000. Finally in 1900 the TVR agreed to an extension to 1902, with a further increase in the price to £60,000. By this time it was clear that the ETV&C had permanent financial problems, and the idea was allowed to lapse, leaving the branch in two ownerships for the next twenty years.

CUTTING THE FIRST SOD (NOVEMBER 1894)

The ETV&C wanted to ensure good publicity for the start of works to encourage further subscriptions locally, and therefore organised a full-scale sod-cutting ceremony on Wednesday 7th November 1894. Although the line had (under the 1882 Act) to be started at the Teign House end, the ceremony was held at Alphington Road on the site of the proposed goods station, this being more convenient for most of the participants and ensuring a conspicuous day's events in the streets in the city of Exeter.

A 'State Procession' was formed up at the Guildhall at 11.30 am and set off for Alphington Road at 11.45 through streets decorated with bunting, in the following order:

City Police
Band of the 1st Volunteer Battalion Devon Regiment
Exeter Committee (i.e., the ETV&C's canvassing committee)
Directors of the Company
Mace Bearers
The Mayor and Sheriff with their Chaplains
The Corporation
The Recorder, Town Clerk, and City Officials
The Bishop of Exeter and Mrs Bickersteth

The Sheriff of Devon
Chagford Committee
Chudleigh Committee
Band of the Chudleigh Company of the 5th Volunteer Battalion
   Devon Regiment

The entrance to the Alphington Road site was spanned by a banner 'Success to the new railway'. A large marquee was provided and this turned out to be a good piece of planning as there was a downpour immediately the procession arrived!

After the directors had received the participants, and Carmichael, the Chairman, welcomed Lady Northcote (wife of the Exeter MP, Sir Stafford Northcote) who was to perform the sod-turning, the Bishop offered prayers. The contractors then asked Lady Northcote to do the honours and presented an oak barrow and spade 'heavily mounted in silver' for the purpose. (These had been on view for some days previously in the window of one of the leading shops in the High Street.) The Mayor had the task of thanking Lady Northcote, and after short speeches — Sir Stafford Northcote referred jokingly to the pressure that there had been on Parliamentary time in recent decades due to 'the attention so frequently given to proposals for a Teign Valley Railway' — the National Anthem was played and the procession returned in reverse order to the London Hotel for a luncheon.

Around 1,000 people were present at Alphington Road and special excursion trains were run from Ashton, Moretonhampstead, and Paignton.

In the afternoon many of the guests watched a football match between Exeter and Blundells School, and in the evening there was a 'Grand Display of Fireworks'. The general view was that everything had passed off very successfully, despite the inclement weather at times.

Serious construction work began shortly afterwards, as described in Chapter 10.

CHANGES OF PLAN 1894–1896

Apart from the omission of the Canal Branch at Exeter (Railway No. 2) and the Lea Cross north curve (Railway No. 5),[5] the 1893 contract was for the railway of the 1883 Act. Full details of the railway as intended in 1893 are given in Chapter 10. However, several developments in the year or so after construction work began were to result in the railway emerging as something rather different in detail, even before the major decision in 1898 to abandon the Chagford branch.

1. Diversion between Ide and Perridge

This must have been done to placate the Ecclesiastical Commissioners who owned most of the affected land. For 1 m 30 ch the line was diverted southwards by up to 300 yds, so that it was now on the south side of the Fordland Brook valley throughout. The diversion was authorised by the 1898 Act but in fact much of the land had been bought and work begun before the Act was passed.

2. Diversion at Culver

Edward Byrom of Culver House had always been a supporter of a railway to Exeter, and indeed had been a TVR director for some years in the 1870s. In 1878 he was a Parliamentary witness in support of the TVR's Exeter Extension, and when asked under cross-examination what he thought of the line's proximity to his house, he replied 'I could certainly see it from some of the windows of my house, and it will be a very pretty object'. However, when the ETV&C came to build its line on all but the same alignment, Byrom's views changed! In order to placate him and obtain his land without difficulties and for payment in shares rather than in cash, it was necessary to draw up a 51 ch diversion (see *Fig. 18*) to remove the line from the immediate view of Culver House. This meant a second tunnel, Culver Tunnel, which had never been anticipated prior to this as it was quite unnecessary in engineering terms, so adding significantly to the cost of the line. The new route was agreed to informally by both sides in January 1896, but Byrom's land was not acquired until the autumn of 1896, by which time construction work was under way on both sides of the 'Byrom gap' (see *Fig. 21*).

3. Additional Station at Longdown

In view of the lack of population, it had never been intended to have any station intermediately between Ide and Lea Cross. However Byrom started pressing for a station to be built at the 'passing place' west of Perridge Tunnel, to serve Culver House which was over two miles from the Lea

Throughout its life, Longdown station lay under the shadow of the 'big house' at Culver, whose owner, Edward Byrom, had, of course, been the prime cause of a station being built here, as explained above. The house was built in 1836, an early example of the neo-Elizabethan style, and Byrom had moved there around 1870. The family group of the 1890s (bottom left) shows Byrom presiding, with his younger son by his second marriage, Luttrell Byrom, at front, and Miss Jerardine Byrom (who was one of the firers of the last shots in Culver tunnel in 1898) at bottom right. Edward Byrom died in 1911 and his son Edward Clement Atherton Byrom took over as 'Squire'. Alf Haywood remembers him as a regular passenger still in the 1920s, but he was an old bachelor by then and did not engage in the sort of house parties which might have brought inwards traffic. He died in 1936 — Alf went to his funeral in Holcombe Burnell church, as any ex-Longdown station employee still living in the area would have been expected to — upon which the house passed by marriage to the Edens, who still live there today. The servant boy from Culver House would come to the station every morning to pick up the London papers from the train. The relationship between the house and the station was somehow epitomised by the fact that the Longdown station masters lived latterly in Culver Lodge (bottom right). The Byroms had given up bothering with a lodge keeper when they bought a car, and left the gates open, so that house had become vacant.   *Cty. Mrs. E. A. Eden*

Cross station. There was also pressure for another station from Sir William Walrond the landowner in the Perridge area (and former Exeter & Chagford Railway Director). At a public meeting in Exeter on 24th February 1896, the Dicksons stated that they 'saw no difficulty in placing a station at Perridge or on Mount Boon', which brought cries of 'Hear! Hear!' The decision taken at this time to move the Lea Cross station to Christow, even further away, added to the pressure for an intermediate station, and within a few weeks of the Exeter meeting it had been decided to have a station at the loop site, to be called 'Longdown' (although it was so far from the hamlet of Longdown that it might more realistically have been called 'Culver'). Byrom wanted the 'power to stop trains by signal' but there is no record that he was granted this (and in the event all trains stopped there anyway). The loop idea was forgotten before the line opened and the station was built on the single line without crossing facilities.

4. Abandonment of Lea Cross Station in favour of new station at 'Christow'

The ETV&C Board of 14th November 1895 had before it a petition from 'the inhabitants in and around Christow' asking to have 'a station at Christow Bridge instead of Leigh Cross as arranged'. (By 'Christow Bridge' they meant a point only a few yards north of the start of the line at Teign House Siding.) The Board resolved to accede to this request, and by February 1896 all was decided.

By this date some work had already been done on the earthworks for Lea Cross station (see 1904 6 in), but the wasted work was not very great. In May 1896 extra land was being bought for the new Christow station.

In connection with this change, it was decided to move the physical junction of the Chagford branch from the south end of Lea Cross station to the north end of Christow station,[6] with the Chagford line and the main line now running side-by-side for 600 yds between the originally-intended junction site and the new junction. Accordingly the cutting at this point, which had already been completed by this date for a single track, had to be widened out to take two lines. This widening was reported complete in October 1896. (In fact, however, inspection shows that it is only 21ft wide between the rock faces at one point).

CHANGES IN THE COMPANY 1895–1899

There were several changes in the Board in the late '90s. In June 1895 the inactive Cory resigned, to be replaced in November by R.J. Jenkins, the TVR director, chosen probably for his railway experience and willingness to be actively involved, as well as for the useful connection with the TVR management. July 1895 saw Carmichael resigning as Chairman, ostensibly on grounds of lack of time but in reality because he, and Lord Norreys also, were unable to pay the calls due on their shares! The company took legal action against both of them in 1896, and eventually in

Frederick Bluett in 1903. He was a Devonian, born in Lydford where his father was curate.

1897 they both resigned as directors. Their places were not filled until the appointment of G.F.S. Warne, the former R&IS Ltd director, in March 1898 (the R&IS Ltd had ceased to function by this date, as described in Chapter 10), and of V.W. Yorke in June 1899 (for whom see Chapter 11). The full Board met regularly in these years but the heart of the company's affairs from November 1895 on was the regular weekly meetings of the 'General Purposes Committee' consisting of Knatchbull-Hugessen, the new Chairman, and R.J. Jenkins as Deputy Chairman.

There was also a change of Engineer. William Lidstone's 17-year association with the valley came to an end early in 1896 when he came into disagreement with the Board over money. Under an agreement dated 6th March 1896 he resigned as Engineer and gave up a legal action for non-payment which he had commenced against the Dicksons, in return for his being paid £200 in cash immediately and a further £216 by instalments. (This was partly in refund of the £450 that Lidstone had given to the Parliamentary costs in 1883.) In the same month of March 1896 Frederick Bluett was appointed as the company's new Engineer, 'on terms arranged by the contractors'. Bluett set up an Engineer's office at Farrants Farm on the Exeter–Moreton road, conveniently sited for the western section of the line then under construction. But in March 1898, with work on the eastern end of the line about to commence, the office was moved to 19 Bedford Circus, Exeter — the same building in which the ETV&C's local office had been located in 1895–6.

THE MID DEVON LIGHT RAILWAY (1897)

The Light Railways Act 1896 provoked an enormous interest in Light Railway schemes, practical and impractical, throughout the country. Amongst those who caught this interest were the Dicksons. They evolved plans in 1896 for a Chagford–Okehampton line, and also toyed with the idea of reviving the Teign Valley's old Crediton Extension as a Light Railway. An October 1896 article in the *Contractors' Chronicle* made much play of these schemes:-

'The value of the proposed Light Railway from Chagford to Okehampton cannot be overestimated. Besides enabling the South Western to secure an easy entry into Torquay, it will connect both the Bude and Bideford bays[7] with Newton Abbot and Torbay . . . [There

is] another suggested Light Railway between Crediton and Dunsford . . . It is not unreasonable to surmise that a considerable volume of traffic from the South Western system must find its way via Chagford, Dunsford [i.e. Crediton–Dunsford] and Lea Cross Jn to South Devonshire by the ETV&C Railway.'

These references to LSWR traffic were probably 'approved' by the Dicksons before the article was published, but one should see them more as an attempt to exaggerate the likely traffic on the ETV&C line than as an anti-GWR comment; the article also stressed that the lines would be of even more importance to the GWR. Nevertheless, some people in the 1890s still had hopes or worries that the LSWR might make a push for Torquay by

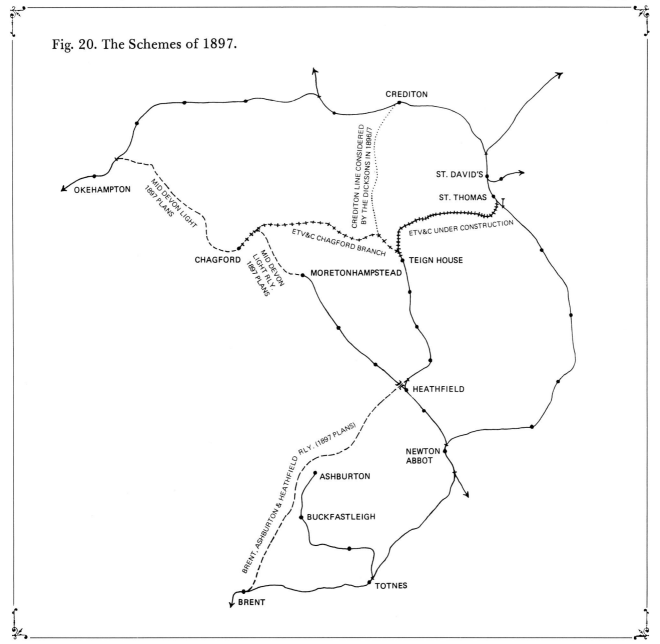

Fig. 20. The Schemes of 1897.

CHAGFORD 12905

Chagford in the early evening sunlight, on a perfect summer's day, c.1913. The view is from above Rushford; the ETV&C station would have been off picture to the left. Despite being fated forever to a railwayless state, Chagford was much cultivated by the railway companies, the LSWR starting a bus service from Exeter Queen Street in 1904 and the GWR a rival service from Moretonhampstead in 1906.

Chapman collection, cty. R. F. D. Sampson

buying up the TVR and ETV&CR companies. John Campfield, the GWR Exeter Divisional Superintendent, was moved to write to Paddington in 1896 to express his concern that the LSWR might try to buy out the ETV&C as 'a stride towards Torquay', and he repeated these warnings in 1898. As had so often been the case in the past, there is no evidence that the LSWR itself had any such intentions!

The Dicksons soon gave up the Crediton line idea, but evolved a further scheme for a Chagford–Moretonhampstead link. This was a strange line for the Dicksons to promote, as it would surely have resulted in most through traffic from Okehampton going to South Devon by the Moretonhampstead branch and not by the ETV&C Chagford branch!

In November 1897, after John Dickson had done full surveys, the Dicksons deposited plans and made a formal application to Parliament under the Light Railways Act for the Okehampton–Chagford and Chagford–Moretonhampstead sections. These involved 14 miles of new construction with one mile of the ETV&C line being used as a connection at Chagford itself. The estimated cost was £87,673, and assistance was to be sought from the Treasury and the Local Authorities.

It was all very optimistic, given that no new settlements would be brought on to the railway map, and that such through traffic as there was between North and South Devon would almost certainly find it more convenient in practice to change at Exeter rather than endure the extra changes and slow journeys on these Light Railways. In the event, the MDLR ideas were to be very quickly abandoned in 1898 when the ETV&C's abandonment of its Chagford branch removed most of the Dicksons' interest.

THE ABANDONMENT OF THE CHAGFORD BRANCH (1898)

In July 1895, Knatchbull-Hugessen had a meeting with the GWR General Manager and Solicitor, with the aim of persuading them to work the Chagford branch for 55% of the receipts instead of 50%. But the GWR would not be persuaded. Much of the land for the branch was bought in 1895/6 and the whole line staked out, but nothing was done beyond that (save for fencing off the first 150 yds at the Lea Cross end), the Dicksons concentrating all their efforts on the main line. Some capital had been taken up in the Chagford/Drewsteignton/Dunsford area on the basis of promises made by the Board that the Chagford line *would* be built, so every month that passed with no sign of activity on the branch meant a more embarrassing position for the Board. There were suggestions that a visible start should be made on the branch works in order to encourage further take-up in Chagford. But as 1897 wore on, and it became ever clearer that there would be difficulty enough financing the Exeter line, the Board's thoughts began to turn rather to abandoning the Chagford line. The

Dicksons were unhappy about this — their Mid Devon Light Railway scheme was largely dependent on the Chagford branch — and, in an attempt to salvage the situation, they made the ETV&C a formal offer in December 1897 'to equip and work your branch railway to Chagford under the Light Railways Act for 2s per train mile on a lease for 7 years'. But the ETV&C's mind was becoming made up.

In November 1897 the ETV&C had made application to Parliament for a Bill in the 1898 session to authorise the diversions at Ide–Perridge and Culver, and for another extension of time for building the line. (The powers had in fact expired in August 1897 but the ETV&C, like the TVR before them, were continuing the construction of the line without authority in the hope that nobody would object.) The Bill as presented had nothing in it about abandoning the Chagford line. But on 11th February 1898 the 'General Purposes Committee' discussed the question of adding such powers to the Bill, and this was approved by the full Board on the 25th. On the 28th the company's solicitors had a meeting with Lord Morley, the Lords' Chairman, and the addition of the extra clauses was agreed.

When this became known, some of the Chagford shareholders called a public meeting in Exeter to muster support against abandonment. But they stood little chance, as the take-up of shares in the area had been very poor. At the company's half-yearly meeting in March, which had to approve the content of the Bill, Knatchbull-Hugessen stated that the Board considered that the Chagford branch 'would ultimately be of great value, but for some years could only be worked at a loss', and that there was no provision in the company's authorised capital for the purchase of stock to work the line which would be necessary given the GWR's continued refusal to do so. The Dicksons' offer was dismissed as 'an offer by private persons to work the line' and generally played down. The organisers of the public meeting, it was claimed, held only £400 of shares between them.

A resolution for abandonment was carried with only one dissentient. It was also resolved to change the company's name to the 'Exeter Railway Company' to reflect the new circumstances.

The Exeter Railway Act 1898 accordingly authorised:

- The diversions at Ide–Perridge and Culver
- The abandonment of the Chagford branch (Railways 4 and 5)
- The change of company name
- The reduction of the company's authorised share capital from £264,000 to £198,000, and the authorised borrowing powers from £88,000 to £66,000 in reflection of the lesser sum needed now that the branch was not to be built. (The company was to regret this later!)
- The extension of time for building the line to August 1901, and a retrospective legalising of the work done in 1897/8.

Negotiations with the Dicksons for the alteration of the contract to take account of the deletion of the branch were

ESTIMATES OF THE EARNINGS OF THE LINE

1896 Prospectus

Main Line	£24,700
Chagford Branch	14,187
	38,888
Less 50%	19,444
Annual earnings	19,444

Which would enable 6% to be paid on the share capital
(£264,000 × 6% plus £88,000 × 4% comes to £19,360).

1898 Prospectus (after abandonment of the Chagford line)

72,000 Tons Through Merchandise[1]	£6,900
745 GWR Special Trains[2]	1,341
15,000 Tons Local Merchandise & Minerals	1,000
200,000 Passengers[3]	5,000
Parcels, Horses, Carriages and Dogs	800
Mails	240
	15,281
Less Working 50%	7,640
	7,640
∴Rebates needed to pay 5% on the share capital and 4% on the debenture stock[4]	2,809
	10,450

1. This figure was based on a survey done at Heathfield, showing that 108,000 Tons of Goods and Minerals passed through per annum, of which 72,000 Tons were to/from Exeter and beyond and (it was therefore assumed) would be routed via the Exeter Rly when opened. In the text of the prospectus it was noted that Candy's had promised to send 35,000–40,000 Tons per annum over the line.

2. Fish, vegetable and excursion trains diverted via Exeter Rly to avoid congestion on the main line at Dawlish. A figure of 1,490 such trains per annum was mentioned in the text and it is not clear why this was halved in the estimates.

3. Based on comparison from the figure of 212,160 passengers passing through Heathfield per annum on the Moretonhampstead line.

4. These figures are based on an assumption of £165,000 issued share capital and £55,000 issued debenture stock, less than what was actually issued. It was estimated that the actual value of the Rebates would be about £5,000 per annum.

to prove prolonged, and it was only in April 1899 that a new sum of £190,000 was agreed upon.

THE BRENT, ASHBURTON & HEATHFIELD RAILWAY

The ETV&C's prospectuses had spoken much of the line being used as an alternative route to the GWR main line, and at the March 1896 shareholders' meeting Knatchbull-Hugessen went so far as to claim 'I have no doubt that eventually the line will become the main line of the Great Western between Exeter and Newton Abbot'. This was not very likely given the nature of the TVR/ETV&C route as a curving single-track line, and even if the line were to be reconstructed at great expense for double track, it was still stuck with 1 in 58 gradients which made it highly unattractive compared to the level route via Dawlish.

However, it was realised that if the line were to be extended from Heathfield to Brent, it would cut a much better picture as an alternative to the main line, as it would enable trains to avoid Dainton and Rattery inclines which

had noticeably worse gradients than the ETV&C line. Accordingly in 1897, interests connected with the ETV&C arranged for William Lidstone to survey a Brent, Ashburton & Heathfield Railway, and plans were deposited in November 1897. This line effectively resuscitated the ideas of 1862, although it was, of course, now anticipated that the line would be used by the GWR instead of being a rival route to Plymouth as had been intended in the 1860s.

However, the GWR decided to oppose the Bill, and the promoters, not fancying the expense of a parliamentary contest, withdrew it in January 1898. The idea did not, however, die immediately. When the Exeter Railway was opened in 1903, the press spoke of its potential in this context. The *Contractors' Chronicle* noted that 'for a long time it has been said that the GWR contemplate the making of two short lines from Heathfield to Ashburton and from Buckfastleigh to a point east of the Marley tunnel', which, in connection with the Exeter Railway, would bring a saving of six miles between Exeter and Plymouth. The *Railway Magazine* talked of the line as a parallel to the cut-off lines via Castle Cary and thought that 'it will be seen that at some future date it may play a very important part in the development of railway communications to the West of England'.

In reality, the GWR's thoughts were turning in a different direction by 1903. The Dawlish–Parson's Tunnel doubling was now under way, and when completed in 1905 it would remove any need for an alternative Exeter–Newton Abbot route on line capacity grounds. There was also little concern over the sea wall at this time. Accordingly the GWR decided to stick to the existing line between Exeter and Newton Abbot, and promote a new line from Newton Abbot to Rattery running close to the old line but with much better gradients. Powers for this line were obtained in 1905. It was never built but it was enough to remove any GWR interest in the Exeter Railway as an alternative route to Plymouth.

---

1. This idea was of course more arguable since the main line had been converted from broad gauge in May 1892.

2. This was not true!

3. The Drewsteignton quarries were north-west of the village over a mile from the proposed railway (see 6 in maps). Worked by Messrs. Ponsford & Co., they are shown as disused on the 1904 OS map but were active again later.

4. Robert Elliott-Cooper, born 1845, set up in private practice 1876, responsible for many railway and other works. Not associated with any one major company in particular. Later Sir Robert, died 1942.

5. It is not clear why these two sections were omitted from the 1893 contract. The Canal Branch, it seems, was always intended to be built, whereas the Lea Cross north curve appears to have been given up in 1893. The abandonment of the Lea Cross north curve, which meant no through service Exeter–Chagford, does not seem to have been picked up by the Chagford interests.

6. 7m 73 ch in the later mileages from City Basin Junction.

7. By means of (a) the LSWR's Bude line then under construction (b) a proposed Okehampton–Hatherleigh–Torrington line which did not come to fruition at this date.

CHAPTER TEN
BUILDING THE EXETER RAILWAY
1894–1903

LIKE the building of the TVR before it, the construction of the Exeter Railway was to prove a protracted affair due to persistent financial problems, punctuated by crises in 1895/6, 1898, and 1901/2 which looked as though they might put a stop to the project altogether. The Dicksons insisted throughout that they could have completed in the two years of the 1893 contract had the money been available. In reality, construction was prolonged for 8½ years. Unlike on the TVR, though, the Dicksons did work continuously throughout these years.

Although there were no major individual works of note apart from the tunnels, the Exeter Railway, passing as it did through the north end of the Haldon Hills and largely against the grain of the land, was an extremely 'heavy' line for most of its length with very considerable earthworks — quite unlike the TVR section. 600,000 cu. yds of excavation was to be needed.

THE START OF WORK (1894–6)

The second Engineer's Certificate of December 1894 included payment for excavation work, so it seems that serious construction work did begin immediately after the November 1894 ceremonies. As the 1883 Act required the Dicksons to start at Teign House, they set up their base there and in January 1895 made arrangements with the GWR and TVR for one of the sidings at Teign House Siding to be extended across the road into their yard (see O.S. map, Chapter 18). The ETV&C construction traffic brought a welcome boost to the TVR's traffic levels at Teign House over the next years (see table, Chapter 12).

The initial 1¾ miles of line from Teign House involved no great problems, and this enabled a reasonably impressive start to be made — although this was always going to be something of a false impression given that there was not even an agreed line for some distance beyond until the agreement of a new line with Byrom in January 1896, and that work on the two tunnels (which were not even started until April 1896) was obviously going to be a major delaying factor. Financial problems slowed down the works right from the start, the R&IS Ltd having failed to do as much as was hoped of it. By August 1895 the Dicksons were telling the Board that they would have to cease work if further cash were not forthcoming, and only reluctantly agreed to carry on unpaid for a further month. In November 1895 the Dicksons complained:

'The Chudleigh shareholders are so dissatisfied that they are convening a meeting with a view to appointing a Committee to enquire into the company's affairs and find out why the works are proceeding so slowly . . . it is the province of the Railway & Industrial Syndicate to provide the requisite finances and we need not repeat the story of its failure to do this and of the trouble and expense involved in efforts to get money in other ways . . .'

The company found itself troubled by defaulters when calls were made on shares, and two of its own directors were amongst the worst offenders. The Dicksons also found difficulty in disposing of the 'paid up' shares, in which they were paid, to the public,[1] which meant that they had to find other sources of ready cash for the present on the security of these shares. To make matters more complex, the Dicksons also took a large number of ordinary unpaid shares themselves, to further the undertaking by improving the facade, and they (thanks to the company having failed to pay *them*) then found that they too could not pay their calls on these shares when the time came.

In 1895 the Dicksons appointed James Dickson's son, John H. Dickson, as their 'Contractor's Engineer' to supervise the contractor's workforce on site. He took up residence at The Grange, Dunsford, and stayed on until completion of the line, after which he became heavily involved in stone quarrying in the valley as described in Chapter 18.

THE 1896 PROSPECTUS

By summer 1895 it was evident that a further general share issue was required; the Board discussed this possibility in July 1895 but it was only in November that their solicitor Hurrell attended to discuss details. It was decided to hold a public meeting in Exeter on 10th January 1896 to launch the prospectus, but this had to be postponed due to an international crisis and was actually held on 24th February. The prospectus offered 10,000 shares and claimed a likely dividend of 6% after opening, in addition to which the contractors were guaranteeing a 4% dividend during the construction period (a common ploy by this date). The well-attended meeting heard Pring complain that 'it had often been thrown out to him at Board meetings that Exeter did not do its part'. A unanimous resolution was passed in favour of the line, but the take-up in Exeter was once again limited. However, the share issue as a whole was reasonably successful; in March the Board heard that 5,013 shares had been applied for, and this saved the day until 1898.

The 1896 prospectus claimed that the works would be completed in 18 months — a claim which Pring repeated at the public meeting. This most unlikely claim brought an anonymous letter to *The Times* from 'A resident on the route of the line' on 20th February 1896, which summed up the ETV&C's situation all too accurately:

'Mr Knatchbull-Hugessen thinks I must have private reasons for pointing out the misrepresentations contained in his company's prospectus. Let me tell him, therefore, publicly what my reasons are. (1) I object to a beautiful landscape being spoilt for all time by the banks and cuttings of an abandoned railway; (2) I object to widows and country parsons being encouraged to throw their money into a hole in the hillside; and (3) I object to railway enterprise in England being discredited by one more fiasco of the Didcot & Newbury or Hull and Barnsley character. I am perfectly aware that the inhabitants of Exeter are very anxious to see the line made. Naturally so, for its construction would render once more tributary to the Exeter Market a considerable district which the existing Teign Valley line now drains into the market of Newton Abbot. If the inhabitants of Exeter will either themselves make or induce the Great Western company to make this new line I have not a word to say. But when the outside public are invited to subscribe, they are entitled to be told the actual facts. These facts are that the Exeter, Teign Valley & Chagford Railway was sanctioned by Act of Parliament as long ago as 1883; that under the powers of the present Act of 1894 the first sod was cut in November 1894; that in the 14 months since then a mile and a half of simple and straightforward earthwork has been finished up to formation level; but that the difficult portion of the work has not even been touched. If, knowing this, would-be subscribers agree with Mr. Knatchbull-Hugessen in thinking it likely that in the course of the next 18 months a long tunnel, with railway access from one end only, can be driven and completed, and after its completion four miles of line, including a junction on an embankment with the main line of the Great Western, can be taken in hand and completed also, why then by all means let them subscribe their money. But when directors state in generalities that considerable progress has been made in 14 months, and that therefore the whole may be expected to be completed in 18 months more, it is surely fair comment to add this particular fact, that certainly not more than 5 per cent of the work has been accomplished, and that therefore, at the present rate of progress, the line might be expected to open for traffic about 1920'.

Knatchbull-Hugessen was obliged to reply to this at length. He conceded that only 1½ miles out of 8 had been done to date and tried to bluff by speaking of progress in railway construction being measured 'not by the linear yard, but by the cubic yard of heavy earthwork' — a singularly irrelevant argument given that, as the anonymous correspondent had pointed out, the difficult parts of the line had not yet been commenced!

The Railway & Industrial Syndicate's role in shuffling paper money seems to have been given up after 1896, and it was wound up in December 1897 with its Secretary Faulkner as Liquidator.

IDEAS OF OPENING TO LEA CROSS
When work got underway in 1894/5, it began to put ideas in local people's heads that the TVR trains might be run through from Heathfield to the Lea Cross station at an early date, before the line opened through to Exeter. This would provide a service that had been desired since the TVR decided in 1882 to run passenger trains as far as Ashton only. The change of station site in 1896 from Lea Cross to Christow, only a few yards beyond the Teign House Siding stops, made such a possibility seem even more achievable. A prime advocate of this course was the ETV&C's eccentric shareholder, W.S. Elphinstone-Stone,[2] who wrote on 22nd October 1896 suggesting:

'that Messrs Dickson should be asked to lay the Permanent Way to Lea Cross and (have) the station [Christow] ready by the 1st of January so that the Great Western may commence to run their trains to Teign House [Christow], if you want a Ticket Collector for the first week until the GW find one of their servants, I will give my services and I should like to drive the first train to Teign House station and decorate the engine by putting the words Success & Prosperity with a bunch of mistletoe and a few flags . . .'

In June 1897 he wrote again:

'I was in hopes that the contractors would have the station for Teign House and a Goods Yard at Lea Cross open for traffic by July. I know Mr. Fulford and the inhabitants of Dunsford would make good use of it'.

But in reality the ETV&C had given up any ideas they might have had of still providing goods facilities at Lea Cross; and the running of passenger trains beyond Ashton was dependent on persuading the impecunious TVR to pay for the upgrading of the Ashton–Christow section to passenger standards, so nothing was done.

PROGRESS 1896–8
In this period work was concentrated on the section between 3 m 7 ch (the boundary of the Ecclesiastical Commissioners' lands west of Ide) and 6 m 64 ch (north of Lea Cross). Most importantly, the two tunnels were pushed ahead. Perridge Tunnel at 829 yds (significantly longer than the 700 yds that had been anticipated in the 1882 deposited plans) was a much longer job than the 251-yard Culver Tunnel, and required nine shafts to be sunk before the headings were begun. The headings of both tunnels were commenced in August 1896 and finished through in February/March 1897. The Dicksons took this as a chance for further publicity, and two separate 'events' were arranged for the benefit of the local press. The 'Last Shot in Culver Tunnel' was celebrated on Saturday 27th February 1897 and was very much the Byroms' day, the last six shots being fired by:

Miss Byrom of Culver House
Mrs Buckingham, the wife of the Rector of Doddiscombsleigh
Mrs Smee of Perridge House
Edward Byrom
Miss J. Byrom
Mrs Byrom,

and the last one duly opened a way through. The party then drank a toast to 'the Contractors', followed by Bluett offering a toast to 'the Chairman and Directors'. The party were then conveyed through the tunnel, which was brightly illuminated by candles, on trolleys, and then continued along the line — presumably a temporary 2 ft gauge tub line — into the west end of Perridge Tunnel, where they watched the miners at work. Bluett and J.H. Dickson, the Contractors' Engineer, were then entertained to lunch at Culver House.

The 'Last Shot in Perridge Tunnel' on Wednesday 3rd March 1897 was a much more Exonian affair (although some of the Culver party were allowed another go!). The Mayoress, Mrs Pople, had been invited to fire the last shot, and Walter Pring was also present, along with a number of other Exeter dignitaries. The party entered the tunnel at the Exeter end but following the ceremony they were able to walk through and leave at the west end. Refreshments were then taken and toasts drunk, and James Dickson made a speech in which he complained, not for the first time, of the small take-up of shares in Exeter.

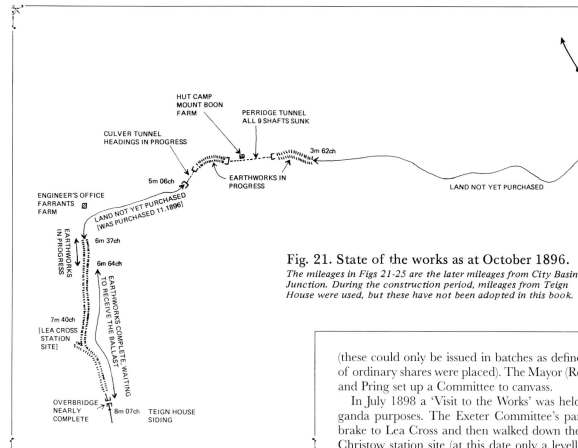

HUT CAMP
MOUNT BOON
FARM

PERRIDGE TUNNEL
ALL 9 SHAFTS SUNK

CULVER TUNNEL
HEADINGS IN PROGRESS

3m 62ch

5m 06ch

EARTHWORKS IN
PROGRESS

LAND NOT YET PURCHASED

ENGINEER'S OFFICE
FARRANTS
FARM

LAND NOT YET PURCHASED
[WAS PURCHASED 11.1896]

EARTHWORKS
IN PROGRESS

6m 37ch

6m 64ch

EARTHWORKS COMPLETE, WAITING
TO RECEIVE THE BALLAST

7m 40ch
[LEA CROSS
STATION
SITE]

OVERBRIDGE
NEARLY
COMPLETE

8m 07ch   TEIGN HOUSE
SIDING

Fig. 21. State of the works as at October 1896.
*The mileages in Figs 21-25 are the later mileages from City Basin
Junction. During the construction period, mileages from Teign
House were used, but these have not been adopted in this book.*

After this the headings had, of course, to be widened out
to full width, and the tunnels lined throughout with brick-
work. This, thanks to financial restrictions, was to prove a
very drawn-out process. The bricks were not delivered to
Teign House siding until the spring of 1899. Culver tunnel
was finished around November 1899 but Perridge tunnel
was not fully lined until around January 1902 — five years
after the 'Last Shot' ceremony!

The impression was given from 1896 onwards that track
laying would begin very shortly, and indeed the Dicksons
had the sleepers stacked at Teign House. But in fact nothing was done until 1899.

THE 1898 CRISIS

Money was beginning to run out again by the spring of
1898. The Dicksons considered that it might still be possible to get a larger take-up in Exeter, and in April 1898 they
entered into talks with the Exeter Chamber of Commerce
in the hope that the Chamber could exert moral pressure
on likely shareholders. If £15,000 could be raised in additional shares, the Chamber was told, the Dicksons had
promises of a large sum being taken in debenture stocks

(these could only be issued in batches as defined numbers
of ordinary shares were placed). The Mayor (Robert Pople)
and Pring set up a Committee to canvass.

In July 1898 a 'Visit to the Works' was held for propa-
ganda purposes. The Exeter Committee's party went by
brake to Lea Cross and then walked down the line to the
Christow station site (at this date only a levelled site with
none of the permanent structures, except the road overbridge, erected). Another party organised by the
'Chudleigh Committee' went by train to Ashton and
walked from there to Christow. They were received by
James Dickson, J.H. Dickson, and Bluett, and treated to a
cold lunch in 'the temporary building which stands on the
site of the proposed goods shed'. They were then subjected to pressure in speeches from James Dickson, who complained that 'so far the contractors had borne the burden
of the day' and that the railway would have been completed by now if Exeter people had done more; and from Pring
who said that he was 'ashamed that the merchants of
Exeter had not done more'. (Dickson also insisted that 'the
construction of a Light Railway to Chagford was practically a certainty', which was rather optimistic by this date!)
After being thus castigated, the parties went on a tour of
the completed sections of the line, and 'everyone was surprised at the enormous amount of work done'. It must be
remembered, of course, that with nothing whatsoever yet
done at the Exeter end, people in Exeter (few of whom
ever went to Lea Cross) were liable to forget that anything
was being done at all.

This time there was a better response. In December the
Dicksons told the Chamber of Commerce that they had

succeeded in getting £17,500 of shares taken up, and thereby been able to place the extra debentures. A large proportion of these debentures were taken up by the Bank of England which thereby acquired a strong influence on the company's Board (as described in Chapter 11). It was estimated in December 1898 that £58,523 of work remained to be done.

PROGRESS 1898–1902

With the financial problems resolved again, work was put back into a higher gear in 1899. The most immediate sign of progress was the long-postponed laying of the track from Teign House to Longdown, between March and November 1899 (Culver tunnel had just been completed,

---

EXETER RAILWAY: TAKE-UP OF SHARES AND DEBENTURE STOCK

Source: Company's half-yearly reports. No figures available from this source prior to June 1896.

	Shares issued £	Money paid up £	Debentures issued £
June 1896	83,890	32,083[1]	Nil
Dec 1896	146,510	73,197	7,530
June 1897	162,700	95,752	17,815
Dec 1897	165,960	99,296	22,765
June 1898	182,970	108,268	27,065
Dec 1898	184,360	116,393	48,870
June 1899	145,480[1]	123,840	53,200
Dec 1899	147,390	129,925	53,200
June 1900	157,380	145,390	53,200
Dec 1900	193,960[2]	161,009	54,200
June 1901	198,000[3]	177,756	66,000[5]
Dec 1901	198,000	194,810	66,000
June 1902	198,000	196,560	66,000
Dec 1902	198,000	196,560	66,000
June 1903	198,000	196,560	66,000
Dec 1903	198,000	196,560	74,580[6]
June 1904	198,000	196,560	74,580
Dec 1904	198,000	196,560	nk
June 1905	198,000	196,560	77,830
Dec 1905	198,000	196,560	77,830
June 1906	198,000	196,560	154,107[7]
Dec 1906	198,000	196,560	154,698

Notes
1. £39,020 'forfeited' in January 1899 due to the persons to whom these shares were issued having failed to make any payments.
2. £36,200 issued unpaid to the Dicksons in August 1900 on the understanding that the shares would become paid out of future Engineer's certificates. This was an (improper) ploy to enable a sufficient increase in the issued capital to allow the remainder of the Debenture stock to be issued.
3. Maximum permitted capital under 1898 Act.
4. Plus £21,618 in 4% guaranteed shares (later included with rest).
5. Maximum permitted Debenture stock under 1898 Act.
6. 1903 Act authorised further Debenture stocks.
7. Lloyds Bonds, previously issued to contractors, converted to Debenture Stock.

In analysing the company's real support, one must bear in mind the large percentage of the shares issued to the Dicksons. There is, of course, no information on this in the half-yearly reports, but figures are available for certain dates. At March 1897, when £160,510 had been allotted, £22,750 was held by the Dicksons fully paid (i.e. issued to them in payment for the works) and £35,000 held by them in 'unpaid' shares taken by them (on which they had in fact paid 1/20 by this date).

---

but the rails had to stop at Longdown because Perridge Tunnel was nowhere near complete).

LOCOMOTIVES USED BY THE DICKSONS ON THE EXETER RAILWAY CONTRACT

Manning Wardle 1087 of 1889, *Chagford*
0-4-0ST. Ex works 1.7.1889 to J.E. Billups, contractor for the Lambourn Valley Railway, as *Lambourn* (or *Lambourne*?). Work on this line ceased in June 1890 and, by a judgement of May 1891, Billups' plant, including the loco, was transferred to the LVR's ownership. Sold by them, at date not known, possibly direct to Dicksons, possibly with an intermediate owner. Sent to the Exeter Railway contract at date not known and renamed *Chagford*. In use on the ER until the end of the work in 1903 and then advertised for sale (see advert at end of this chapter which must refer to this loco although not specifically identifying it). Next known c1907 when acquired by Topham Jones & Railton Ltd, contractors for the Kings Dock, Swansea, and then used by them on the Deep Water Dock, Southampton from c1908, and subsequent contracts. Later, from c1930, at Blaenclydach Colliery, still as *Chagford*. Scrapped 1935.

Fox Walker 278 of 1875, *Earl of Devon*
0-6-0ST. Ex works 10.7.1875 to W.F. Lawrence, contractor for the Banbury & Cheltenham Direct Railway, of which the then Earl of Devon (the same Earl as had been involved in the promotion of Teign Valley schemes earlier) was Chairman. The name is actually quoted as *Earl Devon* originally but it may perhaps always have in fact been *Earl of Devon*. Then to Henry Lovatt who took over part of the B&CDR contract in 1877. After that unknown. In c1890–c1893 with Eckersley, Godfrey & Liddelow on their Canada Branch Dock, Liverpool, contract. Sold to the Dicksons at date not known c1895, and sent to the Exeter Railway contract at date also not known. The *Earl of Devon* name was retained by the Dicksons, being very appropriate given that much of the line was on Powderham Estates land. In use on the ER until the end of the work in 1903 and then advertised for sale. Subsequent fate not known.

Robert Stephenson 2383 of 1879, *Longdown*
0-6-0T. The history of this loco is particularly difficult and has been further confused by regurgitation of errors in previous books, often with additional 'corruptions' added. The known facts were set out at great length by Michael Cook in an article in *Industrial Locomotive* (No. 64, 1992); only those most relevant to the ER can be given here.

Nothing known pre-1887. From RS 6.1887 to William Jackson contractor for the FY&NR, as *Freshwater*. After a court case between Jackson and the FY&NR, two FY&NR Directors bought the loco in 1890 in order to resell it. In December 1890 what was probably this loco was offered for sale by G.N. Dixon, a Liverpool contractors' plant auctioneer, and it was probably then used, along with FW 278, by Eckersley Godfrey & Liddelow on the Canada Branch Dock contract until 1893. It probably came into the Dicksons' possession c1895 along with FW278. It is recorded in secondary sources that it went to the ER contract and was renamed *Longdown*; no original source for this can now be traced, but as the name is unlikely to have been invented and unlikely to have been given unless the loco had been on the ER at the time, one can postulate that this is most likely accurate. If sent to the ER, it cannot have been there very long and may never have worked, as by 1898/9 it had been sold to the Weston Clevedon & Portishead Railway as No.3 *Portishead*. In 1901 it was sold by the WC&PR to the Renishaw Iron Co. Ltd, and was retained by them until scrapped c1936/7.

Peckett 903 of 1901, *Ide*
0-4-0ST. Ex works 28.6.1901, new to the Dicksons at Exeter. There is no mention of a Peckett in the 1903 auction advertisement, which, however, refers to two Manning Wardle 0-4-0STs; as there is no evidence of any second MW on the ER, this may be an error for the Peckett. Subsequent history confused.

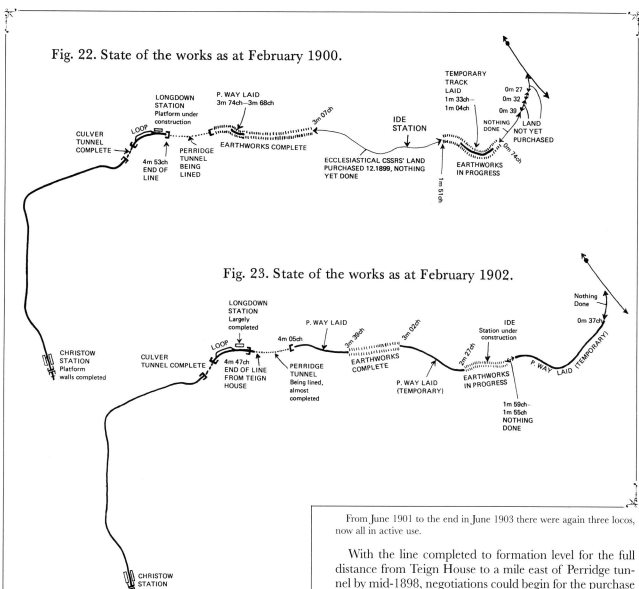

Fig. 22. State of the works as at February 1900.

Fig. 23. State of the works as at February 1902.

From June 1901 to the end in June 1903 there were again three locos, now all in active use.

With the line completed to formation level for the full distance from Teign House to a mile east of Perridge tunnel by mid-1898, negotiations could begin for the purchase of the Ecclesiastical Commissioners' and the Earl of Devon's lands. The Earl's land (between City Basin Jn. and Ide) was acquired first in the spring of 1899, and construction work began immediately on part of this length, including the laying of some track (the permanent rails on temporary sleepers). The materials for the work on this stretch had to be carted by road (from Longdown?) due to the continued inability to enter on the intervening Ecclesiastical Commissioners' land, which was only acquired in December 1899 and on which work started in the spring of 1900.

1900–02 therefore saw work in progress, on different sections at different times, throughout the eastern half of the line (save that the last section at the City Basin Jn. end was not touched until well into 1902). The track was laid

I am grateful to Michael Cook, and other members of the IRS and ILS, for doing their best in the time-consuming task of extracting solid fact from a mass of conflicting and corrupt sources. It will be seen that much still remains obscure.

It is possible that the first three locos (MW1087, RS2383, FW278) were all acquired by the Dicksons early in 1895 and sent to Christow in anticipation of works getting under way vigorously. Two of these locos, RS2383 and FW278, were offered for sale (by persons unknown, but it could well have been the Dicksons) in July 1895; by this date it would have been clear that works were not going to proceed quickly, and therefore that three locos were not required. RS2383 was sold at some date after this although FW278 clearly was not. Until 1899 there would have been no loco work to do on the ER other than shunting the yard at Christow, and it is not proven that locos rather than horses/manpower were used for that.

in discontinuous lengths, and all on temporary sleepers (whereas the Teign House–Longdown section had been laid in permanent form at the start). It was only in the latter half of 1902 that the missing links in the track were all completed so as to give a through line from Teign House to the current end of the works short of City Basin Junction.

Plans of the stations had been sent to the GWR in 1899, and in September 1899 Bluett had a meeting with Campfield, the Exeter Divisional Superintendent, Hill, the Traffic Superintendent, and Gibbons, the District Engineer, including visits to all the station sites. But the GWR did not return the plans approved until 1901, so it was only in the autumn of 1901 that the station buildings at Christow and Longdown were built, followed in the winter of 1901/2 by those at Ide (where, of course, the whole works were running much further behind).

THE 1902 CRISIS

By mid-1901 the whole of the authorised share capital and the whole of the debentures had been issued, but there was still much more work to be done. Relations between the Dicksons and the company deteriorated accordingly. In July 1901 the Dicksons were complaining that the company's behaviour was 'quite intolerable', and threatening to call a special shareholders' meeting if they were not given an immediate cash payment for the previous month's work. The company complained in return of the unpaid calls on some of the shares held by the Dicksons! The situation was resolved by paying the Dicksons in Lloyds Bonds from 1901 on.

In April 1902 a 'Supplemental Contract' was signed requiring completion of the line by 14th August 1902 (a previous deadline of 30th November 1901 having passed unmet). But in fact things moved very slowly after this, the Dicksons having only 50 men on the works in July 1902 against an average of 150–300 in 1899–1901. The new deadline was also unmet and, on 15th August, Faulkner, the ER Secretary, formally informed the Dicksons that the company proposed to take over the works directly. This was not likely to bring much benefit, the real need being rather to find somebody who would advance the Dicksons credit on the security of the Lloyds Bonds (which in themselves were only a 'promise to pay' at some future date). For some time the situation seemed desperate, but rescue came

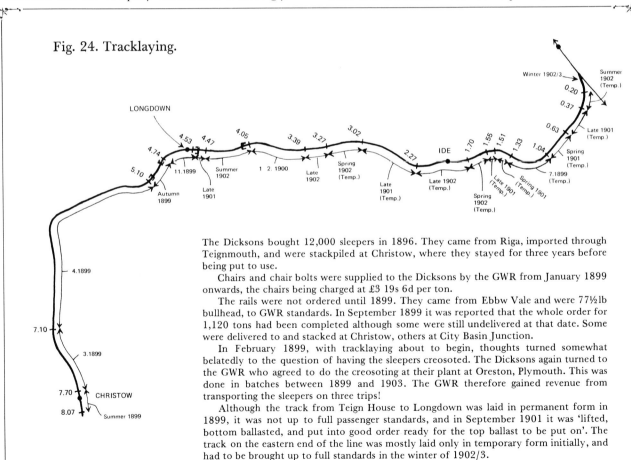

Fig. 24. Tracklaying.

The Dicksons bought 12,000 sleepers in 1896. They came from Riga, imported through Teignmouth, and were stackpiled at Christow, where they stayed for three years before being put to use.

Chairs and chair bolts were supplied to the Dicksons by the GWR from January 1899 onwards, the chairs being charged at £3 19s 6d per ton.

The rails were not ordered until 1899. They came from Ebbw Vale and were 77½lb bullhead, to GWR standards. In September 1899 it was reported that the whole order for 1,120 tons had been completed although some were still undelivered at that date. Some were delivered to and stacked at Christow, others at City Basin Junction.

In February 1899, with tracklaying about to begin, thoughts turned somewhat belatedly to the question of having the sleepers creosoted. The Dicksons again turned to the GWR who agreed to do the creosoting at their plant at Oreston, Plymouth. This was done in batches between 1899 and 1903. The GWR therefore gained revenue from transporting the sleepers on three trips!

Although the track from Teign House to Longdown was laid in permanent form in 1899, it was not up to full passenger standards, and in September 1901 it was 'lifted, bottom ballasted, and put into good order ready for the top ballast to be put on'. The track on the eastern end of the line was mostly laid only in temporary form initially, and had to be brought up to full standards in the winter of 1902/3.

The Dicksons' foreman platelayer. Sadly, his name is not recorded.

in the form of the wealthy Revd Thomas Sheepshanks of Arthington Hall, Yorkshire, and Stokelake House, Chudleigh. By an agreement dated 7th October 1902, Sheepshanks agreed to give the Dicksons £35,000 in cash — enough for the £34,078 now estimated to be needed to complete the line — in return for the £68,650 of Lloyds Bonds issued to date. Another new contract was signed with the Dicksons on the same day (after arbitration on their differences with the company), and from this time on the end was definitely in sight.

Another problem troubling the ER at this time was a legal action brought in May 1900 by the Exeter solicitors, Gidley & Caunter, on behalf of some of the original promoters of the 1883 Act, including Francis Fox, Samuel Jones, and the executors of the late Col. Walker, William Easton, and B.C. Gidley. Back in 1888 the Board had resolved to pay the 1883 promoters £10,000 to recompense them for their Parliamentary costs, and again in 1893 the Dicksons' contract had included a clause requiring them to pay this £10,000 as part of the contract price (this being in effect part of the agreement under which the 'old Board' had let the R&IS Ltd syndicate take over the company). But no payment had ever been made — no doubt because there were always more urgent claims on the available finances! The ER responded to the action with a counter-action for libel but told their solicitors that they 'did not wish it to proceed very far' as it was only a negotiating tactic. The Exeter Chamber of Commerce became rather concerned about the situation and were worried that the completion of the line might be delayed. In fact the case seems to have been largely sorted out in 1901, and in November 1903 a final settlement was drawn up under which the ER was to pay £6,000 in fully paid shares and £3,250 in debenture stock, so largely conceding the correctness of the plaintiffs' action.

COMPLETION OF THE LINE (1902/3)

From October 1902 work resumed at full speed and the fact that the line was nearly completed became more obvious every day. The main work still to be done was in the Ide area, and at City Basin Junction[3] where nothing at all had yet been done on the first 300 yds or so from the GWR junction, or on the Alphington Road and Canal[4] branches. Bluett's regular monthly reports give us a picture of the work in these last months:

3rd December 1902
Land owned by GWR (at City Basin Jn) still not in our possession. Embankment now advanced 0 m 20 ch to 0 m 13 ch. Still much to be done there, and for the goods sidings and the canal Branch.

Rails now laid, either permanently or temporarily, 0 m 13 ch–8 m 07 ch (Teign House) and the engines are running daily over this length.

The GWR Engineers have taken particulars of the junctions (i.e. City Basin Jn, and Christow permanent junction).

250 men on site.

BUILDING OF THE STATIONS

Christow

1894/5	Earthworks commenced. Temporary connection to Contractors' Siding.
1896 (Feb)	Decision to have Station here.
1896	Road diversion and overbridge completed.
1896–8	Station Yard formed (seems that little was done in this period).
1898–9	Excavations for platform and buildings.
1899 (Summer)	Main line laid through station (still using temporary connection to TVR). Some connections laid in for loop, etc, soon after this.
1899–1900	Platform walls built.
1901	Approach road completed.
1901 (Autumn)	Main station building, Goods Shed, Down Platform shelter, and loading dock/carriage shoot built.
1902	Crane delivered. Lamp Hut erected. Final completion of all buildings. Full track layout completed (?).
1903	Cart weighbridge installed. Signal Box and signals erected.

Longdown

1895	Earthworks commenced.
1896 (Feb)	Decision to have Station here.
1896	Approach road completed (not metalled until 1899).
1896–8	Station Yard formed.
1898–9	Excavations for platform and buildings.
1899 (Autumn)	Main line and 'loop' laid.
1901 (Autumn)	Station Building built (but not completed until late 1902).
1901–2	Platform built.
1902	Lamp Hut erected.
1903	Ground Frames installed.

Ide

1900	Earthworks commenced.
1901–2	Station Yard formed. Approach road built.
1901–2	Platform walls built.
1901–2	Station building built.
1902	Loading Dock/Carriage Shoot built (had to be rebuilt 1903 after damage by a runaway truck). Lamp Hut erected.
1902 (Autumn)	Main line laid through station. Siding laid.
1903	Ground Frames installed.

Alphington Road Goods

c.Dec 1902	Start of work on embankment from main line (largely completed c. Jan. 1903).
Jan–Mar 1903	Sidings laid.
Jan–Mar 1903	Goods Lock-Up (20ft × 15ft) built, also Loading Bank, Cattle Pens, Cart Weighbridge, 5 Ton Crane.
April–May 1903	Final completion of all works (except lighting, still unfinished at Sept. 1903).

The west end of Perridge Tunnel, seen in 1921. Complex drainage work was necessary here. Note the complete lack of vegetation on the slopes, but by BR days there was heavy growth. The aqueduct carried a stream over the line and was later removed. The tunnel length was quoted as 829 yds in the 1903 opening notice and the 1903 inspection report. The later official figure of 836 yds given in most GWR sources was almost certainly one of those numerous false figures obtained by taking the difference between the chainages of the portals and multiplying by 22 to convert to yards!

Collection John Owen

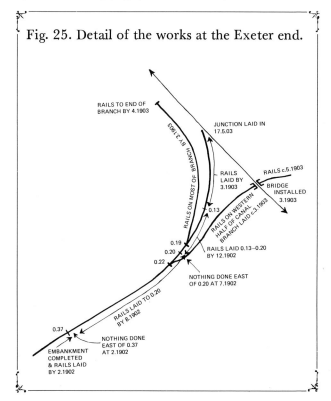

Fig. 25. Detail of the works at the Exeter end.

RAILS TO END OF BRANCH BY 4.1903

JUNCTION LAID IN 17.5.03

RAILS ON MOST OF BRANCH BY 3.1903

RAILS LAID BY 3.1903

RAILS c.5.1903

BRIDGE INSTALLED 3.1903

RAILS ON WESTERN HALF OF CANAL BRANCH LAID c.3.1903

0.13

0.19

0.20

0.22

RAILS LAID 0.13–0.20 BY 12.1902

NOTHING DONE EAST OF 0.20 AT 7.1902

RAILS LAID TO 0.20 BY 8.1902

0.37

NOTHING DONE EAST OF 0.37 AT 2.1902

EMBANKMENT COMPLETED & RAILS LAID BY 2.1902

I have asked the GWR to put in the running timbers for the bridge under their main line for the Canal Branch, they will do this as soon as possible.

6th January 1903

GWR land has been acquired.

The main embankment at Exeter has now reached the toe of the GWR embankment.

The points and crossings at Ide are placed in position.

In many places where the rails were laid temporarily, more sleepers are being added and extra ballast added.

There are no signs of the GWR people putting up the signals, or putting in the Canal Branch timbers.

[For full details of the signalling work, which was all done by the GWR, see Chapter 17].

11th February 1903

All the level crossings (sc.-occupation crossings) and gates are now erected. The telegraph work is in hand, two miles of posts are erected. All the signals are being made. The Signal Box for Christow has been delivered and is ready to put up. The ground frames for Ide and Longdown are delivered and sites for them prepared.

Stations — Christow practically complete except for cart weighbridge.

Longdown practically completed.

Ide - some work still necessary on the station buildings. The line should be ready for the Board of Trade by 1st May.

6th March 1903

Permanent way all in except the junction at Exeter, the Canal Branch, and the sidings at the end of the goods depot.

The abutments of the bridge under the GWR (on the Canal Branch) are built, and the girders are to be placed in position on Sunday next (8th).

6th April 1903
Embankment 7 m 55 ch (0 m 32 ch) to the end of the line (City Basin Jn) is now up to its full height, but additional width is needed for the signal rods.

Goods Depot, and embankment to it, practically completed.

Permanent way laid on half the Canal Branch.

The GWR have put in the junction at Christow.

The GWR are about to relay the line from Ashton to Christow.

Station nameplates and signs are all erected, very little now needs doing on the station buildings.

The GWR have erected all the telegraph poles and are putting the wires up.

The signals at Christow are all up and connected to the cabin but the point rods are not yet finished.

The signals are being installed at Exeter but the rods cannot be laid as the embankment is not wide enough.

The east end of Culver Tunnel, also in 1921. The comments about vegetation again apply. This tunnel was quoted as 251 yds in 1903, the later figure of 253 yds again being suspect.
Collection John Owen

Northwards from Leigh Cross the line was mostly on embankment above the B3193 road, and several under-bridges were required for farm roads. This is the bridge at 6m 33ch (Kingscourt Farm), which would have been built in 1897. It has a round arch but others of the line's masonry (brick arch) under-bridges had segmental arches. *Author*

Perhaps the most interesting engineering feature of the eastern end of the line was this 'road tunnel' at 2m 28ch where Halscombe Lane passes under the high railway embankment. It still exists and is seen here in 1991. There is no reference to the construction but it must have been built (all of brick) as an artificial tunnel on open ground and the earth for the embankment piled on top.   *Author*

7th May 1903

The GWR are laying the points and crossings at the Exeter junction on 17th May.

The relaying of Ashton–Christow is not yet commenced, but the rails have started to arrive.

The heavy rains have interfered with the works.

The GWR are not getting on as well as I think they should be with the signalling.

I expect the line to be completed by the end of the month, except for the Canal Branch.

A first 'passenger train' was run on the afternoon of Wednesday, 1st April 1903, from Alphington Road to Christow, for members of the Exeter Chamber of Commerce. This was entirely the Dicksons' initiative, and they provided for the purpose several wagons hauled by their locomotive *Earl of Devon*. Several journalists were also invited and the *Devon Evening News* duly gave good coverage that same evening.

'The accommodation for the conveyance of the party was somewhat of a primitive description. The saloons are not yet available and a couple of trucks and a car were made as comfortable as may be. Mr R.M. Flint constructed a couple of canopies over the two open conveyances, the sides of which were bedecked with red baize, giving a very holiday-look to the turnout. The cloth-covered planks were not limited to five a side. There was not much sun . . . but the journey altogether was enjoyed . . . The destination was reached after a run of rather less than an hour . . . there were one or two halts necessitated by obstructions in the shape of trucks on the line.'

At Christow tea was provided in the station buildings. Speeches were made by Mr T. Martin of the Chamber of Commerce who noted that 'many of them had never expected to live to see the completion of the scheme', and by 'Mr Dickson' (John?) who confessed that 'it would be a

very long time before they entered into another such contract . . . they had put eight years of hard work into the railway, for which they would get no recompense.'

During the tea a 'Marconigram' arrived addressed to the Dicksons from 'Devonians in India and the Colonies', congratulating them on completion of the work!

'There was no reason why the line should not open by 1st May, bar the weather', said Dickson, adding that the Mayor might like to start a fund for 'sports or some amusement to commemorate the opening'.

This was, as usual in these circumstances, destined to be over-optimistic.

Gibbons, the GWR Divisional Engineer, had made an 'inspection' of the line on 9th February, walking over the full length with Bluett. He was a little concerned by the steep slopes of some of the cuttings and the narrow formation of the line in these cuttings. Then in May the line was 'gone over' by all the local GWR officers. They reported on 27th May, making a number of complaints about incomplete works (notably the rough conditions of the approach roads to Longdown and Ide stations, the poor state of the top ballast between Ide and Longdown, and the absence of gradient boards and quarter-mile posts) and producing a long list of the furnishings needed for the stations, which the GWR was prepared to supply at the ER's expense (see Table).

Meanwhile, Knatchbull-Hugessen and Faulkner had paid a visit to the line themselves on 15th May. They were a little concerned that the GWR might hold up the opening by not completing the Ashton–Christow relaying in time for it to be inspected by the Board of Trade on the

GWR REQUIREMENTS FOR STATION FITTINGS — MAY 1903			
	Ide	Longdown	Christow
Trespass notices — blue enamelled	1	1	1
Seats for Booking Hall	1	1	1
Platform seats, with backs and arms lettered	3	3	5
Luggage barrows flat 4-wheeled	1	1	3
Luggage barrows 2-wheeled	1	2	2
Weighing Machines, platform	1	1	1
Clocks, Dial	1	1	1
Clocks, Office	1	1	2
Fenders	3	3	6
Fire Iron Sets	3	3	6
Office chairs	8	8	12
Tables, Waiting Room, 3ft 6in × 2ft 6in	1	1	2
Stools, Office	1	1	1
Cash safes	1	1	1
Luggage label cases, small	1	1	1
Ladders for platform lamps	1	1	1
Ticket issuing cases	1	1	1

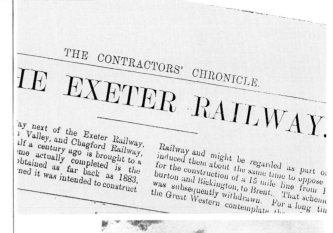

THE CONTRACTORS' CHRONICLE.

THE EXETER RAILWAY.

...ay next of the Exeter Railway, ... Valley, and Chagford Railway, ...lf a century ago is brought to a ...me actually completed is the ...btained as far back as 1883, ...ned it was intended to construct

Railway and might be regarded as part of ...induced them about the same time to oppose ...for the construction of a 15 mile line from ...burton and Bickington, to Brent. That scheme ...was subsequently withdrawn. For a long tim... ...the Great Western contemplate th...

Chagford crossing the Alphington Road bridge (site of the later Halt). The construction of this bridge, with separate masonry arches, either side of the main steel girder span, for the footpaths, is noteworthy. Most of the line's public road under-bridges were steel girder spans.

The junction at City Basin Junction, looking from the Exeter Railway towards the GWR main line, with the hastily-constructed Alphington Road goods station on the left. The nearer signal (City Basin Junction Branch Home with St. Thomas Distant) was already in use and not 'crossed', the signal box (out of sight to the right) having been opened in 1902. The leftmost of the sidings in the goods station, occupied by the line of trucks, was not part of the permanent layout, but the remainder of the layout was as per the 1904 25in map in Chapter 18.

Longdown station.

Christow, looking south. The signal box was all connected up but as the signals were crossed out of use, the photographs must have been taken before the commissioning of this box on 26th June 1903.

same day that the Exeter Railway was inspected. (It will be recalled that this section had not been included in the 1882 inspection because it was not a passenger line, but it was now about to become one.) In the event, the GWR sent in their '10 days notice' on 30th May, a day before the ER sent theirs. Col. Yorke replied on behalf of the Board of Trade on 3rd June, stating that he would come on 11th June and did wish to do both lines on the same day.

EXETER RAILWAY
Highly Important Sale of Contractors' Plant
by order of Messrs. James & John Dickson
owing to completion of contract

A. T. and E. A. Crow, Contractors' Auctioneers,
Manor House, Sunderland,
have been honoured with instructions to sell by auction
On Wednesday & Thursday, 15th & 16th July 1903,
at the Contractor's Yard, Dunsford, near Exeter,
The whole of the valuable contractor's plant and
machinery materials and stores used in the construction
of this railway, comprising: —

Splendid Saddle-Tank Locomotive Engine 13in cyls 6 wheels
  coupled, makers Fox Walker & Co.
Two Excellent Saddle-Tank Locomotive Engines, 9in & 10in
  cyls, 4 wheels coupled, 4ft 8½ gauge, makers Manning
  Wardle & Co.
Three Portable Engines (two 8hp and one 14hp)
Three Mortar Mills (9ft, 7ft, and 6ft 6in pans)
Combined Engine & Mortar Mill 6ft pan
Stonebreaker, 15in by 8in jaw
Saw Bench
120 2½ and 3½ cu yard End-Tip Wagons, 4ft 8½in gauge
5 Rail Trolleys 4ft 8½in gauge
90 1½ and 2 cu yard End and Side Tip wagons, 3ft gauge
24 8 and 10 Ton Permanent Ballast Trucks
Steam Locomotive Travelling Cranes
Scotch Derrick Cranes
100 tons F.B. rails and fastenings, 14 lb to 75 lb per yard
Rock Drills
Pulsometer & Other Pumps
Contents of Blacksmith's and Carpenters' shops and stores
Wood-Built Navvy Huts, Sheds, and Offices; also Horses,
  Dog-Carts, Wagonettes, Dobbin-Carts, Harness &c, &c.

Catalogues now ready, and obtainable from
Messrs. J. & J. Dickson, 48 Grays Inn Road, London WC,
or Contractor's Office, Dunsford, near Exeter; or
A. T. and E. A. Crow, Contractors' Auctioneers and Valuers,
Manor House, Sunderland. Telegrams 'Crow' Sunderland.
National Tel. 731.

The Dicksons sought to dispose of their plant immediately the line was finished, this advertisement appearing in Contract Journal on 1st July 1903. The reference to 'Dunsford' is odd at first sight, as other sources indicate that the Dicksons were based at Christow station yard, and it is inconceivable that locomotives and other heavy plant could have been at Dunsford literally. It is probable that Dunsford was used as the postal address for the Christow site which was, of course, distant from any of the villages and in fact only half a mile beyond the Dunsford parish boundary. The locomotives (for details of which see earlier in the chapter) were not sold at this auction, being repeatedly offered in advertisements up to 1905, although moved elsewhere by then. The list reveals that the Dicksons had used 3ft gauge (assuming that this is not an error for 2ft gauge?) track and wagons during the work, but not with locomotives on this gauge. It might be hypothesised that this had been used in the tunnels.

The GWR's 27th May report also suggested that, if all was satisfactory with the Board of Trade, the new line might open 'from, say 1st July' — the first reference to the actual opening date.

INSPECTION (11th JUNE 1903)
The special train for Col. Yorke on 11th June was booked to comprise:

2 Tank Engines
Exeter 3rd Class saloon No. 2512
Plymouth Inspection Coach at rear

and was to run:

St Davids 9.30 am
St Thomas 9.34/9.36 am
City Basin Jn 9.38 am and on to the new railway to Christow stopping
  as ordered.
Also from Christow to Ashton Level Crossing, and return to Exeter at
  a time uncertain.

In addition to the GWR officials and Bluett, Yorke was accompanied on the train by Knatchbull-Hugessen and his namesake V.W. Yorke, the ER Director.

Yorke did not often find much to criticise on the GWR by this date, and this inspection was no exception. However, he felt that there should be a 25 mph limit over the Exeter Railway 'for the present' and a 15 mph limit between Ashton and Christow for a short period as the ballasting was still incomplete at this date. The Alphington Road and Canal branches, as goods lines, were not inspected.

All was therefore now set up for the opening on 1st July. The signal box at Christow (the only one on the new line, as Christow was to be the only crossing place between City Basin Jn and Heathfield), and the ground frames at the other stations, were brought into use on 26th June.

J.W. Snell, who had been appointed as the first signalman (actually signal porter) at Christow, recalled to the *Express & Echo* in 1958 that he had 'travelled down a day or two [before the opening] by a special train carrying the men and stores for the new stations'. He was then on duty to signal the first train on the opening day.

OPENING
It was discovered that the 1st of July was an inconvenient date for a number of those involved, so the formal celebrations of the opening were changed to Tuesday 30th June. The Exeter Chamber of Commerce took charge of the organisation.

The festivities began with a luncheon for 200 in a large marquee erected in the Alphington Road goods yard — the very same spot where the first sod had been cut some 8½ years previously. This time, however, the day was one of glorious sunshine. Sir Edgar Vincent MP presided, and amongst those present were G.F.S. Warne and Walter Pring representing the Directorate (Knatchbull-Hugessen could not attend), Frank Faulkner the Company Secretary,

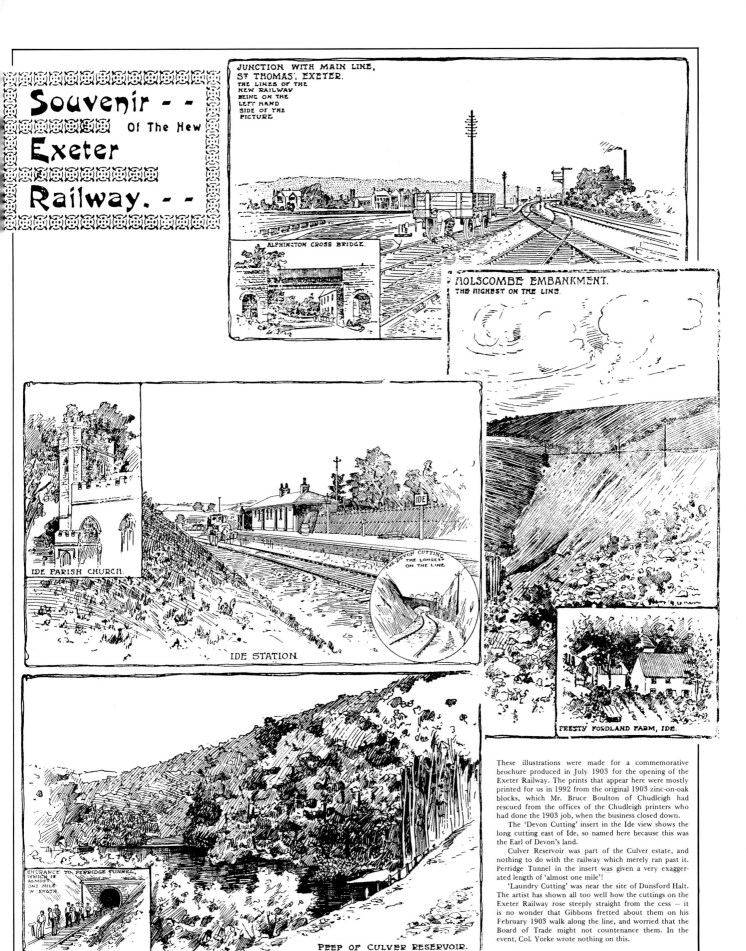

Souvenir - - Of The New Exeter Railway. - -

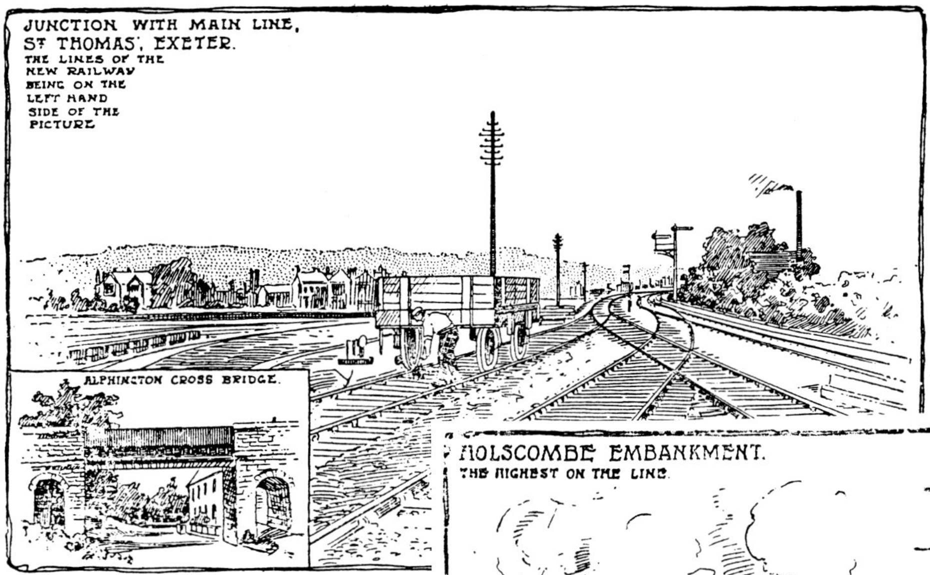

JUNCTION WITH MAIN LINE, ST THOMAS', EXETER. THE LINES OF THE NEW RAILWAY BEING ON THE LEFT HAND SIDE OF THE PICTURE

ALPHINGTON CROSS BRIDGE.

HOLSCOMBE EMBANKMENT. THE HIGHEST ON THE LINE.

PRETTY FORDLAND FARM, IDE.

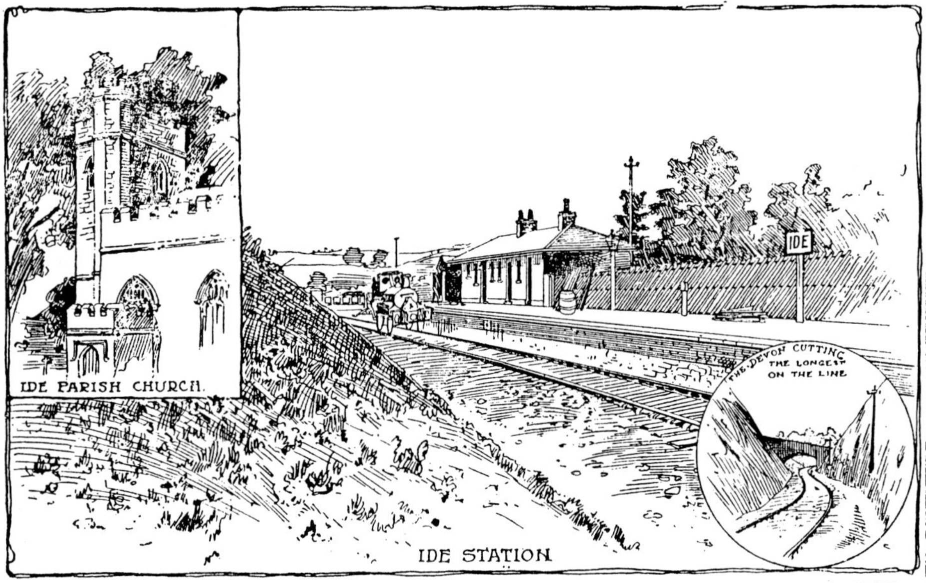

IDE PARISH CHURCH.

THE DEVON CUTTING THE LONGEST ON THE LINE

IDE STATION

ENTRANCE TO PERRIDGE TUNNEL, WHICH IS ALMOST ONE MILE IN LENGTH.

PEEP OF CULVER RESERVOIR.

These illustrations were made for a commemorative brochure produced in July 1903 for the opening of the Exeter Railway. The prints that appear here were mostly printed for us in 1992 from the original 1903 zinc-on-oak blocks, which Mr. Bruce Boulton of Chudleigh had rescued from the offices of the Chudleigh printers who had done the 1903 job, when the business closed down.

The 'Devon Cutting' insert in the Ide view shows the long cutting east of Ide, so named here because this was the Earl of Devon's land.

Culver Reservoir was part of the Culver estate, and nothing to do with the railway which merely ran past it. Perridge Tunnel in the insert was given a very exaggerated length of 'almost one mile'!

'Laundry Cutting' was near the site of Dunsford Halt. The artist has shown all too well how the cuttings on the Exeter Railway rose steeply straight from the cess – it is no wonder that Gibbons fretted about them on his February 1903 walk along the line, and worried that the Board of Trade might not countenance them. In the event, Col. Yorke wrote nothing on this.

LAUNDRY CUTTING.
THE DEEPEST ON THE LINE.

LEIGH CROSS BRIDGE.

Bluett, the Dicksons, J.H. Dickson, and John Campfield, the GWR Divisional Superintendent. After the meal, which was accompanied by 'selections' from the 1st Devon Imperial Yeomanry, Sir Edgar made a lengthy speech in which he thanked those who had assisted the company in the 1898 crisis (making a special mention of Pring) and Sheepshanks for salvaging the situation in 1902, after which he dilated on 'the wonderful continuance of the progress of the railway work which was being carried on in old England'.

After the speeches were ended, the company trooped along Alphington Road and Cowick Street to St Thomas station to join a special train. The 11-coach train, hauled by locomotive No. 1873 decorated with the usual flags and foliage, arrived from St David's (empty) just before 4.0, and departed to the explosion of fog signals exactly on the hour. *The Flying Post's* correspondent continued as follows:

'Passing almost above the luncheon tent the train gently turned from the main line to the branch, and with a slight bump or two settled down into an easy glide for Alphington, slipping through and above gardens and finding a brief seclusion from the direct rays of the sun in the deep cutting leading to Ide, along the edges of which were thick clusters of poppies, forming a brilliant scarlet dado to the earth wall on either side . . . Lifting up a little to the bridge carrying the line over Ide Hill, the procession of carriages ran through an orchard into Ide Station — the background of the village, or "Wessntown" as it is sounded in the soft speech of the neighbourhood. [The west end of Ide Village is known as "West Town"]. "All Ide" was of course on the platform, or as near to it as it could conveniently get, as they say in the shipping charters, and of course as being the metropolis of the line between its extremities there was a very decided halt to allow of a for-

CHRISTOW STATION

SHELDON CUTTING.

mal welcome and the presentation of an address by the local Parliament . . . There was such a crowd on the platform that the railway Directorate and the Parish Council deputation had a difficulty in finding each other, but after some shouting a junction was effected . . .'

Mr. F. Sims, the Parish Clerk, then read the Address, after which Joseph Braddon, the Parish Council Vice-Chairman, presented it to G.F.S. Warne.

On arrival at 'the toy station of Longdown', it was found that there was nobody in formal attendance, so the train set off directly for Christow, where it arrived at 4.40 pm

'. . . to be greeted by a multitude which surprised the visitors by its size. Not only was the station itself crowded, but the road bridge just beyond and all the various approaches had throngs of curious and happily-inclined sightseers who had come from such miles-distant places as Moretonhampstead . . . There was the Christow Band playing 'See the conquering hero comes' in greeting to the passengers, who, as they alighted, noted that the station, the signal box, and the various other appurtenances of a railway depot were rigged out with bunting, and that the air was full of gaiety and festivity . . .'

As Christow, like Ide, regarded itself as a place of importance, the proceedings had to begin with another Parish Council address, read by the Vice-chairman, Mr. J. Northcott, also on behalf of the neighbouring parishes. The company found the afternoon sun 'pouring with unusual mercilessness' during these formalities, and were glad to retire immediately afterwards to a Tea Marquee.

The official party then crossed the river to join the masses in sports and amusements in the meadow in front of the Teign House Inn. The fete had brought in peripatetic vendors from all over, but the most prominent was a local character who had parked a horse and cart with a huge cider barrel in the middle of the field, advertised by the words

'UP DASCOMBSLEIGH!
TO THE VORE!
OLD DEVONSHIRE CIDER
TO QUENCH YER THEST '

The cider was served out to the customers by an assistant who filled a garden watering can from the barrel and took it around the field.

The sports were undertaken with due seriousness, although the sophisticated Exeter reporter noted that 'athletic costumes were at a premium'. Sir Edgar Vincent presented the prizes, and the official party then returned to the

station and departed for Exeter at 7.10 pm, with only the briefest of halts at the intermediate stations. But the local celebrations continued unabated into the summer evening.

'a delightful picture, with the trees catching the slanting rays of the declining sun and making large patches of shade . . . Sun-scorched men gathered in groups to renew acquaintance and prophesy of the things to be made possible by the linking of 'Kestow' with the outside world; varying sizes of boys stood about with eyes opened as wide as possible; and bunches of milkmaids and other maids tripped along with arms around each other's waists as if, like Yum-Yum's schoolmates, "Each a little bit afraid is, Wondering what the world can be" . . .'

The day could not have gone better. Who of the participants would have believed it, one wonders, if they had been told that this was the last time such seemingly-established railway opening festivities would ever be seen in South Devon?

Earlier in the day, another special train provided by the Dicksons had been run from Christow to Exeter and back conveying 300 locals as a treat.[5]

Public services, including goods traffic to Alphington Road, began on Wednesday 1st July 1903, with a service of four passenger and one goods train each way. (The Canal branch did not open at this date, for reasons noted in Chapter 13.) It was reported that 225 passengers booked from St Thomas, and about 100 from St David's, during the course of the day. The timetable, and the GWR's working of the line at large, were, however, already the subject of dispute, and within a few days festivity was to be replaced by acrimony.

It was reported in December 1903 that £340,791 had been expended on the 8-mile line.

---

1. Even at discounted rates; in November 1896 they were offering £10 shares at £7.10s.
2. Webb Smith Elphinstone-Stone was born into a good family but chose to find employment in the GWR Loco & Carriage Dept. in comparatively humble posts. At this date he was employed at Swindon, but he had a large house at Cheriton Bishop (near Dunsford) which brought an interest in the ETV&C. He was forever writing to the ETV&C Secretary Faulkner with his suggestions for promoting the line. In 1897 he was transferred to Newton Abbot but his pro-ETV&C activities began to annoy his employers, the GWR, when relations between the two companies turned sour, and in due course he left the GWR's employ. Around 1915 he moved to Teign Terrace, Christow, and set himself up as a 'Motor Garage, agricultural implement and petrol dealer, etc', also acting as a Coal Merchant and running a 'conveyance' between Christow and Dunsford to connect with trains from Exeter. In later years he developed an unfondness for bathing and once amused the GWR office staff at St David's by recounting to them, on return from an excursion to Scotland, how amazing it was that he had had a compartment to himself both ways on such a crowded train!
3. The junction was strictly 'Exeter Railway Junction' and was (and is) always so called by the Engineers. To the operating side, however, it was always 'City Basin Junction' and that name is used in this book. The adoption of this name was perhaps inevitable given that the signal box so called was actually located at the Exeter Railway junction.
4. The Dicksons were given a separate contract for building the Canal Branch in May 1902.
5. This train probably consisted of Dickson's loco and trucks. Mrs Margaret Howard recalls the passed-on story of how William Slater Howard's wife went from Ashton in her Sunday best to attend the opening ceremonies at Christow, and could not resist the offer of the free trip to Exeter. By the time she got back to Christow after the journey in 'cattle trucks', she was filthy!

MAJOR DATES IN THE COMPLETION OF THE LINE

3.1903	GWR lay in permanent junction at Christow.
17.5.1903	GWR lay in junction at City Basin Jn.
5–6.1903	GWR relay Ashton–Christow section.
11.6.1903	Board of Trade Inspection.
26.6.1903	Christow Signal Box, and Ground Frames at Longdown, Ide and City Basin Jn, brought into use.
30.6.1903	Ceremonial opening.
1.7.1903	Public traffic begins.

Higher Ashton village and Ashton church in 1912.

Chapman collection, cty. Steven Court

A view across the straggling village of Christow.

Chapman collection, cty. Mrs. M. Piller

CHAPTER ELEVEN

THE EXETER RAILWAY COMPANY
1903–1923

ON the very same day that the opening celebrations were being held (30th June 1903), the Exeter Railway Act 1903 received the Royal Assent. This authorised the issuing of a further £100,000 debenture stock, needed primarily to redeem the Lloyds Bonds issued to the Dicksons and now held by Sheepshanks. In fact it was not until 1906 that this was done; it naturally made Sheepshanks a very large and influential debenture holder.

DISPOSING OF BLUETT'S SERVICES

The ER had to maintain the line until 1st July 1904 and Bluett's services were therefore retained for this period. It was agreed that Bluett would take over the company's Bedford Circus, Exeter office himself and be free to act as a Consulting Engineer for others in addition to his ER duties. He retained an ER salary (£120 p.a. less than before) and in addition to maintaining the line he was to generally 'look after the interests of the company and watch the GWR'. So far as the GWR's local officers in Exeter were concerned, Bluett *was* the ER in the 1903/4 period, and his presence on the scene proved very useful to the ER as their relationship with the GWR deteriorated.

When the time came to dispose of Bluett's services, the matter seems to have been badly handled, and Bluett was moved to complain of poor treatment. Matters were sorted out in January 1905, and in due course Bluett found a new job as Engineer to the Buenos Ayres & Pacific Railway and sailed for Argentina in September 1905.

THE BOARD 1903–23

With no large local shareholders to retain a dominant interest (as the TVR had in Lord Haldon), the Exeter Railway provides a good example of how such small companies were likely to fall under the control of debenture holders with no local associations.

Reference was made in Chapter 9 to the election to the Board in June 1899 of V.W. Yorke on the nomination of the Governor of the Bank of England, which held £36,935 of debenture stock by this date and was therefore in a good position to seek a representative on the Board. Yorke had no previous railway experience but soon acquired a strong position on the Board. In December 1899 he was elected to the 'General Purposes Committee' and this brought the edging out of R.J. Jenkins from the centre of things, until in February 1902 Jenkins was asked by Knatchbull-Hugessen to resign so that Yorke could become *de facto* Deputy Chairman (he was never officially noted as such). Jenkins' resignation went down on the record as 'ill health', but he bitterly regretted it afterwards. For the next twenty years he wrote regularly from his new home in Linden Road, Bexhill, asking if there was any pos-

sibility of his being restored to the Board, but he was always either ignored or fobbed off. Eventually the company started ensuring that Jenkins was not sent copies of the notices for the shareholders' meetings! (The Board probably merely saw Jenkins as too old — born in 1839 and part of the Gooch age on the GWR, he was now really out of his time.)

The real changes in the Board came in November 1904 when Knatchbull-Hugessen stood down as Chairman (he remained a Director) so that Yorke could take the post. At the same time Joseph Tiplady, the Revd Sheepshanks' Yorkshire Agent,[1] and John Dickson, the former contractor, were elected to the Board, and Walter Pring resigned (ostensibly on the grounds that the GWR would not give

Vincent Wodehouse Yorke, seen here in later life, was born in 1869 the son of John Reginald Yorke, the squire of Forthampton, Gloucs, and MP for Tewkesbury. Vincent was educated at Eton and Kings College, Cambridge, and became a Fellow of Kings in 1895. However, in 1899 he gave up the scholarly life for marriage and a business career. He became Managing Director of the brewers' engineers H. Pontifex & Sons Ltd., based at the Farringdon Works, Shoe Lane, London EC, who made copper mash tuns and spirit distillation plants. He was also a director of the Westminster Bank. Having been introduced to railways by the Exeter Railway, he became a director and then chairman of the Mexican Railway. On one occasion in the 1920s a bridge collapsed under the chairman's train and he and his wife were reported killed, which enabled him to read his own obituary in *The Times*! Another chairmanship was of the Argentine North Eastern Railway. He died in 1957. *Cty. J. S. Yorke*

THE EXETER, TEIGN VALLEY & CHAGFORD RAILWAY COMPANY
renamed THE EXETER RAILWAY COMPANY 1898

Chairman	1883–1893	Lt. Col. Edwin Fox (*deceased*)
	(1893–1894)	Col. John Walker) (*resigned*)
	1894–1895	David F. Carmichael (*resigned as Chairman*)
	1895–1904	Hon. C(ecil) M(arcus) Knatchbull-Hugessen (*resigned as Chairman*)
	1904–1923	V(incent) W(odehouse) Yorke
Secretary	1883	R.J. Palmer
	1894–1895	E.S. Warne (*temp.*)
	1895–1904	Frank Faulkner
	1904–1923	W.J. Calder
Solicitor	1883–1894	B.C. Gidley of Gidley & Bayliffe (later Gidley & Caunter), and successors.
	1894–1896	Hurrell & Mayo
	1896–1923	Mayo & Co
Engineers	1882–1893	Francis W. Fox & William Lidstone.
	1894–1904	Robert Elliott-Cooper (Consulting Engineer)
	1893–1896	William Lidstone (Engineer)
	1896–1904	Frederick Bluett (Engineer)
Directors	1883–1893	Lt. Col. Edwin Fox (Chairman) (*deceased*)
	1883–1894	Col. John Walker (*resigned*)
	1883–1894	John Norton
	(1888)	F(rancis) D(rummond) Fulford (*lapsed*)
	(1888), 1894–1896	Lord Exmouth (*resigned*)
	(1888), 1894–1904	Walter Pring (*resigned*)
	1894–1897	David F. Carmichael (Chairman 1894–5) (*resigned*)
	1894–1895	Thomas Cory (*resigned*)
	1894–1914	Hon. C(ecil) M(arcus) Knatchbull-Hugessen (Chairman 1895–1904) (*resigned*)
	1894–1897	Lord Norreys (*resigned*)
	1895–1902	R(ichard) J(onathan) Jenkins (*resigned*)
	1898–1914	G(eorge) F(rederick) S(pencer) Warne (*resigned*)
	1899–1923	V(incent) W(odehouse) Yorke (Chairman 1904–23)
	1904–1923	Joseph Tiplady
	1904–1923	John Dickson

EXETER RAILWAY COMPANY : GROSS RECEIPTS OF LINE AND ER's INCOME 1903–1922

	Gross Receipts of line	ER's income	
	£	£	
1903	1451	773	(½ year only)
1904	3394	1799	
1905	3829	2128	
1906	4678	2564	
1907	5445	3044	
1908	5289	2902	
1909	5661	3090	
1910	6429	3499	
1911	7211	3926	
1912	7386	4013	
1913	8764	4776	
1914	9478	5189	
1915	8788	4773	
1916	8794	4778	Government
1917	8794	4774	Control
1918	8790	4774	period — 1913
1919	8790	4774	figures used as
1920	8789	4773	basis of payment
1921	nk	5129	
1922	nk	6005	

Source: RAIL 253/747. Income figures include rebates.

The 1907 figure included a sum of £382 for previous years, as a result of adjustments ordered by the Railway & Canal Commissioners. If this be allowed for, it will be seen that the receipts actually increased regularly every year.

him a free pass to Board meetings in London, but his passing really reflected the fact that the company did not now need an Exeter face). Additionally, the Secretary, Frank Faulkner, was disposed of, and the ER's 'office' address moved to Yorke's Farringdon Works, where W.J. Calder acted as Secretary. The Board meetings were also now held here.

Yorke and Dickson were constituted as a 'Committee' to deal with the company's affairs between Board meetings, and from 1904 to 1923 it was they who really ran the show, with Knatchbull-Hugessen and Warne (who both resigned in 1914 and were not replaced) taking more of a back seat.

Up to 1908 there was still enough work for the Board to meet every three months or so. There was much activity in 1903–5 in the conflict with the GWR over the way the line was being run; this degenerated into a court case and is discussed in detail in Chapter 13 as it was inextricably linked with the development of traffic and train services. The ER Board never really developed a trusting relationship with the GWR. The Board was also kept occupied until 1908 by financial problems, as discussed in the next section, and then by the plans of J.H. Dickson (the former contractors' Engineer) and John Dickson himself to set up stone quarries in the valley in the hope of boosting the ER's revenues, which brought a need for improvements to Christow station.

From 1909 the workload decreased considerably and there were indeed only eight Board meetings held in the years 1910–1922.

FINANCES

As had been the case with the TVR, it became obvious immediately the first traffic returns were drawn up that the ER had nowhere near the income needed to pay the interest on the debenture stocks, let alone pay anything on the ordinary shares. Instead of the £10,000 plus per annum net revenue promised in the 1898 prospectus, the first full year 1904 produced a mere £1,799. This did soon start to improve as the stone traffic grew, but even so it was still clear that the £6,200 a year needed to pay the full interest on the debentures (once the Lloyds Bonds had been converted into debenture stock) was not going to be achieved in the foreseeable future. In fact, no interest was paid at all in 1903–7.

Accordingly, the ER now found itself having to go to the Court of Chancery for an 1867 Act 'Scheme' to reconstruct its finances, to avoid having to appoint a Receiver. The 'Scheme' was authorised in November 1907 and took effect from January 1908. The whole of the old debenture stock (£154,698 had been issued by this date) was called in and replaced by the same sum in debenture stocks, but divided now into two classes, ¼ of the total being first debenture stock (4%) as the priority stock, and ¾ of the total being 'A' debentures on which up to 5% would be paid if sufficient income were available. (In fact it was recognised that the 'A' debentures were never likely to receive their full 5%.) Each holder received new stocks in the same ¼/¾ proportion. A main aim was to make the new first debenture stock a marketable stock; up to this date ER debentures had been all but unsaleable. The 1907 scheme also authorised the issuing of a further £20,000 in new debenture stock, beyond the £166,000 already authorised.

The *Devon & Exeter Gazette* was critical of the arrangement which, they pointed out, was purely in the interest of the debenture holders 'the largest of whom are connected with the Board', and gave no hope to the ordinary shareholders who would now 'never get a farthing for having parted with their money'. (That should have been obvious long before 1907!) The newspaper also suggested that the company had purposely held the meeting to authorise the scheme in London at 11.30 am, instead of the usual lunchtime start, in order to ensure that Exeter people could not get there in time! But the fact was that the debenture holders were entitled to priority.

The full 4% was paid on the new first debentures from the start (1908). With the stone traffic on the line continuing to grow, the interest paid on the 'A' debentures increased from ⅜% in 1908 to a semi-respectable 2% in 1914. It might have increased further but the Government Control period intervened and the 'A' debentures were held to their 1913 interest of 1¾% for the remaining years of the company's life, so that the ER shareholders did not really benefit as they might have from the success of John Dickson's Scatter Rock quarry operations.

ABSORPTION

The Exeter Railway caused the GWR more trouble in the 1922–3 absorption negotiations than any other company. This was partly due to the ER Board's longstanding grudge against the GWR as a result of the events of 1903–5 (see Chapter 13), and partly because the Christow stone traffic had been increasing substantially in the years since 1913 so that the ER was very reluctant to commence negotiations on the basis of the 1913 revenue figures which (thanks to the Government Control period) were all that was available in the way of statistics in 1922. Another factor, no doubt, was that as the ER was a recently-built line, the original shareholders who had parted with their own money were still alive and in positions of influence; with most companies, the original shareholders were long since dead and their heirs were resigned to the fact of their holdings being of little value.

An initial meeting at Paddington on 19th January 1922, attended by Yorke and Calder, the Secretary, did not get anywhere as Yorke would not negotiate until 1921 traffic figures were available. Further meetings in July, November, and December also failed to produce any sign of agreement, so the ER's case ended up being taken to the Railways Amalgamation Tribunal, along with the Midland & South Western Junction (which was, in the event, largely sorted out before the hearing) and the Forest of Dean Central (which caused problems because the company had long since ceased to exist for all practical purposes, so that nobody actually owned the line!).

The GWR took the view that under the 1921 Act the value of each company was to be judged solely on the basis of its 1913 revenue. The ER denied this and argued that the Act required the full circumstances of each case to be taken into consideration. In this view they were supported by Sir Sam Fay who was acting as an adviser to the Association of Smaller Railway Companies (which the ER had joined in 1920). At the initial Tribunal hearing on 5th May 1923 it was ruled that the ER's view on this matter was the correct one, and this enabled the ER to present its full intended case to the Tribunal on 6th and 8th June.

The ER's case concentrated on the large increases of traffic in recent years and the good future prospects of Scatter Rock quarry (Harold Martin the quarry manager was one of the ER's main witnesses, along with Yorke and Fay). By various means they sought to claim that the ER's net income could be £10,677 p.a. instead of the £6,005 actually received in 1922. (The aim was to show that the income could be enough to pay the full interest on the 'A' debentures, in which case the GWR would have to give the 'A' debenture holders GWR debentures at par instead of at a lesser rate.) The ER also pointed out that the line had 'value' to the GWR as a diversionary route, and had been used for this purpose in 1921 and again in March 1923 when (conveniently for the ER's case!) the Teign Valley route had been open 24 hrs for 10 days after a cliff fall at Teignmouth.

The GWR's case sought to show that the ER's recent revenue increases were 'precarious' because they were dependent on a single traffic (the stone at Christow) which might decline in future, and that traffic other than the Christow stone was in fact less in 1922 than in 1913. (This was partly because of the very poor passenger service provided by the GWR in the years after 1919; another factor was the fall-off in Trusham stone traffic routed over the ER.) The GWR also tried to denigrate the line's value for diversionary purposes, and pointed out that (contrary to the 1883 agreement) the ER works were not in fact suited for double track.

In their 'final offer' in December 1922, the GWR had proposed to pay £107,653 for the company (which had a book value of £374,176). The ER had held out for £139,164 although their case to the Tribunal, which was obviously intended as a bargaining posture, had claimed no less than £219,551! The Tribunal's decision, given by letter on 11th June 1923, equated to a value of £115,516. The ER Board seem to have been very satisfied with this. It had always been agreed that the 'First Debenture' holders would receive GWR debentures at par; the Tribunal left it to the ER themselves to decide how the remainder of the payment should be shared between the 'A' debenture holders and the ordinary shareholders, and to this end a private meeting of the leading holders was arranged on

28th June, followed by a Special General Meeting of the ER company on 12th July.

The GWR (Exeter Railway) Absorption Scheme was made on 3rd August 1923 (taking effect as from 1st July 1923) and on 8th August the ER shareholders were sent an explanation of the award. A list of holders was prepared for Paddington, and the Exeter Railway Company ceased to be.

1. Tiplady was a Land Agent living in Killinghall, near Harrogate, and was responsible for Sheepshanks' Yorkshire estates. After his appointment to the Board he took an active interest in the ER's affairs. In 1911 he also became a Director of John Dickson's Scatter Rock Macadams Ltd.

EXETER RAILWAY Co. AUTHORISED AND ISSUED CAPITAL

| | Authorised | | Issued | |
	Shares	Debentures	Shares	Debentures
1883 Act	£240,000	£80,000	see below	
1894 Act	24,000	8,000	see below	
	264,000	88,000		
reduced by				
1898 Act to	198,000	66,000	£198,000	4% £66,000 Deb Stock 88,698 (as at 1907)
1903 Act	–	100,000	–	Above replaced 1908 by new 1907 Scheme stocks to totals (including further issues) of:-
1907 Scheme	–	20,000	–	
				1st Debs (4%) 44,632
				'A' Debs (5%) 132,984
	198,000	186,000	198,000	177,616

CAPITAL OF ER
as at 1923, in order of preference for interest/dividend

1st Debentures	£44,632	— Full 4% interest paid since 1908
'A' Debentures	132,984	— Part interest paid since 1908
Ordinary Shares	196,560*	— No dividend ever paid
TOTAL	£374,176	

*Quoted so, as there were £1,440 unpaid calls on the £198,000.

PAYMENT MADE BY GWR
on takeover of ER Company in 1923

			Sum Paid
1st Debentures	£100 GWR 4% Deb. stock for each £100		£44,632
'A' Debentures	£30 GWR 5% Consol. Pref. stock and £15. 18s. 3d GWR Consol. Ord. stock	for each £100	39,895 / 21,161
Ordinary Shares	10s cash per £10 share		9,828
	Total sum paid by GWR		£115,516

EXETER RAILWAY Co. MAJOR SHAREHOLDERS AT 1923

	1st Debs. £	'A' Debs. £	Ord. Shares £
Lord Brabourne	–	108	6,520
James & John Dickson	2,187	13,425	15,550
James Dickson	180	15,403	15,560
V.W. Yorke	47	1,336	12,220
William Sheepshanks (son of Rev. T.)	21,712	43,411	–
Edith M.L. Dickson, Bridford	136	338	–
Rebecca Tiplady, Killinghall	629	1,978	–
Mrs E. Jenkins (widow of R.J. Jenkins)	–	–	1,730
T.C. Pring (inherited from Walter Pring)	17	52	2,260
The London Trust Co.	–	30,000	22,500
Coutts & Co	1,603	–	–
Alexander Dick & William Whyte, Bishopsgate	8,000	–	–
N. Spens & W.T. Knight, Old Bond St.	2,876	–	–
Stock Conversion & Investment Trust Ltd	–	8,627	–
Viscount Hambleton	461	1,382	3,100
Mrs E. Bullard, Bexhill	22	65	15,570
E.C.A. Byrom	–	–	1,000
F. Bluett	–	–	870

Only the major shareholders and debenture holders are listed here (plus, for interest, a number of other persons associated closely with the company).

It will be seen that the Dicksons had altogether £62,305 (17%) and Sheepshanks £64,712 (17%) of the company's total capital, making John Dickson's and Tiplady's positions on the Board fairly unquestionable.

It will also be seen why the Dicksons and Yorke ensured that the Ordinary Shareholders received some recompense in 1923!

Some people had evidently sold off some of their 1st Debs stock since 1908 (paying their full percentage, these were marketable) and there had no doubt been many other changes over the years. Nevertheless, one can take these figures as a reasonably good guide to the relative influences of people after the company stabilised in 1903–5.

Source: Exeter Railway Co. list prepared for the GWR in 1923, in RAIL 1057/189.

CHAPTER TWELVE

AN ISLAND UNTO ITSELF:
THE TEIGN VALLEY LINE
1882–1903

WE now return in time to 1882, to begin our consideration of the line's traffic and train services throughout its life.

In traffic terms the TVR could not have opened at a worse time. The final collapse of lead mining in 1880 had left only the Bridford Barytes Mine and Great Rock Mine as active industrial locations, and neither of them had a very large output at this period, so to all intents and purposes the Teign Valley had by 1882 reverted to being purely an agricultural area. This was a disastrous change for the economics of the line, which would certainly never have been promoted but for the mineral traffic that had been anticipated.

The line was also lumbered with two further problems which prevented the development of goods traffic in particular. Firstly, there was the break of gauge at Heathfield, which lasted in the event for ten years after the line opened. It is not known exactly what the transhipping charges at Heathfield were, but in similar situations elsewhere (e.g. Exeter) the transhipping charges were such that in practice it was cheaper for traders to cart by road for several miles to the nearest depot of the desired gauge, rather than put the load into 'wrong gauge' trucks at the depot most immediately close at hand. We can safely assume that Chudleigh traders in particular continued to make much use of Heathfield for goods traffic in the years prior to 1892, to the TVR's loss. (In contrast, the break of gauge did not really affect the passenger traffic. Given the practices of the time, the TVR trains would probably only have run to/from Heathfield even if there had not been a break of gauge there, so the compulsory change at Heathfield would not have been seen as a particular disadvantage of the gauge situation.)

Secondly, the line offered a very lengthy (and therefore expensive) route from the valley to Exeter and beyond. It was 32 miles from Teign House to Exeter by railway, compared with only 8 by road, and this actually led to the continued use of road transport in some cases, despite the much higher costs per mile.

These difficulties ensured that, prior to 1892 at least, nobody would regard the railway as offering sufficiently improved transport costs to justify starting up any new industrial activity in the valley.

The TVR's detractors had doubted even in the 1860s whether any railway could pay in such a thinly-populated area. In the changed circumstances of 1882 it stood no chance at all of paying. Traffic on the line in the 1880s and '90s was pathetically low. There was no growth at all in the '80s, and even the removal of the gauge problem in 1892, and the addition of a significant construction traffic for the Exeter Railway in 1895–1902, could not bring a respectable total traffic.

Thanks to the lack of traffic, no changes of significance were needed to the infrastructure prior to 1903. The line was kept in good condition by the GWR despite its poor economics; R.J. Jenkins visited the line in November 1894 to check on the state of things and reported back 'I was much pleased with the character and condition of the Permanent Way, Bridges, Stations and Buildings, &c'.

TRAIN SERVICES: THE OCTOBER 1882 TIMETABLE

In the 1882–1903 period, the provision of good passenger connections to/from Newton Abbot at Heathfield (which was always to be the most important factor in Teign Valley line timetabling) was in fact the sole determinant of the Teign Valley timetable.

When the Teign Valley line opened in October 1882, there were four passenger and one goods train each way on the Moretonhampstead branch, the passenger trains being worked by a single loco and train set stabled overnight at Moreton. The Teign Valley service was arranged to give five minute (or so) connections at Heathfield with all four of the Moretonhampstead passenger trains. The Teign Valley line, too, was worked by a single loco and train set whose daily operations were an exact parallel of the Moretonhampstead train; it began its day at Ashton in time to connect with the first Moreton–Newton train, and after its four return trips (with lengthy layovers at each end) it ended up at Ashton in the evening. One of the Teign Valley services each way was a 'Passenger & Goods' train, the low level of goods traffic making a separate goods train unnecessary until 1901 (see below).

The timetable printed in the October 1882 GWR Timetable showed a 20 minute journey time Ashton to Heathfield (and vice-versa), but this lasted only a week or so before Rich demanded a 12 mph speed limit and the trains had to be decelerated. The new timings involved a journey time of 30 minutes southbound and 31 minutes northbound, giving an end-to-end average of almost exactly 12 mph for the six-mile journey. This enabled a facade of compliance with Rich's edict whilst actually of course requiring running at 20 mph or more! The 'Passenger & Goods' trains were allowed 36 minutes.

There were no Sunday trains on the Teign Valley line; this was to remain the case throughout the line's history.

INITIAL TRAIN SERVICE 9th OCTOBER 1882,
with amended times (following Rich's inspection)
from mid-October (shown in bold)

DOWN

	am		am		pm		pm	
Teign House	–	**–**	–	**–**	–	**–**	–	**–**
Ashton	7.15	**7.5**	10.55	**10.40**	2.10	**2.5**	7.5	**6.55**
Trusham	7.22	**7.16**	11.2	**10.52**	2.18	**2.16**	7.12	**7.6**
Chudleigh	7.29	**7.26**	11.9	**11.6**	2.28	**2.26**	7.19	**7.16**
Heathfield	7.35	**7.35**	11.15	**11.16**	2.35	**2.35**	7.25	**7.25**

connections:

Heathfield	7.40am	11.20am	2.40pm	7.32pm
Newton Abbot	7.53	11.32	2.53	7.45

UP

connections:

Newton Abbot	8.27am	12.0noon	5.33pm	7.32pm
Heathfield	8.39	12.12	5.45	8.37

	am		pm		pm		pm	
Heathfield	8.45	**8.45**	12.20	**12.20**	5.50	**5.50**	8.45	**8.45**
Chudleigh	8.55	**8.56**	12.27	**12.31**	5.57	**6.5**	8.52	**8.56**
Trusham	9.5	**9.6**	12.34	**12.41**	6.4	**6.15**	8.59	**9.6**
Ashton	9.11	**9.16**	12.40	**12.51**	6.10	**6.26**	9.5	**9.16**
Teign House	–	**–**	–	**–**	–	**–**	–	**–**

Note: In the initial 9.10.1882 service in the Working Timetable, all trains are shown as 'Passenger'; but the extended journey times suggest that the 2.10pm down and 8.45am up were actually 'Passenger and Goods'.

The amended times in bold are actually from the May 1883 Working Timetable. The amendments to the October 1882 Working Timetable do not survive, but these amended times must have been introduced in mid-October 1882 in order to comply with Rich's requirement.

In the May 1883 Working Timetable, the 10.40am down and 5.50pm up are shown as 'Passenger and Goods', and have 5 minutes allowed at Chudleigh in both directions (also 2 minutes at Trusham in the down direction).

IMPROVEMENTS TO THE PASSENGER SERVICE

In July 1883 a fifth train, in mid-afternoon, was added to the Moretonhampstead branch timetable. This was a summer-only service, disappearing in October but reappearing in subsequent summers' timetables. It did not have Teign Valley connections in 1883 or 1884, and this brought complaints from Chudleigh people, a memorial being presented to the GWR Board in October 1883. In July 1885 the GWR gave in to the pressure and introduced a Teign Valley connection, but running from Heathfield to Chudleigh and back only. (There was plenty of time to run to Ashton and back, but clearly no justification was seen for this. The loco must have run round the train in the goods siding at Chudleigh.)

From 1892 both the Moretonhampstead and the Chudleigh afternoon trains started to run also on Wednesdays and fourth Tuesdays in the winter, as they were useful for people returning from Newton Abbot market. From 1895 the Chudleigh train was extended to run to and from Ashton.

The slow running introduced in 1882 cannot have been attractive to passengers. In 1892 it was found possible to accelerate the Heathfield–Ashton & vice-versa journey time to 24 minutes — it is not clear that the Board of Trade's permission was sought for this! — and in 1903 it was to be cut further to 18 minutes.

No attempt was made to run the Teign Valley trains through to Newton Abbot when this became possible after

---

TEIGN VALLEY RLY. STATIONS — RETURN OF TRAFFIC for AUGUST 1893

	Passenger Single Tickets				Passenger Return Tickets					Total Passengers	Passenger Revenue	Parcels	Dogs	Misc Revenue	Goods Tons	Goods Revenue
	1	2	3	Parly	1	2	3	Parly	Exc'ns							
Chudleigh	13	28	1092	1719	10	64	583	34	262	3805	£39.15s.8d	446	9	£2.9s.0d	243T. 5Cwts	£15.0s.6d
Trusham	–	2	87	243	1	3	61	4	–	401	£5.18s.5d	89	2	9s.1d	12T.12Cwts	15s.8d
Ashton	1	13	258	516	–	4	111	32	–	935	£23.6s.6d	44	3	19s.0d	95T.8Cwts	£6.19s.11d
Teign House	–	–	–	–	–	–	–	–	–	–	–	–	–	–	225T.11Cwts	£19.1s.0d
TOTAL	14	43	1437	2478	11	71	755	70	262	5141	£69.0s.7d	579	14	£3.17s.1d	576T.16Cwts	£41.17s.1d

Passenger Season Tickets — Nil
Horses & Carriages — Nil

This one month's return is the only one to survive for the pre-1899 period and thus the only one to show in detail the line's traffic before the quarry traffic began. The total revenue of £114 tallies with the 12-months' figure for 1893 of £1,175 given in the TVR revenue table at p.51; the summer months were of course much busier on the passenger front than the winter months.

Counting Returns as double, the number of passenger journeys booked is 6,310; divide this by the 270 trains run per month, and one gets a figure of 23 passengers per train on average. Of course one must add to this the passengers booked to the line from outside; even so one doubts if the total number of passengers per train was above (say) 40 — and that in the busiest month of the year. (Later years' figures show that the number of passengers at the winter low was about 60% of the summer.) The goods figures represent a mere three loaded trucks per day.

The overwhelming importance of Chudleigh on the passenger front is very clear. There are only 1,552 passenger journeys booked north of Chudleigh, probably representing an average of 10 passengers per train north of Chudleigh. Nevertheless, the Chudleigh passengers did not actually bring much revenue to the TVR company because of the short distance they travelled on the TVR line.

The very low number of 1st Class passengers represents only 1 or 2 a day, in other words the 1st Class accommodation was unused on most trains.

On the goods front, Teign House is the most important station in revenue terms (and this before its takings were boosted by Exeter Rly. construction traffic).

Trusham Station does not really justify its existence at all. Who would have guessed that 20 years later it would be the 6th busiest station in the whole Exeter Division?

TEIGN VALLEY BRANCH.

SINGLE LINE, worked by Train Staff without Tickets.   No Block Telegraph.
Only one Engine in steam allowed on this Branch, or two coupled together.
Form of Staff, round ; Colour, Green ; worked between Heathfield and Teign House.   No Train Tickets.

Down Trains. — Week Days.

Distances from Heathfield M C	STATIONS.	1 A Passenger arr.	dep.	3 D Goods arr.	dep.	5 A Passenger arr.	dep.	7 A Passenger arr.	dep.	9 A Mixed arr.	dep.	11 A Passenger arr.	dep.
—	Heathfield	A.M. —	A.M. 8 25	A.M.	A.M.	P.M. —	P.M. 12 22	P.M. —	P.M. 3 45	P.M. —	P.M. 6 17	P.M. —	P.M. 9 5
0 20	Bovey Lane Crossing			..	RR								
1 10	Knighton Crossing												
2 32	Chudleigh	8 33	8 35			12 30	12 32	3 53	—	6 25	6 32	9 13	9 14
4 21	Trusham	8 42	8 43			12 39	12 40			6 40	6 45	9 21	9 22
6 16	Ashton	8 50		—	9 20	12 47	—			6 52	—	9 29	
7 58	Teign House			9 26	—								

Up Trains.

Distances Teign House M C	STATIONS, &c.	1 A Passenger arr.	dep.	3 D Goods arr.	dep.	5 A Mixed arr.	dep.	7 A Passenger arr.	dep.	9 A Passenger arr.	dep.	11 A Passenger arr.	dep.
—	Teign House	A.M.	A.M.	A.M. —	A.M. 9 30	A.M.	A.M.	P.M.	P.M.	P.M.	P.M.	P.M.	P.M.
1 42	Ashton	—	7 13	9 36	—	—	10 32	—	1 48			—	7 8
3 37	Trusham	7 20	7 21			10 40	10 44	1 55	1 56			7 15	7 16
5 26	Chudleigh	7 28	7 29	RR		10 52	10 59	2 3	2 4	—	4 35	7 23	7 24
6 48	Knighton Crossing												
7 38	Bovey Lane Crossing												
7 58	Heathfield	7 37	—			11 8	—	2 12	—	4 43		7 32	—

No Sunday Trains.

April 1894 Working Timetable. The fifth (Chudleigh) train was run daily as early as April in this summer. Note the change in direction of travel (in 1893), and the retitling of the 'Passenger & Goods' trains as 'Mixed' (effected Nov. 1892).

1892; the low traffic did not justify it (and the connection installed in 1892 did not permit through running as a regular signalled move, in any case). It does however seem that Excursions were sometimes run through from Newton Abbot to Chudleigh in the 1892–1916 period.

Further trains were added to the Moretonhampstead branch timetable from the 1890s and 1900s onwards, but Teign Valley connections were not provided.

TEIGN HOUSE SIDING

Although there is little doubt that Teign House Siding did open for traffic along with the rest of the line on 9th October 1882, there were no trains timetabled on the Ashton–Teign House section in the line's first five years. The Working Timetable does not offer any explanation of the situation and one is left to assume that the loco, which had plenty of time available during layovers at Ashton, worked any trucks to/from Teign House as required. In October 1887 a timetabled train was at last introduced, a 9.20 am Ashton–Teign House–Ashton 'Runs as Required' Goods (worked by the branch loco and crew during an Ashton layover). This was allowed only 4 minutes for shunting at Teign House! The outwards trucks could be sent on from Ashton immediately on the daily 'Passenger & Goods' train, but, if the timetable was adhered to, inwards trucks for Teign House would have had to rest at Ashton overnight.

In January 1883, and again in July 1886, local memorials were sent to the GWR asking for a passenger service to

be commenced to Teign House. But with the ETV&C line on the cards, and the low traffic levels, there was little incentive for the TVR and GWR to invest in building a passenger station at Teign House.

Traffic at Teign House Siding was given a noticeable boost by the Dicksons' construction traffic for the Exeter Railway, as the following figures show:

	Ordinary traffic	Contractors' traffic	Total
1898	£147.11s.9d	£ 13. 3s.3d	£160.15s.0d
1899	177. 6s.7d	210.17s.0d	388. 3s.7d
1900	257. 8s.6d	137. 2s.9d	394.11s.3d
1901	234.15s.0d	157.10s.0d	392. 5s.0d
1902	198.18s.6d	117. 2s.6d	316. 1s.0d

After the ETV&C's decision in 1896 to build a full station at Christow only a few yards north of Teign House Siding (see O.S. maps in Chapter 18 for the relationship of the two), it must have become clear that the siding's days were numbered. But no real thought was given to the matter until May 1903 when the ER hinted to the GWR that they might be prepared to make an annual payment to the TVR for loss of traffic if the siding were to be closed and the traffic diverted to the ER's goods yard at Christow. The GWR was left to act as intermediary. In the event the TVR proved amenable, accepting an annual £203 (representing an average of the previous five years traffic minus the ER construction traffic).

The siding therefore closed with effect from 1st July 1903. It was lifted immediately afterwards.

THE FIRST GOODS TRAIN (1901)

In the late 1890s a significant goods traffic arose on the line for the first time, with the start of the first stone quarrying at Trusham. This began to make it difficult for the Mixed trains to keep time or keep within permitted loads. Therefore, as from December 1901, a 'Runs as Required' Heathfield–Trusham–Ashton–Trusham–Heathfield Goods train was introduced.

OPERATING THE LINE 1882–1903

Although the Teign Valley timetable up to 1903 was designed to be worked by one locomotive, it is clear that there were in fact originally two locos shedded at Ashton. Whilst this was unusual for a branch line terminus, it was clearly necessary in this case because of the line's 'wrong-gauge' isolation which prevented another loco being brought in from outside to cover for regular or unplanned maintenance, as would be done on other lines. The need to provide a second loco at Ashton naturally added to the line's unprofitability, the two locos having very low mileage figures.

By 1902, when detailed allocation records begin, there was only one loco at Ashton, and one guesses that the reduction from two to one was made in 1892 when the change of gauge on the Moretonhampstead branch made it possible to bring in a replacement loco from Newton Abbot when necessary.

Although full information is not available, it seems likely that the locomotives at Ashton were always of the '517' class.

The branch remained totally self-contained right up to 1903; its loco and crew did not venture beyond Heathfield, and no locos or crews from elsewhere had any workings over the branch. The branch staff would have been on duty for the full day but their life was not a strenuous one and they had every Sunday off.

TIMETABLE JULY 1902
Showing the new Goods train

DOWN

connections:

Newton Abbot	8.15			12.2	3.0	5.47	9.0
Heathfield	8.25			12.12	3.10	5.57	9.10

	A Passenger am		D Goods (RR) am	D Goods (RR) am*		A Passenger pm	A Passenger pm	A Mixed pm	A Passenger pm
Heathfield	–	8.35	–	–	11.5	–	12.20	–	3.20	–	6.5	–	9.20
Chudleigh	8.43	8.45	–	–		12.28	12.30	3.28	3.29	6.13	6.20	9.28	9.29
Trusham	8.52	8.53	–	11.15	11.23	12.37	12.38	3.36	3.37	6.28	6.33	9.36	9.37
Ashton	9.0	–	–	9.20	11.30	–	12.45	–	3.44	–	6.40	–	9.44	–
Teign House	–	–	9.26	–	–	–	–	–	–

UP

	A Passenger am		D Goods (RR) am	A Mixed am		D Goods (RR am*		A Passenger pm		A Passenger pm		A Passenger pm
Teign House	–	–	9.35	–	–	–	–	–	–
Ashton	–	7.5	9.40	–	–	10.25	–	11.40	–	1.43	–	4.0	–	7.8
Trusham	7.12	7.13	–	10.33	10.37	11.46	11.55	1.50	1.51	4.7	4.8	7.15	7.16
Chudleigh	7.20	7.21	–	10.45	10.52	–	1.58	1.59	4.15	4.16	7.23	7.24
Heathfield	7.29	–	–	11.0	–	12.5	–	2.7	–	4.24	–	7.32	–

connections:

Heathfield	7.34	11.9	2.14	4.29	7.39
Newton Abbot	7.45	11.20	2.25	4.40	7.50

*The Station Master at Trusham to advise Heathfield not later than 7.30pm each day what traffic has to be dealt with on the following day, and the latter will then arrange for this train to run. If the Station Master at Heathfield requires an engine to shunt the yard he must telegraph Messrs. Giles and Mayers, Newton Abbot, not later than 8am.

It will be seen that the trains were still all running within half an hour or so of their original 1882 times.

CHAPTER THIRTEEN

DISAPPOINTMENT AND DISCORD:
TRAFFIC, TRAIN SERVICES, AND THE EXETER RAILWAY'S COURT CASE,
1903–1905

THE opening of the Exeter Railway in July 1903 produced immediate discord between the ER and the Exeter public on the one hand, and the GWR on the other, over the way in which the GWR was working the line.

As was usually the case with new railway lines, the promoters had propagated all sorts of vague ideas about what train services might be run on the line, but had never considered the question of what level of service would be economically practicable. This was left to John Campfield, the GWR's Exeter Divisional Superintendent, to sort out shortly before the line opened (although, to Campfield's annoyance, it was not until as late as 30th May 1903 that Paddington told him definitely that the line would be in his Division, rather than in the Plymouth Division as the Teign Valley line had been up to this time). In March, Campfield was presented with a memorial from local people demanding a level of service which he considered highly over-ambitious, including a Sunday service. The memorial had a detailed draft timetable attached, which had been drawn up by W.S. Elphinstone-Stone on the basis of through running between Exeter and Newton Abbot instead of the established change at Heathfield. As Elphinstone-Stone was a GWR employee, Campfield very much resented having to respond to this memorial, although he did get some pleasure out of being able to ask a clergyman noted for his strict Sabbatarian views why he had signed it!

Campfield had no such grand ideas and on 21st March he wrote to Paddington proposing that the service on the line should simply be based on the prolongation of the existing trains to/from Exeter, so that the all-important connections at Heathfield were still maintained. Although convinced himself that the likely traffic did not merit more than this, Campfield was in sufficiently close contact with the Exeter trading community to know that the GWR was entering into a minefield. 'Local expectations are so wide of what is practicable in the circumstances that we shall be assailed with complaints directly the line is open', he told Paddington in May. In fact the firing began in June when the GWR's summer timetable including the new Exeter Railway service came out.

The ER Board considered the timetable on 23rd June and decided to let the Exeter Chamber of Commerce be the public mouthpiece of complaint. On the 25th the Chamber communicated with the GWR demanding a number of immediate changes, notably that the first down and last up trains should run as Mixed trains on the Exeter–Ashton section instead of as Goods/ECS. The GWR's timetable, they noted, would prevent Exeter labourers and traders from using the line for work purposes, as the first down train was too late, and would 'defeat the chance of the line becoming popular for excursion purposes' unless there were a later evening return train from Chudleigh. The GWR also started receiving letters from private individuals who had expected the line to improve their journeys and now, after all these years waiting, found that it was not going to be of any use to them. Frank Moyle, a London barrister who journeyed regularly to Chudleigh, wrote to complain of the quite useless 'connections' between good London trains and branch trains at Exeter, as a result of which journeys to Chudleigh would still have to be made by Newton Abbot in most cases. The Chudleigh gentry were similarly dissatisfied with this, and with the last down train from Exeter being so early (6.13 pm). They nagged Box, the Chudleigh stationmaster, who wrote to Campfield on 2nd August 'Our people and the Earl of Morley, Lord Clifford, Mr Seale Hayne MP and other big people, think our last train out of Exeter should wait for the 3 pm Paddington'. There was also annoyance at the poor connections to/from Moretonhampstead. 'There are many anxious to [use the line] but cannot', wrote the Rector of Manaton, who wanted to travel from Bovey to Exeter.

The GWR's response was that nothing could be done immediately as the summer timetable was already printed and circulated. At the opening luncheon on 30th June Campfield spoke to Faulkner, the ER Secretary, and pointed out that it was impossible on a line of this sort to accommodate everybody's desires. The unfortunate fact was that people like Moyle were not likely to travel often enough to justify providing the connections they wanted; the needs of the much larger number of purely local passengers had to take priority. The luncheon was spoilt from Campfield's viewpoint by the loud cheers which Walter Pring received when he made some comments about the poor timetable, and on 1st July Campfield despatched another letter to Paddington:

'The local Director Mr Pring made some statements at the luncheon that would have been better avoided, but they were sufficient to show that no one connected with the scheme has yet grasped the idea that the possibilities of a single line are limited and that the arrangements of the GWR Company cannot be readily readjusted to fit in with the individual requirements of everyone who chooses to interfere.'

Attentions were now also focused on the Goods service. When the Alphington Road depot opened on 1st July,

GREAT WESTERN RAILWAY.

Circular No. R. 1223.
T.B. 35125.

CHIEF GOODS MANAGER'S OFFICE,
PADDINGTON STATION, LONDON, W.,
June 29th, 1903.

OPENING OF THE EXETER RAILWAY.

CLOSING OF TEIGNHOUSE SIDING.

On 1st July next a New Line will be opened between Exeter and Ashton.

This Line commences at a Junction with the G.W.R. Main Line at a point about 1¼ miles South of Exeter Station and extends to a Junction with the Ashton Branch about 1½ miles North of Ashton.

The Stations on the New Line, with their respective distances from Exeter, and from Ashton, also accommodation provided at each place, are as shewn below :—

Name of Station.	Distance from Exeter, (St. David's.)		Distance from Ashton.		Accommodation.
	M.	C.	M.	C.	
Alphington Road	1	62	9	55	Goods Lock-up, 5 ton Crane, Cart Weighbridge, Cattle Pens, Goods Siding.
Ide	3	17	7	48	Goods Lock-up, Carriage Shoots, Goods Siding.
Longdown	5	75	4	70	Goods Siding.
Christow	9	20	1	45	Goods Lock-up, 5 ton Crane, Cart Weighbridge, Carriage Shoots, Cattle Pens, Goods Siding.

For the present, Alphington Road Station is to be used only for traffic passing to and from the Stations on the Exeter Railway named above. Traffic from or to Great Western Stations will continue to be dealt with at Exeter St. David's Station and is not to be sent to or from Alphington Road.

Until further arrangements are made, the Company will not undertake Cartage at any of these Stations, and rates must not be quoted as including that service.

Traffic between your Station and these places must be treated as "local," and abstracted accordingly.

If you require any rates for Traffic to or from the Stations, application must be made for the same in the usual manner.

On and from the same date, Teignhouse Siding will be closed and Traffic hitherto dealt with there will in future be dealt with at Christow Station.

Please forward acknowledgment of this Circular to your District Goods Manager.

L. W. MAIDEN.

_____ *Station.*

The Chief Goods Manager's circular for the opening of the line. The Company never did undertake cartage at these stations.

prospective users found to their dismay that a notice was posted up stating that no goods would be dealt with there except for Ide, Longdown, and Christow! They, and the ER Board, had of course been assuming that the depot would be a normal GWR goods station, to serve this industrial part of the city which was remote from the St David's goods station. Although printed under the name of the Chief Goods Manager, this restriction was in reality the doing of Campfield and Hill (the Exeter District Goods Manager), both of whom had always been against the idea of having to work another goods depot in the city, but who had in a correspondence going back to 1899 failed to convince Paddington of the merits of their case. (The GWR was in any case obliged to work the Alphington Road branch under the 1883 agreement.) Campfield and Hill had also succeeded in having Alphington Road left out of the Working Timetable, so that there were no trains booked to call there!

Moreover, the GWR refused to carry any goods for places beyond Christow by the ER route. Goods for Teign

JULY 1903 TIMETABLE

DOWN

	Empty Coaches & Goods K	Passenger B	Passenger to Ashton, Mixed beyond B	Goods RR* K	Passenger B	Passenger B	Dulverton Passenger B
Exeter	5.40am	–	9.42am	–	1.2pm	3.10p.m.	6.5 / 6.13pm
St. Thomas	–	–	9.45 / 9.47	–	1.5 / 1.10	3.13 / 3.15	6.16 / 6.19
City Basin Jn	cs	–	csX	–	1.11csX1.15	cs	cs
Ide	5.55 / 6.3	–	9.53 / 9.54	–	1.20 / 1.21	3.21 / 3.22	6.25 / 6.26
Longdown	6.15 / 6.25	–	10.2 / 10.3	–	1.29 / 1.30	3.30 / 3.32	6.34 / 6.36
Christow	6.35 / 6.44	–	10.10/ 10.13	–	1.37 / 1.39	3.39csX3.44	6.43csX6.54
Ashton	6.50	7.5am	10.18/ 10.25	11.40am	1.44 / 1.45	3.49 / 3.55	6.59 / 7.6
Trusham	–	7.12 /7.13	10.33/ 10.37	11.46/11.55	1.52 / 1.53	4.2 / 4.3	7.13 / 7.14
Chudleigh	–	7.20 /7.21	10.45/ 10.52	–	2.0 / 2.1	4.10 / 4.12	7.21 / 7.22
Heathfield	–	7.29	11.0	12.5	2.9	4.20	7.30
connections:							
Heathfield	–	*7.34*	*11.9*	–	*2.14*	*4.29*	*7.39*
Newton Abbot	–	*7.45*	*11.20*	–	*2.25*	*4.40*	*7.50*

UP

connections:							
Newton Abbot	*8.15am*	–	*12.2pm*	*2.50pm*	*5.47pm*	*9.0pm*	–
Heathfield	*8.25*	–	*12.12*	*3.0*	*5.57*	*9.10*	–

	Passenger B	Goods RR* K	Passenger B	Passenger B	Mixed to Ashton, Passenger beyond B	Passenger B	Goods & Coaches K
Heathfield	8.35am	11.5am	12.20pm	3.10pm	6.5pm	9.20pm	–
Chudleigh	8.43 / 8.45	–	12.28/ 12.30	3.18 / 3.19	6.13 / 6.20	9.28 / 9.29	–
Trusham	8.52 / 8.53	11.15/ 11.23	12.37/12.38	3.26 / 3.27	6.28 / 6.33	9.36 / 9.37	–
Ashton	9.0 / 9.1	11.30	12.45/ 12.46	3.34 / 3.36	6.40 / 6.47	9.44	10.0
Christow	9.6 / 9.8	–	12.51/12.53	3.41 X 3.43	6.52 X 7.2	–	10.7 /10.20
Longdown	9.17 / 9.18	–	1.2 / 1.3	3.52 / 3.53	7.11 / 7.12	–	10.33/10.40
Ide	9.24 / 9.25	–	1.9 / 1.10	3.59 / 4.0	7.18 / 7.19	–	10.49/10.55
City Basin Jn	csX	–	csX	cs	cs	–	cs
St. Thomas	9.30 / 9.33	–	1.15 / 1.18	4.5 / 4.8	7.24 / 7.27	–	–
Exeter	9.36	–	1.21	4.11	7.30	–	11.10

cs Collect/deposit staff
X Crossing of trains
* See 1902 timetable for instructions

ALTERATIONS from 10.8.1903:
5.40am DOWN becomes 6.30am passenger Exeter–Heathfield.
9.20am DOWN Goods added, Exeter–Heathfield.
9.42am DOWN becomes Passenger (not mixed) Ashton–Heathfield section.
11.40am DOWN Goods abolished.
11.5am UP Goods abolished.
4.25pm UP Heathfield–Exeter Goods added.
6.5pm UP becomes Passenger (not mixed) Heathfield–Ashton section.
9.20pm UP becomes through passenger train to Exeter (in place of 10.0pm Ashton–Exeter Goods).

There were minor retimings in October 1903 when, following an Inspection by the District Engineer, it was decreed that journey times between Exeter and Christow would have to be decelerated to allow the 25mph limit to be properly observed. Three minutes were added over this section, but at the same time six minutes were deducted from the standard timings between Heathfield and Ashton, so producing an overall acceleration.

Valley stations (Chudleigh/Trusham/Ashton), and for Heathfield and Moretonhampstead branch stations, were still being sent via Newton, the goods service on the line being split by a 'Berlin Wall' between Ashton and Christow as shown in the timetable. Amongst the traders it was Candy's at Heathfield who were most disgusted at this. They had been cultivated by the ER since 1895 and had been led to believe that their goods for Exeter and beyond would all be sent by the ER once it opened, and their rates reduced on account of the shorter route. But the GWR refused to send any of Candy's traffic by the ER, and said the rates would stay as they were. The ER had been looking to a large income from the Candy's traffic, and were infuriated.

On 10th July the *Flying Post* in Exeter ran an editorial on the subject:

'When the Exeter Railway was under construction, there were not wanting predictions that the policy of the GWR in working it would be first to beggar it with an inconvenient and insufficient train service and general lack of facilities, and then buy it up cheap and develop it when all the profits would flow to Paddington. The attitude taken up in the details of operating the line certainly appears to be by way of justifying the forecast, and for that we are sorry.'

If the GWR proved 'obdurate', perhaps the LSWR could be persuaded to build a line to Lea Cross?

Faulkner commented similarly in a letter to the GWR (which illustrates how bad-tempered the ER/GWR relationship had already become by July 1903): 'Were it the wish of the GWR to kill the Exeter Railway, no better means could have been devised than the present train service . . .'

Matters moved quickly to a point where the GWR had to make concessions. They gave way first on the Alphington Road question, where there was internal dissension. On 22nd July the authorities at Paddington had a notice inserted in the Exeter papers stating that goods would now be accepted at Alphington Road for all stations. This was done without telling Campfield! — when he read it in the paper he fired off a letter to Paddington: 'I can hardly believe this, because it is utterly impracticable . . .' That very same day Messrs. J.L. Thomas & Co. arrived in the yard with three carts of soap and candles for all destinations, and these had to be accepted, although no rates from Alphington Road had yet been advised. Thomas's were hoping to get the same rates as from St David's, but Hill and Campfield wanted higher rates charged because of the extra costs involved in bringing trucks out from St David's. Eventually, in September, Thomas's agreed to higher rates. Others, however, would not and, thanks to this and the GWR's refusal to provide a C&D service, Thomas's were to prove the only significant users of Alphington Road for some time.

On the timetable front, the GWR was forced to act rather more quickly than they might have expected to at first. They could not, of course, do anything in the short term about the poor London and Moretonhampstead connections, but Campfield quickly recognised the force of the

Chamber of Commerce's point regarding the first down and last up trains, noting himself in July that (as the Chamber had predicted) 'Picnic parties to Chudleigh who are very numerous must leave at 6.20 pm or go by road, and I find a good many people are still being driven there'. Other factors also came into play. There were complaints about the slow journey times on the mixed trains; the stone traffic was increasing and requiring more regular running of the Heathfield–Ashton 'RR' goods; and extra Exeter–Alphington Road trains conveying one or two trucks only were having to be run to serve Alphington Road at convenient times. On 30th July, therefore, Campfield proposed to Paddington that a new 9.20 am Exeter–Heathfield–Exeter goods train should be introduced, calling at Alphington Road en route, whereupon

- The mixed trains could become passenger trains throughout.
- The Heathfield–Ashton, and Exeter–Alphington Road goods workings could be abolished.
- The first down and last up trains could run through from/to Exeter as passenger trains.

These changes were agreed and introduced immediately as from 10th August 1903.

The introduction of the through Exeter–Heathfield goods made it more difficult for the GWR to resist the idea of routeing goods to TVR stations by the ER rather than via Newton Abbot, and in August they informed Faulkner that goods to/from TVR and Moretonhampstead branch stations would now be sent by the ER if 'specially consigned' that way. As only the ER's particular supporters would have any motive for so specially consigning, and as the concession did not help in cases like Candy's where special rates were involved, conflict continued on this front.

The concessions made by the GWR in July–August 1903 may have deflated the situation somewhat, but the fact was that the GWR's view of the line was in fundamental conflict with the perceptions of the ER Board and the ER's Exeter supporters. The February 1904 half-yearly report from the ER Board noted that:

'The result of the first half-year's working of the line has been entirely unsatisfactory, but this can be no surprise to the shareholders, who are cognisant of the manner in which the Great Western Railway interprets the obligation to properly develop the traffic on this company's line. Any considerable improvement is impossible so long as the working company entirely disregards the convenience, both as regards passengers and goods service, of the district which this railway was intended to serve, as well as of its duty to the worked company.'

In January 1904 Joseph Tiplady had a secret meeting at Paddington with the GWR General Manager Inglis, to broach the question of whether the GWR would be prepared to buy the line (the assumption being that the GWR would never make full use of the line, so long as it belonged to another company to whom a percentage of the revenue from any through traffic routed by the line would have to be paid). Inglis had a report done by his officers but the recommendation was against acquiring the ER.

THE OPENING OF THE CANAL BRANCH

Another cause of conflict in 1903/4 was the GWR's failure to bring the ER's Canal Branch into use.

The Canal Branch had been built (under a supplemental contract of May 1902) in December 1902–June 1903, and so far as the authorities at Paddington and the ER Board were concerned, it had been opened along with the rest of the line as from 1st July 1903. In reality, however, it was not used. This was partly because the hurriedly-built line had not been maintained properly after completion due to Bluett concentrating his efforts on the ER main line, but more importantly because Campfield and Hill had no wish to use the line when it was simpler to work the very small number of trucks from the ER line for the Basin via St David's (running them through to St David's with the rest of the ER goods train, and taking them to the Basin the next morning on the GWR Basin Branch train). Campfield did not go out of his way to tell his superiors that the line was not being used, no doubt suspecting that this would be 'politically' sensitive. On 9th October, Gibbons, the District Engineer, went over the line with Bluett and prohibited its being used until it was made good. However, Bluett then did the necessary work and on 26th November Gibbons declared the line fit for traffic.

This made life difficult for Campfield, who had to resort to telling Bluett that he had had no specific instructions authorising him to open the line, and that only the Chief Goods Manager had authority to give such instructions. Faulkner then complained to a surprised Inglis, who had been under the impression that the line was open. The ER claimed that it had lost traffic due to the non-use of the line, but it transpired that all the 18 trucks sent to the Basin up to November 1903 had been consigned from TVR stations, so that the GWR was not obliged to work them via the ER Canal Branch anyway! Campfield and Hill now tried to make out that the line had only been repaired in a 'perfunctory manner' in November, but when Gibbons did further tests on 16th March 1904 using loco 1897, he found the results better than he had expected. Paddington therefore now gave Campfield definite orders that traffic from the ER line for the Basin was to be worked by the ER Canal Branch henceforth, and not via St. David's. The 2nd May 1904 was the official opening date of the line, although it was only on 5th May that Hill sent Watkins (his under-official in charge of the Exeter goods trains) copies of Campfield's instructions for working the line, under a covering note which hinted that it might be difficult to persuade the train crews not to work the trucks via St. David's in practice!

The opening of the line did not really benefit the consignors. Trucks for the Basin from the up ER goods were left under the GWR bridge overnight and only taken down to the Basin the next morning by the Basin Branch trip, so they arrived at the Basin at exactly the same time as they had done when worked via St David's! So one can see the force of Campfield's views in this case. The Canal Branch was a total white elephant to the ER; it was a relic of the 1880s dreams of mineral trains running through from the Teign Valley to load ships in the Basin, but no such traffic ever existed (except that there were occasionally odd trucks of stone for the Basin). In 1922 the Canal Branch was noted as 'now practically derelict' due to the infrequent traffic; only when King's Asphalt Siding was added in 1929 did it start to see more use, and latterly it had some small purpose in keeping shunting moves clear of the main line.

THE RAILWAY & CANAL COMMISSION COURT CASE (1904–5)

To understand properly the frustration of the ER Board and its Exeter supporters in 1903/4, we must go back to the aspirations which had been held of the line in the 1890s, and which were still held in July 1903 (cf. the 1898 Prospectus in Chapter 9). These include:

- The GWR using the line for some of its own through trains — fish, vegetable, and excursion trains were anticipated to a total of 1,500 trains per annum, to avoid congestion on the main line on the single-track Dawlish–Parson's Tunnel section.
- The local train service on the line to run through from Exeter to Newton Abbot, including some 'fast' trains.
- The Exeter Railway route to be the main route for Exeter–Moretonhampstead passenger traffic — John Dickson regarded this as having been 'the main feature' of the line as put to him in 1893.
- Alphington Road to be a major goods depot, in particular for coal traffic, and to be shunted by GWR main line goods trains as well as by ER goods trains.
- Goods from the TVR and Moreton branch stations consigned to Exeter and beyond, to all be sent by the ER line.
- A large traffic in summer trippers from Exeter to Christow, Chudleigh (for Chudleigh Rock), and Chagford — including Sunday trips.

In retrospect one might ask why the ER promoters had not engaged in more detailed discussions with the GWR in the 1890s. The GWR had never given any undertaking to use the line for its own through trains, and did not want to do so because of the gradients and speed limits (in any case, the main line at Dawlish was being doubled by 1903). Similarly the GWR had never promised to facilitate Exeter–Moretonhampstead traffic via the line; the ER had just assumed that this would happen because of it being the shortest route.

By the autumn of 1903 it was clear to the ER that the GWR would never develop the line in the way they had anticipated, unless forced to do so by higher authority. The ER's thoughts therefore quickly turned to the possibility of bringing a case against the GWR in the Railway & Canal Commission Court. This, organised primarily by John Dickson, was filed on 14th May 1904.

As had no doubt been anticipated, the filing of the case pushed the GWR into a more concessionary spirit. On the passenger front, the GWR drew up plans for a more frequent service using railmotors and put them to the ER in June 1904. The proposed timetable (reproduced here) involved seven trains each way with some through running to Newton Abbot and Moretonhampstead. It seems to

MOTOR SERVICE PROPOSED BY GWR JUNE 1904 (never introduced)

Mondays to Saturdays, no service Sundays.

DOWN

	Newton Motor	Moreton Motor	Heathfield Goods	Christow Motor	Bovey Motor	Moreton Motor	Christow Motor	Newton Motor
Exeter	6.50	9.50	9.20	11.15	1.12	3.10	4.50	7.10
St. Thomas	6.52	9.52	–	11.17	1.14	3.12	4.52	7.12
Alphington Road Halte	6.54	9.54	–	11.19	1.16	3.14	4.54	7.14
Alphington Road Goods	–	–	9.28/10.20	–	–	–	–	–
Ide	7.3	10.3	10.30	11.28	1.25	3.23	5.3	7.23
Longdown	7.12	10.12	10.45	11.37	1.34	3.32	5.12	7.32
Christow	7.22	10.22	11.8	11.47	1.44	3.42	5.22	7.42
Ashton	7.28	10.28	11.20		1.50	3.48		7.48
Trusham	7.35	10.35	11.40		1.57	3.55		7.55
Chudleigh	7.42	10.42	12.5		2.4	4.2		8.2
Chudleigh Knighton Halte	7.45	10.45	–		2.7	4.5		8.5
Heathfield arr.	7.50	10.50	12.15		2.12	4.10		8.10
Heathfield dep.	7.55	(11.9)			(2.14)	(4.29)		8.15
Newton Abbot	8.5	(11.20)			(2.25)	(4.40)		8.25
Heathfield dep.	(8.27)	10.55			2.20	4.17		(9.12)
Bovey	(8.34)	11.0			2.25	4.24		(9.19)
Moretonhampstead	(8.57)	11.25				4.47		(9.42)

UP

	Newton Motor	Christow Motor	Moreton Motor	Bovey Motor	Christow Motor	Heathfield Goods	Moreton Motor	Newton Motor	
Moretonhampstead	(7.10)		11.40				5.45	(8.10)	
Bovey	(7.27)		11.57	2.40			6.5	(8.26)	MWSO
Heathfield arr.	(7.34)		12.2	2.45			6.10	(8.32)	
Newton Abbot	8.25		(12.0)	(2.48)			(5.45)	8.50	
Heathfield arr.	8.35		(12.14)	(3.2)			(5.59)	9.0	
Heathfield dep.	8.40		12.20	3.10		4.25	6.15	9.15	
Chudleigh Knighton Halte	8.45		12.25	3.15		–	6.20	9.20	
Chudleigh	8.48		12.28	3.18		4.50	6.23	9.23	
Trusham	8.55		12.35	3.25		5.10	6.30	9.30	
Ashton	9.2		12.42	3.32		5.25	6.37	9.37	
Christow	9.8	11.50	12.48	3.38	5.25	5.51	6.45	9.43	
Longdown	9.18	12.0	12.58	3.48	5.35	6.9	6.55	9.53	
Ide	9.27	12.9	1.7	3.57	5.44	6.23	7.4	10.2	
Alphington Road Goods	–	–	–	–	–	6.29/7.25	–	–	
Alphington Road Halte	9.36	12.18	1.16	4.6	5.53	–	7.13	10.11	
St. Thomas	9.38	12.20	1.18	4.8	5.55	–	7.15	10.13	
Exeter	9.40	12.22	1.20	4.10	5.57	7.30	7.18	10.15	

have been intended as a serious proposal; the GWR was becoming very keen on motors at this date and the traffic on the line was so light that it could easily be accommodated in the motors, at a much-reduced operating cost. (Campfield had arranged a survey at Christow in September 1903 which had shown only 1,010 passengers on the trains in six days, i.e. an average of only 16 passengers on each train.) Two 'Haltes' were proposed, at Chudleigh Knighton and Alphington Road.[1] All in all it was quite an attractive service which the ER would have been well-advised to accept in place of its nine-tenths-empty hauled trains. But the ER would have none of it. They seemed to regard the motors as not being 'proper' trains, and they had their own grand ideas of the service they wanted. Accordingly Dickson drew up, and put to the GWR, his own draft timetable, involving seven passenger trains each way all running through between Exeter and Newton Abbot, with connections at Heathfield to give a 1 hr 17 min journey time between Moretonhampstead and Exeter on all trains. One train each way was an 'Express' taking only 50 mins between Exeter and Newton and openly intended to abstract traffic from the GWR's own passenger trains via Dawlish! Three Sunday trains were proposed each way. Needless to say, the GWR had no wish to run a service of this sort.

Nevertheless, the GWR wanted to do something better for the line to improve its position before the court, so in July 1904 it introduced an extra three trains each way on the Exeter–Christow section, making a total of eight each way over this section, distinctly better than most comparable lines enjoyed. This improved service was destined to last for 7½ years, but at the time it was probably regarded as a temporary expedient until motors could be introduced. (In January 1905 the GWR made another attempt

One of the Exeter—Christow short workings, introduced by the GWR in 1904 to placate the Exeter Railway, is seen here c.1905 with the locomotive running round at Christow. The single bogie coach was more than enough for the limited traffic.   *Lens of Sutton*

to interest the ER in a motor service, but once again had a negative reaction, the ER dismissing the motors as something that would 'still further impair the usefulness and carrying capacity of our railway'. After this the subject of motors was not raised again until 1920.)

The GWR also introduced through ticketing to/from all GWR stations in 1905, the original arrangements having been rather restricted.

On the goods front, the GWR agreed in April 1905 to route all goods from TVR stations to Exeter and beyond (and vice-versa) via the ER (instead of just those goods specially consigned via the ER, as conceded in August 1903). They did not concede any liability to do this, but no doubt saw that they could be made to look bad by counsel showing the court on a map how goods were conveyed from Ashton to Exeter via Dawlish to spite the ER. The GWR would not, however, agree to route goods to/from the Moretonhampstead branch via the ER, and in this one can sympathise with them; despite being shorter on the map it would have been more bother in every way.

The GWR's concessions were not enough to prevent the ER from continuing with the case, which was heard on 19th–25th July 1905 before Mr Justice Bigham and Commissioners Sir Frederick Peel and the Hon. A.E.Gathorne-Hardy. John Dickson was the ER's principal witness, supported by Walter Pring, Lord Clifford, M.J.

Dunsford, and several other Exeter traders. The main arguments focused on:

- The GWR's having deprived the ER of Exeter–Moretonhampstead passenger traffic because of the very poor connections at Heathfield which always made it quicker for such passengers to travel via Newton Abbot. The GWR conceded that this was so, but Heathfield was not a crossing place on the Moretonhampstead line and it was therefore impossible to provide Teign Valley line–Moretonhampstead connections without disrupting the far more important Teign Valley line–Newton Abbot connections. Dickson retorted that Heathfield should be made a crossing place, either using the existing goods siding loop (the GWR said that the Board of Trade would not have allowed this) or by altering the layout as necessary (the GWR replied that this would have to be done at the TVR's expense and the court had no power to order a company not party to the case to do anything).[2]
- The GWR's refusal to run its own through trains over the line.
- The lack of Sunday trains.
- The higher charges made for Alphington Road, compared with the St David's rates, to/from all destinations (except the ER and TVR stations, and Moretonhampstead branch stations, where the GWR charged the same rates to Alphington Road as St David's). The ER wanted Alphington Road 'grouped' with St David's for all traffic.
- The GWR's refusal to provide collection & delivery facilities at Alphington Road, which further reduced usage of the depot.

Judgement was delivered on 27th October 1905 and was unfavourable to the ER in almost all respects. The court seems to have felt that the ER was protesting too much and had rushed into the case too quickly. They pointed to the

A view from the east of Christow station in 1905. There was still little vegetation on the road embankment by the overbridge, although it was nine years old by this date.

Chapman collection, cty. Mrs. M. Piller

Longdown station never became a subject of dispute between the Exeter Railway Company and the GWR — no doubt because it must have been obvious from the start, even to the ER, that there was no way any good amount of traffic could be gained there. This was the view that greeted such few passengers as alighted at Longdown and set off down the station approach road. The goods siding was unusually busy on this occasion. *Collection Mrs. M. Piller*

Longdown station in summer 1906. Everything here is in its original form except for the addition of the peculiar down signal worked by a third lever added to the East Ground Frame (and described at page 245). The footpath behind the station building led up the hillside to Longdown village. *Collection J. P. Morris*

'very unsatisfactory' results of the passenger traffic to date as a good reason for the GWR to be cautious about increasing facilities, and declared that there was 'not the least ground to suppose that the defendants (the GWR) have had any desire to do less than justice to the applicants' — a rather one-sided statement since there was plenty of evidence that the GWR had in fact done its best to keep traffic away from Alphington Road wherever possible.

Despite the bad judgment, the ER had benefited from the case in terms of the concessions made by the GWR in 1904. In January 1907 the Railway & Canal Commission made an 'Order' resulting from the case under which the ER received a small backpayment from the GWR in respect of various details of rates where the ER's view had been accepted by the court.

OPERATING AFTER 1903

Ashton shed had no allocation after 1st July 1903 (although it was not deleted from the list of GWR Engine sheds until 1908). The branch was now worked entirely by Exeter

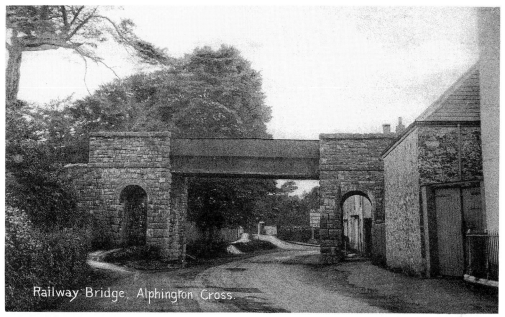

To the inhabitants of Alphington, just as to the Exeter Railway Board, the opening of the ER line in 1903 brought more frustration than pleasure. The line passed through the village but they had no access to it. This frustration lasted until the 1920s when frequent bus services began; Alphington Halt in 1928 (which was accessed from the path at left) came too late. This pre-Halt view is looking northwest towards Exeter.

Collection Mrs. M. Piller

Railway Bridge, Alphington Cross.

This July 1905 Bradshaw extract shows the passenger time-table introduced in July 1904, with the three extra trains to Christow. One defect of this timetable was the long waits at Christow of three of the down trains — 20 minutes on the 9.45 a.m., 18 minutes on the 3.6 p.m., and 23 minutes on the 6.15 p.m. Following complaints in 1903 about the long station stops at Ashton, Trusham, and Chudleigh on one or two trains, all waiting time had been concentrated at Christow. John Dickson noted in 1905 that when these trains were at Christow, 'the Station Master has to go and hide himself, he is so ashamed of the questions which are asked'! These waits were, however, reduced in the following years by better timetabling.

locos and train sets, and this was to remain the case subsequently, save for the fact that some Newton Abbot-based goods services were introduced from 1907 as described in Chapter 14.

From 1903 it was a regular feature for a number of the passenger trains to be advertised through workings to/from Tiverton, Tiverton Junction, or Dulverton. This lasted into the 1920s.

From 1903 to 1923 the line was officially referred to as the 'Exeter Railway and Teign Valley Branch'. After 1923 it became simply the 'Teign Valley Branch' again, and it will be convenient to use this shorter nomenclature throughout in the remainder of this book. (However, the Engineers stuck to the 'Exeter Railway' name for the Christow—Exeter section for their purposes, and, in that small way, that name remains in active railway use in the 1990s.)

---

1. The timings almost suggest that this was to have been situated on the main line between St Thomas and City Basin Jn., rather than at the site of the later Alphington Halt. Note in particular that two trains cross there at 1.16 pm. However one cannot be certain as to what was intended.
2. The TVR Company was not involved in the case, despite its relevance to their line. On 13.4.1904 the TVR Board resolved to assist the ER with evidence, but they never in fact gave any evidence at the hearings.

Lens of Sutton

A '517' class 0—4—2T arriving at Ashton with a down train in 1905.

CHAPTER FOURTEEN

ROADSTONE AND MOTORS:
THE HEYDAY OF THE LINE (AND BEYOND): 1905–1939

An unidentified '517' class 0–4–2T heading a Heathfield–Exeter train at Chudleigh in the summer of 1905. It was unusual to see five coaches, the normal formation of the branch trains being three. The '517s' continued to be the sole motive power for the passenger trains until the motors arrived on the line, and worked the auto and remaining ordinary trains during the 1920s.

Chapman collection, cty. Steven Court

IT is perhaps conventional in books of this kind to deal with passenger traffic before speaking of goods traffic. But in the case of the Teign Valley branch, from the 1900s, it was the goods traffic that predominated and had the major influence on the line's development; it must therefore be discussed first.

Although there had always been small stone quarries in the area, and it had been known that there were large reserves of granite and basalt as yet untouched, it was nevertheless impossible to attempt to increase the quarrying activity prior to 1892 when the line's 'wrong gauge' situation meant high transport costs.

The first person to take up the bait after 1892 was H.L. Hardwicke of the Tytherington Stone Co. (by this date already fully operational at its Gloucestershire base). About 1895 Hardwicke set up the Teign Valley Granite Co. and began quarrying at Crockham, near Trusham station. This quarry, like the others which followed in the valley, pro-

duced a stone that was most suited for roadstone chippings. The company was very successful and in 1904 they had a private siding installed at Crockham to avoid the previous road cartage to Trusham station.

Hardwicke was followed by J.H. Dickson, then still 'Contractor's Engineer' on the Exeter Railway construction, who opened Trusham Quarry adjacent to the station around 1901, followed by Bridford Quarry in 1905. Bridford was a mile from Christow station and in 1910 a Light Railway was opened to connect the quarry and the station (see map, Chapter 18).

The opening of the Exeter Railway in 1903 encouraged further quarrying developments by reducing the costs of transporting to Exeter and beyond, and the rise of the motor car brought greater demand nationally for roadstone. In 1909 Hardwicke opened a large new quarry at Whetcombe a little north of Trusham, and this had its own private siding connection from the start. John Dickson and

TRUSHAM RY. STATION

In the early years of the valley's quarry boom in the 1900s, the greatest impact was felt at Trusham, which had hitherto been a small and insignificant place. By c.1905, when this view was taken, there was a good stone traffic being handled here, although there had not yet been any expansion of the station's facilities. The passenger traffic remained modest and Station Master Honeywill had only his porter, the local postmaster, and a gentleman who looks more like a looker-on than a passenger, for company as this Exeter-bound train, behind the usual '517' class 0—4—2T, arrived. The addition of a fourth coach indicates that the photograph was taken on a Wednesday, Friday, or Saturday, when an additional Third was added to the usual 3-coach set to cater for Market Day traffics and the extra Saturday traffic. Note the 'T' board on the station building, to indicate that all was well with the 'speaking' telegraph instruments used for communication on the line until telephones were installed in 1928, and the 4¼ milepost to the left of the loco. The smoke in the distance was rising from Crockham quarry.

Chapman collection

This c.1905 view, looking towards Exeter, highlights the remote situation of the station in the early days, and its small size. The building of the overbridge for double track is very evident here; this was, of course, a regular practice on single lines but it was soon to be proved necessary at Trusham. These views should be compared with the plans at pages 200 and 208.   *Lens of Sutton*

The third of our c.1905 views shows Trusham Quarry on the left, and the 1893 ground frame hut at the south end points. The quarry's proximity to the line brought restrictions on blasting, but the regulations set out in the 1905 Appendix were only that the quarry foreman must get verbal permission from the station master before blasting, and that the station master must inspect the line afterwards.
Chapman collection, cty. Steven Court

the Exeter Railway Board were themselves very much alive to the possibilities of starting up further quarrying operations, and from 1908 Dickson was involved in planning a large new quarry at Scatter Rock, west of Christow. This opened in due course in 1914, with an aerial ropeway to connect it to Christow station, and succeeded in fulfilling many of the hopes that had been held of it.

Full details of all of these quarries will be found at Chapter 18.

In the late 1900s the roadstone market was booming, and production at the Teign Valley quarries increased year by year, peaking in 1913–14 at over 200,000 tons per annum, almost all of which was sent out by rail. Trusham and Christow stations were the centre of this activity (Trusham much the busier of the two until the 1920s). The line was now very different from what it had been in the 1882–1903 period; the stone traffic so overwhelmed everything else that the total goods traffic on the line in 1913 was

GOODS TRAFFIC

Figures quoted are Tons per annum, In and Out combined.

There are no figures for 1882-1902. Complete figures for 1904-12, 1914-22 exist for Exeter Railway stations only. There are no figures for 1924. There are no figures after 1946/7 as 'Zoning' was introduced with Exeter or Newton Abbot; the 1947 figures themselves exclude smalls traffic for most of the year.

	Chudleigh	Trusham	Ashton	Christow	Longdown	Ide	Alphington Rd
1903	7239	17361	4963	2304	279	122	nk
04	nk	nk	nk	6026	543	454	11136
05	nk	nk	nk	7661	650	788	12175
06	nk	nk	nk	2302	531	1207	17138
07	nk	nk	nk	14509	534	649	17173
08	nk	nk	nk	16414	694	1476	16579
09	nk	nk	nk	21734	533	1427	17463
1910	nk	nk	nk	29034	361	1316	17003
11	nk	nk	nk	35142	490	1911	21267
12	nk	nk	nk	34455	346	2037	19020
13	11488	203275	1873	39482	440	2090	28292
14	nk	nk	nk	55709	848	2058	40095
15	nk	nk	nk	53230	815	790	29369
16	nk	nk	nk	46138	465	1068	33632
17	nk	nk	nk	45121	1110	station closed	35224
18	nk	nk	nk	44273	717	1/1/17–5/5/19	37002
19	nk	nk	nk	56234	384	2487	41303
1920	nk	nk	nk	70319	384	1432	45554
21	nk	nk	nk	64853	698	1983	36161
22	nk	nk	nk	81613	1443	1390	38961
23	6365	85685	2001	60961	709	1100	50055
24	nk	nk	nk	nk	nk	nk	nk
25	12030	82968	1386	55805	448	4273	Zoned with St.
26	13518	83497	1308	nk	457	1945	David's after 1924
27	6194	71278	1465	47677	2019	2951	
28	8403	50484	1331	50600	1373	1748	
29	5745	48130	1325	48012	544	3411	
1930	4496	38916	1450	46603	616	948	
31	4145	35290	3518	55362	173	1521	
32	4020	18473	5138	45976	297	658	
33	4300	10078	4496	36196	239	403	
34	4030	12732	4111	23306	142	414	
35	3879	12255	7327	26957	210	373	
36	4967	6344	4194	27961	82	377	
37	3870	7663	3207	28128	69	300	
38	3596	11262	2554	24653	98	174	
39	3646	8582	1136	37005	72	370	
1940	4744	4166	1377	47654	213	242	
41	5495	9193	1001	41506	49	604	
42	5292	22061	881	35435	294	653	
43	6120	9816	1204	31995	192	1059	
44	7243	11991	875	25503	35	1106	
45	7192	11064	883	31984	8	424	
46	4693	5672	1002	31801	26	439	
1947	nk	nk	869	22547	0	267	

Notes on the goods traffic:

Chudleigh	95% inwards, except in 1940-46.
Trusham	Inwards traffic is 2000-4000 T.p.a., the rest is outwards (stone) traffic.
Ashton	70% inwards, except in 1931-38 when the Ryecroft stone traffic was active.
Christow	Inwards traffic is 1000-4000 T.p.a., the rest is outwards (stone and barytes) traffic.
Longdown	95% inwards.
Ide	80% inwards, except in 1942-48.
Alphington Rd	Approx. half inwards and half outwards.

All this is as one would expect in the circumstances.

sixteen times what it had been in the 1890s. This brought a need for improvements to line capacity as noted in the next section.

The Teign Valley quarries found their markets over most of south-western and southern England (including West London), but could not really compete north of Bristol. The GWR took large amounts of stone themselves as ballast.

The 1914–18 war saw reduced demand for roadstone but was followed by another boom in 1920–22, as Local Authorities made up for the previous years' neglect. Nevertheless, Crockham, Trusham and Whetcombe quarries were never the same after 1914; they had used up their easiest stone and were finding it more difficult to extract stone economically. The 1920s were very much Christow's decade, with the still-young Scatter Rock quarry in full production, and the branch still visibly very busy with stone traffic.

The great days of stone quarrying in the valley came to an end in the early 1930s. Bridford and Trusham quarries had closed c1927, Whetcombe followed c1931, and Scatter Rock suffered a bad loss of business between 1931 and 1934 as changes in the technical specification for road-

THE TEIGN VALLEY QUARRIES

Quarry	Owner	Quarry Opened	Private Sdg. provided	Quarry Closed
Crockham	Teign Valley Granite Co.	c.1895	1904	1976 (but new 'Trusham Quarry' started on part of same site is still open).
Trusham	J.H. Dickson (later became Devon Basalt & Granite Co.)	c.1901	1912	c.1927
Bridford ('Paddy Dixon's')	J.H. Dickson (later became Devon Basalt & Granite Co.) (3 Quarries)	1905	1910	c.1927
Whetcombe/ Tinkley	Teign Valley Granite Co. (2 Quarries)	1909	1910	1931
Scatter Rock	Scatter Rock Macadams Ltd. (2 Quarries)	1914	1914	1950
Ryecroft	Stoneycombe Basalt Ltd.	1930	1930	c.1939

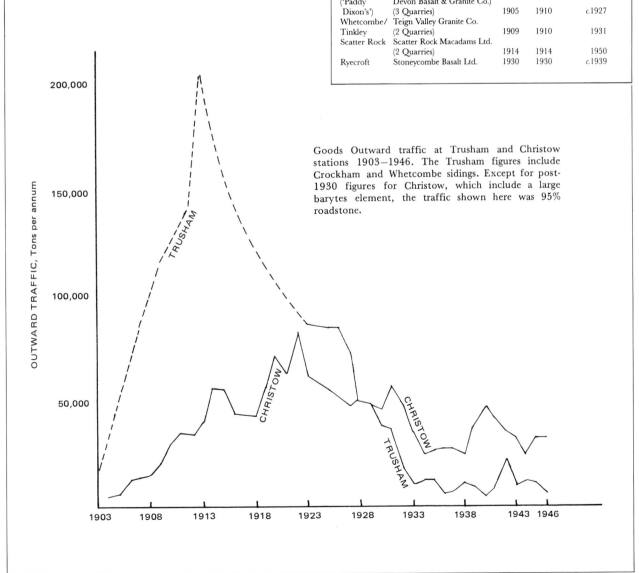

Goods Outward traffic at Trusham and Christow stations 1903–1946. The Trusham figures include Crockham and Whetcombe sidings. Except for post-1930 figures for Christow, which include a large barytes element, the traffic shown here was 95% roadstone.

Ashton, like Chudleigh, remained unaffected by the quarry boom, and had, of course, also lost its importance as 'terminus' and centre of the TVR's little empire, in 1903, when the line was extended to Exeter. Here we see Station Master A. T. Elliott and his signal porter posing on the platform in the summer of 1905, with the village of Lower Ashton in the background. The space opposite the platform was always cultivated as a little garden, but (in later years at least) it never won any prizes in the annual competition. The wire from the Crossing G.F. to the Up Distant signal can be seen passing in front of the plants. *Chapman collection, cty. Steven Court*

stone made its product less wanted. A new quarry at Ryecroft opened in 1930 but was not very successful and closed in 1939. Moreover, road hauliers were now offering competition for the shorter hauls. The railway's stone traffic was down to less than 20,000 tons per annum — only one tenth the 1913/14 figures — by 1934. The 1939–45 war brought a small recovery when competition from seaborne stone — notably North Wales stone brought by sea to Watchet and Bridgwater — was halted for the duration, but Scatter Rock's days were numbered and it closed in 1950, leaving the grass to grow over the sidings at Christow. This left only Crockham quarry which has survived to the present day.

The only major goods traffic on the line apart from the roadstone, was that provided by the Bridford Barytes Mine (handled at Christow). This was a longstanding traffic but

Christow, in its original rural setting before the growth of the quarry traffic, probably in the summer of 1905. The down train waiting in the platform must have been the 9.45 a.m. Exeter–Heathfield, one of the trains whose lengthy waits at Christow so annoyed the Exeter Railway Board! J. W. Snell, the original Christow signal porter, remembered walking along the platform one day, while one of these trains was waiting, and being called to from the train: "Porter, how long are we here for?" He instantly recognised the face of General Buller, then one of the most famous men in Devon, who was on his way to visit Lord Clifford at Ugbrooke. "I told him that the train would be leaving in a minute or two." He then said "Well, have you got any cider here?" "I replied that I was sorry but as I did not drink cider I was unable to oblige, and there wasn't time to make him a cup of tea. He and another gentleman with him laughed heartily at that, and seemed to be enjoying themselves, but I'm afraid the General had to wait until he got to his destination before he could quench his thirst . . ."

The plainness of the Exeter Railway's brick station buildings is evident. From this end the rooms originally (as seen here) were Gents (entrance in end wall), Ladies, Booking Hall, Booking Office, Station Master's Office (entered from Booking Office). There were no doors on the road side and passengers and trolleys entered the platform by gates between the main building and the Goods Shed.

At an unknown date pre-1920 the rather small Booking Office and Station Master's Office rooms were converted to one larger room, the chimney being moved to the end wall (as seen in photo on page 223). Then, in 1924, the building was extended northwards to join up with the Goods Shed, to give more office space. This, of course, blocked the existing entrance to the platform, so a door was put in the road side wall of the Booking Hall and this served as the passenger entrance/exit thereafter; compare with the 'Way Out' sign on page 225. A new gate for trolleys was put in at the south end by the Gents.

The station buildings at Longdown and Ide were originally identical to Christow (save that Longdown was a mirror-image); only Ide remained in original form to the end.

The 300ft platforms provided at Christow, Longdown and Ide were always more than adequate. The platforms were masonry-faced.

Note the 1904 Down Outer Home signal in the distance and the rising gradient towards Exeter through Sheldon cutting.

The original colour scheme of the Exeter Railway's enamel station nameboards is seen here; these original nameboards seem to have survived to the end at Christow and Longdown, but, as later views show, the painting schemes were changed.

This staff portrait was almost certainly taken in the spring of 1905 with Station Master George Haywood in the centre. We cannot be sure who the others were due to the frequent changes of staff.

Lens of Sutton

The line at Ashton, seen from the hill behind Lower Ashton village, in 1912.

Collection Mrs. M. Piller

The very restricted pre-1916 layout at Heathfield is seen in this 1900s view from the A38 overbridge, with a Moretonhampstead–Newton Abbot train arriving. The siding connection which Teign Valley goods trains and excursions had to use pre-1916 is just visible under the rear coaches. Unfortunately, the goods shed all but obscured the Teign Valley platform from this angle. Note how the signal box faced away from the Moretonhampstead line, having been designed in the anticipation that it would only control the TVR lines. The whole scene was dominated by Candy's Great Western Pottery, Brick and Tile Works, whose 1888 private siding is seen at bottom left. Baulk road track still predominated here on the former Broad Gauge side of the station (the Teign Valley side was always cross-sleepered track).

Collection Steven Court

Another 1900s view, with shunting in progress.   *Lens of Sutton*

increased greatly in the 1930s and 1940s when the mine was expanded, producing over 20,000 tons p.a. in some years.

The general goods traffic on the line, which comprised only coal and the miscellaneous needs of a rural community, was never very large, and (as happened everywhere) went into decline after 1919 due to road competition.

IMPROVEMENTS TO THE LINE 1911–1916
The extra trains needed to convey the increasing roadstone traffic in the late 1900s brought a need for improvements to line capacity. In 1911 Trusham was made a crossing station (but for goods trains only until 1943). Then, with Scatter Rock quarry about to open, it became clear that the long Christow–City Basin Junction section, with its steep gradients, was going to become a problem, so in March 1914 the provision of an intermediate block post at

Longdown was authorised. This was delayed by the war but eventually opened in 1916, and proved its worth in the 1920s. There was, however, no loop at Longdown until 1943.

Another improvement made in 1916 was the provision of a direct running connection between the branch and the Moretonhampstead line at Heathfield. Although prompted by thoughts of diversions during sea wall incidents, this also benefited the regular daily goods traffic as some trains were running through to/from Newton Abbot after 1907 and had been obliged to make a double reversal prior to 1916.

GOODS TRAIN WORKINGS 1905–1939
We saw in Chapter 13 how the line was, from August 1903, served by one Exeter–Heathfield–Exeter daily goods train. Although more than adequate in 1903, this quickly

In contrast, this 1925 view shows the '1916' layout at Heathfield, with a direct running connection to the branch (see diagram on page 174). *G. N. Southerden*

MAY 1911 TIMETABLE

The passenger service is the same here as that introduced in 1904, but the Exeter–Christow trains were to be withdrawn only a few months later.

DOWN

	Passenger B	Passenger B	Newton Abbot Goods K	Passenger B	(Station Truck) Goods K	Passenger B	Tiverton Jn Passenger ↓ B	RR Goods K	Passenger B	Goods K	Dulverton Passenger ↓ B	Passenger B
Exeter	6.35am	7.40am		9.45am	9.30am	11.7am	1.5/1.12pm		3.12pm	4.5pm	6.5/6.12pm	7.20pm
St. Thomas	6.39	7.43/7.45		9.48/9.50	–	11.10/11.12	1.15/1.17		3.15/3.17	–	6.15/6.20	7.23/7.25
City Basin Jn.	cs	cs		cs	Xcs	cs	Xcs		cs	Xcs	Xcs	Xcs
Alphington Rd	–	–		–	9.38•10.20	–	–		–	–	–	–
Ide	6.47	7.53		9.58	10.26/10.30	11.20	1.25		3.25	–	6.28	7.33
Longdown	6.56	8.2		10.7	10.41/10.45	11.29	1.34		3.34	–	6.37	7.42
Stop Board	–	–		P	–	–	–		–	P	–	–
Christow	7.6	8.11		10.16/10.34	10.58/11.8	11.38	1.44	2.12	3.43X3.46	4.38/7.15	6.46X6.48	7.51
Ashton	7.11/7.13	–		10.39/10.42	11.15/11.20	–	1.49/1.52	2.17/2.22	3.51/3.54	–	6.53/6.56	–
Whetcombe Sdg	–	–		–	CR	–	–	CR	–	CR	–	–
Trusham	7.19	–	10.10	10.48	11.28/11.40	–	1.58	2.27/2.32	4.0	7.30	7.2	–
Crockham Sdg	–	–	CR	–	CR	–	–	2.33/3.0	–	–	–	–
Chudleigh	7.25	–	–	10.54	11.48/12.5	–	2.4	–	4.6	–	7.8	–
Heathfield	7.31	–	10.25/10.40 ↓	11.0	12.15X	–	2.10	3.10X	4.12X	–	7.14	–
connections:												
Heathfield	7.34	–	to Newton Abbot	11.9	–	–	2.15	–	4.20	–	7.24	–
Newton Abbot	7.45	–	10.55	11.20	–	–	2.26	–	4.31	–	7.35	–

UP

connections:

	Dulverton Passenger B	Passenger B	K	Passenger B	Passenger B	RR Goods K	Passenger B	(Station Truck) Goods K	Passenger B	Passenger B	Stone K	Passenger B
Newton Abbot		8.10am	8.30am		12.6pm		3.1pm		5.52pm			9.3pm
Heathfield		8.20	Newton Abbot Goods		12.16		3.11		6.2			9.14

	Dulverton Passenger B	Passenger B	K	Passenger B	Passenger B	RR Goods K	Passenger B	(Station Truck) Goods K	Passenger B	Passenger B	Stone K	Passenger B
Heathfield		8.33am	8.45/9.0am		X12.22pm	12.47pm	X3.18pm	X4.20pm	6.20pm			9.20pm
Chudleigh		8.40	–	–	12.29	–	3.25	4.30/4.40	6.27			9.27
Crockham Sdg		–	CR		–	12.55/1.20	–	–	–			–
Trusham		8.46	9.12		12.35	1.22/1.27	3.31	4.48/5.8	6.33		8.15pm	9.33
Whetcombe Sdg		–	–		–	CR	–	CR	–			–
Ashton		8.52			12.41	1.32/1.37	3.37	5.16/5.23	6.39		8.23/8.28	9.39
Christow	8.22am	8.58		11.50am	12.47	1.42	3.42X3.45	5.30/5.40	6.44/6.47	8.5pm	8.35/8.50	9.45
Longdown	8.32	9.8		12.0	12.57	–	3.55	5.53/5.58	6.57	8.15		9.55
Stop Board		–	–		–	–	–	P	–	P		–
Ide	8.40	9.16		12.8	1.5	–	4.3	6.8/6.12	7.5	8.23		10.3
Alphington Rd		–	–		–	–	–	6.18X7.25	–	–		–
City Basin Jn	cs	cs		cs	Xcs		cs	cs	cs	cs	cs	cs
St. Thomas	8.47/8.49	9.23/9.25		12.16	1.12/1.14		4.10/4.12	–	7.12/7.14	8.30/8.32		10.10/10.12
Exeter	8.52/9.11	9.28		12.19	1.17		4.15	7.30	7.17	8.35	9.40	10.15

cs — Change staff.
X — Crossing of trains.
CR — Calls when Required.
RR — Runs when Required.
P — Stop to pin down brakes.
The Ashton stops of the 2.12pm down and 8.15pm up were for water only.

9.30 a.m. Exeter to Heathfield.

The Guard of this Train must do all possible to arrive at destination to time, and to attain this he may relieve the Train of any shunting or work that can be done by the 12.47 p.m. ex Heathfield. He must also see that the Engine of the latter Train is utilised to the utmost extent in shunting out traffic at all Stations between Heathfield and Christow, and placed in position for the 4.25 p.m. ex Heathfield to take on in one shunt, and Up Traffic and Coal Empties from Trusham Station and Ashton to be taken to Christow for the 4.25 p.m., **which must reach Alphington Road punctually each day.**

Mr. Williams to provide a Brakesman to work with the 9.30 a.m. Exeter to Heathfield throughout.

Mr. Honeywill to see that as much Stone Traffic as possible is got ready for the Engine of the 12.47 p.m. ex Heathfield to deal with in both directions, so that no delay whatever may take place to the 4.25 p.m. ex Heathfield, and his staff must be in attendance at the Granite Siding on arrival of each train to render every assistance in shunting, &c.

Working of Bank Engine.

Bank Engine to leave Exeter at 4.30 p.m. daily, due Christow at 4.50 p.m., and must shunt out traffic there for the 4.25 p.m. Goods to take on in one shunt. It is very important that this Engine should leave Exeter punctually.

Advices of Traffic.

All stations to wire Christow as usual the number of wagons for the 4.25 p.m. ex Heathfield daily, and the advice from Trusham must reach Christow not later than 3.50 p.m. daily, and in the event of there not being more than a single engine load from that Station must wire Messrs. Williams & Wager, Exeter, to cancel the running of the Bank Engine, and the advice must be despatched not later than 3.55 p.m.

Commenced October 3rd.

Marshalling instructions for the 9.30 a.m. Exeter / 12.47 p.m. Heathfield / 2.12 p.m. Christow / 4.25 p.m. Heathfield, as at January 1908. Mr. Honeywill was the Trusham station master. The 'Granite Siding' is Crockham. After the introduction of the Exeter–Trusham–Exeter evening trip in 1911, it was laid down that the Heathfield–Exeter goods should be kept to a single load only so that no banker would be needed for it.

An unidentified outside-frame 0—6—0 pannier tank leaving Christow for Ashton about 4.15 p.m. on 10th June 1925.   *G. N. Southerden*

became insufficient to cope with the growing stone traffic. The subsequent history of the goods services can be outlined as follows:

- A period of expansion in 1907–1911 to deal with the Trusham stone traffic in particular, followed by eight years of little change.
- A second period of expansion in 1919–1922 to deal with the Christow stone traffic in particular, after which there was little change in the 1920s.
- Reduction from 1932 onwards, in reaction to the fall-off in the stone traffic.

The May 1911 timetable here shows the situation near the end of the first period of expansion. The 8.30 am Newton Abbot–Trusham/10.10 am Trusham–Newton Abbot was introduced in 1907 to enable the bulk of the Trusham/Crockham stone traffic to be taken direct to Newton Abbot, so relieving the Moretonhampstead branch goods trains. The 12.47 pm Heathfield–Christow/ 2.12 pm Christow–Heathfield was also introduced in 1907, to relieve the 9.30 am Exeter and the 4.20 pm Heathfield, and was in fact worked by the same engine and crew as these trains (leaving Exeter 9.30 am, back 7.30 pm). The full Marshalling Instructions for these trains are appended. Note the references to banking, which was regularly necessary from this date until the 1930s and is discussed further in Chapter 18. Finally, the 4.05 pm Exeter–Trusham/ 8.15 pm Trusham–Exeter 'Stone' train was introduced in

January 1911 to further relieve the 9.30 am Exeter and 4.20 pm Heathfield, by taking most of such Trusham/Crockham stone traffic as needed to be taken out via Exeter rather than via Heathfield, and the Christow stone traffic (almost all of which always went out via Exeter). This train was timetabled to run to/from Crockham Siding from August 1911.

The May 1911 timetable just predates Trusham's conversion to a crossing station and shows why this was necessary. Note in particular the tight timings of the 12.47 pm Heathfield/2.12 pm Christow in relation to the passenger trains. After Trusham became a crossing station, the 9.30 am Exeter/4.20 pm Heathfield were given more relaxed timings (thanks to being able to cross the 12.22 pm up and 3.12 pm down passenger trains at Trusham) and were thereby enabled to do all the necessary shunting en route, so that the tightly-timed 12.47/2.12 was withdrawn.

From 1911 to 1919, therefore, there were three goods trains on the branch; Newton Abbot–Trusham–Newton Abbot, Exeter–Heathfield–Exeter, and Exeter–Crockham–Exeter. The March 1919 timetable shows this. However, in addition to the timetabled trains there was at one time a daily GWR ballast train from Crockham; and almost certainly other specials ran at the busiest times.

The changes of 1919–22 were too complex to narrate in full detail, but left a situation through the 1920s, shown in the September 1931 Timetable, in which there were usually five daily goods trains *(page 138)*:

- Newton Abbot–Exeter
- Exeter–Newton Abbot (a separate train)
  These workings were introduced in 1921 and replaced the previous Exeter–Heathfield–Exeter and Newton Abbot–Trusham–Newton Abbot services. They did the bulk of the shunting at Crockham, Trusham, and Whetcombe.
- Exeter–Christow–Exeter (extended to Ryecroft from 1930) in the middle of the day. This was introduced in September 1919 in

reaction to the increased stone traffic at Christow, and did the bulk of the shunting at Christow. (Its locomotive also banked the Newton Abbot–Exeter train from Christow to Longdown.)
- Exeter–Trusham–Exeter, in the afternoon/evening, as before. (No longer shown to/from Crockham in the timetable, but it still took Crockham stone traffic.) This train became 'Runs as Required' latterly, as traffic fell off.
- Exeter–Alphington Road–Exeter, in the late afternoon, introduced 1922. The traffic at Alphington Road had increased considerably in the years before this, and was now such as to require a separate train. However, some of the other trains continued to call at Alphington Road also.

MARCH 1919 TIMETABLE

Showing the very poor passenger service at this period. The Goods trains are as in 1912; there could be no retraction on the Goods front.

DOWN

	Passenger B	Passenger B	Newton Abbot Goods K	Goods K	Goods K	Passenger B
Exeter	7.25am	9.55am		10.10am	2.35pm	5.0pm
St. Thomas	7.28	9.58		–	–	5.3
City Basin Jn	cs	cs		cs	2.43 / 2.48	csX
Alphington Rd	–	–		10.20 / 11.0	–	–
Ide	–	–		–	–	–
Longdown	7.46	10.17		11.21 / 11.26	cs	5.22
Stop Board	–	–		11.27 P 11.29	3.1 P 3.4	–
Christow	7.56	10.26 / 10.28		11.39 / 11.55	3.14 / 6.0	5.31 / 5.33
Ashton	8.1 / 8.3	10.33 / 10.36		12.2 / 12.20	6.7 / 6.10	5.38 / 5.40
Whetcombe Sdg	–	–		12/25 / 12.40	6.15 / 6.30	–
Trusham	8.9	10.42	12.0	12.43 X 1.18	6.32 X 6.50	5.47
Crockham Sdg	–	–	CR	1.21 / 1.40	6.52	–
Chudleigh	8.15	10.48	CR	1.47 / 1.55	–	5.53
Heathfield	8.21	10.54	12.20	2.5	—	6.2
connections:						
Heathfield	*(8.29)*	*(11.4)*	12.55	–	–	–
Newton Abbot	*(8.40)*	*(11.15)*	1.15	–	–	–

UP

connections:						
Newton Abbot		8.50	*(12.40)*	–	*(6.10)*	–
Heathfield	–	9.10	*(12.50)*	–	*(6.19)*	–

	Passenger B	Newton Abbot Goods K	Passenger B	Goods K	Passenger B	Goods K
Heathfield	8.35am	11.00am	1.5pm	2.30pm	6.35pm	–
Chudleigh	8.42	CR	1.12	2.40 / 2.50	6.42	–
Crockham Sdg	–	CR	–	2.57 / 3.5	–	7.5pm
Trusham	8.48	11.20	1 X 18	3.7 / 3.20	6 X 48	7.6 / 7.15
Whetcombe Sdg	–		–	3.22 / 3.30	–	CR
Ashton	8.54		1.24	3.35 / 3.40	6.54	7.25 / 7.30
Christow	9.0		1.30 / 1.47	3.47 X 4.25	7.0	7.40 / 8.20
Longdown	9.9/9.12		1.56 / 1.59	4.38 ST 4.43	7.9 / 7.13	8.33 / 8.40
Stop Board	–		–	4.44 P 4.47	–	8.41 P 8.44
Ide	–		–	P	–	–
Stop Board	–		–		–	9.12 P 9.15
Alphington Rd	–		–	5.4 X 7.45	–	–
City Basin Jn	cs		cs	cs	cs	cs
St. Thomas	9.25		2.12	–	7.27	–
Exeter	9.28		2.15	7.55	7.30	9.27

Note that there are no trains through to/from the Exe Valley line in this timetable. (This soon resumed, however.) There were only 4 trains each way on the Moretonhampstead branch at this period. The Ashton stop of the 7.5pm up was for water only. Note that the 10.10am down goods takes advantage of the new Block Post at Longdown by passing City Basin Jn as soon as the previous train has reached Longdown. Also the very (impossibly) tight timing by which the 2.30pm up goods arrives at Alphington Rd at 5.4, upon which the fireman has to walk to City Basin Jn signal box with the staff and the signalman have the staff ready again for the down passenger booked off St. Thomas at 5.3pm!

cs – Change staff.   P – Stop to pin down brakes
CR – Calls when Required   ST – Stops for Station Trucks purposes only.

No. 1244 waiting at Trusham with an up goods in September 1924. By the 1930s, the 45XX 2—6—2Ts had replaced these pannier tanks on the Teign Valley goods workings.
G. N. Southerden

It will be noted that there was now only one train each way over the Heathfield–Trusham section (previously two), but three each way over the Exeter–Christow section (previously two). This reflected the decline of the Trusham stone traffic.

STATION TRUCKS WORKINGS

As on all lines, goods 'smalls' were conveyed in a 'Station Truck' van in the branch goods train, which stopped in the passenger platform at each station for the porters to load/unload from the van any consignments for that station.

Originally, of course, all goods had to be transhipped between Broad Gauge and Standard Gauge trucks at Heathfield. After 1892, though, the Teign Valley Station Truck ran through from Newton Abbot in the Moretonhampstead branch goods train, exchanging trains at Heathfield. This continued until 1921 after which the Station Trucks ran in the new through Exeter–Newton Abbot and v.v. goods trains.

The Station Trucks came to an end in 1947/8 under the GWR's 'Zoning' scheme, by which smalls were delivered by road from the nearest large station. Zoning dates for the Teign Valley stations were:-

	smalls	full loads	Zoned
Chudleigh	1/3/47	1/3/47	Newton Abbot
Trusham	1/3/47	1/3/47	Newton Abbot
Ashton	1/2/47	1/10/48	Exeter
Christow	1/2/47	1/10/48	Exeter
Longdown	1/2/47	1/10/48	Exeter
Ide	1/2/47	1/10/48	Exeter

(Full loads continued by rail to each station, the 'zoning' being for accounts purposes in this case.)

The 1930s decline was very sudden. 1932 saw the end of the Exeter–Trusham–Exeter evening train, and 1935/6 a recasting of the remaining services into the following workings only:

- Newton Abbot–Christow–Newton Abbot (mornings).
- Exeter–Trusham–Exeter (late mornings; effectively an extension of the Christow train to compensate for the withdrawal of the other trains).
- Exeter–Alphington Road (early mornings, to bring in empties; returns Engine & Van to Exeter).
- Exeter–Alphington Road–Exeter, late afternoon, as previously.

Most of the line therefore now saw only one goods train each way, and the daily goods train mileage was 47, instead of 104 in 1931.

PASSENGER TRAFFIC AND SERVICES 1905–1919

Passenger traffic increased gradually in the years up to 1914, as on most lines. The service introduced in 1904 (five trains Exeter–Heathfield, and three extra trains Exeter–Christow) was kept until the winter of 1911/12, when the Exeter–Christow trains were withdrawn, bringing the service back to its August 1903 form. It is doubtful whether the Christow trains had ever really been justified; they had been introduced for political purposes rather than traffic need, and it is clear from the traffic figures that the

Railmotor No. 81 leaving Exeter St. Thomas on its way to Heathfield in April 1924. No. 81 worked from Exeter from 1922 until 1925, when she was transferred onto the Cambrian section.
G. N. Southerden

south end of the branch was in fact busier than the north end, notably on the Chudleigh–Heathfield section. The withdrawal of these trains may have been due in part to a desire to clear the single line of these unremunerative passenger trains so that the timetabling of the goods trains could be made easier. It brought a significant loss of custom at Ide station (where, thanks to its proximity to Exeter, passenger figures were always very sensitive to train frequency), but had only a small impact on the Longdown and Christow figures.

The 1914–18 war brought drastic reductions in the line's passenger service, and usage figures tumbled as a result. In the early part of the war the 1.12 down/3.18 up was cut out, leaving 4 trains each way, and the time of the last up train advanced from the time-honoured 9 pm-plus to 7.40 pm (it never returned to the later times). Ide station was closed to all traffic from 1st January 1917 (to 5th May 1919) as part of a general programme of closing stations to release staff; and St Thomas, which was used by most local passengers for Exeter, was closed from 2nd April 1917 (to 3rd March 1919). Then in 1918 a further train each way was deleted, leaving until 1920 the dreadful 3-trains-a-day service shown in the March 1919 Timetable here, the worst service ever provided on the line. The last train from Exeter was now at 5 pm, the last train from Chudleigh to Newton Abbot at 10.48 am (!), and it was quite impossible to get from Newton Abbot to anywhere on the branch and

return the same day. This was what the railway had to offer at the moment bus competition began.

BUS COMPETITION AFTER 1919

Prior to 1914 the GWR's Moretonhampstead–Chagford service (introduced 1906 in place of a long-established horse bus service), and the LSWR's Exeter–Chagford service (commenced 1904, and running via the A30 to Whiddon Down), had been the only serious bus operations in the area. Neither of these had affected the Teign Valley line.[1] But after 1919 the line was hit seriously by bus competition, as happened everywhere.

In 1919 the newly-established Devon General Company began an Exeter–Haldon–Chudleigh–Kingsteignton–Newton Abbot service (Service 1) and this quickly took away the majority of the railway's Chudleigh traffic, thanks to its more convenient timings and, of course, the remote situation of Chudleigh station. The railway made no attempt to respond and would not have retained the traffic even if they had. By 1923 Chudleigh was dealing with only one third of its previous traffic, and from this time always had less traffic than Trusham and Ashton; people soon forgot that it had once been the busiest station on the line.

At the other end of the line, Devon Motor Transport Ltd began an Exeter–Longdown–Leigh Cross–Dunsford–Moretonhampstead service in 1920. This route was transferred to Devon General (Service 19) in 1924 and the timings improved in 1927. As the buses ran through Longdown village and Dunsford village, which had been Longdown station's main sources of traffic prior to this date but which were both a long walk from the station, they succeeded in reducing Longdown's trade to one third of its former level by the late 1920s. It has to be said, though, that as the passenger numbers at Longdown had never been very large, this was not a loss to the line comparable to the loss of the Chudleigh traffic.

Ide gained an Exeter bus service around 1931 (an Exeter–Ide–Dunchideock route run by Milton's Services of Crediton, and taken over by Devon General in 1935). This immediately took traffic away from Ide station, which had been doing increased trade in the 1920s after train services were improved; by the late '30s the traffic at Ide was down to a quarter of the 1930 level.

In contrast, nobody considered it worth starting a bus service to Trusham, Ashton, or Christow in the interwar years. As a result, the traffic at these stations held up well in the 1920s, and only began to decline gradually in the '30s as private car ownership increased.

The Teign Valley line therefore provides an excellent example of how the passenger traffic at different stations on a rural branch line could be affected in quite different ways in the 1920s–50s period, according to the level of bus service provided at each place.

PASSENGER TRAFFIC AND TRAIN SERVICES 1919–1939

Despite the loss of some traffic as noted above, the 1920s were a very positive time for the branch's passenger traffic on the whole. By the mid-1920s the GWR's management had thrown out the inheritance of the 1914–18 cutbacks, and were setting out to improve services on their rural branches to combat competition. The Teign Valley line benefited greatly from this and by the late '20s had a better service than ever before (as described in detail below). The '20s and '30s also saw the GWR engaged in a second burst of rural halt building, as extensive as that of the 1900s. This time the Teign Valley line, which had not benefited in the 1900s due to the Exeter Railway's opposition to motors, did share in the programme, with halts being opened at Chudleigh Knighton in 1924 and Dunsford and Alphington in 1928. All the trains on the line called at these halts. Chudleigh Knighton (which should have been provided long before) was very successful. Dunsford and Alphington were less obvious, both villages having good

This row of cottages in the lower part of Ide village was known as 'The College' and featured road access via the 'water lane', which vehicles drove along in the stream. The view dates from the 1920s and most of the cottages lost their thatch just after this.

Collection Mrs. M. Piller

This view of Christow is believed to date from the summer of 1922, in which case the trains would be the 12.57 Heathfield–Exeter and the 12.50 Exeter–Heathfield motor. The contrast between the two illustrates the passenger service's early 1920s 'transitional' period, prior to the near-takeover by motors in 1923. The five-coach trains of these years were the longest ever regularly seen on the line.

Collection Paul Strong

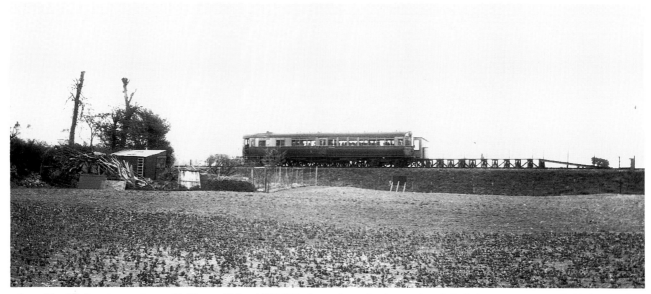

An unidentified motor pausing at Alphington Halt c.1930. This shows the embankment site of the halt.

G. N. Southerden

bus services by the time the halts were opened; Dunsford was also a very long way from the village it purported to serve, and Alphington was too near Exeter to bring in much traffic, especially as the trains could not deposit people in the city centre as the frequent buses could.

The postwar recovery of the passenger timetable began in July 1920 when a Motor trip was added on the line (Exeter d.12.55 pm/Heathfield d.3.15 pm/Christow d.4.30 pm/Heathfield d.5.45 pm to Exeter) to fill in the long afternoon gap in the services. This was the first appearance of Motors on the line and this time the Exeter Railway Board does not seem to have raised any objections! (They were no doubt glad to see any improvement in the service.) It was also the first instance of a Heathfield–Christow–Heathfield short working; these were to become a regular feature in the interwar timetables. By 1923 a further Motor trip had been added in the mornings, so bringing the service back to five trains each way. Then in October 1923 the ordinary passenger trains were changed over to Auto or Motor operation, bringing an entirely Auto and Motor timetable. All this enabled a reduction in costs as well as an improvement in services, and as part of the same package the station master at Ide

---

The April 1928 Passenger Timetable, as shown in the opening notice for Alphington Halt. In this timetable, the Saturday late train from Exeter (9.40 p.m.) ran on to Heathfield, but still returned to Exeter via the branch.

The 8.45 p.m. Exeter–Heathfield was another late train, for general passengers, introduced in the mid-20s. It ran every summer until 1939 but never ran in the winter. Usually it returned as the 9.55 p.m. Heathfield–Exeter, but in this timetable it ran through to Newton Abbot instead and did not return to Exeter via the branch.

With Heathfield having been made a crossing station for Moretonhampstead line trains in 1927, there are now at least some good Moretonhampstead–Exeter and v.v. connections. However, most people wanting such a journey would now go by bus!

GREAT WESTERN RAILWAY.

On Monday, April 2nd, 1928,

A NEW HALT
WILL BE OPENED AT

ALPHINGTON

SITUATE BETWEEN
EXETER (ST. THOMAS) AND IDE HALT.

TRAIN SERVICE. Week-days only.

(timetable details)

Tickets should be obtained from the Guard on the train.
The Third Class Single Fares from ALPHINGTON HALT will be as under:—

CHEAP THIRD-CLASS RETURN TICKETS will be issued each week-day by ANY TRAIN—

Parcels and Goods traffic will not be dealt with at the Halt.

Paddington,
March, 1928.

FELIX J. C. POLE,
General Manager.

Railmotor 97, seen here at Ashton on 24th July 1930, was at Exeter shed from 1928 to 1931.

F. M. Gates

Railmotor 53 departing from Christow on a down service with a six-wheel trailer on August Bank Holiday Monday, 3rd August 1931. The train in the up platform also had a trailer, six-wheel Brake Third No. 1685. From the 1930s the new fashion for country rambling started to bring extra traffic to the line on fine Saturday afternoons and Bank Holidays. In particular, youth groups from Exeter would come out to Christow or Ashton for a walk up to the Tottiford Reservoirs.

G. N. Southerden

Destination of almost all branch passengers prior to 1903, and still for a large proportion after that date, was Newton Abbot's splendid 1860/1 station. Although John Dickson's 1904 ideas of frequent fast Teign Valley through trains never came to fruition, and very few Teign Valley trains ran through at all prior to the 1940s, the platform signing at Newton Abbot nevertheless gave proper prominence to the branch. Moretonhampstead (as they were in reality!) trains used the middle line platforms. This station was taken down in 1925/6 and the new station erected, partly on the same site.

National Railway Museum

was abolished in October 1923 and the station renamed 'Ide Halt' to signify that it was now unstaffed on the late turn.

From 1923 to 1935 the branch was largely a Motor preserve. Some timetables indeed saw 100% Motor operation, but others had one or two Autos or ordinary passenger trains.

By 1927 there were seven daily trains each way over the full length of the line, an unprecedentedly good service, and the number remained at 6, 7, or 8 in subsequent timetables of the interwar years, plus some short workings in most cases.

The world was a different place after 1919 and this brought changed social habits and changed travelling patterns to which the branch timetable had to respond. Most significantly, there was the emergence of a 'commuter' (not that that word was used then) and schoolchildren's traffic to Exeter and Newton Abbot, something which we regard as a normal feature of a rural branch line but which did not really exist before 1914. The Newton Abbot traffic

On the reverse of the original photograph, G. N. Southerden noted this unidentified steam railmotor, with a van third in tow, as departing from Newton Abbot on a Newton, Heathfield & Exeter service during the spring of 1935. He also noted this as his last photo of a GW steam railmotor. The service was most probably the 3.0 p.m. ex Newton which ran during the currency of the winter timetables on Wednesdays and Saturdays only from around 1928. This was shown as a 'Motor' service until the mid-1930s, working down from Heathfield to Newton Abbot at 2.40 p.m., but thereafter becoming an auto duty, continuing as such until the 1950s, latterly on a daily basis.
G. N. Southerden

The new 1927 crossing loop and down platform at Heathfield, giving good connections both ways for Teign Valley trains, are seen in action here on the afternoon of Saturday, 9th September 1933, with the 3.45 p.m. Kingswear–Moretonhampstead arriving, the 4.58 p.m. Bovey–Newton auto (propelled by a '517' class 0–4–2T) waiting for it to clear, and motor No. 80, with a six-wheel trailer, in the Bay ready to work the 5.10 p.m. Teign Valley service. Trailers were regularly carried by the motors on Saturdays and other busier days (see page 270).

G. N. Southerden

Railmotor No. 74 at Christow on the 2.45 p.m. service from Exeter on 10th June 1925. Like most of the cars, No. 74 moved around the system a great deal, moving to Exeter from the Cambrian line (Penmaenpool) in 1924, and was transferred to Southall around 1927.

G. N. Southerden

must not be exaggerated; it consisted only of those few children from Christow, Ashton, and Trusham who had won 'scholarships' to Newton Abbot Grammar School, and the odd shop girl. Even on Wednesdays, when they were accompanied by farmers' wives from the valley taking eggs and butter to Newton Abbot market, the Motor was nowhere near full. The first down train was already suitably timed for this Newton traffic, delivering people in Newton around 8.30 am, but for some reason the passengers were always subjected to a 20-minute wait at Heathfield for their connection to arrive from Moretonhampstead. They had to sit in the train in the platform, waiting patiently or impatiently. There was no reason why the Teign Valley train could not have run 20 minutes later (and eventually, in 1957, this happened). The return times from Newton Abbot in the evenings were also already reasonably suitable.

For the Exeter traffic, however, the existing service did not really provide. Since the abolition of the Christow extras in 1911/12, the first up train only arrived in Exeter around 9.15 am, and this was too late. Pressure was therefore brought on the GWR to run another train before this, and in 1929 they introduced an 8.0 am Christow–Exeter. This was a costly train to run as the down train to form it,

the 7.20 am Exeter, ran almost empty; but it remained a fixture of the timetable from this time onwards. (In 1947 it was extended to start from Trusham.) The late afternoon down service was improved at the same time by the addition of a 4.30 pm Exeter–Christow (soon extended through to Heathfield) which also stayed as a fixture in the timetable afterwards. The last down train had been running at 5.45 pm in the '20s and was now put back to 6.15 pm (its traditional pre-1914 time); it drifted to 6.30 pm in the '40s before reverting to around 6 pm in the '50s.

A particular feature of the line, from its introduction in 1923 (as the 9.20 pm Exeter–Trusham), was the Saturday-only[2] late-night down train provided to give valley people, the quarrymen in particular, a 'night out' in Exeter. It was a great sight to see this train arrive back at Christow or Trusham, as the happy crowd poured out of the station and set off on their long treks back home to Christow, Doddiscombsleigh, Bridford, Teign Village, or Trusham villages. This train remained in the timetable to the end, save that it was withdrawn during the 1939–45 war. In some years it ran through to Heathfield or Newton Abbot instead of returning to Exeter up the branch, as there was little or no passenger traffic for the up return working. The train's departure time from Exeter was always too early for

National Railway Museum

Exeter St. David's station in April 1931.

An unidentified steam railmotor heading away from Exeter St. David's towards St. Thomas, probably on a Teign Valley service c.1925.
G. N. Southerden

the satisfaction of cinema addicts; Teign Valley children never saw the end of a film and had to run down the hill to St Thomas at the last minute! (As often as not they then found the train left late anyway, as it had to wait for a character called 'Jimmy the Fiddler' from Bridford who rarely presented himself on time.)

Less frequent but no less noisy were the 'Pantomime -Trains' run on one or two Saturdays in January for many years in the '20s and '30s. This involved a very late train, at about 11.10 pm from Exeter, to bring home the valley children after a night at the pantomime at the Theatre Royal, Exeter. It was organised at the behest of Percy Dunsford, the theatre owner, but did appear in the public timetables. The train returned from Heathfield as a passenger (in theory) working at the unlikely hour of 12.15 am!

The use of Motors and Autos facilitated odd workings terminating at intermediate stations and halts (something which had not been seen since the Heathfield–Chudleigh train of the 1880s). For example:

- In 1927 one train from Exeter ran through to Bovey.
- A 5.10 pm Heathfield–Chudleigh–Heathfield in 1928.
- A 2.45 pm Exeter–Chudleigh for some years (although, as will be seen from the 1931 Timetable here, any passengers for Chudleigh had to alight at Trusham whilst an up Motor was crossed, and then get back in again!).

The exact occasion on which this view was taken is not remembered, but the window labels in coach 3938 read 'Teign Valley Schools' and clearly someone had arranged a special train. The photograph was taken at Christow c.1933 and Christow signalman Wilf Cox's younger daughter Cynthia (with bonnet) is seen in the nearest compartment with her aunt. Cynthia was later to marry Frank Edworthy, signalman at Longdown 1944-1949. *Cty. Frank & Cynthia Edworthy*

DOWN TRAINS. TEIGN VALLEY BRANCH. Week Days.

SINGLE LINE worked by Electric Train Staff. The Staff Stations are City Basin Junction, Longdown, Christow, Trusham and Heathfield. The Crossing Stations are City Basin Junction and Christow. When absolutely necessary a Passenger Train may cross Goods or Empty Trains at Trusham on the understanding that the Passenger Train is always kept on the Running Line, and that if the Passenger Train has to stop at Trusham, it must stop at the Platform.

M. P. Mileage M.	C.	Distances from Exeter M.	C.	STATIONS.	Station No.	Ruling Gradient.	Point to Point Times.	Allow for Stop.	Allow for Start.	B Motor. arr.	dep.	B Passenger. arr.	dep.	K Newton Abbot Goods. arr.	dep.	K Goods. RR arr.	dep.	B Motor. arr.	dep.			B Motor. arr.	dep.	B Motor. arr.	dep.	K Goods. arr.	dep.
							Mins.	Mins.	Mins.	A.M.	A.M.	A.M.	A.M.	A.M.	A.M.	A.M.	A.M.	A.M.	A.M.			A.M.	A.M.	A.M.	A.M.	A.M.	A.M.
—	—	—	—	**Exeter** ..	1552	—	—	—	2	—	**7 0**	—	**7 20**	—	6 0	..	..		**9 25**	..	..	—	**10 55**	—	**11 25**	—	10 40
—	—		74	St. Thomas	1554	—	—	—	—	7 3	7 4	7 23	7 24	—	—	....	....	9 28	9 29	....	..	10 58	10 59	11 28	11 30	—	—
—	—	1	19	City Basin Junc	1555	—	—	—	—	C	S	C	S	C	S	..	..	C	S	..	..	C	S	11 31	X11 33	C	S
0	19	1	38	Alphington Road Goods Junc.	1628	264 R	6	1	1	—	—	—	—	6 9	6 30	..	..	—		..	..	—	—	SUS-PENDED		10 49•	X12 0
0	62	2	1	Alphington Halt	—	56 R.	—	—	—	7 8	7 9	7 28	7 29	—	—	....	....	9 33	9 34	....	....	11 3	11 4	11 36	11 37	—	—
2	0	3	19	Ide Halt ..	1629	58 R.	7	1	2	7 13	7 14	7 33	7 34	C	R	..	..	9 38	9 39	..	..	11 8	11 9	11 41	11 42	C	R
4	58	5	77	Longdown	1630	58 R.	10	1	1	7 22	7 23	7 42	7 43	C	R	....	....	9 47	9 48	...	....	11 17	11 18	11 50	11 51	C	S
4	68	6	7	Stop Board ..	—	L.	—	—	—	—	—	—	—	6 50	P6 53	..	..	—	—	..	..	—	—	—	—	12 20	P12 23
6	1	7	20	Dunsford Halt	—	64 F.	—	—	—	7 27	7 28	7 47	7 48	—	—	...	...	9 52	9 53	..	..	11 22	11 23	11 55	11 56	—	—
8	3	9	22	Christow	1631	64 F.	8	2	1	7 34	7 36	7 54	—	7 4•	P7 50	..	..	9 59	10 1	..	..	11 29	X11 31	12 2	X12 3	12 33	P—
		10	29	Ryecroft Quarry	—	—	—	—	—	—	—			—	—	....	....	—	—	....	....	—	—	—	—		
Terminates at 8M. 7C.		10	68	Ashton ..	1632	132 F	4	1	1	7 41	7 42	....	....	7 56	8 6	..	..	10 6	10 7	..	..	11 36	11 37	12 8	12 9	R	R
		12	33	Whetcombe Sdg.	1667	198 F.	4	1	1	—	—	..	..	—	—	....	....	—	—	....	....	—	—	—	—	to Ry	ecroft.
		12	63	Trusham ..	1634	384 F.	2	1	1	7 47	7 48	....	....	8 •14	X12 0	—	9 30	10 12	X10 13	..	..	11 42	X11 43	12 14	12 15	...	...
		13	8	Crockham Siding	1635	84 F.	2	1	1	—	—	..	..	—	—	—	—	—	—	....		—	—	—	—	..	..
		14	51	Chudleigh ..	1636	132 F.	4	1	1	7 53	7 54	....	....	12 8	12 30	9 38	—	10 18	10 19	..	..	11 48	11 49	12 20	12 21	....	..
		15	74	Chudleigh K. Hlt.	—	—	—	—	—	7 57	7 58			—	—			10 22	10 23	..	..	11 52	11 53	12 24	12 25	..	..
		17	3	**Heathfield** ..	1641	66 R.	6	1	—	**8 2**	—	....	....	12 38	1 15	....	....	**10 27**	—	....	....	**11 57**	—	**12 29**	—	....	....

Down Trains—continued. Week Days. STATIONS.	B Motor. arr.	dep.	B Motor. arr.	dep.	B Motor. arr.	dep.	B Motor. arr.	dep.	K Goods. RR arr.	dep.	B Passenger. arr.	dep.	K Goods. arr.	dep.	B Auto. arr.	dep.	B Motor. arr.	dep.	B Newton Abt. Pass. SO arr.	dep.		Sundays. K Goods. arr.	dep.
	P.M.	P.M.	P.M.	P.M.	P.M.	P.M.	P.M.	P.M.	P.M.	P.M.	P.M.	P.M.	P.M.	P.M.	P.M.	P.M.	P.M.	P.M.	P.M.	P.M.		A.M.	A.M.
Exeter	—	**12 55**	—	**2 45**	..	..	..	..	—	3 5	—	**4†18**	—	4 45	—	**6 15**	—	**8 45**	-	9 40	...	—	5 30
St. Thomas	12 58	12 59	2 48	2 50	....	....	....	....	—	—	4†21	4 30	—	—	6 18	6 19	8 48	8 49	9 43	9 44	..	—	—
City Basin Junction ..	C	S	XC	S	..	..	..	..	3	14	C	S	C 4 53	S	C	S	SUS-		C	S	....	C	S
Alphington Road Goods Junc.	—	—	—	—	..	....	....	....	—	—	—	—	4 55	—	—	—	PENDED		—	—	..	5 40	—
Alphington Halt	1 3	1 4	2 54	2 55	..	..	..	..	—	--	4 34	4 35			6 23	6 23½	8 53	8 54	9 48	9 49	....		
Ide Halt	1 8	1 9	2 59	3 0	....	....	....	....	—	—	4 39	4 40	..	..	6 27½	6 28	8 58	8 59	9 53	9 54	..	..	..
Longdown	1 17	1 18	3 8	3 9	..	..	..	..	C	S	4 48	4 49	..		6 36	6 36½	9 7	9 8	10 2	10 3	....	....	....
Stop Board	—	—	—	—	....	....	....	....	3 34P	3 37	—	—	K		—	—	—	—	—	—	..	....	....
Dunsford Halt ..	1 22	1 23	3 13	3 14	..	..	..	..	—	—	4 53	4 54			6 40½	6 41	9 12	9 13	10 7	10 8	....	..	..
Christow	1 29	X 1 31	3 20	3 22	....	....	—	4 11	3 47P	X5 40	5 0	X—	Goods.		6 47	X6 50	9 19	X 9 20	10 1[illegible]	X10 16	..	....	....
Ryecroft Quarry	—	—	—	—	..	..	—	—	—	—	..	..			—	—	—	—	—	—	....	....	....
Ashton	1 36	1 37	3 27	3 28	....	....	4 16	4 17	—	—	..	..	arr.	dep.	6 55	6 56½	9 25	9 27	10 21	10 22	..	..	..
Whetcombe Siding ..	—	—	—	—	..	..	—	—	C	R	....	....	P.M.	P.M.	—	—	—	—	—	—	....	....	....
Trusham	1 42	1 43	3 33	X—	—	3 45	4 22	4 23	5 55	—	..	..	—	6 30	7 1	7 2	9 32	9 33	10 27	10 28	..	..	..
Crockham Siding	—	—	—	—	—	—	—	—	....		....	....	—	—	—	—	—	—	—	—	....	....	....
Chudleigh	1 48	1 49	..	..	3 50	—	4 28	4 29	..	..	..	..	—	—	7 7	7 8	9 38	9 39	[illegible]	10 34	..	..	..
Chudleigh Knighton Halt	1 52	1 53	....				4 32	4 33	....	....	....	....	—	—	7 11	7 12	9 42	9 43	10 37	10 38	....	....	....
Heathfield	**1 57**	—		..	..	..	**4 37**	—		..	..	..	6 44	6 48	**7 16**	—	**9 47**	—	[illegible]	[illegible]	..	..	..

UP TRAINS. TEIGN VALLEY BRANCH—*continued*. Week Days.

M. P. Mileage M.	C.	STATIONS.	Ruling Gradient.	Point to Point Times	Allow for Stop.	Allow for Start.	B Passenger. arr.	dep.	B Motor. arr.	dep.	K Goods. RR arr.	dep.	B Motor. SUS-PENDED arr.	dep.	B Motor. arr.	dep.	B Motor. arr.	dep.	K Newton Abbot Goods arr.	dep.			B Motor. SUS-PENDED arr.	dep.	
				Mins.	Mins.	Mins.	A.M.	A.M.	A.M.	A.M.	A.M.	A.M.	A.M.	A.M.	A.M.	A.M.	P.M.	P.M.	A.M.	A.M.			P.M.	P.M.	
0	0	**Heathfield**	—	—	—	1	....	....	—	**8 23**	....	....	—	**10 35**	—	**11 0**	—	**1 0**	7 2	8 40	..	....	—	**2 57**	....
1	9	Chudleigh Knig'ton Ht	—	—	—	—	..		8 27	8 28	..	..	10 39	10 40	11 4	11 5	1 4	1 5	—	—	..	..	3 1	3 2	..
2	32	Chudleigh	66 F.	6	1	1	..	....	8 31	8 32	—	9 55	10 43	10 44	11 8	11 9	1 8	1 9	8 48	9 15	....	...	3 5	3 6	....
3	75	Crockham Siding ..	132 R.	4	1	1	..	..	—	—	—	—	—	—	—	—	—	—	—	—	..	..	—	—	..
4	20	Trusham	84 R.	2	1	1	....	....	8 37	X 8 38	10 3	—	10 49	X10 50	11 14	X11 15	1 14	1 15	9 23	X•1145	....	....	3 11	3 12	....
4	50	Whetcombe Siding ..	384 R.	2	1	1	..	..	—	—			—	—	—	—	—	—	—	—	..	..	—	—	..
6	15	Ashton	198 R	4	1	1	....	....	8 43	8 44	....	....	10 55	10 56	11 20	11 21	1 20	1 21	11 53	12 0	....	....	3 17	3 18	....
6	53	Ryecroft Quarry ..	—	—	—	—	..	....	—	—	..	..	—	—	—	—	—	—	C	R	..	..	—	—	..
		Christow	132 R.	4	1	2	—	8 0	8 49	8 50	....	....	11 1	11 4	11 26	X11 32	1 26	X 1 31	12 7	•X1 45	....	....	3 23	X 3 25	..
		Dunsford Halt ..	64 R.	—	—	—	8 7	8 8	8 56	8 57	..	..	11 11	11 12	11 39	11 40	1 37	1 38	—	—	..	..	3 32	3 33	..
		Longdown	64 R.	18	1	1	8 12	8 13	9 1	9 2	....	....	11 16	11 17	11 44	11 45	1 40	1 43	CR	ST	....	...	3 37	3 38	..
Terminates at 7M 57C.		Stop Board 5m. 66c.	—	—	—	—	—	—	—	—	.	..	—	—	—	—	—	—	2 5	P2 8	..	..	—	—	..
		Ide Halt	58 F.	12	2	1	8 19	8 20	9 8	9 9	....	....	11 23	11 24	11 51	11 52	1 49	1 50	CR	ST	....	...	3 44	3 45	..
		Alphington Halt ..	58 F.	—	—	—	8 24	8 25	9 13	9 14	..	..	11 28	11 29	11 56	11 57	1 54	1 55	—	—	..	..	3 49	3 50	..
		Stop Board 1m. 39c.	L.	8	2	1	—	—	—	—	....	....	—	—	—	—	—	—	2 28	P2 31	....	....	—	—	....
		Alphington Rd. Gds. Yd	56 F.	1	1	2	—	—	—	—	..	..	—	—	—	—	—	—	—	—	..	..	—	—	..
		City Basin Junction	—	—	—	—	C	S	C	S	....	....	C	SX	C	SX	C	S	2 35	X*2 55	....	....	C	SX	....
		St. Thomas	—	—	—	—	8 30	8 32	9 17	9 19	..	..	11 32	11 35	12 0	12 2	1 58	2 0	—	—	..	..	3 53	3 56	..
		Exeter	—	7	1	—	**8 35**	—	**9 22**	—	....	....	**11 38**	—	**12 5**	—	**2 3**	—	3 5	-	....	....	**4 1**	—	....

Up Trains—continued. Week Days. STATIONS.	B Motor. arr.	dep.	D Empty Motor. arr.	dep.	K Goods. arr.	dep.		B Motor. arr.	dep.	K Goods. arr.	dep.	B Passenger. arr.	dep.	B Auto. arr.	dep.	K Stone. arr.	dep.	B Motor. SUS-PENDED arr.	dep.	B Auto. SO SUS-PENDED arr.	dep.	Sundays. G Engine and Van. arr.	dep.
	P.M.	P.M.	P.M.	P.M.	P.M.	P.M.		P.M.	P.M.	P.M.	P.M.	P.M.	P.M.	P.M.	P.M.	P.M.	P.M.	P.M.	P.M.	P.M.	P.M.	A.M.	A.M.
Heathfield	—	**3 26**	....	....	....	....	....	—	**5 10**	5 20	5 30	....	....	—	**7 55**	....	....	—	**9 55**	—	10 55	....	....
Chudleigh Knighton Halt ..	3 30	3 31	..	..	..	..	..	5 14	5 14½	—	—	..	..	7 59	8 0	R	R	9 59	10 0	10 59	11 0	..	..
Chudleigh	3 34	3 35	—	3†52	....	....	....	5 17½	5 18	—	—	....	....	8 3	8 4	....	....	10 3	10 4	11 3	11 4	....	....
Crockham Siding	—	—	—	—	..	..	..	—	—	—	—	..	..	—	—	..	..	—	—	—	—	..	..
Trusham	3 40	X 3 41	C	S	....	....	....	5 23	5 23½	5 40	—	....	....	8 9	8 10	—	7 20	10 9	10 10	11 9	11 10	....	....
Whetcombe Siding	—	—	—	—	..	..	..	—	—			..	..	—	—	C	R	—	—	—	—	..	..
Ashton	3 46	3 47	—	—	....	....	....	5 28½	5 29	....	....	....	....	8 15	8 16	—	—	10 15	10 16	11 15	11 16	....	....
Ryecroft Quarry	—	—	—	—	..	..	..	—	—	..	..	..	..	—	—	C	R	—	—	—	—	..	..
Christow	3 52	X 3 53	4† 5	—	—	X 5 1	....	5 34	X 5 35	K		—	X 7 0	8 21	8 22	7 33	• 8 35	10 21	X10 22	11 21	11 22	....	....
Dunsford Halt	4 0	4 1			—	—	..	5 42	5 42½			7 7	7 8	8 29	8 30	—	—	10 28	10 29	11 28	11 29	..	..
Longdown	4 5	4 6	....	....	—	—	....	5 46½	5 47	Goods.		7 12	7 13	8 34	8 35	8 55	9 0	10 33	10 34	11 33	11 34	....	....
Stop Board 5m. 66c. ..	—	—	..	..	5 21P	5 23	.	—	—			—	—	—	—	9 1P	9 4	—	—	—	—	..	..
Ide Halt	4 12	4 13	....	..	—	—	....	5 53	5 54			7 19	7 20	8 41	8 42	C	R	10 40	10 41	11 40	11 41	....	....
Alphington Halt	4 17	4 18	..	..	—	—	..	5 58	5 59	arr.	dep.	7 24	7 25	8 46	8 47	—	—	10 45	10 46	11 45	11 46	..	..
Stop Board 1m. 39c.	—	—	....	..	5 43P	5 45	....	—	—	P.M.	P.M.	—	—	—	—	9 24P	9 27	—		—	—	....	....
Alphington Road Goods Yard	—	—	..	..	—	—	..	—	—	—	7 30	—	—	—	—	C	R	—	—	—	—	—	5†50
City Basin Junction	C	S	....	....	C	S	....	C	S	C	S	C	S	C	S	9 30	9* 36	C	S	C	S	C	S
St. Thomas	4 21	4 23	..	..	—	—	..	6 2	6 5	—	—	7 28	7 30	8 50	8 52	—	—	10 49	10 51	11 49	11 51	—	—
Exeter	**4 26**	—	....	....	5 55	—	....	**6 8**	—	7 40	—	**7 33**	—	**8 55**	—	9 45	—	**10 54**	—	11 54	—	6†0	—

The 14.9.1931 Timetable. This was the last timetable of the line's heyday, before the goods services were cut back. The 5.30 p.m. Heathfield–Trusham–Heathfield goods was a shortlived service, and it is not clear why it was found necessary to have such a service at this date. The Sunday train to Alphington Road ran in most years in the 1930s. The 11.25 a.m. Down and 10.35 a.m. and 2.57 p.m. Up motors were alternative times to the 10.55 a.m. Down and 11.0 a.m. and 3.26 p.m. Up, not extra trains that had been suspended for economic reasons. The 8.45 p.m. Down and 9.55 p.m. Up motors were genuinely 'suspended' at this date, as they were every winter. The 9.40 p.m. SO Down ran through to Newton Abbot in this timetable, therefore the 10.55 p.m. Up did not run. Note that the 9.40 was booked to be an ordinary passenger train, not a motor.

CR	Calls as required
CS	Collect or put down staff
P	Pick up or put down brakes
RR	Runs as required
ST	Calls for Station Trucks purposes only

- A 5.5 pm Heathfield–Chudleigh Knighton at 1937.
- A 2.25 pm WSO Heathfield–Chudleigh Knighton in the late 1930s, for people returning from Newton Abbot market.

These workings were all shortlived, depending on the availability of stock and a path at the time in question, and did not reappear after 1939.

Through running to/from Newton Abbot had been made possible in 1916 but was only very occasionally engaged in in the interwar years, and then usually for operating convenience rather than passenger convenience. (The 1927 timetable went a step further with an evening through train from Paignton to Exeter via the Teign Valley, but such things were never seen again.) If it had been engaged in more, it might have eased the whole timetabling of the line in the busiest years, by removing the need to make connections at Heathfield; but the low traffic levels did not encourage such improvements. In fact, connections at Heathfield also deteriorated in some cases from the 1920s; most trains still had good connections, but with the once-important Chudleigh–Newton traffic gone, connections at Heathfield were no longer the be-all and end-all of Teign Valley timetabling as they had been before 1914. In the 1937 timetable, for example, connections at Heathfield were 21, 2, 4, 4, 29, 11, 9 and 15 minutes off down trains, and 19, 24, 4, 3, 37, 7, 8, 3 and 2 minutes into up trains.

The Motors lasted on the line until their final withdrawal by the GWR in September 1935. After this all trains on the line were worked by Autos (until 1957), more often than not with only one coach.

The 1930s were a much less happy time for the branch than the 1920s. Not only did the line lose its real *raison d'être* with the collapse of the stone traffic, but the passenger traffic everywhere began to decline year by year as the impact of increasing car ownership made itself felt even at those stations where there was no bus competition. There were still seven passenger trains each way in 1939, but it cannot be said that the traffic justified this; it had become more a social service at the expense of the GWR shareholders than a commercial operation. The GWR had in fact given serious consideration to withdrawing the passenger service as early as 1930. This was made known in the local press in September/October 1930, and the GWR admitted that the matter was being given thought to. The *South Devon Weekly Express* tried to stir up opposition and predictable letters were written about the railways being a 'public servant', but no very coherent campaign was staged. In November the GWR announced that the idea had been given up. Although no statement was made as to why, it is probable that it was considered that the line would have had to be maintained to passenger standards for use by heavy trains during emergency diversions — this was only a few months after the 1930 breach at Dawlish — so that the savings would have been less than normal. Nevertheless, by 1939 there had been much more traffic lost, and one suspects that, but for the outbreak of war,

even the GWR's benevolent management would ere long have once again been provoked into thoughts of withdrawal.

In another way, though, the falling back of the traffic to a small number of 'regulars' made the daily life of the branch a more friendly one. The branch guards — Jack Harvey, Ted Boyle, and Charlie Snell — knew most of the passengers and would never let the train leave a station until the proper complement had arrived.

The loss of traffic brought a need for staff economies, most notably the abolition of the stationmasters' posts in 1929–32. Chudleigh, Trusham, and Ashton were now put under the Christow stationmaster, and Longdown under the St Thomas stationmaster. Additional porters' posts created at Trusham and Christow in the stone traffic's heyday were also now axed.

---

1. The LSWR bus service had inspired John Dickson in 1906 to evolve plans for a 'Motor Track' (flanged wheelway) from Christow to Chagford, along the formerly-proposed railway route. It was estimated that a 1 hr 30 min. journey time from Exeter to Chagford would be possible by the train to Christow and motor bus along the 'Track' to Chagford, 50 min. faster than the 2 hr 20 min. of the LSWR buses. But Dickson's scheme did not get off the ground, and no Chagford passengers ever travelled on the Exeter Railway.
2. For a few years in the mid-'30s it ran on Thursdays as well.

Perhaps the best-remembered character amongst the branch's regular guards was Jack Harvey, who came to the line about 1930 and is seen here c.1955. He would stand on the platform ends calling out to latecoming schoolchildren: "Come on, what have you had? Fish for breakfast?" Guards on lines such as this often acquired other functions for the local community, and Jack had an arrangement with the farmer at Horrowmore Farm, near Dunsford Halt, under which he delivered a copy of the *Express and Echo* each evening (if one can use the word 'deliver' for a newspaper thrown out of the window of a passing train into a field!). There were also arrangements between the branch guards and several of the shops in Cowick Street by St. Thomas station, under which, if a customer in the valley wanted something but could not get into Exeter, the shop would entrust the required item to the guard at St. Thomas and the customer would pick it up and hand over the money at their nearest station. Alas, such conveniences could not really be mentioned when the line was put up for closure!

PASSENGER TRAFFIC

There are no figures for 1882-1902 (save odd months). Complete figures for the years 1904-12 and 1914-22 exist for Exeter Railway stations only. There are no figures for 1924. 1958 figures are, of course, for five months only. The Ide figure for 1955 is for nine weeks only. Christow/Longdown/Ide figures for 1903 are for six months only.

	Chudleigh Passenger Tickets sold	Chudleigh Seasons sold	Trusham Passenger Tickets sold	Trusham Seasons sold	Ashton Passenger Tickets sold	Ashton Seasons sold	Christow Passenger Tickets sold	Christow Seasons sold	Longdown Passenger Tickets sold	Longdown Seasons sold	Ide Passenger Tickets sold	Ide Seasons sold
1903	15496	nk	5111	nk	6192	nk	5417	nk	2789	nk	5276	nk
04	nk	nk	nk	nk	nk	nk	12153	nk	5774	nk	10686	nk
05	nk	nk	nk	nk	nk	nk	12271	nk	5878	nk	10314	nk
06	nk	nk	nk	nk	nk	nk	12763	nk	5955	nk	10256	nk
07	nk	nk	nk	nk	nk	nk	12467	nk	6114	nk	9473	nk
08	nk	nk	nk	nk	nk	nk	12464	nk	6196	nk	8378	nk
09	nk	nk	nk	nk	nk	nk	13757	nk	6048	nk	8793	nk
1910	nk	nk	nk	nk	nk	nk	13846	nk	5993	nk	9163	nk
11	nk	nk	nk	nk	nk	nk	14329	nk	6072	nk	9192	nk
12	nk	nk	nk	nk	nk	nk	13080	nk	5527	nk	6593	nk
13	19895	nk	9377	nk	6872	nk	14480	nk	5359	nk	7782	nk
14	nk	nk	nk	nk	nk	nk	13765	nk	4903	nk	6945	nk
15	nk	nk	nk	nk	nk	nk	13073	nk	5141	nk	5764	nk
16	nk	nk	nk	nk	nk	nk	13069	nk	5769	nk	6907	nk
17	nk	nk	nk	nk	nk	nk	8914	nk	3946	nk	Station closed	
18	nk	nk	nk	nk	nk	nk	9072	nk	4843	nk	1/1/17–5/5/19	
19	nk	nk	nk	nk	nk	nk	13611	nk	6137	nk	5021	nk
1920	nk	nk	nk	nk	nk	nk	15190	nk	6441	nk	8941	nk
21	nk	nk	nk	nk	nk	nk	14468	nk	5508	nk	8952	nk
22	nk	nk	nk	nk	nk	nk	14875	nk	4811	nk	7906	nk
23	7100	27	9833	40	7261	24	16115	24	5058	22	7819	6
24	nk	nk	nk	nk	nk	nk	nk	nk	nk	nk	nk	nk
25	7145	38	10412	39	8585	15	15861	10	4422	23	7872	0
26	6011	36	9144	23	7839	6	10802	18	3817	26	8037	10
27	6538	23	10357	42	8071	7	15693	37	3693	15	9932	4
28	5351	14	9449	46	7888	8	15725	26	2115½	14	10095	2
29	4309	14	9428	35	7352	21	13555	46	2278	7	10442	5
1930	3391	1	8827	50	6511	31	12750	86	2266	31	10435	6
31	3350	9	9208	44	6139	21	12474	56	2078	94	9373	8
32	3263	21	8432	42	5659	42	11054	67	1895	79	8691	19
33	2695	20	8269	27	5695	30	11592	94	1826	56	7149	26
34	2519	30	8245	15	5974	47	11708	97	1936	33	6351	16
35	2580	24	7790	19	6503	78	12002	106	1456	3	5270	36
36	2672	16	7414	44	6559	70	10829	120	904	3	4364	57
37	2506	13	6925	60	6352	53	10502	153	838	4	3819	73
38	2463	14	6768	34	6369	87	10009	179	1015	0	3244	84
39	2277	16	5320	45	5145	52	8613	184	924	1	3137	57
1940	3073	19	6247	14	4743	26	8943	223	1176	1	2594	16
41	5752	28	8342	20	8538	98	11328	301	1395	19	2716	23
42	8674	74	9815	110	9866	237	14560	827	2047	205	4087	36
43	6593	62	10103	72	10068	166	13235	706	1668	272	3941	26
44	6566	78	11571	150	9952	131	12916	768	1773	139	4745	31
45	5787	129	11781	143	9835	170	12821	691	1237	93	4554	35
46	3586	107	11133	167	9743	136	10656	555	745	46	3861	43
47	2967	44	10354	122	8164	100	10134	367	755	72	3782	72
48	2464	40	9420	60	7351	131	9283	157	667	47	2897	90
49	2284	27	7811	95	6800	112	7610	120	519	21	2425	105
1950	1575	9	6583	94	5992	202	4865	92	435	11	2222	61
51	1292	3	7045	111	5702	243	4436	90	344	7	2553	58
52	1643	18	6659	96	6237	219	4466	74	304	3	2607	79
53	1072	3	6639	76	5138	207	4270	34	188	3	3033	70
54	1465	3	6661	75	5541	154	3977	67	108	3	3064	66
55	1329	3	5957	85	5687	243	3830	58	143	3	417	15
56	1345	23	5883	72	5496	457	3618	36	90	0	nk(Unstaffed)	nk
57	2195	34	5903	27	5408	349	4531	204	228	0	nk(Unstaffed)	nk
58	571	2	1459	12	1996	129	1459	12	192	0	nk(Unstaffed)	nk

Chudleigh also sold 19 tickets in 1959 — presumably to railway enthusiasts!

SUMMARY OF TRAFFIC AND REVENUE (WHOLE BRANCH)

	Staff	Paybill	Tickets sold	Seasons sold	Total Coaching Receipts	Goods traffic (Tons)	Goods Receipts	Total Receipts
1903*	15	£570	40,281	nk	£2,886	35,829	£7,087	£9,973
1913	22	£1,156	63,765	nk	£4,147	291,109	£59,447	£63,594
1923	26	£3,902	53,186	143	£4,620	206,876	£73,287	£77,907
1934†	16	£2,053	36,733	238	£2,942	44,731	£19,894	£22,836

Notes * ½ year's figures only for Exeter Railway stations
† 1934 figures exclude Alphington Road (zoned with Exeter for accounts)

The £63,594 taken at the branch stations in 1913 may be compared with the £18,147 'Gross receipts' of the TVR and ER lines (combined) in the same year, this difference being due to the traffic being largely outward stone traffic, which was on GWR (and other companies') metals for most of its journey and so had only a small part of the takings credited to the TVR and ER accounts. But no doubt the TVR and ER Directors sometimes reflected at this period on the cruelty of a line whose annual takings were 55 times the staffing (excluding train crew) costs, still being unable to produce a penny of dividends for the ordinary shareholders!

NOTES

Chudleigh — the busiest station on the line pre-1919. Disastrous loss of traffic after bus services began in 1919. Small revival in 1939-45.

Trusham — slow decline in 1930s from losses to the private car, followed by recovery in 1939-45.

Ashton — Very similar to Trusham but better figures in the post-1945 period. By 1955 Ashton was actually the busiest station on the line!

Christow — similar to Trusham/Ashton up to 1939. Very large increase in commuter traffic in 1939-45, followed by disastrous decline when bus services began in the late 1940s. Between the collapse of Chudleigh c.1920 and its own collapse c.1947, Christow was much the busiest station on the line.

Longdown — always quiet, and collapsed badly in the mid-1920s in the face of bus competition.

Ide — traffic fell off after 1911 due to poor train services, recovered in the 1920s as services improved, and then collapsed in the 1930s in the face of bus competition.

Note — there is no information available as to the period of validity of the season tickets sold. Nevertheless, it is clear that season ticket holders were an important part of the total users from the late 1930s onwards, and an estimate has to be made. The adjustments shown here are based on a guess of each season representing 10 ordinary tickets.

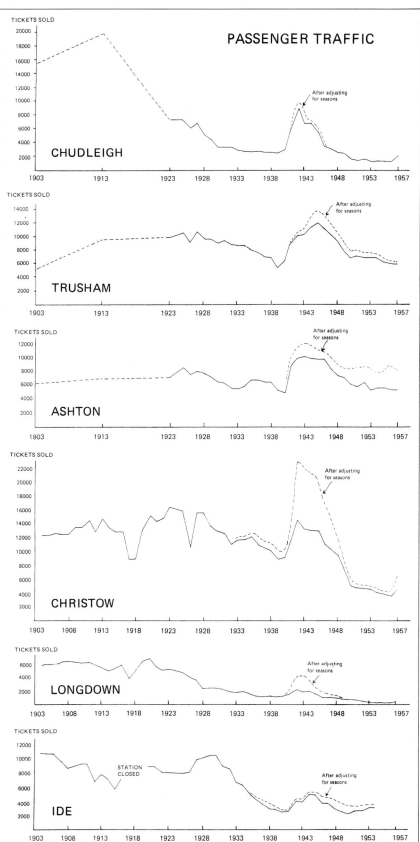

PASSENGER TRAFFIC

MISCELLANEOUS TRAFFIC

Details are only available from 1925 on.

MILK

The former traffic declined to nil by 1930 under road competition. But a significant traffic was regained from the late 1940s, at Trusham and Ashton in particular, and this continued until some time after the passenger closure (all still in churns). Traffic depended of course on the personal preferences of individual farmers.

Chudleigh — Some until 1929, none 1930–34, some 1935–41, none after 1941.

Trusham — None to 1945. Substantial traffic from 1946, maximum 24,628 gallons in 1957.

Ashton — None to 1934, some from 1935 increasing to maximum of 23,727 gallons in 1949, much less after 1954.

Christow — Some 1925–27, none 1928–29, some 1930–35, none 1936–38, some 1939–40, none 1941–45, some 1946–57.

Longdown — None.

Ide — None.

LIVESTOCK

Only Christow and Ide ever had a significant traffic, and all was gone by 1947.
No. of wagons handled per annum:

Chudleigh — 1 to 3 up to 1939, nil later.

Trusham — 5 in 1931, 1 in 1938, 1 in 1939, nil all other years.

Ashton — 1 to 3 in 1925 and 1933–37, nil other years.

Christow — Traffic in all years up to 1946, varies 85 to 128 in the 1920s, 11 to 57 in the 1930s, 1 to 9 in the 1940s.

Longdown — 1 in 1931, nil all other years.

Ide — Nil to 1931, varies 2 to 57 in the 1930s, 1 to 4 in the 1940s, nil after 1946.

PARCELS

There was very little parcels traffic at Trusham, Ashton, Longdown and Ide. Chudleigh had a fair traffic and indeed after 1948 the parcels revenue was higher than the passenger revenue!

STATION STAFF AT 1921

Chudleigh	1 Station master
	1 Porter (?)
Trusham	1 Station master
	3 Porters
	2 Signalmen
Ashton	1 Station master
	1 Porter
Christow	1 Station master
	1 Porter
	1 Goods Porter
	1 Lad Porter
	2 Signalmen
Longdown	1 Station master
	1 Signalman
Ide	1 Station master
	1 Porter
Alphington Rd	1 Clerk
	1 Foreman
	1 Checker
	1 Goods Porter

STATION STAFF AT 1934

Chudleigh	2 Porters
Trusham	2 Porters
	2 Signalmen
Ashton	2 Porters
Christow	1 Station master
	2 Porters (Summer — 1 Junior Porter extra)
	2 Signalmen
Longdown	2 Signalmen
Ide	1 Porter
Alphington Rd	nk

STAFF CHANGES 1922–1936

from the *GWR Magazine*
(It cannot be assumed that this is a complete listing. Also a few were probably cancelled.)

1922	March	F.J. Loram, Signalman Christow to Brixham.
	May	W.A. Cox, Ashburton to Signalman Christow.
	August	A. Wonnacott, Moretonhampstead to Signalman Christow.
	September	W.W. Wills, Signalman Christow to Stoke Canon.
	November	T. Way, Churston to Signalman Longdown.
	December	P.J.A. Baker, Station master Ide to Thornfalcon.
1923	January	C. Edbrooke, Wellington to Station master Ide.
	May	R.G. Short, Christow to Porter Signalman Brixham.
	July	H. Cockram, Station master Longdown to Culmstock.
	September	G.S. Cook, Christow to Porter Signalman Williton.
		W.G. Roost, Signalman Trusham to Kingskerswell (this must have been cancelled — see below)
		J.W. Balsdon, Tiverton Junction to Longdown Station master.
	December	W.D. Farmer, Porter Ashton to Kingswear.
1924	April	W.G. Roost, Signalman Trusham to Dunball.
	May	W. Lugg, Signalman Milverton to Trusham.
1925	August	T. Way, Signalman Longdown to Blue Anchor.
1926	October	E. Davies, Station master Longdown to Rowden Mill.
1927	February	W. Lugg, Signalman Trusham to Dainton.
	June	W.J Edwards, to Exeter District Relief Porter.
1928	April	A.W. Wonnacott, Signalman Christow to Exminster.
		J. Cooper, Exeter to Longdown Station master.
	May	E.J. Valentine, Station master Ashton to Kingskerswell.
		C. Pyke, Ashton to Porter-Signalman Hatch.
		H.R. Hamilton, Brixham to Signalman Longdown.
		E.J. Tucker, Station master Longdown to Thornfalcon.
		A. Haywood, Signalman Longdown to Christow.
	June	F.W. Matravers, Hatch to Signalman Trusham.
		J. Webber, Hele & Bradninch to Station master Longdown.
	July	C.W. Gardner, Churston to Signalman Trusham.
	September	J. Cooper, Station master Longdown to Culmstock.
		C.H. Hutchings, Bridgwater to Station master Ashton.
	October	H.R. Hamilton, Signalman Longdown to Exeter.
		C. Pyke, Hatch to Signalman Longdown.
		H. Brimscombe, Athelney to Station master Longdown.
	December	C. Pyke, Signalman Longdown to Exeter.
		A.J. Cornish, Dunball to Signalman Longdown.
1929	May	C.H. Hutchings, Station master Ashton to Stogumber.
1930	January	H. Brimscombe, Station master Longdown to Culmstock.
	October	A.W. Brooking, Station master Chudleigh to Heathfield.
	November	G.F.D. Cuddeford, Station master Christow to Cullompton.
1931	May	R.G.T. Churchill, Station master Longdown to Swimbridge.
		H.C. Goodland, Hatch to Signalman Longdown.
	June	F.J. Channing, Station master Stoke Canon to Christow.
	August	A.J. Cornish, Signalman Longdown to Moretonhampstead.
1932	December	J.G. Hulme, Station master Trusham to Tiverton.
1933	May	J.H. Horn, Brixham to Signalman Longdown.
		H.A. Payne, Station master Dunster to Christow.
		H.C. Goodland, Signalman Longdown to Bampton.
1934	March	H.A. Payne, Station master Christow to Watchet.
	April	C.J. Webber, Exeter to Station master Christow.
	August	A.E. Keates, Dunball to Signalman Longdown.
1936	January	F. Nichols, Ashton to Shunter Newton Abbot.
	February	A.J. Salter, Wellington to Grade 1 Porter Ashton.
	April	A. Haywood, Signalman Christow to Teignmouth.
		A.E. Keates, Signalman Longdown to Somerton.
		A.B. Smith, Signalman Somerton to Christow.
	May	H.A. Pike, Ashton to Newton Abbot District Relief Porter.
		W.G. Bissett, Brixham to Signalman Longdown.
		A.F. Billing, Signalman Longdown to Somerton.
	July	S.J. Elson, Station master Athelney to Chudleigh.
		E.J. Tucker, Station master Bampton to Christow.
		H.J. Wallace, Paignton to Signalman Longdown.
		T. Pavey, Stoke Canon to Grade 1 Porter Ashton.
	August	C.H. Pullen, Grade 1 Porter Christow to Exeter.
	December	W.A.E. Salter, Trusham to Porter Guard Barnstaple.

The careers of those staff who stayed longest on the line are featured in more detail in Chapter 18. However, whilst it is always pleasant to feature those staff who worked on a line for many years and became closely associated with it, it must nevertheless be realised that (as the above listing should make clear) most of the staff at small branch line stations were young men there as a necessary rung on the promotion ladder and were anxious to be away to fill a main-line vacancy as soon as one arose. Promotion was in fact quite slow in the depression-hit interwar years; in the 1900s, when the railway was still expanding and promotion was accordingly quicker, almost nobody (except the Station masters) stayed on the branch for more than a year or two. Promotion was normally within the Exeter Division (there is only one case in the above listing of promotion to or from another Division).

CHAPTER FIFTEEN
THE LINE AS DIVERSIONARY ROUTE

DESPITE the importance laid on this aspect by the Exeter Railway's promoters in the 1890s, the Teign Valley line was not looked upon by the GWR as a Diversionary Route for some years after 1903. There were three reasons for this:

- The line's 'wrong-gauge' origins and subsequent lack of a running connection at Heathfield even after 1892, led to it being regarded as an Exeter–Heathfield line only. It was only when the stone traffic enforced the through running of goods trains from Newton Abbot from 1907 on that people began to perceive the line as a possible through route.
- The ownership of the line by the independent TVR and ER companies militated against making improvements (notably the provision of a running connection at Heathfield) and ensured that the GWR had no wish to use the line for diversionary purposes in any but the direst emergencies.
- There had been no significant trouble on the Dawlish sea wall, or with the cliffs, since 1873, and by the 1900s the GWR officers had come to see sea wall breaches as a thing of the past which the improvements made to the wall in the 1870s had put paid to. There was therefore no demand seen for a Diversionary Route.

The line's role as Diversionary Route really began as the result of a (comparatively insignificant) case of undermining on the wall at Dawlish in February 1916. This threw the GWR Engineers into a sudden concern over the state of the wall and the cliffs, and one result was the authorising of a £2,015 scheme for a direct connection at Heathfield by the Traffic Committee on 9th March 1916. This was brought into use in October 1916 and used daily by the goods trains, but it was to be five years in the event before it was actually needed for diversions.

It will be recalled that the TVR section of the branch had a number of timber bridges, and the GWR now decided that these would have to be replaced if the line were to be used regularly by main line trains. (It is also likely that the GWR wanted to do this work now because it would have to be paid for by the TVR if started before the 1923

absorptions took effect!) New steel girder bridges were authorised as follows:

0m 25½ ch Bovey Marsh bridge (completed 1920).	March 1920	estimate £1,461
0m 33½ ch Bovey River bridge (completed 1922).	June 1921	estimate £2,922
1m 24½ ch Teign River bridge (completed 1923).	July 1921	estimate £8,993

The work on the Bovey River Bridge brought the branch's most disruptive accident on Sunday 11th June 1922, when the crane came off the line and ended up in the river. Fortunately, the driver, Sam Broom of Newton Abbot and his fireman both jumped clear. It took some days to recover the crane and in the duration buses had to be run between Chudleigh and Heathfield.

Later, in 1933, the girder bridges at Huxbear (3m 13½ ch) and Crockham (3m 77½ ch) were also replaced. The drawings of the latter show that preparation was included for a possible future doubling of the line.

The first actual use of the line for diversions was on 22nd September 1921 when the main line was blocked for some hours by a collision at Dawlish. The most important occasions subsequently were during sea wall breaches and cliff falls:

12–22 March 1923	Cliff fall at Sprey Point.
4–8 January 1930	Sea wall breach at Dawlish.
10–12 February 1936	River wall breach at Powderham.
18–19 and 21 December 1945	Sea wall damage at Starcross.

But there were many other occasions, particularly during the 1920s and '30s when so many cliff slips were experienced at Teignmouth, when single line working was in force on the main line and some trains ran via the Teign Valley. It was (as one would expect) quite unpredictable; some years would pass without a single train having to be diverted via the line, in other years there might be three or four consecutive incidents.

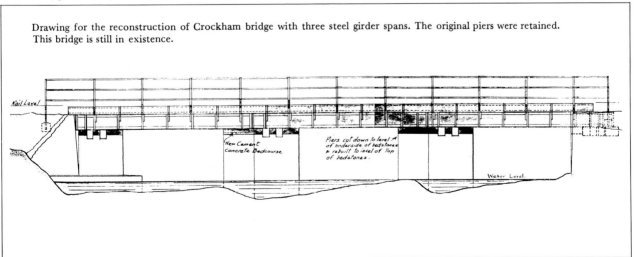

Drawing for the reconstruction of Crockham bridge with three steel girder spans. The original piers were retained. This bridge is still in existence.

Diversion of passenger trains over the# Teign Valley line.
10-0pm January 4th to 12-0 noon January 8th 1930.
DOWN.

Train	Approximate times Dep.Exeter	Arr.Newton A.	Remarks.
9-50pm Paddington to Penzance	2-50am	4-0am.	
1-40am Paddington to Penzance (Newspapers)	4-40am	5-50am.	
7-0am Exeter to Newton Abbot	7-0am	8-20am	Ordinary # to Newton Abbot
7-20am "	7-20am "	11-20am	" to Christow
9-25am "	9-25am "	11-20am	" to Newton Abbot
10-55am "	10-55am "	12-45pm	" " to "
10-10am Bath to Plymouth	12-50pm	2-10pm	To run non-stop to Christow. To cross 11-25am Kingswear and leave Christow at 1-31pm in times of 12-55pm Exeter calling all stations to Newton Abbot except Teigngrace.
1-37pm Exeter to Plymouth	1-37pm	3-20pm	To call at all stations except Teigngrace. Cross 11-20am Plymouth at City Basin Jct 1-10pm Kingswear at Christow and11-0am Penzance at Heathfield.
12-0 noon Paddington to Kingswear (Torbay Limited)	2-59pm	4-0pm	Tp cross 1-10pm Kingswear at City Basin Jct 11-0am Penzance at Christow.
3-40pm Exeter to Kingswear	3-40pm	4-50pm	To call all stations except Teigngrace and cross 11-0am Penzance at City Basin Jct.
10-32am Crewe to Plymouth	4-40pm	5-45pm	To call at St Thomas Longdown and Christow.
10-12am Bradford to Paignton	6-15pm	7-25pm	Not to leave Exeter before 8-15pm and call at all stations except Teigngrace.To cross 4-20pm Plymouth at Christow and 6-20pm Plymouth at Newton Abbot.
4-30pm Paddington to Plymouth	8-40pm	9-45pm	To cross 6-25pm Kingswear at City Basin Jct.
6-30pm Paddington to Plymouth	10-50pm	11-55pm	To cross 8-40pm Penzance & at City Basin Jct.

Diversion of passenger trains over the Teign valley line.
10-0pm January 4th to 12-0 noon January 8th 1930.
UP.

Train	Approximate times Dep.Newton	Arr.Exeter	Remarks.
8-0am Christow		8-35am	ordinary train.
7-38am Paignton to Paddington (mondays only)	8-18am	9-5am	
7-5am Kingswear to Swansea	8-10am	9-23am	To take up times of 8-23am Heathfield to Exeter.
8-10am Kingswear to Exeter	9-5am	10-25am	To cross 9-25am Exeter at Christow.
8-45am Plymouth to Crewe	9-48am	10-50am	To cross 9-25am Exeter at Christow.
9-10am Plymouth to Exeter	10-48am	12-5pm	To take up times of 11-0am Heathfield, to cross 9-25am Exeter at Heathfield and 10-55am Exeter at Christow.
10-28am Kingswear to Exeter	11-33am	12-40pm	10-28am Kingswear to Newton Abbot to be extended to Exeter. To cross 10-55am Exeter at Christow.
11-25am Kingswear to Paddington (Torbay Limited)	12-20pm	1-25pm	To cross 10-55am Exeter at 8 Heathfield and 10-10am Bath at Christow.
11-20am Plymouth to Exeter	12-43pm	2-5pm	To take up times of 1-0pm Heathfield to 10-10am Bath at Christow.
1-10pm Kingswear to Exeter	2-5pm	3-10pm	To cross 10-10am Bath at Newton Abbot 1-37pm Exeter at Christow and 12-0 noon Paddington at City Basin Jct.
11-0am Penzance to Paddington (Through Aberdeen Coach)	2-55pm	3-55pm	To cross 1-37pm Exeter at Heathfield 12-0 noon Paddington at Christow and 3-40pm Exeter at City Basin Jct.
4-20pm Plymouth to Taunton	5-50pm	7-33pm	To call at all stations except Teigngrace. To cross 3-55pm Bristol (10-12am Bradford) at Christow and take up times of 7-0pm Christow to Exeter.
6-20 pm Plymouth to Paddington	7-25pm	8-25pm	To cross 3-55pm Bristol at Newton Abbot.
6-25pm Kingswear to Exeter	7-34pm	8-50pm	To call all stations except Teigngrace to cross 4-30pm Paddington at City Basin Jct.
8-49pm Penzance to Paddington (Post Office Mail)	10-10pm	11-5pm	To cross 6-30pmPaddington at City Basin Jct.

Plymouth and Cornish trains were usually sent by the 'Southern' route via Okehampton even though this involved payment being made by the GWR; it was a much more suitable route. The Teign Valley line was hardpressed enough dealing with the Torbay traffic. However, the 'Cornish Riviera' and other Cornish expresses did sometimes find themselves travelling along the valley, for example if they had already left Plymouth when the blockage occurred. During diversions, non-urgent goods traffic was held back at Newton, Exeter, or beyond, and only urgent traffic sent in special workings via the Teign Valley. In 1936 at least the Teign Valley local passenger trains were replaced by buses in order to increase line capacity.

The signalmen on the branch were always very pleased when diversions were necessary, because they were put on 12-hour days, 7 days a week, the only overtime they ever received.

In the 1920s diverted passenger trains were normally double-headed by two 45XX tank locos, the heaviest locos allowed on the line. But around 1930 'Bulldogs' were tried on the line and found to be suitable, and were commonly used on the passenger trains after that, although not to the exclusion of the 45XXs.

EMERGENCY TIMETABLE JANUARY 1930

By good fortune a copy has survived of the DSO Exeter's Special Notice of 6th January 1930 giving full instructions for the passenger train operations in that week, during the sea wall blockage at Dawlish. The listings reproduced here seem to have been typed up as a 'record' after it was all over and give most of the necessary facts rather more succinctly than the Notice itself.

The normal branch passenger service at this date was as per the 1931 timetable reproduced in Chapter 14, save that the last up train was 7.40pm from Heathfield rather than 7.55pm.

All the regular branch trains were withdrawn as such (save for the 7.20am Exeter/8.0am Christow), as the Motors could not have accommodated the extra traffic. The 7.0am, 9.25am, and 10.55am Exeter down trains ran in their normal timings on the Exeter–Christow leg but were severely held up at Christow awaiting crossings; these trains were all formed of loco + coaches and extended to Newton Abbot for the benefit of 'through' passengers. The remaining trains on the line were all long-distance services, many of which, however, called at branch stations in lieu of the cancelled Motors; the trains leaving Exeter at 6.15pm, and Heathfield at 8.23am, 11.0am, and 1.0pm and Christow at 7.0pm, ran in the exact times of regular branch trains, which made life easier for local passengers and facilitated the timetabling exercise. The only local passengers left without any reasonable alternative service were the users of the 3.26pm Heathfield which was cancelled, with no stopping train off Newton Abbot between 12.43pm and 5.55pm in the emergency service.

One can readily see, however, why the GWR decided in 1936 to take the 'simpler' course of running the diverted trains non-stop along the branch and putting on buses for the valley passengers as a separate operation.

The graph shows the tightness of the workings in the midday period. Exact timings are not available for all points and some have had to be estimated. At Heathfield one train would have had to 'shunt' at each crossing. The time given for the 7.0am Exeter, to arrive Newton Abbot 8.20am, is impossible as it conflicts with up trains. In the evening there were gaps between the passenger trains, and goods trains must have been run then.

There was no attempt to use the loop at Trusham and the graph shows very clearly how useful converting the goods loop to passenger use would have been. Only minor signalling alterations would have been needed to enable this (the work eventually done at Trusham in 1943 was

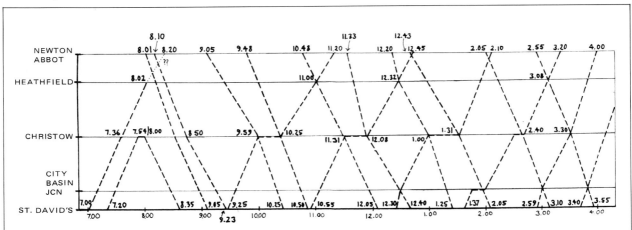

This graph has been prepared on the basis of the January 1930 Emergency Timetable opposite, to illustrate the single-line working involved at the busiest part of the day.

more expensive, as someone else was paying!). There was criticism in the papers after the January 1930 diversions regarding the GWR's unwillingness to make relatively minor improvements that would reduce delays during diversions, and in particular of the manner in which costly alterations had been done at Heathfield in 1927 in such a way that it was still impossible to cross two Teign Valley trains there without time-consuming shunting moves. After the 'closure' ideas (see Ch. 14) in 1930 were given up, the GWR did in fact make it known that, whilst they would certainly not double the line as some had sought,

'a scheme is contemplated whereby passing places will be provided at intervals, thus doing away with much delay when main line trains

have to use the branch. It is also proposed to generally strengthen the existing line.'

(*Mid Devon Times* 29.11.1930)

However, nothing was done prior to the war.

WARTIME IMPROVEMENTS

Under the shadow of war, arrangements for diversions were made more formalised in 1938 with the introduction of 'Emergency Working' arrangements under which locomotives of classes 2251, 2301, 41XX, 51XX, and 43XX–73XX were allowed subject to a maximum speed of 25mph. (There had been a general speed limit over the whole branch of 25mph since 1922, but this was increased

---

Obstruction between City Basin Junction exclusive and Newton Abbot East exclusive
CODE **E.D. 12**

ALTERNATIVE ROUTES.
Route No. 1.—Via Southern Railway between Exeter and Plymouth.
Route No. 2.—Via Christow and Heathfield.

LOCAL SERVICES.
Teign Valley Branch.—The Local Passenger Rail Service will be suspended and the traffic will be conveyed by busses provided by the Devon General Bus Co. To be run at times as near as possible to the times advertised in the Railway Time Tables.
Moretonhampstead Branch.—To be worked by Moretonhampstead Engine, Train, and Guards between Moretonhampstead and Bovey, and by the Devon General Busses between Bovey and Newton Abbot.
Arrangements to be made by the Bus Company for passengers to join or alight at the nearest convenient point to Brimley and Teigngrace Halts.
Exeter and Newton Abbot Local Train Service.—Train and Bus Services will be arranged to meet traffic requirements.

ENGINE RESTRICTIONS.
Route 1.—As in Section E.D.11.
Route 2.—The following types of Engines are sanctioned over this route :

2-6-0—43XX, 53XX, 63XX, 73XX.		0-6-0T.
2-6-2T—41XX, 44XX, 45XX, 51XX, 55XX.	Subject to maximum speed of 25 m.p.h.	2-4-0T—Metro.
4-4-0—32XX, 33XX, 34XX.		0-4-2T—48XX, 58XX.
0-6-0—2251 to 2290, 23XX, 24XX, 25XX.		Uncoloured Engines.

4-6-0 78XX "Manor" class are permitted subject to the speed not exceeding 20 m.p.h. at any point.
Note.—Two 51XX Class Engines must not run coupled. Engines must not run Chimney to Chimney. When Tank and Tender Engines are coupled the Tender Engine must be leading and work Chimney first.
Subject to these restrictions, trains may be double-headed.

"Point to Point" Running Times—*continued.*
15—Between Exeter and Newton Abbot via Heathfield.

Between	Passenger Trains		Express Freight Trains	
	Down	Up	Down	Up
	Mins.	Mins.	Mins.	Mins.
Exeter and Christow	25	25	31	31
Christow and Newton Abbot	27	27	33	33
4-6-0 78XX Manor Class Engines at 20 m.p.h.				
Exeter and Christow	30	29	33	33
Christow and Newton Abbot	39	39	42	42

WATER COLUMNS.
Exeter, Christow, Newton Abbot.

STOP BOARDS.
Down Trains.—Between Longdown and Dunsford Halt, 4m. 68¼ch. To Put Down.
At Christow 8m. 54¼ch. To Pick Up.
Up Trains.—Between Longdown and Ide Halt, 4m. 51ch. To Put Down.
Alphington Halt and City Basin Junction 0m. 22ch. To Pick Up.

SINGLE LINE CROSSING LOOPS.
City Basin Junction, 625 feet ; Christow, 670 feet ; Trusham, 1096 feet ; Heathfield, 1040 feet.

CATCH POINTS.
City Basin Junction Down Branch .. .. 62 yards from Signal Box.

WORKING AT TRUSHAM.
During these emergency arrangements, two Passenger Trains may cross at Trusham, provided the Line is clear in accordance with Electric Train Staff Regulation 4 (i).
No Passenger Train must be permitted to enter the Loop Line until the Points are clipped and padlocked.

Extracts from Notice 464 of May 1941, relating to diversions via the Teign Valley line. It is not to be assumed that everything listed here ever actually happened. In addition to the major sea wall incidents, Teign Valley diversions were occasionally called upon for a few hours as a result of relatively minor operating incidents on the main line.

ASSISTING TRAINS IN REAR.
A Bank engine to be stationed at City Basin Junction and another at Christow to assist trains to Longdown. Trains may be assisted in the rear in clear weather only provided the following instructions are rigidly observed :

CITY BASIN JUNCTION—LONGDOWN SECTION.
Passenger, Coaching Stock, and Freight Trains.
Bank engine to run coupled in rear. Train to stop at Longdown Stop Board, situated on the Christow side of Longdown Station at 4 miles 68 chs., banker to be uncoupled and follow train to Signal Box.
When the load of a Passenger train necessitates a Bank Engine, two engines will, when possible, be provided to work through from Exeter to Newton Abbot to save additional stops en route for Bank Engine purposes.

CHRISTOW—LONGDOWN SECTION.
Passenger and Coaching Stock Trains.
Bank Engine to run uncoupled and ease regulator on emerging from Culver Tunnel at 4 miles 75¼ chs., and follow the train to Longdown Signal Box.
When the load of a Passenger train necessitates a Bank Engine, two engines will, when possible, be provided to work through from Newton Abbot to Exeter to save additional stops en route for Bank Engine purposes.

Freight Trains.
Bank engine to run coupled until the train comes to a stand at the Stop Board near Longdown Up Starting Signal. Banker uncoupled to follow train to Longdown Signal Box, unless required to work through to City Basin Junction, when the instructions on Page 80 of the Appendix to No. 5 Service Book must apply.

EXTRA STAFF TO COVER EMERGENCY WORKING.

EXETER DIVISIONAL SUPERINTENDENT'S OFFICE AND PLYMOUTH DISTRICT TRAFFIC MANAGER'S OFFICE.
The Passenger Train Offices and the Freight Train Control Offices in the Exeter D.S.O. and the Plymouth D.T.M.O. to be open continuously.
Exeter Control Office. Staff to be augmented.
Guards Working. Staff to be provided to cover the 24 hours.

EXETER STATION.
Train Regulators to be provided at Exeter East and at Exeter Station to control the working into or out of Exeter Yard and Station, and from Cowley Bridge Junction, and to and from City Basin Junction.
The Station Master to arrange for two Inspectors to work on each turn of duty.
The Traffic and Locomotive Departments to keep in close touch with all concerned in connection with Engine working.
Telephonists to be provided continuously at :
Exeter Middle Signal Box. Exeter Down Side Platform Inspector's Office.
Exeter West Signal Box.
A Shunting Engine and two shunters to be provided continuously to deal with the Goods traffic in Exeter "New Yard."

CITY BASIN JUNCTION.
An appointed Porter to be stationed at City Basin Junction to transfer the Electric Staff from Trainmen to Signalman, and vice versa, also to assist Guards, when necessary, in dividing Down Freight Trains to enable them to be held on the Loop Line and, when foul of the Junction, to be drawn in clear by crossing the front portion to Alphington Road Yard or towards the City Basin Branch Line and so avoid having to send the train on to Christow at the expense of an Up Train which should have the preference.

LONGDOWN.
A competent man to be provided at Longdown to assist Guards Braking Freight trains in each direction and assist the Signalman in exchanging the Electric Train Staff on Passenger trains.

CHRISTOW, TRUSHAM and HEATHFIELD.
Relief Clerk to be provided at each of these stations to take turns with the Station Master and be responsible for regulating the working of the trains over the Branch. The Station Masters at these stations to provide a man to assist the Signalman in changing the Electric Train Staff.

NEWTON ABBOT.
Train Regulators to be provided at Newton Abbot East Signal Box to control traffic to and from the Moretonhampstead Branch.

SIGNAL BOXES at :
Sampford Peverell, Stoke Canon Junction.—To be open continuously from 5.0 a.m. Monday to 10.0 a.m. Sunday, or as ordered.
St. Thomas.—To be open continuously.
A Signal Department Lineman to be on duty on Teign Valley Branch to transfer Electric Train Staffs as required.

The 1943 alterations at Heathfield also involved changes at the north end, where the Goods Loop was taken out of use as such; although not directly related to Teign Valley trains, this was an integral part of the same scheme. In these 22nd April 1943 views the Goods Loop points *(below)* are still in situ, but they had been decommissioned on 11th April, hence the removed signal arm. The Up Siding (as it now was) was extended northwards beyond the footbridge. See also pp. 174 & 176.   *NRM*

in 1938, for the ordinary branch motive power, to 35mph Exeter–Christow and 45mph Christow–Heathfield). In 1941 the 78XX class was added to the list, with a 20mph maximum speed.

It was during the 1939–45 war that the line really came to be appreciated as a potential Diversionary Route. After Dunkirk there was concern over the vulnerability of the coastal line to enemy action, especially with it being the main supply route to Plymouth. The Teign Valley line was (like many other secondary lines on the GWR) therefore kept open continuously 7 days a week from 1941 to the summer of 1945. In May 1941 notices were issued detailing at great length the diversionary arrangements to be adopted in the event of blockage of the line at any point on the GWR system, and extracts from Notice 464 relating to the Exeter Division are reproduced here. It was also felt necessary to do something to improve line capacity. The only passenger loop on the branch, at Christow, was, at 670ft, too short for diverted passenger trains, and to effect a crossing there the up train had to be shunted back into the up siding. Trusham loop was lengthy but was a

goods loop only, so (whilst its use was permitted under 'Emergency Working' for passenger trains) point clipping was necessary. Finally Heathfield, although provided with a loop for Moretonhampstead branch trains in 1927, could not cross two Teign Valley trains without the up train being shunted (plan, Chapter 18). The whole situation was far from ideal, so in 1942/3 plans were drawn up for major improvements to the line to be carried out at the Government's expense as part of the national programme of 'Insurance Works' for increasing the capacity of diversionary routes. These improvements comprised:

Heathfield	—	Provision of double line junction to Teign Valley line, to enable the station to be used as a crossing place for diverted trains. Estimate £12,223.
Trusham	—	Conversion of Goods Loop to Passenger Loop. Estimate £5,747.
Christow	—	Extension of Loop. Estimate £6,669.
Longdown	—	Provision of Loop. Estimate £6,408.

Total Estimate £31,047. These works were all carried out between May and September 1943, as described in

Chapter 18. The loop at Longdown was not intended to be used in normal service and was arranged to be worked by ground frames during 'Emergency Working' only. The new loops were of 1,100ft length.

In the event, there were no troubles with the sea wall and the cliffs during the war years, and so far as is known no diversions via the Teign Valley were ever needed at this period. The signalmen had nothing to do on their night turns until June 1944 when Ambulance Trains began run-

ning from the ports to convey American wounded from France to American Military Hospital 316 at Stover (situated where the Polish Hostel was built subsequently). These trains ran down the Teign Valley line from Exeter and unloaded at Chudleigh station. (Heathfield station was nearer the hospital but there was better road access at Chudleigh for parking the large number of ambulances required.) Most ran at night time, mainly, it is believed, because the lengthy time which it took to unload them

The four views here give an excellent illustration of the development of the south end of Heathfield station (and should be compared with the diagrams at page 174). The 1925 view above shows the '1916' layout; the Down Home, in accordance with then practice, had splitting arms for Main and Branch, although there was only the one line through the platform. Also shown is the 1917 Timber Siding and the 4-lever covered North ground frame which controlled this connection until it was transferred to the signal box in 1927.

G. N. Southerden

Right: The '1927' layout with reversible working. *Below:* A 22nd April 1943 view looking north from the new loop connection, 166 yds nearer Newton Abbot, which had been laid in on 28th March 1943, but is clipped and padlocked here as it was not brought into use until 2nd May 1943. In this five-week period there was no loop available at all, as the old south end points had been taken out; hence the 'Down to Up Main' Home arm had been removed from the bracket post at centre. The two up signals at right were fixed, temporarily. The main 'changeover' at Heathfield took place between 1st and 11th May.

P. J. Garland

NRM

Finally, a 1959 picture of the '1943' layout, with the lengthened loop evident. The loop points, some 400 yds from the box, were worked by Westinghouse point motor, and had a sand drag. An Auxiliary Token Instrument was provided here. *S. J. Dickson*

Trusham, also on 22nd April 1943. The works here were commissioned in July (see pp. 208/9 for details) and the upper view shows the 1911 south end loop points intact, but with the embankment widened to accommodate the very short extension of the loop. A footpath crossed the line here, hence the notice. In contrast the lower view shows the new pointwork at the north end already partly installed.

National Railway Museum

Two views of Christow on the same date, the upper looking south from the new loop connection which was already laid in, the lower looking north from the cattle pens where the new trackwork had not yet commenced, the loop extension being laid as far as the Down Inner Home signal only. Note the new block retaining wall for the Scatter Rock sidings. Although there was clearly a lot of work still to be done at this date, the new layout at Christow was commissioned in May, only four weeks after this; see pp. 226/7 for details.

National Railway Museum

Still on 22nd April 1943, these four photographs show Longdown where the new crossing loop is seen to have been at an advanced stage (although it was not commissioned until 19th September). Some sloping back of the cuttings either side, and widening of the embankment through the station, had been necessary. The old Down Home signal had been temporarily relocated outside the new loop; it was abolished in September, but the old Up Starting signal, seen in the bottom right view looking towards Perridge Tunnel, survived the 1943 alterations.

National Railway Museum

would have disrupted the branch timetable had they run during the day.[1] After unloading, they continued down the line to Newton Abbot and returned via the main line. Initially the trains used were the Westinghouse-braked trains built for the use of the US Army on the continent, and these were hauled by ex-GE B12 4-6-0s which could be used on the branch thanks to their light axle loading; observers in June–August 1944 saw 8516 and 8530. But during the autumn of 1944 these trains were all sent over to the continent to fulfil their intended purpose, and the 'home' work taken over by vacuum-braked trains. On the Teign Valley line pairs of 43XX 2-6-0s were noted on these trains. The running of the trains was erratic depending on the level of fighting in France, perhaps two or three

Exeter shed received six of the Collett 48XX 0–4–2Ts new in 1932/3 but their duties on the Teign Valley line were comparatively limited until the demise of the motors in 1935. They then had a near-monopoly of the branch passenger services from 1935 to the early 1950s when other classes began to appear also. Here we see the now-renumbered 1469 with the usual single-coach auto (trailer 157) in Platform 1 at Exeter St. David's in August 1947. Auto-trains on the branch normally ran with the loco at the Exeter end. *Tom Reardon*

a week on average. They continued until around May 1945. It had been anticipated that there would be rather more casualties, and therefore more trains, than actually proved to be the case. Another special wartime traffic on the branch comprised trains to the American petrol dump at Knighton Heath where special sidings were provided (Chapter 18). The line also saw occasional patrols by the armoured train based at Newton Abbot, which contrived to demolish the level crossing gates at Ashton on one trip.

After the 24hr opening ceased in 1945, special arrangements were made for the speedy opening up of the line at night time in emergencies. Every night, after the passage of the last trains:

- the City Basin Jn–Longdown staff was taken out at City Basin Jn box
- the Longdown–Christow staff was taken out at Longdown
- points 25 at Christow were left reversed so that a train could run into the platform from Longdown
- the Newton Abbot East–Heathfield token was taken out at Newton Abbot East box
- the Heathfield–Trusham token was taken out at Heathfield box and Points 28 at Heathfield left reversed so that a train could run on to the branch.

By these means a down train could proceed as far as Christow, and an up train as far as Trusham, before the signalmen reported for duty. The instructions provided that when an emergency opening was necessary, Chief Inspector Long and District Inspector Vickery of Exeter, along with Frank Edworthy, the Longdown signalman, who lived in Exeter, were to travel out on the first down train. District Inspector Saffin and Assistant District Inspector Court of Newton Abbot were to travel on the first up train and work Heathfield and Trusham boxes respectively until the regular signalmen arrived. Christow Signalman Wilf Cox was to be alerted by a direct phone call from Control and was to wake up the Christow station master on his way down to the station. It is not clear that all this was ever actually called upon, in the event!

The Longdown loop was taken out of use in 1954. But diversions continued from time to time up to 1958, and, when the closure of the line was proposed, there were inevitably suggestions that the line should be retained for its value as a diversionary route. Few would have suspected in 1958 that only ten years later British Railways would close the Southern route to Plymouth also, leaving the whole railway system west of Exeter dependent on the sea wall.

---

1. All the former staff interviewed agreed that the trains ran at night time. But there were also occasional daytime workings: a report on an accident to one of the lady porters from Trusham at Crockham siding at 11.47am on 29.7.1944 refers specifically to the fact that attempts were being made to shunt the goods as quickly as possible because 'an Ambulance Train was shortly to be dealt with at Chudleigh'. It is possible that Heathfield station was used for unloading on some occasions latterly, but there is no definite confirmation of this.

CHAPTER SIXTEEN

DECLINE: 1939–1958

THE Second World War had quite the opposite effect on the line's traffic to the First. Thanks to the restrictions on private transport, both passenger and goods traffic shot up to 1½ times their 1930s levels. The passenger traffic at Trusham, Ashton, and Christow, where there were no buses, reached an all-time high; but even where there were buses they were often overcrowded, and this brought Chudleigh people back to their station again in larger numbers, and saw Dunsford people trekking it to their eponymous but distant halt. A new traffic in the converse direction was brought about by the Exeter air raids, which saw Exeter people coming out on the last down train to sleep in the fields in the valley, returning to Exeter in the morning.

So far as the line's permanent future was concerned, the wartime boom was a fool's dawn. The late 1940s saw a dramatic decline in the passenger traffic, exacerbated by the introduction of a bus service to Christow village for the first time in 1947. The village had asked for an improved rail service but was not granted it. The loss of most of the Christow traffic left Ashton and Trusham as the line's only solid sources of passenger revenue, and given that they did not produce more than 25 or so journeys a day each, the writing was on the wall by the early '50s.

The unhappy-looking Christow of the last years is seen in this 14th October 1950 view, just after Scatter Rock closed. The Scatter Rock sidings were quite unused at this stage as the barytes traffic did not start using them until 1952. The train was the 11.45 Exeter–Heathfield auto, with trailers 156 and 147. Note the new lighting standards, a GWR system of the 1930s for Tilley lamps which were wound up to the top of the tall posts (for a better light) by a winding down on the posts.   *W. A. Camwell*

DOWN TRAINS. TEIGN VALLEY BRANCH. WEEK DAYS.

Single Line City Basin Junction to Heathfield worked by Electric Train Staff. The Staff Stations are City Basin Junction, Longdown, Christow, Trusham, and Heathfield. Crossing Stations are Christow and Trusham. Intermediate token instrument at Chudleigh Knighton Sidings. Longdown is a crossing station, only by special arrangement during emergency working, but the Down Loop may be used, when required, for side-tracking a Freight Train.

M.P. Mileage M.	C.	Distances from Exeter M.	C.	STATIONS	Ruling Gradient	Point-to Point Times (Mins.)	Allow for Stop (Mins.)	Allow for Start (Mins.)	K Freight arr. a.m.	K Freight dep. a.m.	B Auto. arr. a.m.	B Auto. dep. a.m.	B Auto. arr. a.m.	B Auto. dep. a.m.	B Newton Abbot Auto. arr. a.m.	B Newton Abbot Auto. dep. a.m.	K Newton Abbot Freight. arr. a.m.	K Newton Abbot Freight. dep. a.m.	B Auto. SO arr. p.m.	B Auto. SO dep. p.m.
—	—	—	—	**EXETER**	—	—	—	2	—	7‡ 0	—	6 30	—	7 0	—	9 46	....	....	—	12 5
—	—	—	74	St. Thomas	—	—	—	—	—	—	6 33	6 34	7 3	7 4	9 49	9 50	..	..	12 8	12 9
—	—	1	19	City Basin Jct.	—	—	—	—	C7	11 S	C	S	C	S	C	S	....	....	C	S
0	19	1	38	Alphington Road Goods Yard	264 R.	6	1	1	7‡13	—	—	—	—	—	—	—	....	....	—	—
0	62	2	1	Alphington Halt	56 R.	—	—	—			6 38	6 38½	7 8	7 9	9 54	9 54½	....	....	12 13	12 13½
2	0	3	19	Ide Halt	58 R.	7	1	2	‡—RR to City Basin.		6 42	6 42½	7 13	7 14	9 58	9 58½	..	..	12 17	12 17½
4	58	5	77	Longdown	58 R.	10	1	1			6 49½	6 50	7 21½	7 22½	10 6	10 6½	..	..	12 25	12 26
4	68	6	7	Stop Board	L.	—	—	—			—	—	—	—	—	—	....	....	—	—
6	1	7	20	Dunsford Halt	64 F.	—	—	—	..	..	6 53	6 53½	7 25½	7 26½	10 9½	10 10	..	..	12 29	12 30
8	3	9	22	Christow	64 F.	8	2	1	....	....	6 58	7 0	7 31	7 33	1014½	1015½	—	11 0	12 35	12 36
—	—	10	29	Ryecroft Quarry	—	—	—	—	..	..	—	—	—	—	—	—	—	—	—	—
		10	68	Ashton	132 F.	4	1	1	....	....	7 4	7 5	7 37	7 38	1019½	10 20	C	R	12 40	12 41
		12	33	Whetcombe Sdg.	198 F.	4	1	1	..	..	—	—	—	—	—	—	—	—	—	—
		12	63	Trusham	384 F.	2	1	1	....	....	7 10	—	7 43	X7 44	10 25	1025½	11 10	•11 55	12 46	12 47
		13	8	Crockham Siding	84 F.	2	1	1	..	..			—	—	—	—	—	—	—	—
		14	51	Chudleigh	132 F.	4	1	1	....	....	....	....	7 48	7 49	1029½	10 30	12 2	•12 20	12 51	12 52
		15	74	Chudleigh K. Hlt.	—	—	—	—	..	..	..	..	7 52	7 53	10 33	1033½	—	—	12 55	12 56
		15	74	Chudleigh K. O.S.	—	—	—	—	....	....	....	....	—	—	—	—	C	R	—	—
		17	3	**HEATHFIELD**	66 R.	6	1	—	....	....	....	....	7 57	—	10 38	10 42	12 27	1 3	1 0	—

Terminates at 8m. 7c.

STATIONS.	B Newton Abbot Auto. arr. p.m.	dep. p.m.	K Newton Abbot Freight. SX arr. p.m.	dep. p.m.	K Newton Abbot Freight SO arr. p.m.	dep. p.m.	K Freight. FO arr. p.m.	dep. p.m.	K Freight. arr. p.m.	dep. p.m.	B Auto. arr. p.m.	dep. p.m.	B Auto. arr. p.m.	dep. p.m.	B Auto. arr. p.m.	dep. p.m.	B Auto. SO arr. p.m.	dep. p.m.
EXETER	—	12 50	—	2 8	—	1 15	—	1 30	—	4 10	—	4 30	....	....	—	6 30	—	9 55
St. Thomas	12 53	12 54	—	—	—	—	—	—	—	—	4 33	4 34	..	..	6 33	6 34	9 58	9 59
City Basin Junction	C	S	C2	14S	C1	21S	C1	36S	C4	16S	C	S	....	....	C	S	C	S
Alphington Road Goods Yard	—	—	—	—	—	—	1 38	—	4 18	—	—	—	..	..	—	—	—	—
Alphington Halt	12 58	12 59	—	—	—	—					4 38	4 38½	....	....	6 38	6 38½	10 3	10 4
Ide Halt	1 3	1 4	—	—	—	—	..	..	..	..	4 42½	4 43	..	..	6 42½	6 43	10 8	10 9
Longdown	1 11½	1 12½	C	S	1 41	X2 24	....	....	....	....	4 50½	4 51½	....	....	6 50½	6 51½	1016½	1017½
Stop Board	—	—	2 35	P2 38	2 26	P2 29	..	..	..	..	—	—	..	..	—	—	—	—
Dunsford Halt	1 15½	1 16½	—	—	—	—	....	....	....	....	4 54½	4 55	....	....	6 54½	6 55	1020½	10 21
Christow	1 21	1 25	2 49	P2 52	2 40	P2 43	..	..	..	..	4 59½	5 2	—	5 52	6 59½	X7 1	10 26	1027
Ryecroft Quarry	—	—	—	—	—	—	....	....	....	....	—	—	—	—	—	—	—	—
Ashton	1 28	1 29	—	—	—	—	..	..	..	..	5 5	5 6	5 56	5 57	7 4	7 4½	10 31	10 32
Whetcombe Siding	—	—	—	—	—	—	....	....	....	....	—	—	—	—	—	—	—	—
Trusham	1 34	X1 39	3 4	*3 6	2 55	*3 6	..	..	..	..	5 10½	5 11½	6 1½	6 2½	7 9	7 9½	10 37	—
Crockham Siding	—	—	—	—	—	—	....	....	....	....	—	—	—	—	—	—		
Chudleigh	1 43	1 44	—	—	—	—	..	..	..	..	5 15½	5 16½	6 6½	6 7	7 13½	7 14	..	..
Chudleigh Knighton Halt	1 47	1 48	—	—	—	—	....	....	....	....	5 19½	5 20	6 10	6 11	7 17	7 17½	....	....
Chudleigh Knighton O.S.	—	—	—	—	—	—	..	..	..	..	—	—	—	—	—	—	..	..
HEATHFIELD	1 52	1 55	3 20	X 3 30	3 20	X3 30	....	....	....	....	5 24	—	6 15	—	7 22	—	....	....

UP TRAINS. TEIGN VALLEY BRANCH—continued. WEEK DAYS.

M.P. Mileage M.	C.	STATIONS.	Ruling Gradient.	Point-to Point Times. (Mins.)	Allow for Stop. (Mins.)	Allow for Start. (Mins.)	G Engine and Van. arr. a.m.	dep. a.m.	B Auto. arr. a.m.	dep. a.m.	B Auto. arr. a.m.	dep. a.m.	K 7.0 a.m. Newton Abbot Freight. arr. a.m.	dep. a.m.	K 9.20 a.m. Newton Abbot Freight. arr. a.m.	dep. a.m.	B 11.5 a.m. Newton Abbot Auto. arr. a.m.	dep. a.m.
0	0	**HEATHFIELD**	—	—	—	1	....	....	....	....	—	8 20	7 27	8 40	9 31	•1011	11 13	11 15
1	9	Chudleigh Knighton O.S.	—	—	—	—	..	..	..	..	—	—	C	R	—	—	—	—
1	9	Chudleigh Knighton Halt	—	—	—	—	....	....	....	....	8 25	8 25½	—	—	—	—	11 19	11 20
2	32	Chudleigh	66 F.	6	1	1	..	..	..	..	8 28½	8 29	8 48	9 20	—	—	11 23	11 24
3	75	Crockham Siding	132 R.	4	1	1	....	....	....	....	—	—	—	—	—	—	—	—
4	20	Trusham	84 R.	2	1	1	..	..	—	X7 45	8 33½	8 34	9 28	9 40	10 24	X10 30	11 28	11 29
4	50	Whetcombe Siding	384 R.	2	1	1	....	....	—	—	—	—	—	—	—	—	—	—
6	15	Ashton	198 R.	4	1	1	..	..	7 50	7 51	8 39	8 39½	9 48	10 0	—	—	11 33	11 34
6	53	Ryecroft Quarry	—	—	—	—	....	....	—	—	—	—	—	—	—	—	—	—
		Christow	132 R.	4	1	2	..	..	7 55	8 0	8 43½	8 45½	10 6	—	C10	45S	1137½	1139½
		Dunsford Halt	64 R.	—	—	—	....	....	8 5	8 6	8 50½	8 51			—	—	1144½	1145½
		Longdown	64 R.	16	1	1	..	..	8 10	8 11	8 55	8 56	....	....	—	—	1149½	1150½
		Stop Board 4m. 51c.	—	—	—	—	....	....	—	—	—	—	..	..	11 0	P11 4	—	—
		Ide Halt	58 F.	11	2	1	..	..	8 16½	8 17½	9 1½	9 2½	....	....	—	—	11 56	11 57
		Alphington Halt	58 F.	—	—	—	....	....	8 20½	8 21½	9 5½	9 6½	..	..	—	—	12 0	12 1
		Stop Board 0m. 22c.	L.	5	2	1	..	..	—	—	—	—	....	....	11 23	P1127	—	—
		Alphington Rd. Gds. Y.	56 F.	1	2	1	—	7†47	—	—	—	—	..	..	—	—	—	—
		City Basin Junction	—	—	—	—	C7	50S	C	S	C	S	....	....	C11	30S	C12	4S
		St. Thomas	—	—	—	—	—	—	8 25½	8 27	9 10½	9 12	..	..	—	—	12 5	12 7
		EXETER	—	5	1	—	7†55	—	8 30	—	9 15	—	....	....	11 36	—	12 10	—

Terminates at 8m. 7c.

STATIONS.	B Auto. SO arr. p.m.	dep. p.m.	K Freight. FO arr. p.m.	dep. p.m.	B 2.55 p.m. Newton Abbot Auto. arr. p.m.	dep. p.m.	B Auto. arr. p.m.	dep. p.m.	K Freight. arr. p.m.	dep. p.m.	B Auto. arr. p.m.	dep. p.m.	B Auto. arr. p.m.	dep. p.m.	B Auto. SO arr. p.m.	dep. p.m.
HEATHFIELD	—	1 20	....	....	3 4	3 25	—	5 28	....	....	—	6 30	—	8 23	....	....
Chudleigh Knighton O.S.	—	—	..	..	—	—	—	—	..	..	—	—	—	—	..	..
Chudleigh Knighton Halt	1 25	1 26	....	....	3 29	3 30	5 32	5 32½	....	....	6 35	6 36	8 27	8 28	....	....
Chudleigh	1 29	1 30	..	..	3 33	3 34	5 35½	5 36	..	..	6 39	6 40	8 31	8 32	..	..
Crockham Siding	—	—	....	....	—	—	—	—	....	....	—	—	—	—	....	....
Trusham	1 35	X1 48	..	..	3 38	3 39	5 40	5 41	..	..	6 44½	6 46	8 36½	8 37½	—	10 45
Whetcombe Siding	—	—	....	....	—	—	—	—	....	....	—	—	—	—	—	—
Ashton	1 52	1 52½	..	..	3 43	3 44	5 45	5 45½	..	..	6 51	6 52	8 42½	8 43	10 50	10 51
Ryecroft Quarry	—	—	....	....	—	—	—	—	....	....	—	—	—	—	—	—
Christow	1 55½	1 56½	..	..	3 47½	3 49½	5 49	—	..	..	6 56	X7 2	8 47	8 49	10 55	10 56
Dunsford Halt	2 1½	2 2	....	....	3 54½	3 55½			....	....	7 7	7 7½	8 55	8 56	11 1	11 2
Longdown	2 6	2 6½	..	..	3 59½	4 0½	..	..	..	..	7 11½	7 12	9 0	9 1	11 6	11 7
Stop Board 4m. 51c.	—	—	....	....	—	—	....	....	....	....	—	—	—	—	—	—
Ide Halt	2 12	2 12½	..	..	4 6	4 7	..	..	..	..	7 18	7 18½	9 7	9 8	11 12	11 13
Alphington Halt	2 15½	2 16	....	....	4 10	4 11	....	....	....	....	7 21½	7 22	9 11	9 12	11 16	11 17
Stop Board 0m. 22c.	—	—	..	..	—	—	..	..	..	..	—	—	—	—	—	—
Alphington Road Goods Yd.	—	—	—	3 45	—	—	....	....	—	5 50	—	—	—	—	—	—
City Basin Junction	C2	20S	C3	47S	C	S	..	..	C5	52S	C	S	C	S	C	S
St. Thomas	2 21	2 22	—	—	4 15	4 17	....	....	—	—	7 26	7 27	9 19	9 21	11 21	11 22
EXETER	2 25	—	3 53	—	4 20	—	..	..	5 58	—	7 30	—	9 24	—	11 25	—

The timetable applicable from 6th October 1947. The early morning Exeter–Christow train was newly extended to run through to Trusham in this timetable, for the benefit of those travelling to work in Exeter from Trusham and Ashton, and continued to run from Trusham subsequently. There is one timetabled crossing of trains at Longdown per week, and one timetabled crossing of two passenger trains at Trusham per week. One improvement made when the timetable was reduced at the start of the war, was the extension of two of the five trains daily to/from Newton Abbot. This is still the case in this timetable but the early 1950s saw a gradual reduction in the number of trains working through. The extra Saturday lunchtime train now runs through to/from Heathfield, and the 9.55 p.m. Exeter SO has been restored after its wartime disappearance.

There was a closure scare in the local papers in March 1952 when it was revealed that BR were carrying out 'investigations', but nothing came of this immediately.

PASSENGER SERVICES 1939–1957

In the early part of the war, one morning and one afternoon trip each way were cut out, leaving five trains each way plus the early morning Exeter–Christow–Exeter commuter working and an afternoon Heathfield–Christow–Heathfield trip. In 1941 an additional 12.20pm Exeter–Trusham SO (and return) had to be introduced to cater for the demand at Saturday lunchtime which had always been one of the busiest times on the line.

This service was really more appropriate to the level of demand than the more frequent service of the 1930s had been, and although intended no doubt as a wartime econ-

In the early 1950s, the previous near-monopoly of the 14XXs started to break down as Exeter shed began to put 54XXs and 57XXs on the Teign Valley services. The 57XXs were not auto-fitted (although all trains remained booked for auto operation until June 1957) and had to run round at Heathfield. Taken on the evening of 5th August 1953, this picture shows No. 7716 running into Christow with the 6.20 p.m. Exeter while No. 1469 was waiting in the up platform with the 6.20 p.m. Heathfield.
P. W. Gray

The relatively few appearances of the 'Manors' on the line were but little photographed. Here, however, is a splendid view from the signal box steps at Christow, with 7806 *Cockington Manor* waiting in the up platform whilst a down auto crosses. The photograph comes undated and uncaptioned, and it had been postulated that the loco was on a special working to test clearances for the class. But the fact that it was taken about 10.0 a.m. suggests that this is more likely the ordinary Newton Abbot–Christow goods, halfway through its activities at Christow. Note also the 'J' headlamp code rather than 'K' as one might expect.
I. D. Beale

No. 5412 propelling the 9.44 a.m. from Exeter out of Chudleigh station on 13th October 1956.

P. W. Gray

Table 88 — EXETER, CHRISTOW and HEATHFIELD
WEEK DAYS ONLY (Second class only)

DOWN

Miles	Station	am E	am S	am S	am	am S	pm E S	pm S E	pm E S	pm S
—	Exeter (St. David's) .. dep	6 30	6 55	7 0	9 20	9 25	12 50 12 55	4 25 4 42	5 55 9 30	
½	(St. Thomas)	6 34	6 58	7 3	9 23	9 28	12 53 12 58	4 29 4 45	5 58 9 33	
2	Alphington Halt ..	6 38	7 3	7 8	9 28	9 33 12 5	12 58 1 3	4 34 4 50	6 3 9 38	
3½	Longdown	6 43	7 8	7 13	9 33	9 38 12 10	1 3 1 8	4 39 4 55	6 8 9 43	
6	Ide Halt	6 51	7 17	7 22	9 42	9 47 12 18	1 12 1 17	4 47 5 4	6 17 9 51	
7½	Dunsford Halt ..	6 55	7 21	7 26	9 46	9 51 12 22	1 16 1 21	4 52 5 8	6 21 9 55	
9½	Christow	7 0	7 28	7 32	9 51	9 58 12 28	1 28 1 28	4 58 5 15	6 38 10 0	
10½	Ashton	7 7	7 33	7 38	9 59	10 4 12 33	1 34 1 34	5 4 5 21	6 44 10 5	
12½	Trusham	7 13	7 39	7 44	10 5	10 10 12 39	1 40 1 40	5 10 5 27	6 50 10 12	
14½	Chudleigh		7 44	7 49	10 10	10 15 12 44	1 45 1 45	5 15 5 32	6 55 10 17	
16	Chudleigh Knighton Halt		7 48	7 53	10 14	10 19 12 48	1 49 1 49	5 19 5 36	6 59 10 21	
17	Heathfield .... arr		7 53	7 58	10 19	10 24 12 53	1 54 1 54	5 24 5 41	7 5 10 26	
20½/90	Newton Abbot .. arr		8 25	8 25	10 50	10 50	2 9 2 9	5 46 5 55	7 34 10 35	

UP

Miles	Station	am S	am E	am E S	am E S	am S S	pm S S	pm S E	pm S
—	90 Newton Abbot .. dep			7 50 7 50		10 30 10 30	12 44	2 15	6 5 8 15
—	Heathfield .... dep			8 5 8 20	10 43 10 45	1 5	2 10 2 40	6 15 8 35	
1	Chudleigh Knighton Halt			8 9 8 24	10 47 10 49	1 9	2 14 2 44	6 20 8 39	
2½	Chudleigh			8 13 8 28	10 51 10 53	1 13	2 18 2 48	6 23 8 43	
4½	Trusham	7 45		8 18 8 33	10 56 10 58	1 18	2 23 2 53	6 28 8 48	
6½	Ashton	7 49 7 50		8 23 8 38	11 1 11 3	1 23	2 28 2 58	6 33 8 53	
7½	Christow	7 56		8 29 8 46	11 8 11 10	1 30	2 34 3 4	6 40 9 0	
9½	Dunsford Halt	8 2		8 35 8 53	11 14 11 16	1 38	2 41 3 10	6 45 9 6	
11	Longdown	8 7 8 6		8 40 8 58	11 19 11 21	1 43	2 46 3 15	6 50 9 11	
13½	Ide Halt	8 14 8 21		8 47 9 5	11 26 11 28	1 50	2 52 3 22	6 57 9 18	
15	Alphington Halt	8 18 8 21		8 51 9 9	11 30 11 32 11Z37	1 54	2 56 3 26	7 1 9 22	
16½	Exeter (St. Thomas)	8 23 8 27		8 56 9 14	11 35 11 41	11Z41 1 59	3 3 3 31	7 7 9 27	
17	(St. David's) .. arr		8 34	9 3 9 18	11 41	11Z46	3 4 3 35	7 11 9 31	

■ Except Saturdays S Saturdays only Z By Exeter Corporation Omnibus (heavy luggage not conveyed)

For OTHER TRAINS between Exeter (St. David's) and Exeter (St. Thomas), see Table 81

On summer Saturdays in the 1950s it was necessary for some of the branch trains to run to/from Alphington Halt only, so far as the passengers were concerned. In reality, they ran through to City Basin Jcn for ETS purposes, or ran through to/from St. David's, but with such long waits for pathing purposes at City Basin Jcn that they were not deemed advertisable as through trains to St. David's. Here, in the 17th June 1957 timetable, one train has a bus connection advertised.

Other trains were shown as terminating at St. Thomas, so that they could run into the yard at St. David's instead of into the passenger platforms.

Some of the Newton Abbot connections in this timetable are rather poor, and none of the trains ran through, save the 9.30 p.m. SO, which by this date was returning to Exeter up the main line.

In this timetable only the 12.50 SO down/2.10 SO up, and the 4.25 down/6.15 up, were booked for auto working.

Through workings from and to the Exe Valley, reintroduced in this timetable after many years, were as follows:

DOWN

9.20 a.m. SO/9.25 a.m. SX is 8.10 p.m. Dulverton
4.42 p.m. SO   is 3.25 p.m. Dulverton

UP

8.20 a.m. SO   is through to Dulverton
10.43 a.m. SX   is through to Dulverton
2.40 p.m. SX   is through to Dulverton
8.35 p.m.   is through to Dulverton
        (SO)

This through working was not publicly advertised.

omy, it remained the established service on the line through to 1957 (see 1947 Timetable here).

THE SEPTEMBER 1957 TIMETABLE

In September 1957, with closure already planned, major changes were made to the timetable. Most of the branch services were now run through to/from Newton Abbot, and for the first time ever a Newton Abbot loco and train set took half the workings.[1] This enabled the withdrawal of the 6.30am Exeter—Trusham and the 8.35pm up train, both of which had run nearly empty. Crossings were concentrated at Christow.

At the same time the auto trailers were withdrawn and all trains worked as ordinary hauled trains. (Up to June 1957 all the branch services were Autos. All but two trips (see timetable here) became ordinary trains from June

The regular auto-trailers were normally used even when a non-auto-fitted loco was provided, but here a very clean 7761 had an ordinary coach in tow as the 11.45 a.m. SO Exeter—Heathfield on 13th October 1956. This picture was taken in the open countryside between Ide and Perridge.

P. W. Gray

The 45XXs, which, like the 57XXs, were not auto-fitted, only began to make regular appearances on passenger trains on the line in June 1957. This 9th November 1957 view shows No. 5536 passing Chudleigh flood platform with coaches W5052W and W4076W, as the 9.25 a.m. from Exeter.
P. W. Gray

1957, and all became ordinary trains from September 1957.) *See p. 265 for the full September 1957 timetable.*

GOODS WORKINGS 1939–1958

It will be recalled from Chapter 14 that the cuts of the 1930s had left the line with daily Newton Abbot–Christow and Exeter–Trusham workings, plus two Exeter–Alphington Road trips. The Exeter–Trusham train was cut back to Christow around 1941 and then in 1947 it was withdrawn altogether, a reflection of the decline of the Scatter Rock traffic. This left Ide and Longdown without any booked goods service even though they remained open for goods traffic (in theory) until 1955 and 1958 respectively. (It was stated officially in 1958 that the Newton Abbot–Christow goods ran to Longdown if required but in practice this never was required in the last years.)

A more curious development in 1947 was the introduction for the first time ever of a 'main line' through goods train booked to run via the branch instead of via Dawlish. This train, the 9.20am Newton Abbot returning from Exeter at 2.8pm, can be seen in the October 1947 timetable here. It had no traffic stops on the branch.[2] It lasted until 1954, whereupon the line ceased to be used by goods trains between Christow and Alphington Road.

Auto-trailer W215W and 14XX in the Moretonhampstead bay platform No. 9 after arriving with the 12.47 p.m. Exeter on 29th September 1956. At that time this was the only through trip to Newton Abbot (save for the 9.30 p.m. SO down). They would return to Exeter as the 2.30 p.m.
R. M. Casserley

In 1955 the remaining goods train (Newton Abbot–Christow) was reduced to TThSO (Tuesdays, Thursdays, Saturdays Only) operation.

---

1. As noted earlier, Newton Abbot had had a share in the branch goods workings since 1907.
2. On 1.7.1954 C.A.S. Honnor noted 7815 on this train. Whether the 78XXs were regularly used is not known.

CHAPTER SEVENTEEN
SIGNALLING & OPERATING

HAD the TVR been opened in 1866 or 1870, it would have been able to make do without interlocking and with only the most primitive signalling arrangements. But by 1877 the Board of Trade's demands were very different, and it would have been clear to everybody from the resumption of activity on the works in 1877 that the line would have to be fully interlocked with a full set of signals at every station. As was usual with a new line being built by a small company, it was left to the contractor to arrange for a signalling contractor to do the necessary work under sub-contract, the cost being included within the main contractor's overall price. Richard Walker's 1877 contract merely stated that signalling was to be provided in accordance with the requirements of the Board of Trade, a fairly common way of arranging things. In fact, though, nothing was done in respect of the signalling prior to the August 1881 contract, which laid down in great detail the signalling equipment to be provided. 'Ground Locking Frames' and Starting, Home, and Distant signals were to be installed at each station (except the goods-only Teign House terminus, where no signalling was called for), and a two-wire telegraph provided, with 'single needles and blocks' (i.e., a single needle 'speaking instrument', and Block Instruments) at each station. As ever, the actual installations differed in several ways from what had been specified. The contract clearly anticipated that the signal box at Heathfield would control the TVR lines only, but it was decided in the event that it should control the broad gauge lines also, so the '9 or 10' levers specified was increased to 25. The contract seems to have foreseen ground level signal boxes throughout, but they were actually built as elevated cabins, as the Board of Trade would probably have insisted anyway. And the signals which the contract specified for the level crossings seem not to have been provided.

Signalling was usually one of the very last matters to be dealt with in the building of a new railway, and the TVR was no exception. The signalling contract was let by Walker some time in the winter of 1881/2[1] but nothing was done on the ground until March 1882, largely because the GWR sent a Signalling Inspector to look over the line in late January and then took a month to let the TVR have his report. On 13th March 1882 S.W. Jenkin told the TVR Board that the GWR's agreement had now been obtained and that 'the signal boxes are commenced'. Work proceeded as fast as possible but on 8th June it was reported that the signals and points were still not connected up to the signal boxes, so the signalling work can only just have been finished in time for Yolland's inspection of the line on 30th June.

The four signal boxes (Heathfield, Chudleigh, Trusham, and Ashton) were all built to the same design, with brick bases (Candy's bricks) and hipped roofs. The design would

have been S.W. Jenkin's and indeed is almost identical to that of Moorswater box designed by Jenkin for the Liskeard & Caradon Railway in 1879.

The TVR provides a good example of the excessive sums of money spent on the signalling of rural branches at this period, when the Board of Trade was at its most demanding. The sum actually expended by the TVR on signalling is not known but Jenkin's estimate was £2,000 — an enormous sum for the impoverished company. The real needs of such a line were much less; the points could have been locked by a key on the staff, as they were latterly. But in 1882 the Board of Trade demanded signals at all stations irrespective of real need, and if there were signals they had to be interlocked with the points, which meant the building of signal boxes. In fact, however, the TVR went beyond what the BoT would have demanded and also installed Block Instruments so that the passenger section of the line, with its one train, could be worked as three separate Block Sections (Heathfield–Chudleigh, Chudleigh–Trusham, Trusham–Ashton). This may have been done because the TVR, still with inflated notions of the likely traffic, perhaps still anticipated in 1881 the running of separate goods trains which might be on the line at the same time as the passenger train, in which case Block working would have been necessary. Alternatively, the TVR may have been under the false impression that the BoT required Block working on all passenger lines (when in fact they were quite happy for a single line without crossing stations to be worked on a 'One Engine in Steam' basis without Block).

Yolland's initial inspection on 30th June 1882 resulted in his requiring that 'Starting signals [are required] at all the stations . . . A repeating signal is required at Chudleigh and Ashton stations. The Up Distant signal at Trusham should be fixed on a bracket so as to be seen from the Signal Box.' It is rather odd that there were not already Starting Signals everywhere, as they had been specified in the contract. The 'repeating signals' demanded were probably repeaters in the box due to these Distant signals being out of sight.

Apart from this, and his odd views on the arrangement of the goods sidings (Chapter 6), Yolland was satisfied with the signalling. He made no criticisms of the proposed method of working the line, and one would not have expected him to, since what the TVR was proposing was exactly what the BoT was enforcing on the GWR in the West of England at this period whenever it could. However, when the TVR and GWR sent the BoT the usual 'Undertakings' as to the working of the single line, difficulties started to arise. The first Undertakings sent in July seem to have been lost by the BoT officials, which did not help matters, as it was only on Friday 6th October, three days before the finally-decided opening date, that the TVR became apprised of the fact that the BoT claimed not to have any Undertaking from them. Further copies were therefore quickly signed and sent to the BoT, in the hands of a messenger instructed to wait for an answer! — but Rich (who had taken over from Yolland) would not accept the wording, which was 'to work the line on the Train Staff & Ticket system in connection with the Block Telegraph'. As this was an accurate description of what the TVR proposed, and a form of wording regularly approved by the BoT, one wonders what Rich was objecting to; nevertheless, he insisted that there must instead be an Undertaking that the line be 'worked by one engine in steam or two or more coupled together'. Rich's reaction may perhaps have been due in part to the eccentricity of the TVR's adoption of the Block system on a line where it was clearly not actually necessary.

At any event, Lake, the TVR Solicitor, who was in charge of dealings with the BoT, found himself on the afternoon of Friday 6th October 1882 with only one working day in which to get a new Undertaking in the form desired by Rich drafted, signed by the authorities at Paddington, and sent to the BoT for approval. Fortunately, Gooch and Saunders, whose signatures as GWR Chairman and Secretary were required, were both in their offices late on Friday, and Lake was able to get the necessary package to the BoT at the start of the day on Saturday.

These third, and agreed, Undertakings read: 'The Teign Valley Railway Company/Great Western Railway Company hereby undertake that the single line between Heathfield station and Ashton station shall be worked by an (sic) engine in steam or two or more coupled together'.

WORKING 1882–1893

From 1882 to 1893 the line was worked by Block telegraph Heathfield–Chudleigh–Trusham–Ashton in conjunction with a single Train Staff Heathfield–Teign House (this providing the only protection needed on the goods-only section from Ashton to Teign House). The wording of the Undertaking ruled out the use of Tickets (which would have enabled one train or engine to follow another in the same direction); this hardly mattered in the context of the TVR's one-train timetable, but it did have the effect of rendering the use of the Block System totally pointless! Although there was a second engine at Ashton shed, there was no way in which it could leave Ashton whilst the first loco was on the line.

The Down direction from 1882 to 1893 was Teign House to Heathfield. This followed the direction of the Moretonhampstead branch which had no doubt arisen as a result of that line making a down-facing junction with the SDR main line.

In October 1890 the GWR for some reason sent the BoT a new Undertaking with the wording 'worked by one engine in steam (or two or more coupled together) in conjunction with the train staff'. There was no change in the actual working and it may be that the GWR wished to

assure the BoT that the train staff was in use on the line (some single lines elsewhere were still worked without any staff at this date, which the BoT was now more actively turning its face against).

THE ABOLITION OF BLOCK WORKING: 1893–1903

Although the standard-gauge TVR line did not, of course, need any alterations done to it in 1892/3 as the rest of the GWR system west of Exeter did, it was probably the general atmosphere of 'sweeping away the old' then prevalent that brought major changes to the method of working the line some time in the spring of 1893. The quite pointless Block Working was abolished, thereby saving a fair sum in annual upkeep costs, and at the same time all the signals on the line (except at Heathfield) were removed as unnecessary. In this removal of the signals, the GWR were taking advantage of a recent relaxation in the Board of Trade's demands; from c1890 the BoT no longer demanded signals at single line stations that were not Block Posts, provided that the points were locked by a key on the staff.

From 1893 to 1903, therefore, the line was worked by the much more appropriate system of the One-engine-in-steam Train Staff Heathfield to Teign House, without Block. The signal boxes at Chudleigh, Trusham, and Ashton were reduced to Ground Frames released by a key on the Train Staff (unlocking the FPL levers). The removal of the signals naturally left a lot of levers spare. This situation is shown in the 1896 diagrams in Chapter 18. At Trusham a second Ground Frame was added to work the south end points. There was, of course, no real need to have elevated signal box structures at these stations any more, and in due course (Chudleigh in 1910, Trusham in 1911, Ashton in 1920) they were replaced by simple two-lever ground frames (or, in the case of Trusham, by a new Block Post signal box provided for the new loop there).

Heathfield signal box remained in use to control the full layout at Heathfield and act as a Block Post on the Moretonhampstead branch.

The Down direction was changed in 1893 to become Heathfield to Teign House, a similar change being made on the Moretonhampstead branch also.

THE OPENING OF THE EXETER RAILWAY AND THE INTRODUCTION OF THE ELECTRIC TRAIN STAFF ON THE LINE (1903)

In 1882 the GWR had still been letting much of its own signalling work out to contractors, and so had been happy to let the TVR carry out its own signalling arrangements. But by the turn of the century the GWR had a very standardised signalling policy, and insisted that it was to do the Exeter Railway's signalling work using standard GWR equipment. The argument put to the ER was that 95% of the work was at the GWR junctions at City Basin Jn and Christow which the GWR would do itself in any case, so it might as well do the rest of the work too!

The GWR dithered for two years (1900–02) over what to do at City Basin Jn. In addition to the opening of the Exeter Railway, the date of which was very uncertain thanks to the ER's financial problems, there was a second question in the air, the working of the GWR's Basin Branch. At this date the Basin Branch junction was still controlled by a non-Block-Post ground frame hut ('City Basin Junction Box') opened in 1892 and situated in the fork of the junction. There was no crossover road at the junction and trains from the branch still had to run back up the down line to St Thomas station. But traffic on the main line was increasing (from 24 trains booked each way in 1891, to 48 in 1905) and this method of operating was becoming ever more unsatisfactory. In addition, the Basin Branch traffic itself was increasing since Willey's Engineering works had moved to this site.

In the autumn of 1900 a definite plan was drawn up to make the ground frame hut at the junction a Block Post, and put a 13-lever frame in it (the idea being that it would be in circuit only when the Basin Branch train was about, worked by a Porter-Signalman sent from St Thomas). A mains crossover was to be installed as part of this plan, and this was authorised in October 1900 and laid in by April 1901; but nothing else was done and the new crossover remained unconnected and unusable. The reason for this was that, whilst in 1900 it had been anticipated that the Exeter Railway junction would be worked by another new box, a rival idea had now come into favour of working the Basin Branch junction and the Exeter Railway junction from the same box. Campfield, the Exeter Divisional Superintendent, did not like this new idea, because of the uncertainty over the ER's completion and consequent like-lihood that the relief of his Basin Branch problems would be postponed for longer; he requested that if things were to be done this way he should at least be allowed a temporary signal box to work the Basin junction crossover until the new permanent box were built, but this, although agreed to by Paddington, was not actually done.

Thanks to this indecision over the junction signalling, it was not until 23rd October 1901 that the GWR sent the ER the proposed plans for the signalling of the line. The GWR volunteered to pay £338 of the total cost of £1,788 of the works at City Basin Jn itself, this representing half the cost of the crossover already installed.[2] The scheme to work both junctions from a single box was then proceeded with and, to placate Campfield, this was done before the Exeter Railway itself was completed, the new box (City Basin Junction) opening in August 1902, and the old ground frame box of the same name being abolished. The new box was located 7ch from the Exeter Railway junction points and 13ch from the Basin Branch points. But for its historical origins, one wonders if it might not have been named instead after the Exeter Railway junction which was after all the more important of the two junctions.

The GWR had received provisional sanctions for the original scheme in November 1900, but never told the

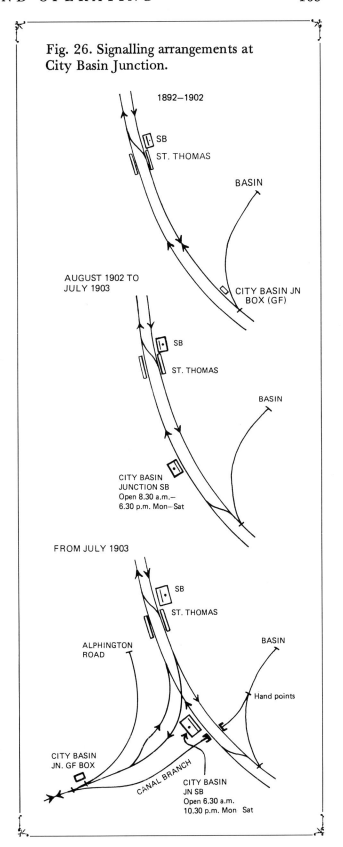

Fig. 26. Signalling arrangements at City Basin Junction.

GREAT WESTERN RAILWAY

OPENING OF·THE EXETER RAILWAY

Exeter City Basin Junction to Christow.

Notice to Station Masters, Enginemen, Guards, Signalmen

AND ALL CONCERNED.

On WEDNESDAY, July 1st, 1903,

The New Line between the Exeter City Basin Junction, about half-a-mile south of St. Thomas, and Christow Station, and from Christow to the present Ashton Station, will be opened for traffic.

The Line from Exeter City Basin Junction to Christow, and from Christow to Heathfield Sation, is Single throughout, and will, on and from WEDNESDAY, July 1st, be worked on the Electric Train Staff system, under the Regulations shewn on Pages 41 to 59 of the General Appendix to the Rules.

The Train Staff Sections, and the persons who alone must exchange the Staffs at the Stations are as under :—

Staff Sections.	Station or Signal Box.	Persons authorised to Exchange the Staffs.
Between City Basin Junction and Christow. Between Christow and Heathfield.	At City Basin Junction. } At Christow. At Heathfield.	Signalman. Signal Porter. Signalman.

The Crossing Stations will be Exeter City Basin Junction and Christow.

The speed of all trains must be slackened at Exeter City Basin Junction to 10 miles an hour to receive and deliver the Train Staff.

The Train Staffs are marked with the names of the stations between which they apply, and the Drivers must not on any account leave the station or Junction unless he has given up the Staff for the Section behind him and has received the Staff for the Section in advance.

No person must be allowed to work the Electric Train Staff Instrument or to withdraw a Staff except the person specially appointed for that duty.

The last Train to carry the Wooden Train Staff will be the 7-8 p.m. Train from Ashton to Heathfield on Tuesday, June 30th, 1903.

The first train to carry the Electric Staff will be the 9-20 p.m. train from Heathfield to Ashton on Tuesday, June 30th, 1903, which train will run through to Exeter.

After the arrival of the 7-8 p.m. train from Ashton at Heathfield on Tuesday, June 30th, the present Wooden Train Staff will be taken out of use, and the 9-20 p.m. train from Heathfield will be worked through to Exeter by the Electric Train Staff.

Chief-Inspector Shattock will travel with both trains and will take charge of the disused staff.

The following are the Stations and Mileage :—

Stations.	Distance from Exeter.	
	Miles.	Chains.
Exeter	—	—
St. Thomas	—	71
City Basin Junc.	1	37
Ide	3	37
Longdown	6	15
Christow	9	40
Ashton	11	5
Trusham	13	0
Chudleigh	14	69
Knighton Crossing	16	11
Bovey Lane Crossing	17	1
Heathfield	17	21

Trusham's longest-serving signalman was Fred Court, seen here after his retirement. He was brought up in Stoke Canon and joined the GWR as a porter there. After his first signalman's job at Watchet, he came to  Trusham box around 1927 intending to stay a couple of years, but he soon acquired too much of an affection for the friendly Valley branch to want to move elsewhere. In 1942 he was persuaded to go to Stoke Canon Crossing box after being told that he would be in line for a station master's post if he got some main-line experience, but after a few months there, he was begging to be allowed to go back to Trusham, which the GWR granted; he stayed there until the box closed in 1958.

From 1929 Fred lived in one of the Exmouth Cottages at Ashton (see page 214) and one of the line's amusing stories arose from his habit, when on late turn, of travelling home to Ashton on the last up train (he would wait in the office at Ashton station for the Christow signalman to ring him to report that the train had arrived complete!). One night in the 1950s some misunderstanding occurred and the driver started away from Trusham while Fred and guard Jack Harvey were still preoccupied with the necessaries. Off went the train into the night with both of them standing on the platform. When the train arrived at Ashton and the driver found himself

guard-less, the train had to set off back to Trusham again! Fred and Jack were eventually found trudging up the line near Whetcombe.

Cliff Gardner was Fred's mate at Trusham from 1928 to 1948; he lived latterly in the station master's house at Trusham. For a while during the war there was a third signalman's post to allow for the 24-hour opening of the line. The picture above shows Fred in Trusham box in 1942. Note the removal of the signal box nameplate for security reasons.

Cty. John Court

Board of Trade about the change of plan. Despite this, Yorke made no reference, when inspecting the new box in June 1903, to the fact that it was nothing like the scheme that provisional sanction had been granted for!

The signalling on the ER line itself was commenced in December 1902 and completed in May 1903. The GWR took full advantage of the relaxation of the Board of Trade requirements, and at the intermediate stations of Ide and Longdown no signals were provided, only two 2-lever open ground frames at each station to work the siding points, released by a key on the train staffs. A ground frame hut (City Basin Junction Ground Frame) had to be provided to work the Alphington Road and Canal Branch junctions, which were too far away from City Basin Jn signal box to be worked directly. But the only full-size signal box on the new line was that at Christow. The new signalling was commissioned on 26th June 1903, five days before the opening of the line.

It was decided to work the ER line on the Electric Train Staff system and to convert the TVR section to the same system. The ETS had been first used on the GWR in 1891 and by 1903 it was the GWR's standard system of working all but the quietest single-line passenger branches (the Moretonhampstead branch had been converted to ETS in 1901). The ETS was brought into use throughout on the evening of 30th June 1903 (see notice reproduced here) and the old Heathfield–Teign House train staff abolished. The ETS sections were Heathfield–Christow–City Basin Jn. The ER's 'Undertaking' to work the line by the ETS

was sent to the Board of Trade on 16th June, and the TVR had to send in a new Undertaking to the same effect.

The Down direction was changed once again on 1st July 1903, now City Basin Jn to Heathfield, to fit in with the main line at City Basin Jn. This meant that the Teign Valley line and the Moretonhampstead line were now opposed in direction at Heathfield.

1903–1958

The basic method of working was not altered in this period. However, several important alterations were made:

- Additional Block Posts/ETS Posts at Trusham (from 1911) and Longdown (from 1916). Longdown was not a crossing station until 1943.
- Provision of intermediate sidings, worked by 2-lever ground frames released by a key on the ETS, at Crockham (1904), Whetcombe (1910) and Ryecroft (1930).

  This, and the running of Motors to intermediate stations/halts, led to the branch having an unusually large number of cases where working under ETS Regulation 8A (Trains requiring to return to Station in rear, without going though the whole Block Section) was authorised:

  Christow to Ryecroft
  Trusham to Whetcombe
  Trusham to Crockham
  Trusham to Chudleigh
  Heathfield to (Chudleigh Knighton Halt or) Chudleigh.[3]

  Propelling of goods trains was also permitted in these instances, in one or both directions.
- Conversion of the Heathfield–Trusham section to Key Token in 1943. This was done to facilitate the provision of 'shutting in' facilities at the siding at Chudleigh Knighton installed at that date (it being more difficult to provide such a facility under the ETS system).

This view of Longdown station office in 1957 illustrates the single line working equipment in use on the line (it was located in the signal boxes at the other stations, but there was no room in the small box at Longdown). This view shows the Electric Train Staff instruments for the Christow–Longdown (left) and Longdown–City Basin Junction (right) either side of the window, with the respective block bells on the wall above them. The 'box' between the two ETS instruments was the Economical System of Maintenance control instrument for the City Basin Junction–Longdown section (the instrument for the Longdown–Christow section was at Christow). Signal lamp repeaters can be seen on the wall at upper right.

P. W. Gray

Distant signals on the branch were made fixed in 1906 (except those for Ashton Crossing) and painted yellow on 4th December 1930.

Methods of working after 1958 are discussed in Chapter 19.

For full details of the signalling installations at each location, see Chapter 18.

In the GWR's marks system of signal box grading introduced in 1923, City Basin Jn and Heathfield boxes were Class 4, Christow and Trusham Class 5, and Longdown Class 6 (the lowest). However, all of them (except Longdown) managed to move up one class before long.

PERMANENT WAY

Originally there were small Permanent Way gangs at each station, but as from 1st April 1935 the 'Economical System of Maintenance' was introduced on the line with one 11-man gang based at Christow responsible for the whole line. Under this system, by then standard on GWR single lines, the gang were provided with two

The Christow gang passing through Ashton in the large trolley, with its trailer for tools attached, in 1958. Ashton Middle Ground Frame on the left was disused by this date.

Arthur C. Palmer, cty. M. A. King

Private and not for Publication   Notice No. 25

GREAT WESTERN RAILWAY.

(For the use of the Company's Servants only)

EXETER DIVISION.

TEIGN VALLEY BRANCH

Introduction of Motor Trolley System of Maintenance.

MONDAY, APRIL 1st, 1935

On and from the above date the Motor Trolley System of Maintenance will operate on the above Branch which will be under the control of an Engineering Gang with headquarters at Christow

A small petrol motor driven inspection car will be provided for the use of the Ganger. The gang will be provided with a petrol motor driven trolley capable of carrying men and a small quantity of tools. A trailer is also supplied fo¹ the conveyance of materials and tools.

The general instructions for working are as shewn on Pages 34—36 of No. 5 Appendix, dated June 1934.

PLACES WHERE TELEPHONES AND KEY BOXES ARE FIXED.

	m.	chs.	
CITY BASIN SIGNAL BOX			
No. 1	1	9	Exeter Railway Mileage.
No. 2	2	8	
No. 3	2	75	
No. 4	3	79	
* LONGDOWN SIGNAL BOX			
No. 5	5	44	
No. 6	6	35	
No. 7	7	31	
† CHRISTOW SIGNAL BOX			
No. 8	6	74	Teign Valley Mileage
No. 9	6	2	
No. 10	5	10	
¶ TRUSHAM SIGNAL BOX			
No. 11	3	22	
No. 12	2	20	
No. 13	1	14	
HEATHFIELD SIGNAL BOX			

*—Control Instrument and Telephone—City Basin—Longdown Section.
†—Control Instrument and Telephone—Longdown—Christow—Trusham Sections.
¶—Control Instrument and Telephone—Trusham—Heathfield Section

---

PLEASE NOTE, ADVISE ALL CONCERNED AND ACKNOWLEDGE RECEIPT TO HEAD OF DEPARTMENT.

H. A. ALEXANDER,   R. W. HIGGINS,
Divisional Engineer,   *Divisional Superintendent*
Taunton.   Exeter.
H—2260   G—40637 W
    March 1935.   371—300

An additional Key Box was provided at 4m 20ch (Trusham) in 1958.

SIGNAL BOX REGISTER INCLUDING GROUND FRAMES

		Opened	Closed	SB Design	SB Size	Frame Design	Frame Pitch	Frame Size	Frame Date	Status BP – Block Post NBP–Not a block post
HEATHFIELD	1	c. 9.10.1882	1916	TVR	nk	nk	nk	25	1882	BP (No Switch)
HEATHFIELD	2	1916	12.10.1965	GWR 7d	33'6" × 12' × 9'	1.VT 3 Bar	4	42	1916	BP
						2.VT 5 Bar	4	58	1927	(No Switch)
Heathfield GF		1893	1916	nk	–	gf	nk	3	1893	NBP Released from SB
Bovey Lane Crossing		Crossing staffed 1882–1958. Type 29 Hut provided. No signalling.								
Chudleigh Knighton Sidings GF		22.8.1943	c. 1952 (oou c. 1945)	(*open) gf	–	gf	–	2	1943	NBP Released by KT
Knighton Crossing		Crossing staffed 1882–1958. No signalling.								
CHUDLEIGH		9.10.1882	12.1910	TVR	nk	nk	nk	13	1882	BP until 1893 (Released by NBP from 1893 Staff/ETS)
Chudleigh South GF		12.1910	1.7.1968	covered gf	–	gf	–	2	1910	NBP Released Later by ETS/KT uncovered
Chudleigh North GF		12.1910	1.7.1968	covered gf	–	gf	–	2	1910	NBP Released Later by ETS/KT uncovered
Crockham Siding GF		c. 7.1904	1.7.1968	open gf	–	gf	–	2	1904	NBP Released by ETS/KT
Trusham GF		*1893	c. 6.1911	GWR Hut	nk	nk	nk	3	*1893	NBP Released by Staff/ETS
TRUSHAM	1	9.10.1882	c. 6.1911	TVR	nk	nk	nk	13	1882	BP until 1893 (Released by NBP from 1893 Staff/ETS)
TRUSHAM	2	c. 6.1911	1.5.1961	GWR 7d	29' × 11' × 8'	Stud conv.VT 5 Bar Locking 1943	5¼	25	1911	BP GF from (No switch) 9.6.1958
Whetcombe Quarry Siding GF		c. 1.1910	23.3.1952	covered gf	–	gf	–	2	1910	NBP Released by ETS
ASHTON		9.10.1882	5.1920	TVR	nk	nk	nk	17	1882	BP until 1893 (Released by NBP from 1893 Staff/ETS)
Ashton South GF		5.1920	1.5.1961	covered gf	–	gf	–	2	1920	NBP Released Later uncovered by ETS OOU 10.1960
Ashton Middle GF		5.1920	11.1956	covered gf	–	gf	–	2	1920	NBP Released Later uncovered by ETS
Ashton Crossing GF		7.1903	* 9.6.1958	open gf	–	gf	–	3	1903	NBP (G)
Ryecroft Quarry Siding GF		10.11.1930	25.6.1956	(* open) gf	–	gf	–	2	1930	NBP Released by ETS
Teign House Siding GF		c. 3.1903	30.6.1903	open gf	–	gf	–	nk	1903	NBP Released by Staff
CHRISTOW		26.6.1903	1.5.1961	GWR 28b	21' × 11' × 7'	1. Double Twist	5¼	21	1903	BP GF from 9.6.1958
						2. VT 3 Bar	4	30	1914	(No switch) OOU 10.1960
Longdown West GF		26.6.1903	19.9.1943	open gf	–	gf	–	2	1903	NBP Released by ETS
Longdown East GF		26.6.1903	1916	open gf	–	gf	–	2	1903	NBP Released 3rd lever added by ETS 3.1906
LONGDOWN		1916	9.6.1958	21	nk	1. Stud	nk	5	1916	BP
			Bricked up 1943			2. Stud, Class 6	5	9	1943	(No switch)
Longdown West Loop GF		19.9.1943	20.7.1954	gf	–	gf	–	2	1943	NBP Released from SB
Longdown West Siding GF		19.9.1943	18.11.1956	open gf	–	gf	–	2	1943	NBP Released from SB
Longdown East Siding GF		19.9.1943	18.11.1956	open gf	–	gf	–	2	1943	NBP Released from SB
Longdown East Loop GF		19.9.1943	20.7.1954	gf	–	gf	–	2	1943	NBP Released from SB
Ide West GF		26.6.1903	1955	open gf	–	gf	–	2	1903	NBP Released by ETS
Ide East GF		26.6.1903	1955	open gf	–	gf	–	2	1903	NBP Released by ETS
City Basin Jn GF		26.6.1903	19.10.1939	21 Gable to track	nk	gf (Class 6)	nk	4	1903	NBP Released by ETS (Exeter Rly line, Alphington Rd & Basin Branch Jn points)
City Basin Jn Box		1893	8.1902	nk	nk	nk	nk	2	1893	NBP (At GWR Basin Branch Jn)
CITY BASIN JUNCTION		8.1902	9.12.1962	27c	25' × 11' × 8'	Double twist	5¼	33	1902	BP (switch)
EXETER CITY BASIN		9.12.1962	14.11.1986	37a	25'9" × 13' × 9'	VT 5 Bar	4	27	1962	BP (switch) Frame ex Culham

*Indicates uncertain information.

The old Ide gang, looking fashionable and debonair as only a Permanent Way gang can, in the 1920s. From left to right: Mark Bond, Alf Hallet, — Farley, Sid Beer, and 'Queenie' Down.
Cty. Mrs. M. Piller

petrol trolleys, the smaller one being for the ganger's daily inspection of the line, and the large one for conveying the gang and their tools. These trolleys could only be run on the line after withdrawal of a 'Ganger's Occupation Key' from one of the 'Key Boxes' located at the signal boxes and in huts along the line at approximately one-mile intervals, and released by the signalman in the nearest box by means of a 'Control Instrument'. When the Ganger's Occupation Key was withdrawn, the Electric Train Staff for the relevant section was locked in the instrument, and vice-versa.

The system was, of course, reliant on the gang returning the key to one of the key boxes before the next train was due, and this could bring worries to the signalmen! One occasion is remembered in 1958 when the gang were putting in new fence posts along the line using the large trolley, and the ganger found himself obliged to ring up the Longdown signalman to say that he had lost the key. Someone eventually had the bright idea that the key might have dropped into one of the holes dug for the new posts, so the posts were all taken out again one by one until the key was located under one of them! But by this time the train was rather late.

The Christow gang (Gang 104) in the 1950s comprised:

Ganger	George Horwill (of Doddiscombsleigh)
Sub-Ganger	Stanley Cox (brother of Christow signalman Wilf Cox)
	Leslie Matthews
	Harry Andrews
	George Amery
	Jack Brooks
	Ronald Baxter
	Jack Webber ⎤ who had both been signalmen at
	Bernard Cann ⎦ Christow for a short time
	? Conway
	Alf Stonelake

After June 1958 the gang was reduced to seven. The 'Economical System' was retained, with the key boxes all being reconnected to Heathfield signal box.

DIRECTION

9.10.1882	DOWN	Teign House to Heathfield.
1893	DOWN	Heathfield to Teign House.
1.7.1903	DOWN	City Basin Jn. to Heathfield.
9.6.1958	⎰ DOWN	City Basin Jn. to Alphington Road.
	⎱ DOWN	Heathfield to Christow.

Note: To avoid confusion, the expressions 'Up' and 'Down' are only used in this book when the 1903–58 period is being referred to.

MILEAGES

0.00 at Heathfield to 7.57 at Christow (former Teign House siding stops)
— Teign Valley Railway mileage.
0.00 at City Basin Jn to 8.07 at Christow
— Exeter Railway mileage.

These mileages were never altered (and are still used by the BR Engineers today).

METHOD OF WORKING — SUMMARY

9.10.1882	Block Telegraph Heathfield–Chudleigh–Trusham–Ashton, in conjunction with OEIS Train Staff Heathfield–Teign House.
1893	OEIS Train Staff Heathfield–Teign House, no Block. Form of staff–round; colour — green.
1.7.1903	Electric Train Staff Heathfield–Christow–City Basin Jn.
6.1911	Electric Train Staff Heathfield–Trusham–Christow–City Basin Jn.
1916	Electric Train Staff Heathfield–Trusham–Christow–Longdown–City Basin Jn.
22.8.1943	Key Token Heathfield–Trusham, Electric Train Staff Trusham–Christow–Longdown–City Basin Jn.
9.6.1958	OEIS Train Staff Heathfield–Christow.
1.5.1961	OEIS Train Staff Heathfield–Trusham.
(actually 1.10.1960)	
10.2.1965	OEIS Train Staff Heathfield–Crockham Sdg.
10.1965	'C2' working under control of Person-in-Charge Heathfield, no train staff.

ELECTRIC TRAIN STAFF CONFIGURATIONS POST–1943

Trusham–Christow	C
Christow–Longdown	B
Longdown–City Basin Jn	A

Some uncertainty attaches to the earlier configurations.

TELEPHONE CIRCUIT

Telephone communication was installed between Exeter and Heathfield in 1928, in place of the former single-needle telegraph. (Authorised by Traffic Committee 16.2.1928 at an estimate of £500.)

Exeter St. David's Exchange	Special
Exeter West Box	1–3
Exeter St. Thomas Box	2
Exeter City Basin Jn Box	3
Ide Office	2–1
Longdown Office	3–3
Christow Box	4
Christow Office	3–2
Ashton Office	5
Trusham Box	3–1
Trusham Office	2–3
Chudleigh Office	6
Chudleigh Knighton Halt	1–4
Bovey Lane Crossing	2–2
Heathfield Box	1–2
Heathfield Office	4–2

SIGNAL & TELEGRAPH

Throughout its life the signalling on the branch was maintained by linemen based at Exeter, Newton Abbot, or Teignmouth; but there were many changes in the linemen's 'sections' over the years and it would be neither possible nor profitable to attempt to give a full history of them now.

Originally the GWR had separate 'Signal' and 'Telegraph' departments. In 1905 it is known that the branch was divided on the 'Signal' side between the Exeter No 1 Lineman who covered to Ide, and the Newton Abbot No 2 Lineman who went as far as Longdown; whereas on the 'Telegraph' side the Exeter No 2 Telegraph Lineman covered the whole branch. In 1909, in contrast, a Signal Lineman at Teignmouth covered the branch (in addition to his more important function of St Thomas to Bishopsteignton on the main line), the Exeter No 2 Telegraph Lineman remaining in charge on his front.

From 1928, however, there was a combined 'S&T' Depot at Teignmouth and the same linemen did both sides of the job. In the last years of the branch in the 1950s the Teignmouth No 2 Lineman (based at the depot itself, unlike most linemen who continued to be outbased) was

LINE SPEEDS

- As noted in Chapters 7 and 12, a 12mph limit was imposed on the Heathfield–Ashton section for some time after October 1882. Never strictly adhered to in the timetabling, this limit was in due course forgotten.
- After this there was no defined speed limit on the Heathfield–Ashton section until 1922.
- As noted in Chapter 10, a 15mph limit was imposed on the Ashton–Christow section in June 1903, but was withdrawn in September 1903, after which there was no defined limit on this section until 1922.
- As noted in Chapter 10, a 25mph limit was imposed on the City Basin Jn–Christow section in June 1903. Although originally meant to be temporary, it stayed in force as a permanent limit until 1938.
- In 1922 the 25mph limit was extended to the Christow–Heathfield section also.
- In 1938 the limits were increased to
  35mph City Basin Jn to Christow
  45mph Christow to Heathfield.
  This brought a need for a number of additional 25mph or 35mph restrictions; the total list of restrictions after this was:

City Basin Jn to/from branch	15mph
City Basin Jn to/from ER Canal branch	10mph
City Basin Jn to/from Alphington Road	10mph
City Basin Jn to ¼ MP	30mph
Longdown Loop (added 1943) down trains	10mph
Christow Loops	15mph
Ashton, through station	35mph
Whetcombe Crossing	15mph Down
	25mph Up
Trusham Loops	15mph
Trusham and 4 MP	up trains 25mph
Chudleigh and 2 MP	30mph
Heathfield to/from bay	10mph
Heathfield, junction	10mph pre-1943
	15mph post-1943

- The 45mph limit was kept after 1958 for a time, but reduced to 15mph in the 1960s.

STOP BOARDS for goods trains were located at the following positions:
DOWN 4m 68ch (west end of Longdown station) to put down brakes.
        8m 5ch (south end of platform at Christow) to pick up.
UP   4m 51ch (east end of Longdown station) to put down brakes.
        0m 22ch (City Basin Jn Up Home signal) to pick up.

MAXIMUM LOADS OF PASSENGER (PARCELS, MILK & FISH) TRAINS (Tons)

Source: 1946 Service Book. The special allowances for Emergency working were introduced in 1938; the other figures were the same from the first appearance of these tables in the Service Book *c.* 1930.

Exeter–Heathfield	280	200	200	170	100	90
Heathfield–Exeter	300	200	220	200	110	100
	Specially agreed for 41xx, 51xx, 43xx–73xx in connection with Emergency working.	Specially agreed for 2251 class in connection with Emergency working	3306– 3455 (44xx) 45xx 55xx 36xx 37xx 46xx 57xx 77xx 87xx 96xx 97xx	0-6-0 0-6-0T 0-6-2T 45xx 'A' Group	2-4-0T Metro. 0-4-2T 48xx, 58xx	'517' class

Classes in brackets did not work on the line in practice.

MAXIMUM LOADS OF GOODS TRAINS (number of trucks)

As given in the Service Book from the 1920s.

R.H. figures for 45xx class locos; L.H. figures for other tank engines.*

	Class 1 traffic	Class 2 traffic	Class 3 traffic	Empties
Exeter–Longdown	13/16	16/19	20/24	30/35
Longdown–Christow	40/40	45/45	45/45	45/45
Christow–Heathfield	20/30	24/36	30/43	40/45
Heathfield–Christow	28/30	34/36	40/43	40/45
Christow–Longdown	15/17	18/20	23/26	30/34
Longdown–Exeter	40/40	45/45	45/45	45/45

Class 1 traffic includes coal, coke, etc; Class 2 traffic includes roadstone; Class 3 traffic is general goods.

* 48xx class Auto engines were restricted to lesser loadings than these (but were not in practice used on the goods trains).

No train to exceed 45 trucks in any circumstances.

From 1938, under Emergency Working the following loads were permitted for Classes 41xx–51xx, 43xx–73xx:

Exeter–Newton Abbot via Teign Valley Line	30 wagons Class 3
Newton Abbot–Exeter via Teign Valley Line	33 wagons Class 3

or the corresponding number of Class 1 or Class 2.

responsible for the branch, covering the Moretonhampstead branch also. E.G. Mills was the lineman and his brother, F.J.Mills, the assistant lineman. From 1956 they had Derek Turner with them for a time as a 15-year-old 'probationer', and Derek recalls how, having to start from Teignmouth every morning and travel everywhere by the infrequent trains, they spent a large part of each day getting to where the job was! They had the use of the ganger's motor trolley for transferring staffs between boxes for 'balancing'. On several occasions the signalmen happily disappeared for an hour or two to carry out business of their own and left the youthful Derek in charge of the box! But with the simple traffic of that date there was not much that anyone could do wrong.

Sometime in the 1930s the main Paddington–Plymouth trunk 'Tye Lines' were transferred from the Dawlish route to the Teign Valley between Exeter and Newton Abbot, and new telegraph poles carrying up to 20 wires erected along the branch to carry them as well as the local wires. (The old, and new, poles can be seen in many of the photographs here.) These Tye Lines remained in use for some years after 1958 even though the Christow–Exeter track had been lifted. Unfortunately, when Perridge tunnel was let to a mushroom grower, he seems to have been insufficiently informed of this vital fact, and one day the lineman got a call to say that communication between London and Plymouth had failed because the mushroom man had cut the wires!

1. It is not known who the signalling contractor was. There is no reference in TVR records, and all the equipment was gone by 1920. One might hazard a guess at Stevens & Sons, who had been the contractors for Moorswater in 1879. The supplier of the original telegraph and block instruments is also unknown (in 1884 the GWR demanded that the block instruments be replaced by new instruments to a different design, again unspecified). The signal box structures would almost certainly have been built by Walker. There are no known interior photographs of the 1882 boxes, and no photographs of the 1882 signals.
2. It had originally been intended to have a crossover at the Exeter Railway junction itself, but it was now decided that the crossover already installed at the Basin Branch junction 18ch further south would suffice for all needs. In fact the GWR did very well to only pay half the cost of this crossover themselves, since it was never used in the event by Exeter Railway trains! (The ER had anticipated down main line goods trains shunting Alphington Road, but this never happened.)
3. Also in practice, pre-1928, Christow to Ashton and Trusham to Ashton, for locos to take water.

Life at Trusham was rather dull on wartime Sundays when the boxes were open but no trains were running. However, on this Sunday in 1942 Fred Court had managed to get some company. Fred is seen halfway up the pre-1943 Down Home bracket signal with, above him, his brother-in-law Bill Staddon from Stoke Canon and his daughter-in-law Mary Court. *Cty. John Court*

Longdown signal box interior on 9th November 1957. By this date levers 3 and 4, which had worked the Down Loop signals, and 5, 6 and 7, which had released the ground frames (hence the short handles), were all spare. The plungers on the front of the block shelf had been used to give the electrical releases to the Loop ground frames. The arm repeaters on the shelf itself were for signals 1 & 3 (left) and 9 (right). For the Booking Office interior see page 166. *P. W. Gray*

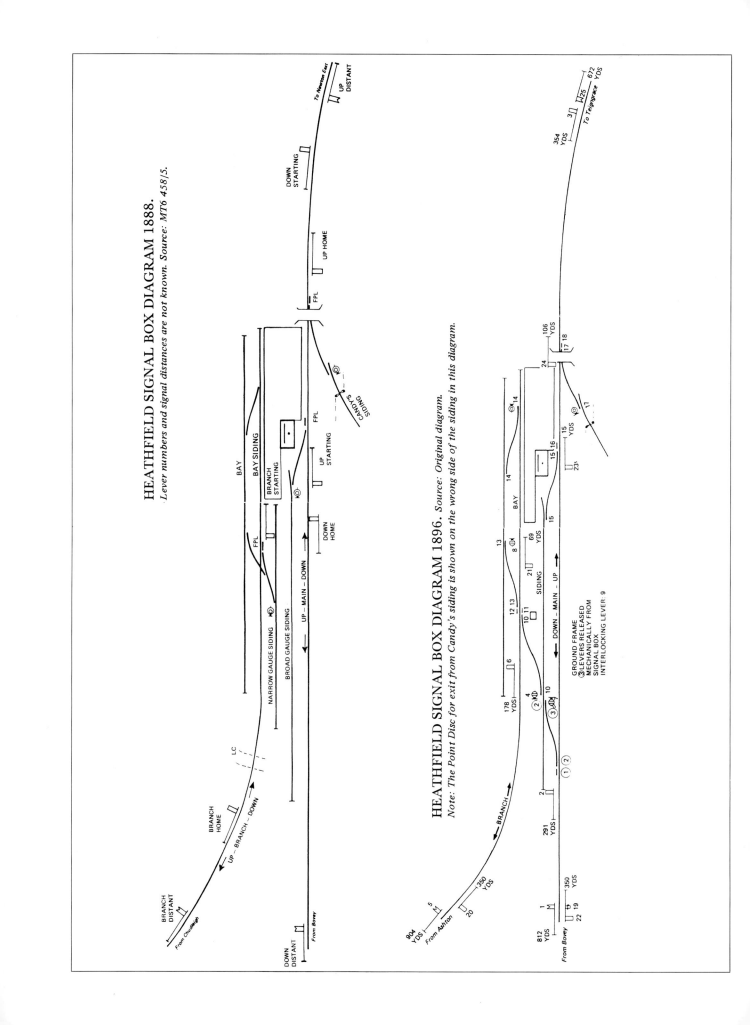

HEATHFIELD SIGNAL BOX DIAGRAM 1888.
Lever numbers and signal distances are not known. Source: MT6 458/5.

HEATHFIELD SIGNAL BOX DIAGRAM 1896. *Source: Original diagram.*
Note: The Point Disc for exit from Candy's siding is shown on the wrong side of the siding in this diagram.

CHAPTER EIGHTEEN

THE LINE AND STATIONS

HEATHFIELD

The pre-1916 layout at Heathfield was seen at pp. 118/9. This 1924 view (see also that at pp. 120/1) shows the 1916-27 arrangements, with the new 1916 signal box and, opposite it, the Down Inner Home signal with three arms reading to Moretonhampstead/Siding/ Branch. The great width of the platform suggests that even in 1874 allowance had been made for a future doubling through the station. The 1874 SDR goods shed was extended 35ft by the TVR in 1881, as is particularly evident in the p.121 view. *Lens of Sutton*

It is not intended to give a full history of Heathfield station here; for this the reader is referred to John Owen's forthcoming book on the Moretonhampstead Branch. This account will focus only on the station's role as the terminus of the Teign Valley trains.

1882–1893: The station's origins, and opening in 1874 as 'Chudleigh Road', were noted in Chapter 4. It was renamed 'Heathfield' on 1st October 1882 and the new standard-gauge Teign Valley side of the station came into use on 9th October 1882. At the same date the whole layout was interlocked. There are no plans showing the original 1882 signalling, but the 1888 diagram here, showing the arrangements after the installation of Candy's siding in April 1888, does show the track layout on the Teign Valley side still in its original form, comprising run-round facilities plus a transhipment siding alongside the broad gauge siding. There was a level crossing over the Teign Valley line for road access to the broad gauge siding; this did not last into the present century, and it became the practice to use the Teign Valley 'Bay Siding' for any trucks where road access was

required. All arriving Teign Valley trains originally stopped outside Heathfield for a ticket check.

The 1909 Appendix refers to a 'Ticket Platform' which must have been a very small construction as it is not evident on maps.

1893–1916: After the gauge of the Moretonhampstead line was narrowed in 1892, a connection was put in between the two sides of the station and the Teign Valley transhipment siding taken out. A ground frame had to be provided to work one set of points as the 1882 signal box's 25 levers were insufficient to cope with the new layout, which was inspected in August 1893 and is shown in the 1896 diagram here. The new layout gave a 360ft 'loop' on the Moretonhampstead side but this was not signalled as a running loop and could not be used to cross passenger trains.

The connection between the Teign Valley side and the Moretonhampstead line was initially used only for goods shunting moves transferring individual trucks, but (as noted in Chapter 14) a daily Teign Valley goods train was run through from 1907, and the connection was also used for

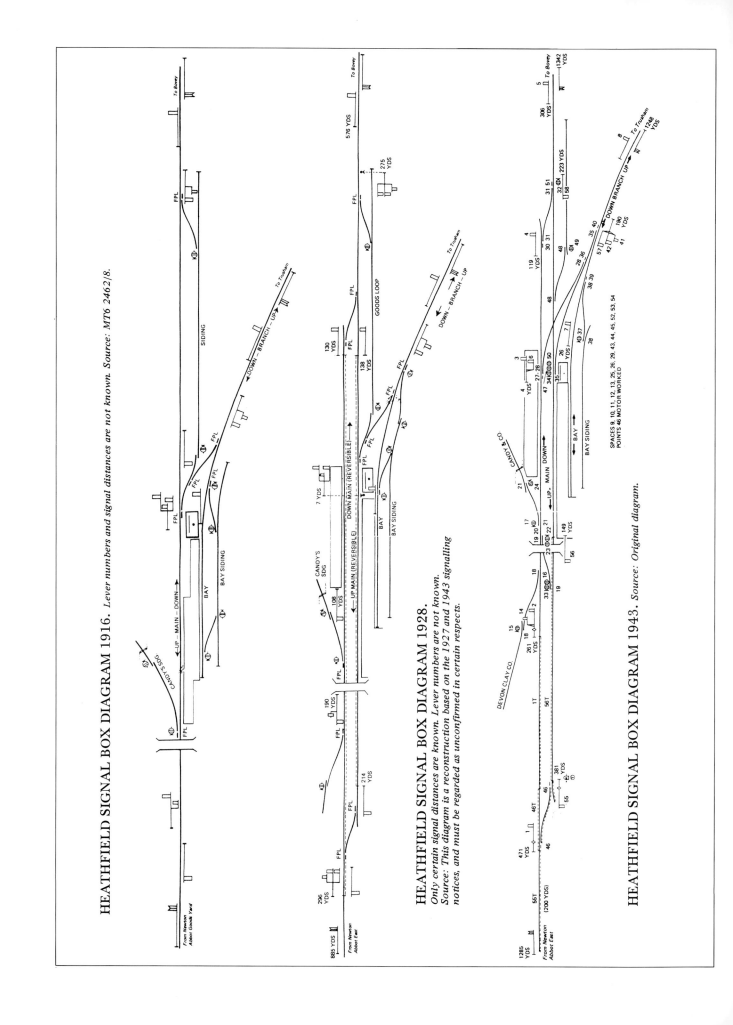

HEATHFIELD SIGNAL BOX DIAGRAM 1916. *Lever numbers and signal distances are not known. Source: MT6 2462/8.*

HEATHFIELD SIGNAL BOX DIAGRAM 1928.
Only certain signal distances are known. Lever numbers are not known.
Source: This diagram is a reconstruction based on the 1927 and 1943 signalling notices, and must be regarded as unconfirmed in certain respects.

HEATHFIELD SIGNAL BOX DIAGRAM 1943. *Source: Original diagram.*

passenger excursion trains from time to time. It will be seen that through running required a double reversal.

1916–1926/7: As noted in Chapter 15, a new direct running connection between the Teign Valley and Moretonhampstead lines was brought into use on 2nd October 1916, to facilitate diversionary workings as well as the daily goods trains. This required a new signal box. The works were inspected in October 1917 by Col. Pringle, who was not entirely happy about the simple single-line junction; it was normal Board of Trade practice to require that a double line junction should be formed in such cases. However, Pringle decided not to press the point.

The great majority of Teign Valley passenger trains continued to terminate in the bay platform.

1926/7–1943: In 1926 the Teign Valley bay siding connections were altered so that the run-round loop was now located further north. This may have been done to enable the motors to run with a trailer; it is possible that the head-shunt in the Bay platform road, which had, of course, been designed for small tank engines, was not quite long enough for a Motor, and the station buildings prevented any extension at the stops end.[1] Another benefit of the new arrangement was that it gave a greater length of the 'Bay Siding' clear for the use of local goods traffic.

1927 saw more drastic changes with Heathfield at last made a crossing station for Moretonhampstead branch trains. The layout adopted was rather curious. A new down loop with a second platform was provided, but the Teign Valley line was not given a conventional double junction;

'517' class 0–4–2T No. 1487 in the up main platform at Heathfield, with an auto-train from Moretonhampstead, and Railmotor No. 80 and 4-wheel saloon in the Teign Valley bay on 9th September 1933. The 'Clifton Downs' auto-train coaches were 3331 (leading) and 3275.
G. N. Southerden

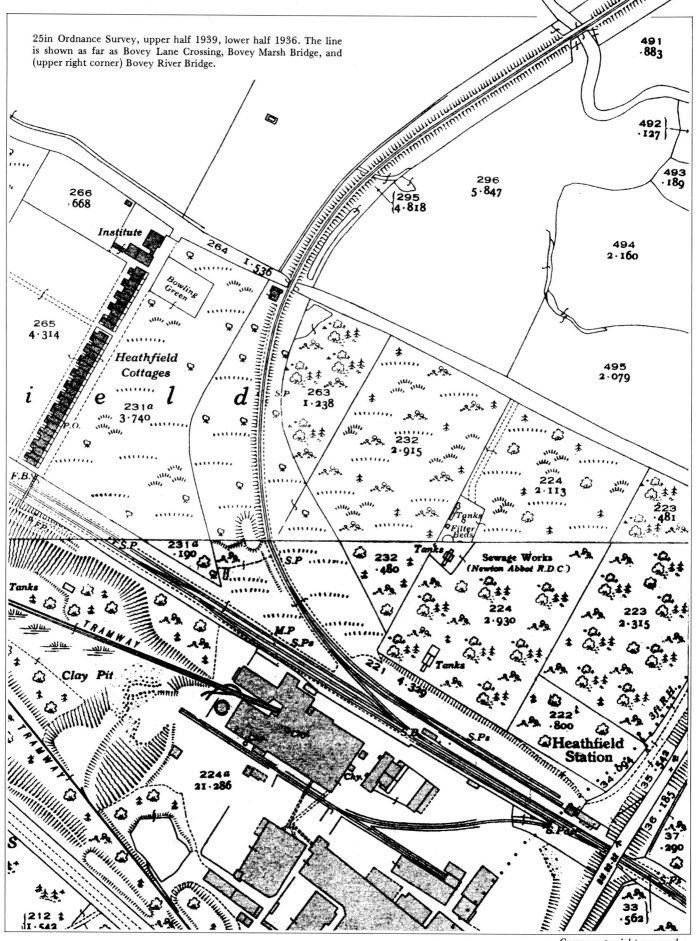

25in Ordnance Survey, upper half 1939, lower half 1936. The line is shown as far as Bovey Lane Crossing, Bovey Marsh Bridge, and (upper right corner) Bovey River Bridge.

This further 1933 view shows more clearly the 1927-43 layout. In the 1927 scheme, the up main (as it now was) was slewed through the station, remaining on its original alignment past the signal box but passing through the road bridge some 10ft north of its previous alignment. The platform was cut back accordingly. Half of the goods shed was removed altogether, and the remaining half re-erected further back and nearer the station building. Also, the (up) platform was extended northwards from 200ft to 413ft so that it now ended at the same point as the Bay platform. The new 1927 down platform is seen at left.   *G. N. Southerden*

The signal seen on page 173 was physically removed to the opposite side of the line in May 1927, and is seen in its new position in this picture taken on 11th April 1928 with the Bay Starting signal on the right.   *G. N. Southerden*

instead it remained connected to the up line (as it now was) only, as before. As a result of this the up line had to be reversible, and it was decided to make the new down line reversible also. The whole scheme cost £4,520 and involved the signal box being given a new 58-lever frame. Track circuiting was provided on both platform lines to remove the risk (arising from the reversible signalling) of a

signalman directing a train into an occupied platform. When Col. Pringle inspected the new layout in July 1928, he was concerned (quite reasonably) that there was no footbridge to the new platform, only a foot crossing by the signal box. The GWR were once again treated generously, however; Pringle decided that 'in view of the restriction of speed upon trains to 10mph when they are not booked to

Above & top right: These 1930s views of shunting in progress at Heathfield serve to suggest the difficulties that must have arisen on this front with the pre-1927 layout. The 1927 connection between the Bay and Bay Siding lines is seen more clearly here.

G. N. Southerden

Looking south from the up platform in the 1930s. The pre-1927 single line passed through the right-hand side of the arch. For more on the development of the south end of the layout see pp. 148/9.

P. J. Garland

'Metro' class 2—4—0T No. 3590 at Heathfield with a Moretonhampstead train on 22nd July 1939. The auto-trailers were 156 and 158.

G. N. Southerden

stop at the station, it is not in my opinion at present necessary to provide a footbridge'.

1943–1960s: Under the 1927 layout trains to/from the Teign Valley line could only cross each other at Heathfield by dint of the Exeter-bound train making a double reversal, which one assumes happened during diversions. The 1943 plans for turning the Teign Valley line into a more suitable main line Diversionary Route demanded more convenient arrangements at Heathfield, and to this end a conventional double junction to the Teign Valley line was brought into use in May 1943. The loop was extended at the south end to give a clear length of 1,100ft for crossing Teign Valley trains; the new south end points had to be Motor worked. The reversible use of the lines through the station was abolished and this simplified the signalling to the extent that only 44 working levers were now required instead of 53.

Finally, the post-1943 layout, in a May 1958 view. There was no need to alter the platforms or buildings in 1943. For more on the 1943 work at Heathfield, see pages 147-9, and for a closer view of the double junction, see page 264.   *P. Rickard*

The 1916 signal box is seen here on 23rd January 1965, in the last year of its life. Like the earlier brick structures on the TVR line, it was built of white Candy's bricks (instead of the red brick normally favoured by the GWR). The Fixed Distant arms on Heathfield Nos. 6 and 7 signals were added after June 1958 when Bovey Lane Crossing was converted to traincrew operation.
                    C. L. Caddy

These views of the 1874 SDR Heathfield station building are of particular interest in so far as they enable comparison with the TVR's 'copy' building at Chudleigh (p. 187). Heathfield had no road side entrance door, being built above the yard level. *A. Attewell*

Also in May 1943, the engine release crossover in the Teign Valley Bay was removed, and the 'Bay Siding' became a purely goods siding. This was possible because all Teign Valley trains were now worked by Autos. However, it made life difficult in the 1950s when non-auto-fitted locos started to appear on Teign Valley trains in practice, and more so when Auto working was abolished in June/September 1957. Such ordinary hauled trains had to back out of the Bay platform and then run round in the Up Main platform after the connecting Moretonhampstead–Newton Abbot train had left, before backing into the Bay from the branch line.

After 1943 through trains from Newton Abbot to the Teign Valley line used the Down Main platform (whereas from 1927 to 1943 they had used the Up Main platform). However, it is said that latterly Teign Valley trains which

had terminated at Heathfield sometimes departed back to Exeter from the Up Main platform to avoid the trouble of having to run back into the Bay, so that in practice the Up Main platform was still used for Teign Valley departures in addition to the Down Main and Bay platforms.

There were no changes to the layout at Heathfield in 1958. The Bay platform line became in practice an additional goods siding, and was sometimes used for storing trucks that were wanted out of the way at Newton Abbot. 1961 saw the Bay Siding slewed into a new Banana Siding. Even the abolition of the signal box on 12th October 1965 did not result in any changes to the layout, the whole layout being converted to hand points as it stood. Further rationalisation only came after the closure of the Teign Valley line.

BOVEY LANE CROSSING

The line left Heathfield on a sharp right-hand curve across scrub ground, to Bovey Lane Crossing at 0m 21ch. This was worked by a resident crossing keeper. A Block Indicator and Bell were provided, but no signals.

As noted in earlier chapters, this crossing was built illegally and only authorised retrospectively by the TVR's 1884 Act. This Act specified that 'the speed of trains in passing the said level crossing shall not exceed the rate of 4mph, and a notice board to that effect shall be placed in a conspicuous place at such level crossing' — a provision which was soon forgotten about!

The crossing keeper was withdrawn sometime after June 1958 and the crossing converted to traincrew operation. The gates were now kept locked across the railway, and fixed distant signals were installed.

Bovey Lane Crossing came into view immediately on departure from Heathfield, as seen in this shot from the last up train, the 8.0 p.m. from Newton Abbot on 7th June 1958. Heathfield Nos. 41, 42 and 57 signals feature in the foreground.   *P. W. Gray*

The TVR did not devote any unnecessary expense to the Bovey Lane crossing house which was built in 1880 of Candy's bricks. A Mrs. Bovey (!) was resident keeper in the postwar years, and when she gave up around 1953, the post was taken over by Emily Edwards, wife of Tom Edwards, the eldest son of Mrs. Edwards, the Chudleigh Knighton crossing keeper. Emily and Tom (a lorry driver) were already living in the area and now moved into the crossing house here, which they found had no lighting but plenty of rats! They managed to get the railway to put in a gas cooker and gas lighting. The house had a bedroom (left) and living room (behind porch) at rail level, but the ground fell away sharply to the rear and there were also a kitchen and coal cellar underneath, reached by the *ad hoc* covered timber stairs alongside this end of the house. The toilet was, of course, 'down the garden'. The standard GWR 'Type 29' hut at right was for the use of reliefmen, who, however, could usually rely on getting their dinner provided in the living room; it also housed the flags. The block indicator and bell were in the living room. The road was quiet but the gates were in later years normally left open to the road, which resulted in an unexpected engineer's train on Sunday morning running through them on at least one occasion!

Emily and Tom continued to live here after the keeper's job ended but the house was in poor condition and hardly worth repairing in the circumstances. They moved out in 1964 and the

house was demolished immediately. Surprisingly, one of the crossing gates, and the rails across the road, are still in situ in 1995.

In this 7th July 1956 view, 5412 is seen passing with the 10.50 a.m. Heathfield—Exeter. The 54XXs were often seen on the line at this time.   *P. W. Gray*

CHUDLEIGH KNIGHTON SIDINGS

From Bovey Lane the line ran immediately onto embankment across the flat Bovey River water meadows, with underbridges at 0m 25½ ch (Bovey Marsh flood channel) and 0m 33½ ch (Bovey River). On the far side of the valley there followed a ¼ mile shallow cutting across Bovey Heath, and here were situated the short-lived Chudleigh Knighton Sidings.

These sidings were provided on the Government account in 1943 to serve an American Forces' petrol dump on Knighton Heath. They were brought into use on Sunday 22nd August 1943 when a new 2-lever ground frame, Chudleigh Knighton Sidings Ground Frame, was commissioned at 0m 68ch, released by a key on the Heathfield–Trusham Electric Train Token (which, as noted in Chapter 17, replaced the Electric

Train Staff on this section on the same date). An Intermediate Instrument was provided so that trains could be shut in the siding, and the layout of the sidings gave 550ft of line clear of the main line to enable a shut-in train to shunt.

The sidings saw activity only for a few months before and after D-Day. The petrol came in jerry cans in open trucks, always on special workings from Heathfield, and was stacked on concrete bases nearby, guarded by American troops. It was also taken out again by rail. The sidings were already noted as out of use when they were inspected on 16th August 1946, and the Private Siding Agreement was terminated in 1949, followed by lifting around 1952. The heath soon reclaimed the site.

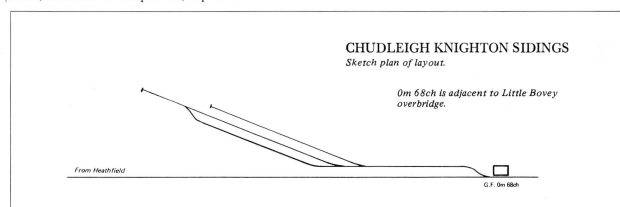

CHUDLEIGH KNIGHTON SIDINGS
Sketch plan of layout.

0m 68ch is adjacent to Little Bovey overbridge.

From Heathfield

G.F. 0m 68ch

Sketch plan of the layout of the 1943 Chudleigh Knighton sidings. The ground frame at 0m 68ch was adjacent to Little Bovey road bridge; the OS 6in maps at page 275 will make the location clear. The northernmost siding was the traffic siding where unloading, and later loading, took place; the other two sidings were for run-round purposes. The depot was known as a 'POL Depot' (Petrol, Oil and Lubricant) by the military. The stocks started arriving in 1943 before the sidings were commissioned and had to be brought by road transport from Heathfield initially.

Cecil Edwards was stationed as a relief porter at Heathfield for a time in 1944 to help work the Chudleigh Knighton traffic out at the height of the Normandy campaign, when there were three trips a day from Heathfield. When bringing empty wagons for loading, they would bring 30 wagons (the maximum the loading siding could take) and stop with the rear of the train just west of the ground frame to detach the brake van. The loco then propelled the empties into the siding, and once it was clear of the points, the brake van would be manhandled over the points (on the falling gradient of 1/143) and stopped just to the east, so that the return to Heathfield could be locomotive-first.

When collecting the loaded wagons, they came Engine & Brake from Heathfield and again stopped just west of the ground frame to detach the brake. The loco took a first lift of 15 wagons from the loading siding, shunted them into the run-round sidings, and ran round. Whilst this was happening, the brake was being manhandled over the connection, and stopped some way to the east so that the loco could then propel the wagons on to it. The loco then repeated this with the second lift of 15 wagons, after which the train could leave for Heathfield locomotive-first.

None of those involved recalls the facility for shutting a train into the sidings actually having to be used.

The Halt in its original form, seen in September 1925. The oil lamps were tended by a porter from Chudleigh.   *G. N. Southerden*

CHUDLEIGH KNIGHTON HALT
and KNIGHTON CROSSING

After passing in cutting under the Little Bovey and Knighton overbridges, the line arrived at Chudleigh Knighton Halt (1m 09ch). Authorised by the GWR Traffic Committee on 31st January 1924 at an estimate of £300, this was one of the earliest halts in the GWR's 1920s–30s burst of halt-building. It was opened on Monday 9th June 1924 and comprised a 150ft long timber platform with a 20ft by 7ft 6in 'Pagoda' shelter and oil lamps. When it was inspected in April 1925, Col. Pringle was told that it was intended to use it for Motors only, this being at a time when all the services on the line were worked by Motors and Autos; but in practice it was subsequently used by some hauled trains also, as all trains always stopped here.

The Halt was supervised by the Chudleigh station master until that post was abolished in 1930, and thereafter by the Heathfield station master.

In postwar days the platform was reconstructed in blocks.

Adjacent to the Halt was Knighton Crossing which was very much the 'twin' of Bovey Lane Crossing, having the same illegal origins and a similar crossing house. It, too, was provided with Block Indicator and bell but no signals. After the Halt opened, it tended to be referred to as 'Chudleigh Knighton Crossing' instead. Again, the crossing keeper was withdrawn some time after June 1958, the crossing converted to train crew operation with gates normally locked across the railway, and fixed distant signals provided.

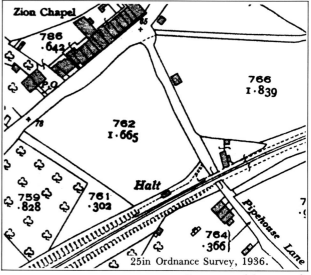

25in Ordnance Survey, 1936.

These views from the Edwards family album show everyday life in the Chudleigh Knighton crossing house in the 1930s-50s period. Like many GWR crossing keepers, Mrs. Louisa Edwards got the job because her husband Tom (William Thomas) Edwards had 'died in service'. Tom had himself had to move from Devizes and take the quiet crossing keeper's job at Great Somerford in 1930 owing to poor health, and then died in 1932, leaving his wife with two small children to support. (Their eldest son, Tom, who we have already come across in connection with his later residence at Bovey Lane, had remained back in Devizes.) Chudleigh Knighton was vacant, and so it was to there that Mrs. Edwards and the children removed, having had no previous connection with the area. This Chapman's postcard (there was hardly a house in rural South Devon whose occupants could not buy a Chapman's card of it!) was sent by Mrs. Edwards to her sister in Ebley soon after their arrival in Devon. We are looking south-east down the lane, over the railway which hardly impinges on the scene at all save for the wicket gate at right. The house here was built on flat ground and was entirely single-storey, with three rooms (one window each), which the Edwards used as two bedrooms (this end) and living room (next the line). The similarity of the crossing houses to the contemporary station buildings at Trusham and Ashton is evident.

Mrs. Edwards' children Eva and Cecil in the front garden of the crossing house c.1935 (the dogs belonged to the local doctor) with period GWR impedimenta by the gate to the halt in the background. The large board at left was headed 'Rail Motor Cars Will Leave This Halt Chudleigh Knighton For - - - '. When Cecil left school in 1941, he joined the GWR, starting as a booking boy at Newton Abbot East and then doing many jobs (including a spell as relief porter at Heathfield in 1944, as just related in connection with Chudleigh Knighton Sidings), ending up as a shunter in Hackney Yard before leaving in 1946.

'Uncle Jim' and Cecil's daughter Jenny shelling peas in the back garden c.1956. This domestic view might be thought to have little 'railway' relevance at first glance, but we cannot pass over Chudleigh Knighton without mentioning Uncle Jim (Jim Ford), whose role illustrates the convenient informality that often attended the staffing arrangements at these quiet crossings. Jim was never on the GWR payroll but, thanks to him, no reliefman ever had to go to Chudleigh Knighton in the twenty-plus years of Mrs. Edwards' occupancy. He was Mrs. Edwards' brother and was already living with the family at Great Somerford. When her husband died, Mrs. Edwards felt that she 'needed a man about the house', so he came with them here and acted as crossing keeper whenever she was away or ill. The station master at Heathfield was fully au fait with this arrangement. Jim never had a regular job until the war years, so it was all very useful. The second purpose of this view is that it shows the house's 'kitchen' extension, which was built of (sliced) old sleepers. It was not, of course, an original feature, but an ad hoc addition by a previous occupant; thanks to this, the railway, who were always good enough at repairs to the house proper, refused to recognise its existence and would not touch it when work needed doing on it!

No. 7761 running in to Chudleigh Knighton Halt past the 1881-built crossing house, on a train from Exeter on 1st February 1958. The hut by the telegraph pole was never needed for reliefmen (for reasons explained in the other captions) and only served to house the obligatory red and green flags — even they had been in the living room, but they kept falling off the shelf! — and, perhaps more importantly, gardening tools and a sack of potatoes. The wooden boxing leading from the telegraph pole to the house, seen above the hut, carried the wires for the block repeater and bell, and the telephone, which were all located on a shelf on this end wall of the house's living room. Crossing keepers' families did not need alarm clocks as the ringing of bells when the signal boxes opened in the morning was enough to awaken all!

P. W. Gray

A view towards Exeter around 1930. The motor appears to have been No. 97 which was at Exeter from 1928-1931. A passenger can be seen in this view! The overbridge was built for double track in the usual way. The ornamental hedge was a feature of the station for many years; the regular flooding probably prevented horticultural efforts of the less robust kind. Chudleigh was the only station on the Teign Valley branch to boast a platform canopy, a reflection of its greater importance pre-1919. The station building and goods shed at Chudleigh were all but identical to those at Heathfield save for being arranged on the opposite hand. For the road side see page 268.

Lens of Sutton

CHUDLEIGH

The standard view of Chudleigh station, looking south from the A38 overbridge, in 1925. Comparison with the 1905 photograph at page 109 reveals only one change of note, the 1910 North ground frame in lieu of the signal box (which still stands, boarded up). For a later view see page 264. *G. N. Southerden*

After leaving Chudleigh Knighton Halt, the line immediately entered the Teign Valley bottom, with the first Teign river bridge at 1m 24½ ch, then running through the flat meadows close to the river all the way to Chudleigh station.

Chudleigh was one of those stations where 'nothing ever changed'. The 1877/8 station building and the 1882 track layout served unaltered until the closure of the line. The only significant alterations were on the signalling front, as noted below.

Although the station lost most of its passenger traffic after 1919, it remained important to the town on the goods front. The primary users of the goods yard were Taverners, the main Chudleigh coal merchants throughout the railway period. In the 1920s Walter George Taverner had three horse carts driven by Harry White, Frank Stone, and Fred Dodge, but then he bought a motor lorry. The Chudleigh Gas Works also brought coke in for their own purposes. Another particular traffic was animal feed for Mr Rayment of Bellamarsh Mills. Outwards traffics remembered in the 1930s were pit props and Christmas trees from the

Forestry Commission at Haldon, and swedes for Hitchin.

The smalls and parcels traffic was heavier than elsewhere on the line, as one would expect given the size of the town compared to the villages (and the large number of 'big houses' in the vicinity). There was always a collection and delivery service in Chudleigh, the only station on the line to offer one. The original Agent was William Tremeer who had begun in the 1870s carting from Chudleigh Road before the branch opened, and who was also the proprietor of the then connecting bus service. He died in 1899 and his son Ernest Tremeer was appointed Agent in his place. Ern Tremeer bought a mule from the Army to haul the cart, and this became a well-known sight in the town; it had the large letters 'W.D.' branded on its rear! When Ern died in the 1920s his daughter Ruby took over for a number of years, still with the mule-cart, but then she gave up and the Agency went to Bernard Pike who had a motor lorry.

In 1915 there were complaints in the papers because it was not possible to load vehicles at Chudleigh. The GWR proposed altering the loading bank for the pur-

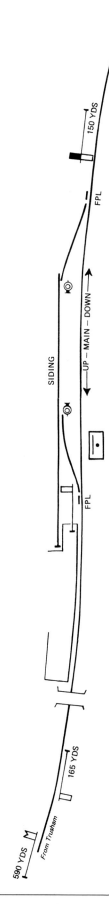

CHUDLEIGH SIGNAL BOX DIAGRAM 1882
Source: Reconstruction based on O.S. map. All details to be regarded as unconfirmed.

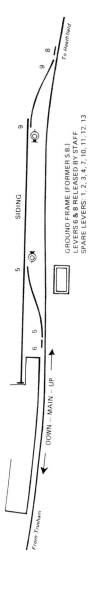

CHUDLEIGH SIGNALLING DIAGRAM 1896
Source: Original diagram.

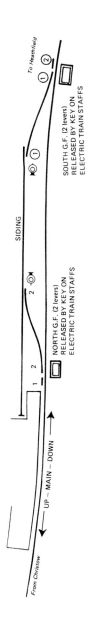

CHUDLEIGH SIGNALLING DIAGRAM 1910
Source: RAIL 282.

One of Chudleigh's regular floods, brought about by Parliament's refusal to let the line cross the road on the level. For this 5th December 1929 view, the photographer (who must have got wet for the cause!) had climbed up to the old signal box. Fortunately, it was only rarely that the water came over platform height, so little serious damage was done. After the introduction of Motors, which could turn round anywhere, a 'flood platform' was built 100 yds north of the station, on higher ground, so that trains from Exeter could terminate there when the station was flooded. This platform is seen in one of the views in Chapter 16.
Dartington Rural Archive

pose, but the TVR Board was unenthusiastic about the expenditure and nothing was done.

There was originally a 3-ton crane, but this was removed around the 1940s.

SIGNALLING

1882–1893: Chudleigh was originally a Block Post with full signalling controlled from the signal box. An attempted reconstruction of the 1882 signalling, based on the signal positions shown on the 1887 Ordnance Survey, is given here.

1893–1910: In 1893 the signal box was reduced to ground frame status and the signals removed, this situation being shown in the 1896 diagram. The frame was released by a key on the Train Staff (the Electric Train Staffs from 1903).

1910–1968: In 1910 the signal box was abolished completely and replaced by two ground frames, Chudleigh North GF and Chudleigh South GF. These were released by a key on the Electric Train Staffs as before (from 1943, ET Tokens). The GFs were covered originally but later were open.

The 1882 signal box lasted intact until around 1930 when its upper half was removed and the brick base roofed over as a Permanent Way mess hut, in which form it lasted until the end of the line.

Northwards from Chudleigh, the line ran through the meadows in the flat valley bottom, crossing the river again at Huxbear Bridge (3m 13½ ch) to run on the west bank for ¾ mile until Crockham Bridge (3m 77½ ch). Shortly before Crockham Bridge was the junction with the Crockham Quarry sidings.

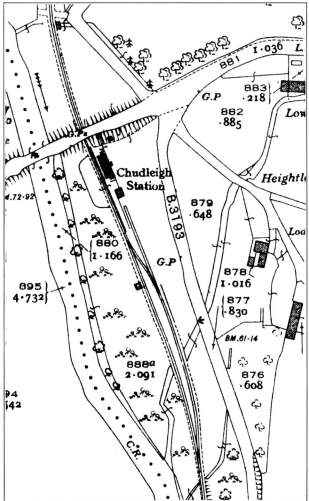

25in Ordnance Survey for 1936. The 'flood platform' is seen by the bend in the road at upper left. *Crown copyright reserved*

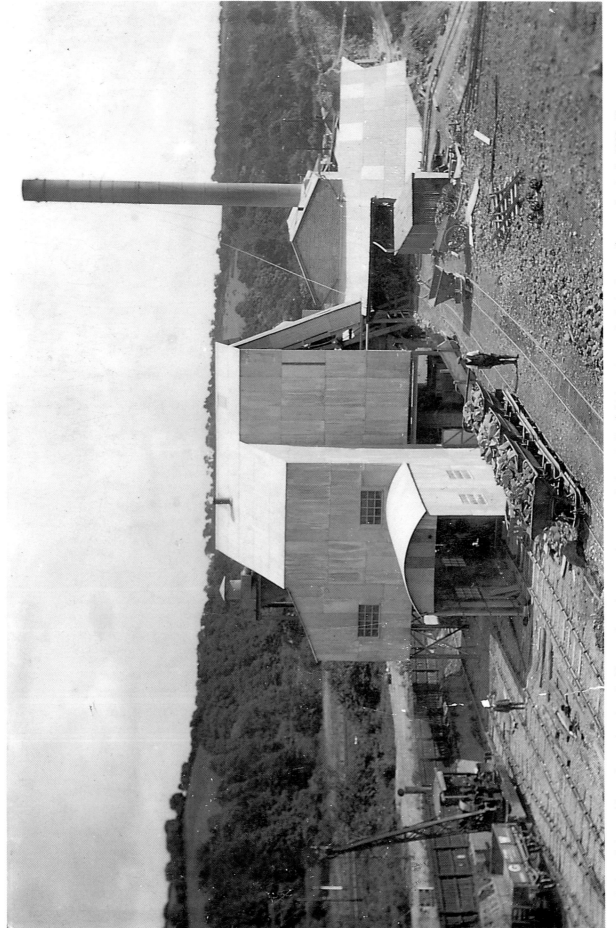

A view of the crushing and screening plant, looking east from the quarry slopes towards the main line (which can be seen in the background), some time in the 1920s. The narrow gauge lines terminated inside the plant.

Collection D. Lystor

CROCKHAM QUARRY and SIDINGS

Crockham Quarry was commenced around 1895 by the Teign Valley Granite Co., set up for the purpose by H.L. Hardwicke of Tytherington, Glos (also the owner of the Tytherington Stone Co.). The stone was a basalt diabase most suited for use as roadstone chippings or railway ballast. Operations were on a low scale in the first few years, but output increased quickly in the early 1900s, and on 13th January 1904 a Private Siding Agreement was made with the GWR (the stone, up to this date, having been carted the short distance to Trusham station by road). The sidings[2] were brought into use around July 1904 and were located at 3m 74ch, ¼ mile south of Trusham station.

The late 1900s and the years up to 1914 were the quarry's best period. In 1909 Hardwicke turned the company into a limited company, The Teign Valley Granite Co. Ltd, this being done partly to help finance the opening of the company's new quarry at Whetcombe. At this date there were 130 employees under Managing Director Robert Bathurst and output was approaching 500 tons (50 trucks) a day at times. The main markets were Devon, Somerset, Dorset, Glos, Wilts, Berks, Hants, Bucks, Oxon, Surrey, and Sussex. In addition to the extra timetabled trains introduced at this period (Ch.14), special trains were having to be run. The GWR was running a complete 'Trusham Ballast Train' for its own purposes to different destinations as required — the workings of this train for a sample period in 1909 are given in the Table here — and sending out many more individual ballast trucks in the ordinary

With the exception of the GWR ballast, the vast majority of the output of Crockham was carried in the Teign Valley Granite Co's own private owner wagons. At least eighteen can be seen in this view of the Crockham sidings, which must date from the 1920s as the company's postal address was changed from 'Hennock' to 'Trusham' in 1918. The photographer was looking north from the Concrete Works building, with the dead-end Concrete Works siding immediately below and the two main through sidings at centre. The ramshackle shed seen in this view was known as the 'Marcroft Shed', being used by the wagon repairers of that name. The trees in the background are on the river bank.

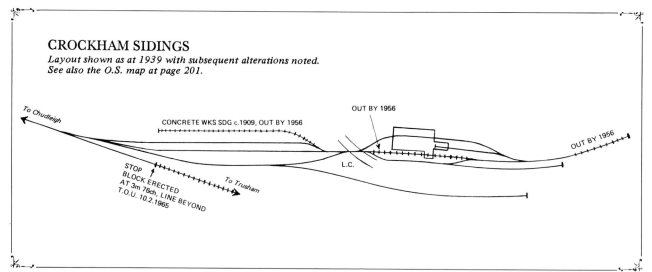

CROCKHAM SIDINGS
Layout shown as at 1939 with subsequent alterations noted.
See also the O.S. map at page 201.

To Chudleigh

CONCRETE WKS SDG c.1909, OUT BY 1956

OUT BY 1956

OUT BY 1956

L.C.

STOP
BLOCK ERECTED
AT 3m 76ch, LINE BEYOND
T.O.U. 10.2.1965

To Trusham

goods trains to other destinations including new works at such places at Ashendon Junction, Camerton, and Reading Central Goods. An extra GWR traffic in 1910 was special trains of 'refuse stone' for tipping on Hackney Marshes for the new Hackney Yard (followed in 1913/14 and 1915/16 by further trains for additional sidings there).

Sales dropped badly in 1914 when the rival Scatter Rock Quarry opened, and things were never as good again. Figures are available for 1925–29 (these are of the quarry's output per annum, but it can be assumed that almost all was going out by rail):

	1925	1926	1927	1928	1929
Stone (Tons)	39,978	35,691	31,009	29,341	23,003
Rubble (Tons)	3,563	3,954	2,986	3,798	9,584

These show how the quarry was declining in importance through the interwar years, its operations being hampered by a very heavy 'overburden' which meant that debris removed to spoil was twice the volume of the saleable stone. By the 1930s the amount being sent out by rail was down to 4,000–9,000 tons per annum, only one or two trucks a day on average. There were, however, still 47 employees in 1937.

Over the years the company was involved in several amalgamations (although it continued to trade under the 'Teign Valley Granite Co. Ltd' name until 1967). These also affected the rival Teign Valley quarries which were all under the same control by 1938. Details are given in the Table here.

The 1950s saw the quarry's fortunes revived as (unlike the other Teign Valley quarries) its stone was suited to the changed specification now required for roadstone, and it still had good reserves. Although much of the output now went out by road, the revival brought an increased rail traffic compared to the 1930s. Complete trainloads were being sent out to Tytherington and West Drayton, and stone was also being brought in to Crockham by road from other quar-

ries (notably Kingsteignton) for loading into rail trucks there. In 1965 BR were still referring to 'your valued traffic', but during 1966 stone ceased to be taken out by rail and the sidings were allowed to get into unusable condition. As noted in Chapter 19, they were declared unfit in November 1967 and BR then put pressure on ARC to agree to the termination of the Private Siding Agreement, which took place on 31st March 1968. The sidings were lifted immediately after this. Crockham quarry itself was abandoned in 1976 as there was now

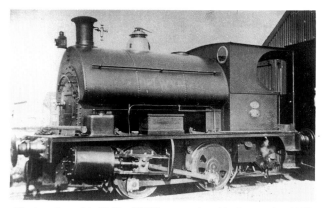

Finetta, Avonside 1565 of 1911, was ordered in September 1908 but not supplied to the Teign Valley Granite Co. until the spring of 1911. It was one of two Class SS1 locomotives with 14in x 20in outside cylinders and 3ft 3in wheels. By 1917, with traffic at Crockham falling away, the company seem to have decided that the steam cranes could do the shunting, and *Finetta* was disposed of to the War Office, being noted at Codford in 1919 as WD No. 16. But in autumn 1919 it was returned to the Teign Valley Granite Co's subsidiary Sandford & Conygar Quarries at Sandford Quarry (off the Yatton–Wells line). Later it served at Conygar quarry, which was connected to the Weston Clevedon & Portishead line. In the 1930s it was sold to A. R. Adams & Son of Newport, and then to the Glamorgan Canal Co. at Cardiff who renamed it *Delwyn*, in which form it is seen here. Finally, it was sold to ICI Winsford in 1947, renamed *John L. Deuchar*, and scrapped c.1953. (Information from article by K. P. Plant in *Industrial Railway Record* Vol. 5, p. 90.)

A view from the roadside. The chute leading down from the narrow gauge line level was probably used for tipping rubble from the tubs direct into railway trucks below.
Collection D. Lystor

too much shale in the stone, but a new quarry known as 'Trusham Quarry' (not to be confused with the old Devon Basalt & Granite Co's Trusham Quarry) had been started in 1973 on another part of the site, and this was still active in 1991.

Until replaced by dumper trucks around 1951, the quarry had the usual ever-changing system of narrow gauge tub lines worked by hand and horse power. These led down to the crusher/screening plant which was located above the railway sidings (two of which passed through it), so enabling the overhead loading of the railway trucks. There was also a tarmacadam plant, making a product known as Targranix (granite chippings blended with tar) which was claimed to make an ideal road surface. For a few years after 1911 the company had a locomotive to shunt the sidings, but after this steam cranes were used for shunting until the 1960s when they were taken out of use and road vehicles used for shunting instead. The long, ungated, level crossing over the B3193 road started causing difficulties when road traffic grew, and in 1922 the then Quarry Manager Mr H.A.G. Hough was obliged to assure Newton RDC that 'a boy with a red flag' had now been stationed there and that 'as soon as they received the official level crossing signs they would be pleased to erect them'.

In addition to the stone traffic, the railway brought in coal for the quarry engine house and the tarmacadam

One of the cranes that served for shunting during most of the quarry's rail-served life is seen here in the 1930s, with Bill Hooper, the crane driver, on the right and Jim Hodge, who worked in the Concrete Works, on the left. *Cty. Mrs. D. Hodge*

Horsepower on the narrow gauge system, and one of the cranes shunting a number of the company's private owner wagons, 925, 975, 1255 and 1120 being identifiable.
Collection D. Lystor

plant boilers, tar in tankers, and vans of dynamite for the quarry's use.

Originally there were 'Calls as Required' by the goods trains in both directions; the northbound trains must, however, have served Crockham by a shunt from Trusham station as, with GWR locos not allowed beyond the siding gates, it was impossible for a north-bound train to actually shunt Crockham en route. From the early 1920s the Working Timetables did not show any booked calls at Crockham Siding at all; the traffic was mostly worked to and from Trusham station (the outward traffic being weighed at Trusham) by the loco-motives of the goods trains during their booked waits at Trusham. Locomotives were (necessarily) permitted to propel wagons from Crockham to Trusham, without a Brake Van; 'a man must accompany the wagons and either ride in or walk beside the leading . . . vehicle . . ., and be prepared to hand-signal the driver as required'. A porter went with the train from Trusham to assist the guard. From the 1940s, the Christow–Newton goods normally shunted Crockham en route instead. Finally, after the line from Crockham to Trusham was closed in

1965, trains were propelled from Heathfield to Crockham, so that the loco would be at the right end for the shunt.

SIGNALLING
The siding points were worked by a 2-lever ground frame, Crockham Siding Ground Frame, on the up side of the line. The ground frame was released by a key on the Electric Train Staffs (from 1943, ET Tokens).

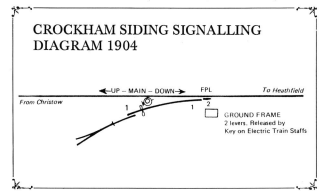

CROCKHAM SIDING SIGNALLING DIAGRAM 1904

←UP – MAIN – DOWN→   FPL   *To Heathfield*

From Christow

GROUND FRAME
2 levers. Released by
Key on Electric Train Staffs

From the level crossing, looking west, in the opposite direction to the previous views. The crushing and screening plant seems to have lost its sheeting temporarily. Tramps used to go into the quarry engine house on the left to stay warm at night time and it was a hard job to persuade them to move off before the start of work in the morning!   *ARC SW Ltd.*

The increasing labour force at Crockham brought a housing shortage locally, and about 1910 the Teign Valley Granite Co. built 54 houses for its employees on the Crocombe Bridge–Hennock road. The settlement was named 'Teign Village' and survives intact today.
Chapman collection, cty. Devon C.R.O.

TRUSHAM BALLAST TRAIN PROGRAMME
22nd February–7th April 1909

Monday	22 February	Exeter	10 Hoppers Ballast (W.S. Marsh)
Tuesday	23	Menheniot	12 Hoppers Ballast Resleepering, 2 engines
Wednesday	24	Exeter	10 Hoppers Ballast (W.S. Marsh)
Thursday	25	Bodmin Road	12 Hoppers Ballast Relaying, 2 engines
Friday	26	Bodmin Road	12 Hoppers Ballast Relaying, 2 engines
Saturday	27	Bodmin Road	12 Hoppers Ballast Relaying, 2 engines
Monday	1 March	Bodmin Road	12 Hoppers Ballast Relaying, 2 engines
Tuesday	2	Bodmin Road	12 Hoppers Ballast Relaying, 2 engines
Wednesday	3	Weymouth	10 Hoppers Ballast
Thursday	4	Bodmin Road	12 Hoppers Ballast Relaying, 2 engines
Friday	5	Heathfield	10 Hoppers Ballast Maintenance
Monday	8	Langport East*	10 Hoppers Ballast (Mr Marsh)
Tuesday	9	Laira	10 Hoppers Ballast Maintenance
Wednesday	10	Langport East*	10 Hoppers Ballast (Mr Marsh)
Thursday	11	Heathfield	10 Hoppers Ballast Maintenance
Friday	12	Cogload Jn	10 Hoppers Ballast (Mr Marsh)
Saturday	13	Cogload Jn	10 Hoppers Ballast (Mr Marsh)
Monday	15	Bodmin Road	12 Hoppers Ballast Relaying, 2 engines
Tuesday	16	Bodmin Road	12 Hoppers Ballast Relaying, 2 engines
Wednesday	17	Bodmin Road	12 Hoppers Ballast Relaying, 2 engines
Thursday	18	Bodmin Road	12 Hoppers Ballast Relaying, 2 engines
Friday	19	Menheniot	12 Hoppers Ballast Resleepering, 2 engines
Monday	22	Bodmin Road	12 Hoppers Ballast Relaying, 2 engines
Tuesday	23	Heathfield	10 Hoppers Ballast Maintenance
Wednesday	24	Bodmin Road	12 Hoppers Ballast Relaying, 2 engines
Thursday	25	Kingsbridge	10 Hoppers Ballast Maintenance
Friday	26	Bodmin Road	12 Hoppers Ballast Relaying, 2 engines
Saturday	27	Newton Abbot	15 Hoppers Ballast (to stable at Newton for following day for Liskeard & Looe)
Monday	29	Liskeard & Looe†	15 Hoppers Ballast Relaying, 2 engines
Tuesday	30	Burngullow for Drinnick Mill	12 Hoppers Ballast Relaying, 2 engines
Wednesday	31	Liskeard & Looe†	15 Hoppers Ballast Relaying, 2 engines
Thursday	1 April	St Austell	12 Hoppers Ballast Resleepering, 2 engines
Friday	2	Liskeard & Looe†	15 Hoppers Ballast Relaying, 2 engines
Monday	5	Liskeard & Looe†	12 Hoppers Ballast Relaying, 2 engines
Tuesday	6	Bodmin Road	12 Hoppers Ballast Relaying, 2 engines
Wednesday	7	Bodmin Road	12 Hoppers Ballast Relaying, 2 engines

* To unload on Up line 128-130 MP.

† These hoppers are only to be loaded to the 9¾ line and run to Liskeard with Newton engines. Mr Turpin will arrange Liskeard & Looe engine to run train from Liskeard to relaying. Enginemen and guard to be relieved at Newton at 9am before starting west.

ACCIDENT AT CROCKHAM SIDING, 1944

On 29th July 1944 there was a minor (as it turned out, by good luck) accident to Trusham Porter Mrs B.M. Bradley at Crockham Sidings, during the shunting of the 11.0am Christow–Newton Abbot goods (loco. 4582, driver R.J. Newman, Guard T.H. Snell). Mrs Bradley had come with the train from Trusham along with Porter Josie Gerring, the former to operate the ground frame and the latter to label the wagons. (Normally only one of them would have come, but an Ambulance Train was expected and it was therefore desired to get the goods train away as soon as possible.) The train came to a stop north of the siding connection and the Guard 'cut off' behind the 5th wagon. Mrs Bradley went to the cab to collect the Token and started walking down the line towards the ground frame. As she approached the ground frame she moved in to walk on the sleeper ends, to avoid the point rodding, and was struck on the left-hand side of her head by the engine which was now moving forward to clear the points preparatory to doing the shunt. Guard Snell had shouted a warning, but Mrs Bradley had not heard this or the approaching engine itself, owing to the noise made by the concrete mixer in the concrete works. She was off work for 12 days as a result of her injuries. An inquiry was held at Exeter but made no recommendation as 'the mishap was due to Mrs Bradley failing to exercise sufficient caution to ensure her own safety'.

Mrs Bradley was 43 and had entered the company's service at Newton Abbot on 15.3.1943, transferring to Trusham on 15.6.43.

Josie Gerring (née Ridler) was a Teign Village girl and had joined the railway on 3.8.1943. Shortly after this incident her husband George Gerring was killed serving in the forces in Italy, and she left the railway feeling too shocked to continue work. But this was not the end of her railway connections, as in 1947 she married Christow signalman George Bissett. George had started as a Porter in North Devon and had come to Christow via Porter Signalman Dunball, Porter Signalman Brixham, and Signalman Longdown. He later moved to one of the Newton Abbot boxes but increasing deafness forced a transfer latterly to a platform job at Newton. He died in 1972.

CHANGES IN OWNERSHIP OF THE TEIGN VALLEY QUARRIES

1924 Teign Valley Granite Co. Ltd merged with Mendip Mountain Quarries Ltd of Cranmore and renamed Roads Reconstruction Ltd. This group also controlled the Tytherington Stone Co. and Sandford & Conygar Quarries Co.

1931 Assets of Devon Basalt & Granite Co. Ltd taken over (the disused Trusham and Bridford quarries).

1934 Roads Reconstruction Ltd company dissolved, new company Roads Reconstruction (1934) Ltd formed.

1936 New joint marketing company Devon Basalts Ltd formed by Roads Reconstruction (1934) Ltd, Scatter Rock Macadams Ltd, and the Stoneycombe Basalt Co., the new company to purchase the whole output of the remaining Teign Valley quarries (Crockham, Scatter Rock and Ryecroft) and have sole responsibility for sales.

1938 Roads Reconstruction (1934) Ltd takes control of Scatter Rock Macadams Ltd (although the latter company was retained in existence until 1977).

Except for Ryecroft Quarry (closed in c. 1939), Roads Reconstruction (1934) therefore owned all the Teign Valley quarries, active and disused, from 1938 on. Roads Reconstruction (1934) Ltd was later taken over by the Amalgamated Roadstone Corporation Ltd, which was itself taken over in 1967 by the Amey Roadstone Corporation Ltd (ARC).

Looking north-west across the Concrete Works stacking ground in the 1920s (the photograph was taken from about where the number '152' appears on the O.S. map at page 201). The Concrete Works was the building in the centre. The quarry engine house can be seen on the left, and several Teign Valley Granite Co. trucks and a 'Princess Royal' coal truck feature in the siding on the right. *ARC SW Ltd.*

THE TEIGN VALLEY CONCRETE WORKS

The Teign Valley Concrete Works was started around 1908/9 by Harry C. Colvin Smith who had experience of the use of concrete blocks for building railway stations in Chile and Cuba and wanted to promote their use as a building material in this country. Colvin Smith was assisted by Archibald P. Fisher, a Newton Abbot Civil Engineer who had been Resident Engineer for the last of the Torquay Corporation reservoirs at Hennock. The works was built on Crockham Quarry lands leased from H.L. Hardwicke, and throughout its life has been closely associated with the quarry. A limited company, the Teign Valley Concrete Works Ltd, was formed in October 1909.

Production was originally limited to the concrete blocks. These were made of cement (brought in by rail) and granite chippings (supplied by the quarry). The blocks took 12 hours to set and then had to be watered for 10 days and left for a further 6 weeks to mature. They were made in various colours (reds, yellows and browns), and blocks with a 'granite' face were also produced.

In more recent decades, however, the works has specialised in concrete sewer pipes.

The works had a 'consent' to use the Teign Valley Granite Co's siding facilities and at one time provided a sizeable rail traffic. But rail transport was largely given up in the 1950s, due to the excessive number of breakages of pipes experienced. Nevertheless, occasional loads were still despatched by rail until 1968.

The works was still active in 1991, now owned by ARC.

From Crockham Sidings it was but ¼ mile into Trusham station, crossing the river back to the east bank at Crockham bridge.

This c.1933 view shows the 1911/12 layout, with everything still the same as in the 1921 scene opposite. Motor No. 96 had just arrived from Chudleigh but the signalman had not yet restored the signals. The train in the sidings (to the right of the 1911 signal box) was the 2.45 p.m. Exeter–Chudleigh, one of the odd workings referred to in Chapter 14, which had a quarter-hour sojourn in the yard here in order to cross the up motor (the goods loop not being available to passenger trains). The large galvanised iron hut on the platforms was the goods lock-up, added in 1903 at a cost of £40; the smaller hut at the end of the platform was the lamp hut. The gate by the main building at bottom right was the main station entrance as there were no doors in the rear of the building.

G. N. Southerden

TRUSHAM (including Trusham Quarry)

Trusham in its heyday in 1921 (compare the views of the original arrangements at p. 110/111). The station buildings at Trusham and Ashton were built of Candy's yellow bricks, like the 1882 signal boxes. The Trusham building in its original form (p. 110) comprised (left to right) Gents, Ladies, Booking Hall, Booking Office, and a lean-to extension at this end which was an 1882 afterthought and may have been the 'coal and lamp house' demanded by the GWR. However, in 1914, to give an extra office, the lean-to section was made into a full-height room as seen here. An additional chimney was provided and the original Booking Office chimney relocated. The 1911 extension of the platform is clearly seen here. The 1912 Devon Basalt & Granite Company's siding can be seen on the left.   *L & GRP*

The original facilities at Trusham comprised a 160ft long passenger platform, a loop siding, and a dead-end siding ending at a loading bank. These were more than adequate in the 1880s and '90s when Trusham was the quietest station on the line, but were soon found insufficient in the 1900s when Trusham suddenly grew into a very busy place thanks to the Trusham Quarry traffic (see below) and the shunting of trucks from Crockham and Whetcombe quarries.

In July 1910 the GWR Traffic Committee authorised a £3,353 scheme to provide a bidirectional goods loop through the station and make Trusham a crossing station. Included were a new signal box, a weighbridge on the goods loop line for weighing loaded trucks from the quarries, and an extension of the passenger platform to 316ft. These works were all completed by summer 1911. At the same time the staff had to be increased. The original station master and porter were augmented by a second porter in 1904 and a third in 1907; when the two signalmen were added in 1911, there were five staff under the station master's control. A station master's house was provided in 1912, reflecting the increased

The Trusham staff posing for the camera c.1930, with Station Master George Hulme in the centre and Fred Court second from left; the others cannot be identified.   *Cty. John Court*

importance of the place, and the station building was extended.

TRUSHAM QUARRY

In September 1899 J.H. Dickson, then still acting as Contractor's Engineer on the Dicksons' Exeter Railway contract, took a lease of land adjacent to Trusham Station from the Commercial Union Assurance Co. for use as a quarry. Production began around 1901 and by 1904 there was a fair-sized quarry face as shown in the O.S. map. Although the quarry was adjacent to the railway, there were no loading facilities on this side of the line, and the stone was at first carted by road over the bridge to the goods yard. Dickson traded, for some reason, as 'J.H. Dixon', and indeed he was always known in the valley as 'Paddy Dixon' rather than by his proper name. After the Exeter Railway contract was completed he took up residence at Prospect Park, Exeter, and until the 1920s was a regular traveller out on the first down train from Exeter to Trusham; he is remembered as 'a little dapper chap, who always wore a trilby and carried a Gladstone bag'. In 1909 he formed a limited compa-

The provision of a station master's house at Trusham was first authorised in December 1908 at an estimate of £359, but nothing was done until 1912. The house was built to a standard GWR design (compare the photograph of Savernake at Plate 294 of Adrian Vaughan's *Great Western Architecture*) but instead of the usual brick construction, it was built of concrete blocks from the Teign Valley Concrete Works, an appropriate local touch. It was sold off by BR in 1966.   *Author*

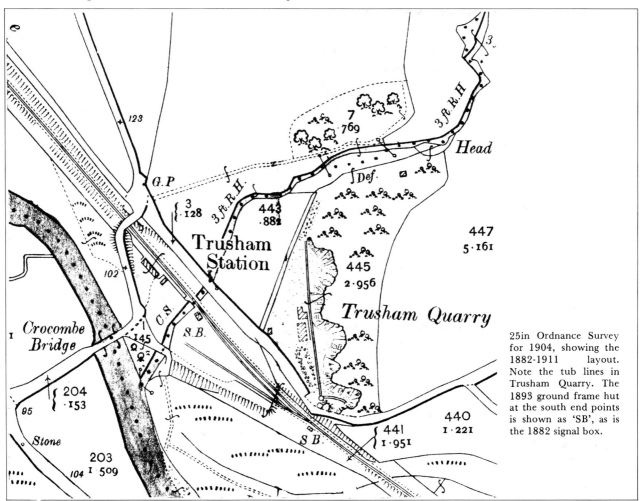

25in Ordnance Survey for 1904, showing the 1882-1911 layout. Note the tub lines in Trusham Quarry. The 1893 ground frame hut at the south end points is shown as 'SB', as is the 1882 signal box.

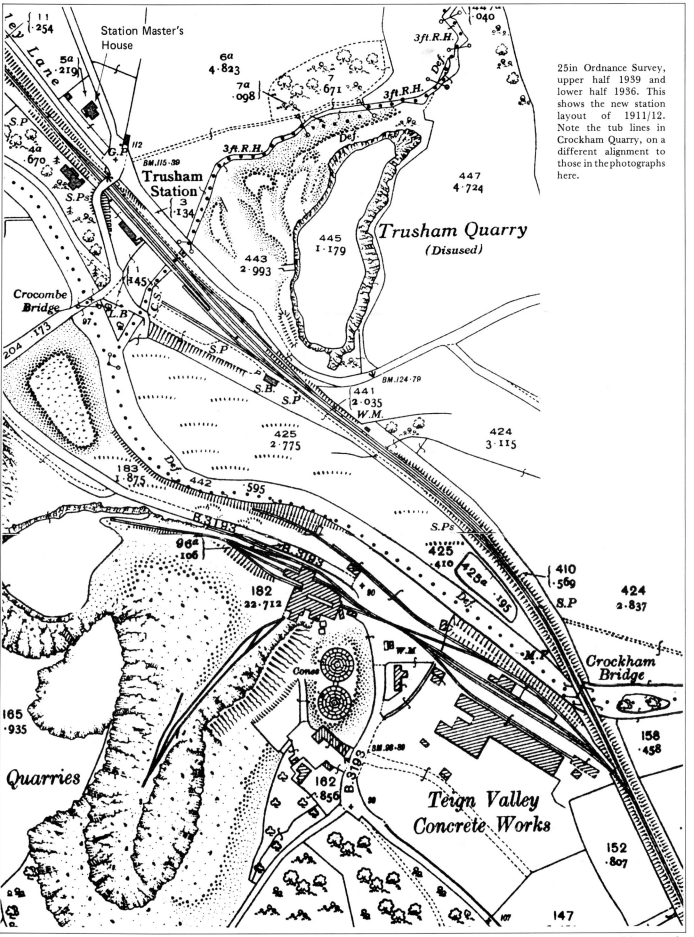

25in Ordnance Survey, upper half 1939 and lower half 1936. This shows the new station layout of 1911/12. Note the tub lines in Crockham Quarry, on a different alignment to those in the photographs here.

Crown copyright reserved

Motor 96 about to depart for Exeter with a trailer, c.1933. Trusham Quarry (still active in the view at page 204, where stone trucks can be seen waiting to be loaded at the chutes) *was* *several years closed by this date, but we get a good view here of the abandoned quarry face, since obscured by vegetation.*

G. N. Southerden

Almost certainly the same train a few seconds later, looking towards Whetcombe with a view up the valley. The 1911 Down Main/Down Main to Loop Home signal was later altered to the form seen at page 171.   *G. N. Southerden*

ny, the Devon Basalt & Granite Co. Ltd, to take over the Trusham quarry, Westcott quarry (west of Bridford) which he had leased since 1899, and the new quarry which he had opened at Bridford in 1905.

In August 1911 the Devon Basalt & Granite Co. told the GWR that better accommodation was needed for their traffic at Trusham if the quarry was to be retained. The DB&G Co. agreed to pay the £355 cost of a siding, to be refunded by rebates on the traffic, and to build the loading facilities; the GWR bore the £165 cost of signalling alterations themselves. On this basis a Private Siding Agreement was made on 23rd January 1912, and a loop siding off the new goods loop installed.

The quarry installed extensive new plant in 1915–17 but fell into bad times in the 1920s and seems to have closed around 1927. The DB&G Co. passed into liquidation in 1931 (the Bridford quarry having also closed). However, the 1912 siding at Trusham was allowed to remain, no doubt being found of use by the GWR for other purposes, until it had to be removed in connection

with the 1943 works (see below). The Private Siding Agreement was then terminated with effect (retrospectively) from 31st December 1942.

From the mid-1900s to the early 1930s Trusham station was the scene of frequent shunting operations for much of the day, as trucks were taken to or from Whetcombe

---

TRUSHAM STATION MASTERS

October 1882	Henry Huddison (from Laira)
c. 1895	James Elliot Towillis
c. 1902	John Pellow (to Station master Chudleigh)
September 1903	Sidney Honeywill (from Signal Porter Ashton)
c. 1915 to 1932	(John) George Hulme (from Station master Ide, to Station master Tiverton).

With the quarry traffic reduced by the 1930s to low figures and at Crockham only, the Station master's post was abolished on George Hulme's departure and the station put under the Christow Station master. Further retrenchment came in 1934 when one of the porter's posts was also abolished, leaving but one porter on each turn. In 1950 the staffing was reduced to one porter only.

These three photos, taken at the same time as the one on page 125, show No. 1244 waiting in the goods loop at Trusham with an up goods in September 1924. It was waiting for a down railmotor which was signalled in the top picture. No. 1244 worked mostly in the Exeter area from 1920 until 1930, when it was withdrawn from service from Exeter shed.   *G. N. Southerden*

and Crockham as necessary. In the 1920s a total of 6–8 hours shunting time was allowed at Trusham by the various goods trains calling, and the up and down Exeter–Newton Abbot goods trains were to be seen at the station together mid-morning. But things became very much quieter in the '30s.

The inability to cross two passenger trains in normal working under the 1911 layout must have been felt a nuisance on occasion, and in 1943, as part of the Government-funded works to improve the line's suitability as a diversionary route, it was decided to convert the loop into a passenger line and adopt normal directional working through the station for all trains. This required the provision of a second passenger platform on the loop line for use by down trains, partly on the site of the former DB&G Co. private siding; and this was brought into use in July 1943.

The 1943-built down platform is seen to advantage in this view towards Exeter, in the 1950s. The shelter was not provided until 1946. For contemporary views of the 1943 works at Trusham, see page 150.

J. H. Moss

A down train running into Trusham in 1957.
Cty. Mrs. S. Wheeler

Looking towards Heathfield (compare with view on page 199). The elegant oil lamps had gone since the 1920s. Note the milk churns, Trusham having a substantial milk traffic in the 1950s. It was unusual to see the yard so empty of trucks. *J. H. Moss*

SIGNALLING

1882–1893: Trusham was originally a Block Post with full signalling controlled from the signal box. An attempted reconstruction of the 1882 signalling, based on the signal positions shown on the 1887 Ordnance Survey, is given here.

1893–1911: In 1893 the signal box was reduced to ground frame status and the signals removed. At the same time control of the south end points was transferred from the signal box to an additional Ground Frame hut provided for the purpose. This was presumably designed to speed up shunting (still being done by tightly-timed mixed trains at this date) but it is odd that

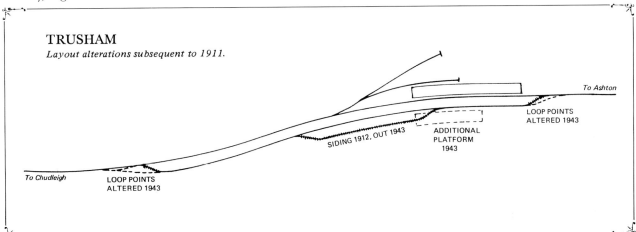

TRUSHAM
Layout alterations subsequent to 1911.

To Ashton

LOOP POINTS
ALTERED 1943

SIDING 1912, OUT 1943

ADDITIONAL
PLATFORM
1943

To Chudleigh

LOOP POINTS
ALTERED 1943

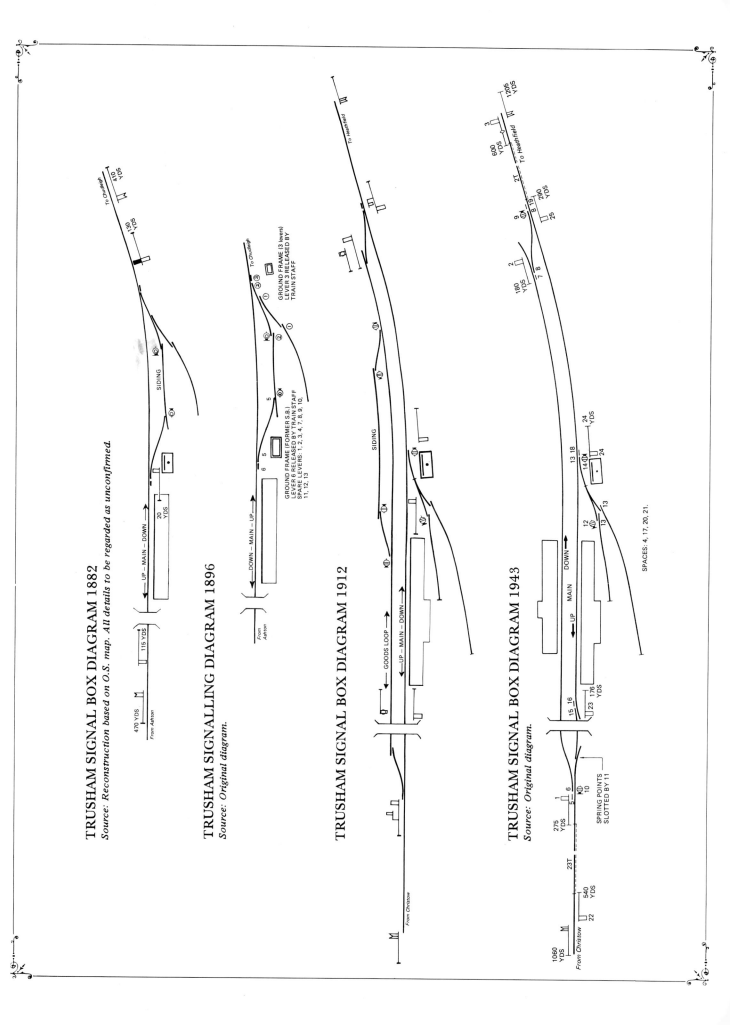

TRUSHAM SIGNAL BOX DIAGRAM 1882
Source: Reconstruction based on O.S. map. All details to be regarded as unconfirmed.

TRUSHAM SIGNALLING DIAGRAM 1896
Source: Original diagram.

TRUSHAM SIGNAL BOX DIAGRAM 1912

TRUSHAM SIGNAL BOX DIAGRAM 1943
Source: Original diagram.

LOCKING TABLE TRUSHAM 1943

	Released by	Locks in Normal Position	Locks in Either Position	Releases
1 Down Main Home	5. 7	9. 22		
2 Down Main Starting	7. 8	9	5. 6	
3 Down Main Advanced Starting		9. 14. 25. (24 when 8N)	8. 19. 13. (7 when 8R)(18 when 8N)	
4 –	x			
5 FPL for 6	6			1
6 Down Main Facing		15		5. 9
7 FPL for 8			8	1. 2
8 Up & Down Main Facing		11. 13. 19		2. 9
9 Disc for 8	6. 8	1. 2. 3	5. 7	
10 Disc at 6	11	22	16. 18. 19	
11 Spring points in Up Main (slotted)	15	8. 13. 23. 24. 25		10
12 Disc for 13	13	14	19	
13 Up Main Facing		8. 11. 18		12. 14
14 Disc for 13	13	3. 12	19	
15 Up Main Facing		6		11. 23
16 FPL for 15			15	23. 24
17 –	x			
18 FPL for 13		13		24. 25
19 FPL for 8		8		25
20 –	x			
21 –	x			
22 Up Main Advanced Starting		1. 10	5. 6. 11. 15. (16 when 15R)	
23 Up Main Starting	15. 16	11	13. 18	
24 Up Main Inner Home	16. 18	11 (3 when 8N)	8. 19	
25 Up Main Home	18. 19	3. 11		

Table dated 1.4.1943

it was only done at Trusham which at this date had the least traffic. The 1893 arrangements are shown in the 1896 diagram.

1911–1943: A new Block Post signal box was brought into use around June 1911 in connection with the alterations carried out that year and a complete resignalling effected. It had a 25-lever frame of which 20 were originally in use, but the addition of the Devon Basalt & Granite Co's siding in 1912 saw all levers now in use, as shown in the 1912 diagram.

1943–1958: The 1943 works required major alterations in the signalling (detailed in the Table here). The lever frame was relocked with VT5 Bar locking in consequence. The loop points were relaid in revised form so as to enable two trains to run into the station simultaneously (in contrast to normal practice at single-line crossing places). Track circuiting was provided in rear of the Advanced Starting signals which were some distance from the box; this was the only track circuiting on the whole branch after 1943.

1958–1961: On closure to passengers (9.6.1958) the signal box was reduced to ground frame status. The loop was spiked out of use and only 13 points left workable for access to the yard. Full details of the 1958 changes are given in the Table.

However, after the floods of 1st October 1960, the Trusham loop had to be brought back into use. It is not

known exactly what arrangements were made for this initially.

1961–1965: On 1st May 1961 the signal box (ground frame) was abolished altogether, and the layout controlled from hand points. The line was cut back to 4m 20ch in summer 1963 (see plan) and then taken out of use north of Crockham on 10th February 1965.

TRUSHAM
SIGNALLING ALTERATIONS 1943

4.4.1943 Private siding (DB&G Co) disconnected.
16.4.1943 Down Main Home re-erected temporarily at 268yds.
Up Main Home re-erected temporarily at 281yds.
4- 8.7.1943 Former Up and Down Goods loop becomes Down Passenger loop, Former Main line becomes Up line.
New connections at both ends of loop.
New Down Main Home, Down Main Starting, Down Main Advanced Starting, Up Main Home, Up Main Advanced Starting signals.
New discs 9 and 10.
(Old Up Main Inner Home, Up Main Starting, and Discs 12 and 14, retained.)
Old Down Main Home, Down Main to Loop Home, Down Loop to Down Main Starting, Down Main Inner Home, Down Main Starting, Up Main Home, Up Main to Loop Home signals recovered.

SIGNALLING ALTERATIONS 1958

9.6.1958 Signal Box reduced to GF, all levers except 13 and 18 bolted normal.
All signals removed.
Track circuits disconnected.
15/11 points reset, spiked, & padlocked.
8 and 6 points spiked & padlocked.
13 points set for main line, clipped & padlocked, padlock key attached to train staff.

Whetcombe Quarry, looking north in the 1920s. The narrow gauge tub lines in the quarry bottom all radiated from a central turntable. Tubs can be seen being loaded by hand at the quarry face on each line. The line running off the bottom of this view ran up to the crushing plant. Petrol engines were used on these lines, driven by Leslie Langdon and Fred Turner. The long Transfer Siding features on the left, running parallel to the main line. The stop board for GWR locos, seen here, was located well inside this siding, enabling GWR locos to shunt as necessary. However, the main shunting was done by the quarry company's steam crane (similar to those at Crockham).

Collection D. Lystor

The Whetcombe 'ton a minute' crushing and screening plant (which also served Tinkley Quarry). Three of the sidings ran underneath the screens for loading from above. The connection with the main line can be seen on the bottom right of this photo.   *ARC SW Ltd.*

WHETCOMBE QUARRY and SIDING

Whetcombe quarry was but 30 chains north of Trusham station. The quarry was opened in the winter of 1909/10 by the Teign Valley Granite Co. as an expansion of their activities at Crockham. The stone was a basalt diabase as at Crockham. A private siding was provided from the start under a Private Siding Agreement of 11th October 1909, the railway works being completed in January 1910. The company paid the GWR £386 for the siding connection plus a further £80 for stone to be quarried on railway property. A new road (including a new river bridge) was built for access from the main Teign Valley Road, and this involved a level crossing of the railway line.

There were actually two quarries, Whetcombe and Tinkley, but the railway always referred to the location as 'Whetcombe'. The quarries were a large scale operation during their brief life, but were already in decline in the '20s, as the following figures show (Whetcombe & Tinkley combined).

	1925	1926	1927	1928	1929
Stone (Tons)	47,048	42,693	35,953	28,127	30,232
Rubble (Tons)	—	—	—	212	—

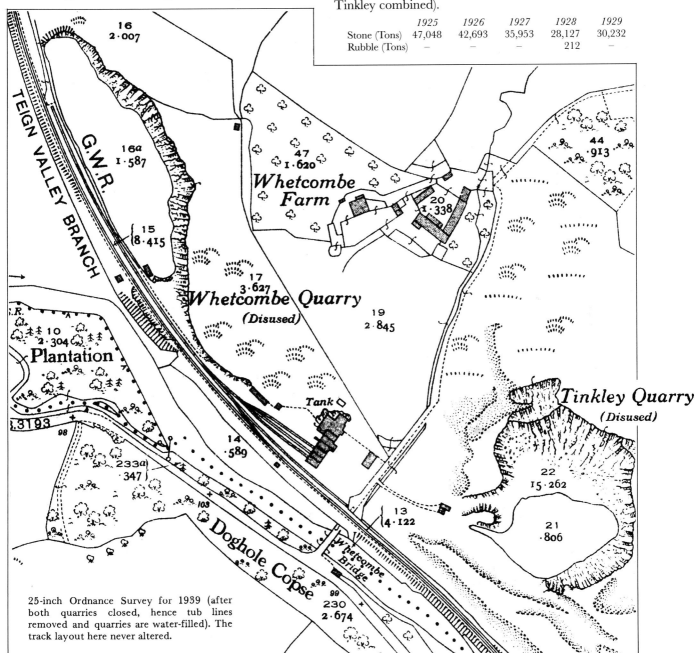

25-inch Ordnance Survey for 1939 (after both quarries closed, hence tub lines removed and quarries are water-filled). The track layout here never altered.

In 1930 the company decided to concentrate on Crockham, and Whetcombe closed in 1931. No hurry was shown in removing the sidings and the Private Siding Agreement was not terminated until May 1952, the sidings being lifted shortly after this.

Although the goods trains had timetabled calls at Whetcombe throughout the siding's active life, the regular practice was for the siding to be worked by a trip from Trusham made by the loco of one of the goods trains during the time allocated for shunting at Trusham. Locomotives were permitted to propel or haul between Trusham and Whetcombe without a Brake Van. All trucks from Whetcombe had to be taken to Trusham station for weighing.

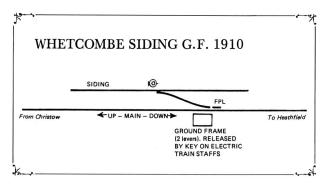

SIGNALLING

The siding was controlled from a 2-lever ground frame, released by a key on the Electric Train Staffs. This ground frame was brought into use in January 1910 and taken out of use on 23rd March 1952.

Before blasting was permitted at Whetcombe or Tinkley quarries, the quarry foreman (Jack Middlewick) was required to obtain the permission of the Trusham signalman, and after blasting to report back that the railway line was unaffected by debris.

From Whetcombe the line continued in the valley bottom for 1½ miles to Ashton.

ACCIDENT AT WHETCOMBE CROSSING, 1941

On 11th October 1941 the 3.15pm Newton Abbot–Exeter Auto (which fortunately had the engine 4835 leading) collided at Whetcombe Crossing with an Army lorry 'understood to have been in charge of Capt. Steward attached to a Battery stationed at Chagford'. The lorry was carried 10 yards before the train came to a stop, but nobody was injured and there was no damage to the train which was able to proceed on its way only 10 minutes later after the lorry had been pushed off the track.

The Accommodation Crossing had been little used since the quarry closed, but the military were now making use of the quarry for firing practice. The GWR inquiry concluded that 'the cause of the collision was negligence on the part of the lorry driver', but their report conceded that the view that a road vehicle driver had of approaching up trains was 'practically Nil'!

Shunting in progress at Whetcombe Siding in the 1920s. The photographer was by the level crossing, and the ground frame hut appears at left.
G. N. Southerden

ASHTON

This photograph, taken on 26th September 1928, shows the splendid oil lamps which were later removed and Tilley lamps used instead.

G. N. Southerden

Ashton was the focal point of the line in the 1882–1903 period, and retained some importance even after the engine shed passed out of use in 1903, as the locomotive water supply (the only one on the line) was retained. Indeed, as the stone traffic, and hence the amount of shunting, at Christow and Trusham grew, the importance of the Ashton water supply was enhanced, and light engine movements from Christow or Trusham to Ashton to take water became common. The arrangements at Ashton were looked after by a character known as 'Pumper' who came out from Exeter every day. It was only in 1928, when new water facilities at Christow came into use, that those at Ashton were given up. The water tower was then demolished. The long-disused engine shed itself, though, managed to last until 1959.

The staffing at Ashton was a station master and one porter (graded signal porter for many years) until April 1929 when the station master's post was abolished, and after that two porters until 1958. Because of the level crossing, Ashton had to be staffed at all hours trains were running, so the complement could not be reduced below two prior to the passenger closure. From 1958 to 1961 there was one porter only.

Passengers came to Ashton station from some parts of Christow which were nearer Ashton than Christow station, as well as from Higher and Lower Ashton. The main users of the goods yard were W.S. Howard & Sons, agricultural suppliers and coal merchants, of Ashton Mills. They had a coal stack in the station yard and also brought in fertiliser by rail. The porters had to 'measure up excess space' (see how much the coal stack was extending beyond the area actually rented), and also had a regular job in going up to the Mill to collect demurrage due on the coal wagons. There had been a significant cattle traffic pre-1903 but the GWR withdrew the facility when Christow station opened (although the annual returns show a few wagons handled in the interwar years).

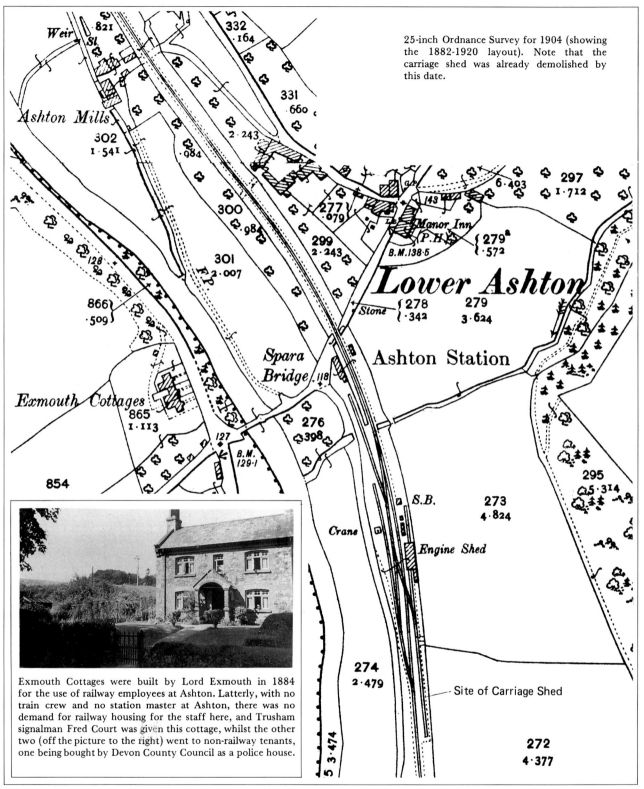

25-inch Ordnance Survey for 1904 (showing the 1882-1920 layout). Note that the carriage shed was already demolished by this date.

Exmouth Cottages were built by Lord Exmouth in 1884 for the use of railway employees at Ashton. Latterly, with no train crew and no station master at Ashton, there was no demand for railway housing for the staff here, and Trusham signalman Fred Court was given this cottage, whilst the other two (off the picture to the right) went to non-railway tenants, one being bought by Devon County Council as a police house.

Ashton received a camping coach in 1934, the very first year of the scheme on the GWR. The public brochure noted:

> 'The village of Ashton lies in the charming middle Teign Valley, which is one of the most densely wooded districts in South Devon. The scenery in the vicinity is particularly enchanting. Delightful walks may be taken to Chudleigh Rocks, Lustleigh Cleave, Moretonhampstead, Haldon Moor, and many other famous beauty spots on the fringe of Dartmoor.'

The GWR clearly expected energetic campers! The coach was removed after 1939, and no coach was pro-

ASHTON STATION MASTERS	
October 1882	Matthews (from Goods Dept., Buckfastleigh)
c. 1885	James Symons
c. 1895	George Bowden
c. 1900	George Alfred Haywood (to Station master Christow)
June 1903	Alfred Thomas Elliott (from Signal Porter Williton)
c. 1912	Edward G. Coles
c. 1921	Charles Harvey
c. 1925	Ernest J. Valentine (to Kingskerswell)
1928	C.H. Hutchings (from Bridgwater; to Stogumber April 1929)

Looking towards Heathfield from the level crossing in 1921, with the Crossing G.F. in the foreground. The single-storey block on the left was added at the GWR's request just before opening in 1882, and contained a porters' room (not used as such latterly), coal shed for the station supply, and lamp room.

L & GRP

Happy campers at Ashton, c.1937.   *Cty. John Court*

A view from the platform end on 26th September 1928, with the covered Middle G.F. on the left. The water tank still seems to have been in use at this date, but did not have many weeks to go. The timber in the yard was presumably waiting to be taken out by rail.

G. N. Southerden

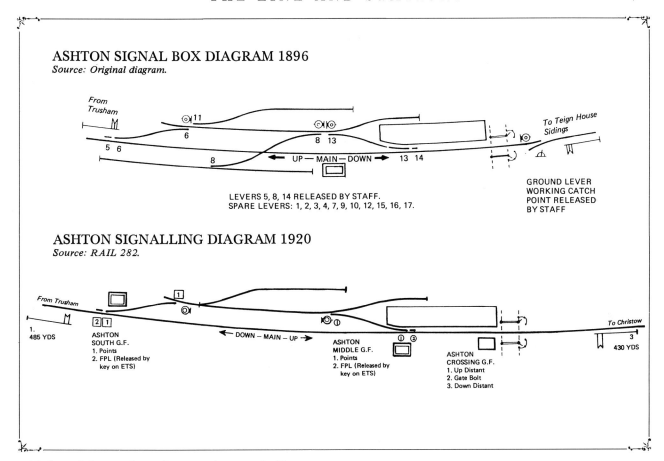

ASHTON SIGNAL BOX DIAGRAM 1896
Source: Original diagram.

From Trusham

To Teign House Sidings

← UP — MAIN — DOWN →

GROUND LEVER WORKING CATCH POINT RELEASED BY STAFF

LEVERS 5, 8, 14 RELEASED BY STAFF.
SPARE LEVERS: 1, 2, 3, 4, 7, 9, 10, 12, 15, 16, 17.

ASHTON SIGNALLING DIAGRAM 1920
Source: RAIL 282.

From Trusham

To Christow

← DOWN — MAIN — UP →

1.
485 YDS

ASHTON SOUTH G.F.
1. Points
2. FPL (Released by key on ETS)

ASHTON MIDDLE G.F.
1. Points
2. FPL (Released by key on ETS)

ASHTON CROSSING G.F.
1. Up Distant
2. Gate Bolt
3. Down Distant

3
430 YDS

vided at Ashton when the camping coach idea was revived in BR days.

SIGNALLING

1882–1893: Ashton was originally a Block Post with full signalling controlled from the signal box. However, no signalling diagram is known for this period.

1893–1903: In 1893 the signal box was reduced to ground frame status and the signals removed. The frame was released by a key on the Train Staff. This situation is shown in the 1896 diagram here.

1903–1920: Up to 1903 Ashton was effectively worked as a terminus from both directions, so Fixed Distants had sufficed to protect the level crossing. But when the line became a proper through route in 1903, a 3-lever ground frame (Ashton Crossing Ground Frame) was installed at the level crossing, with working Distant signals. The ground lever and and catch point at the north end were taken out. Beyond this, things remained as before, the various connections still being worked by the ex-signal box ground frame (now released by a key on the Electric Train Staffs).

1920–1958: In May 1920 the former signal box was abolished, the connection to the former Engine Shed line taken out, and two new small covered ground frames (Ashton

The level crossing in 1958.   *Arthur C. Palmer, cty. M. A. King*

South Ground Frame and Ashton Middle Ground Frame) installed to work the remaining connections. These were released by a key on the Electric Train Staffs in the usual way and worked by the train crew. The 1903 Crossing Ground Frame was unaffected.

In November 1956 the Middle GF, and the connection worked from it, were taken out of use. In 1957 the outer siding was removed.[3]

The goods yard from the south in the 1950s, with Howards' coal stacks conspicuous. The single-storey enginemen's room/storeroom, to the right of the main part of the engine shed, managed to survive when the rest of the shed was demolished in 1959 and was indeed still standing in 1992. Howards were (and are) based at Ashton Mills, and were the valley's main coal merchants. W. S. Howard had an interesting life; born in Bridford, he went to Australia in 1881 and worked in the mines at Broken Hill; he sailed to Paraguay in 1893 as part of an Australian utopian colony settlement. and then came back to the valley in 1896 after the colony broke up in disagreement. Taking Ashton Mills in 1901, he built up the coal merchants, and later road haulage and agricultural contractors, business. Ashton Mills had a private crossing over the line (top left of map at page 204) which was left open from morn to night; if the branch was about to be visited by management, the Christow signalman had to ring to get the Howards to shut the gates! They had 'a lot of three-legged dogs' as a result, and a fatality on one occasion.   *John Court*

Although Maurice Freeman had no connection with the railway, this picture of him on Fred Court's son's bike provides another delightful view of the lane alongside the station.

Ashton c.1957, with passengers! The station building was identical to Trusham except for the additional portion at this end (this side of the chimney) which was added in 1882 at the GWR's request to provide a 'Goods Shed'. There were no changes to the buildings after 1882. The 160ft-long platform was never extended and was the shortest on the line (apart from the Halts). *Lens of Sutton*

1958–1961: It is believed that the Crossing GF was taken out of use in June 1958, the gates henceforth being worked by the train crew. This left only the South GF (now released by a Key on the wooden Train Staff) in use until closure of this section of the line in 1961.

The Crossing GF was worked (1903–58) by the porters, relying on a block indicator and bell in the station office. The gates were normally kept across the line, and were shut when 'Train Entering Section' was given (i.e. when the train was leaving Christow or Trusham). However, in the case of up goods trains which had to shunt at Ashton, the gates were left open and the Up Distant sig-

Ashton in May 1941 with Mrs. Milford, the wartime porter, on the left and Fred Court's daughter-in-law Mary Court at right. Mrs. Milford's husband Herbert was also a porter at Ashton during the war. Note the removal of the station nameboard (the posts are still there, right of lamp-post) as a security measure. This, of course, did nothing to help non-local passengers, and one of the posters on the wall read as follows: 'An Appeal to the Regular Traveller — Fellow travellers may not be as familiar with the line as you are and may miss their destination in the blackout. Railwaymen do their best to call station names but your help would be invaluable.' *Cty. John Court*

JIM SERCOMBE

Jim Sercombe became the longest-serving employee at Ashton in BR days. Unlike the majority of the line's staff, he was a Teign Valley man, born in Christow in 1919. As a schoolboy in the early '30s he travelled to Newton Abbot Grammar School every day on the train. He joined the railway as a Lad Porter at Chudleigh on 14th June 1937, under Station master Elson. (For reasons unknown, the GWR had seen fit in 1936 to reappoint a Station master at Chudleigh after a 6-year gap; Elson was only there two years.) In 1938 he transferred to Hackney Yard, and was away in the Army from 1940 to 1946. He then came back to the valley in 1946 as Porter at Ashton, and stayed there until July 1959 when, foreseeing the destaffing of the station, he left for Starcross. Starcross was still a busy place in 1959, but suffered badly in the Beeching years, and by 1968 Jim was the only member of staff left; he was made redundant there on destaffing in 1971 and ended his days at Dawlish.

nal left on, the gates being shut only when the train had finished its work and was ready to leave. One relief porter, who had more concern for the running of trains than the convenience of motorists, used to go off to the pub for lengthy periods and always left the gates shut before he left in case a train should appear before his return; the drivers would sit honking, assuming that he was in the station office, but he was too far away to hear!

Another relief porter brought trouble from his habit of travelling home to Exeter on the last up train when on late turn. This meant that the train had to stop and wait north of the crossing while he reopened the gates for the night behind it. One night the driver stopped with the rear of the train very close to the gate, and then set back a little on restarting, smashing the gate. Not an easy accident to explain to management!

In the 1950s, Ashton, situated as it was in the heart of the valley and away from the scars of the quarry developments, was perhaps the most idyllic of the branch stations, and these views emphasise how little had really changed here since the line opened.

J. H. Moss

RYECROFT QUARRY and SIDING

Opened in 1930 (on the site of a small earlier quarry shown on the 6in map at p.278) and closed in 1939, Ryecroft was the last and least productive of the Teign Valley roadstone quarries. It was owned by Stoneycombe Basalt Ltd.

In July 1930 the company agreed to pay the GWR £1,670 for laying in a private siding connection, of which £1,257 was to be returned to them in due course in traffic rebates. The Private Siding Agreement was dated 13th October 1930 and the siding, controlled by a 2-lever Ground Frame released by a key on the Electric Train Staffs, was brought into use on 10th November 1930.

Although up goods trains had 'CR' calls at the siding, it was normally worked by special trips from Christow. The train was propelled from Christow to the siding with a brake van leading, with a porter from Christow to assist the guard. On arrival at the siding the van was uncoupled and left on the main line south of the siding points. Outgoing wagons from the siding were drawn out first and coupled on to the van. The incoming empties were then propelled into the siding. It is not known what form of motive power the quarry used to move wagons between the end of the GWR siding and the quarry.

The company built a new road bridge over the river for access to the quarry from the main Teign Valley road, and improved an existing occupation crossing for use by their lorries. (To encourage rail use, the Private Siding Agreement required the company to pay the GWR 1d per ton on all roadborne stone passing over the crossing!) Permission to use this crossing had to be sought from the Christow signalman. The quarry foreman also had to obtain the Christow signalman's permission before blasting at the quarry. Provided no train was in section, Christow would send the special bell code 4–3 ('May We Blast?') to Trusham, and, upon this being repeated by Trusham, a staff was withdrawn at Christow and both signalmen placed a collar on their starting signals and three detonators in front of the boxes. After the foreman advised that all was clear, Christow sent 'Obstruction Removed' to Trusham, the staff was restored and the detonators removed.

The siding points were spiked out of use when the quarry ceased production in 1939, but the quarry company were unwilling to terminate the PSA as they had not made a final decision on the quarry's future. This they eventually did in 1953, and the PSA was then terminated, but the GF was not taken out of use until 25.6.1956.

From Ryecroft it was just over a mile, still in the valley bottom and with bridges over the river at 6m 53½ ch and 6m 75¾ ch, to Christow station.

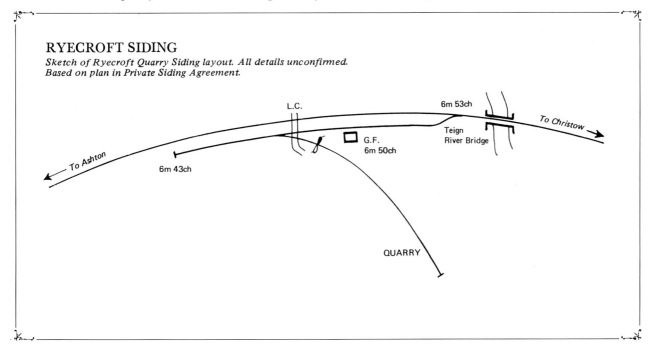

RYECROFT SIDING
Sketch of Ryecroft Quarry Siding layout. All details unconfirmed.
Based on plan in Private Siding Agreement.

L.C.

6m 53ch

To Christow

Teign
River Bridge

To Ashton

6m 43ch

G.F.
6m 50ch

QUARRY

This 25in Ordnance Survey for 1887 shows Teign House Siding and the site of Christow station. Dicksons' private siding installed in 1895 was an extension of the western of the two sidings, crossing the road by a level crossing initially until the overbridge was built. When the 'permanent junction' was put in in March 1903, this siding must have been cut back to the old stops, and (with the new running line taking the position of the former eastern siding) one imagines it served as the only active siding in in the weeks between March 1903 and its closure after traffic on 30th June 1903. The point was worked by a ground frame released by a key on the train staff in this period, instead of the former hand point. It was quickly lifted after closure and the 1904 OS clearly shows the vacant trackbed here. The level crossing to the north of the cattle pen, which was a private road for Sheldon Manor, was reduced to footpath status after the Scatter Rock sidings were put in, and the new road 'Sheldon Lane' was built on the east side of the railway.

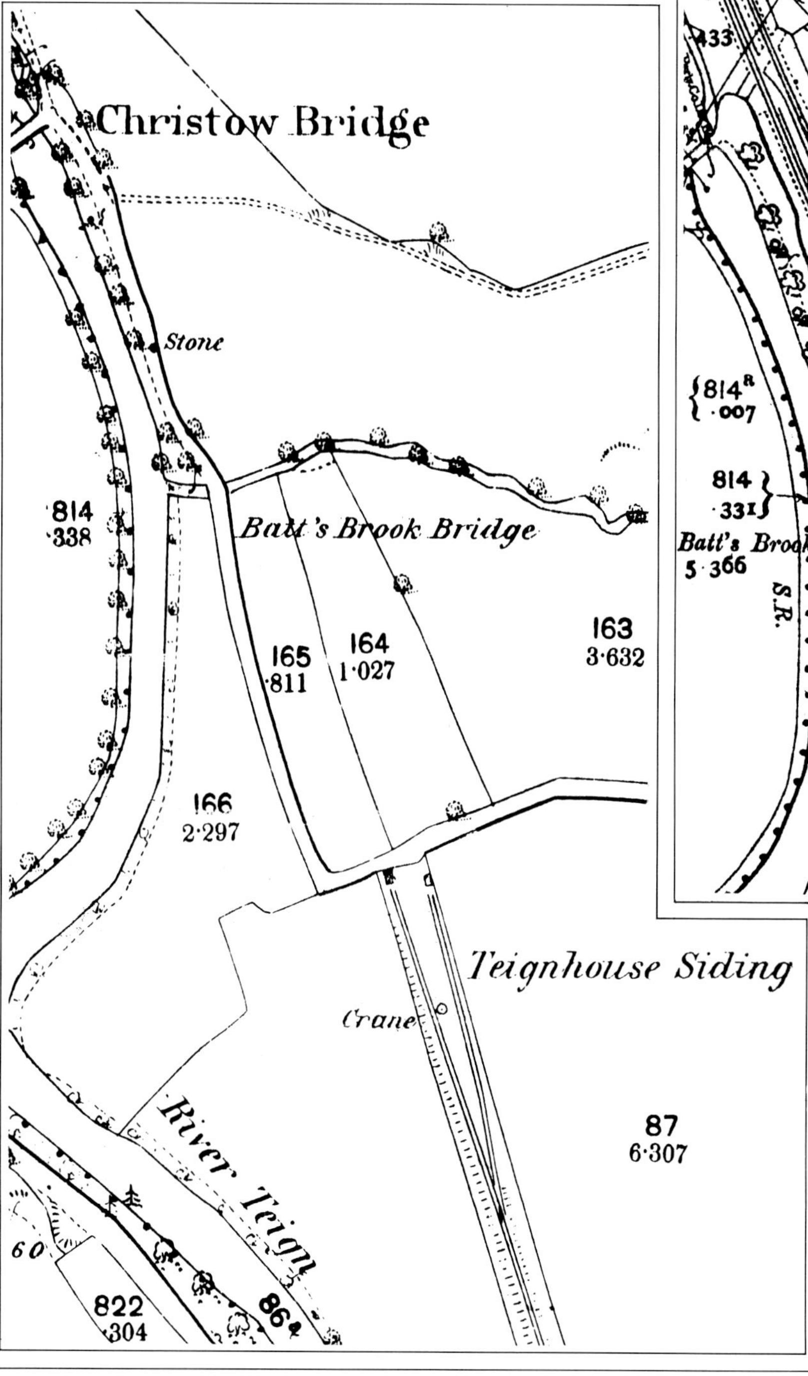

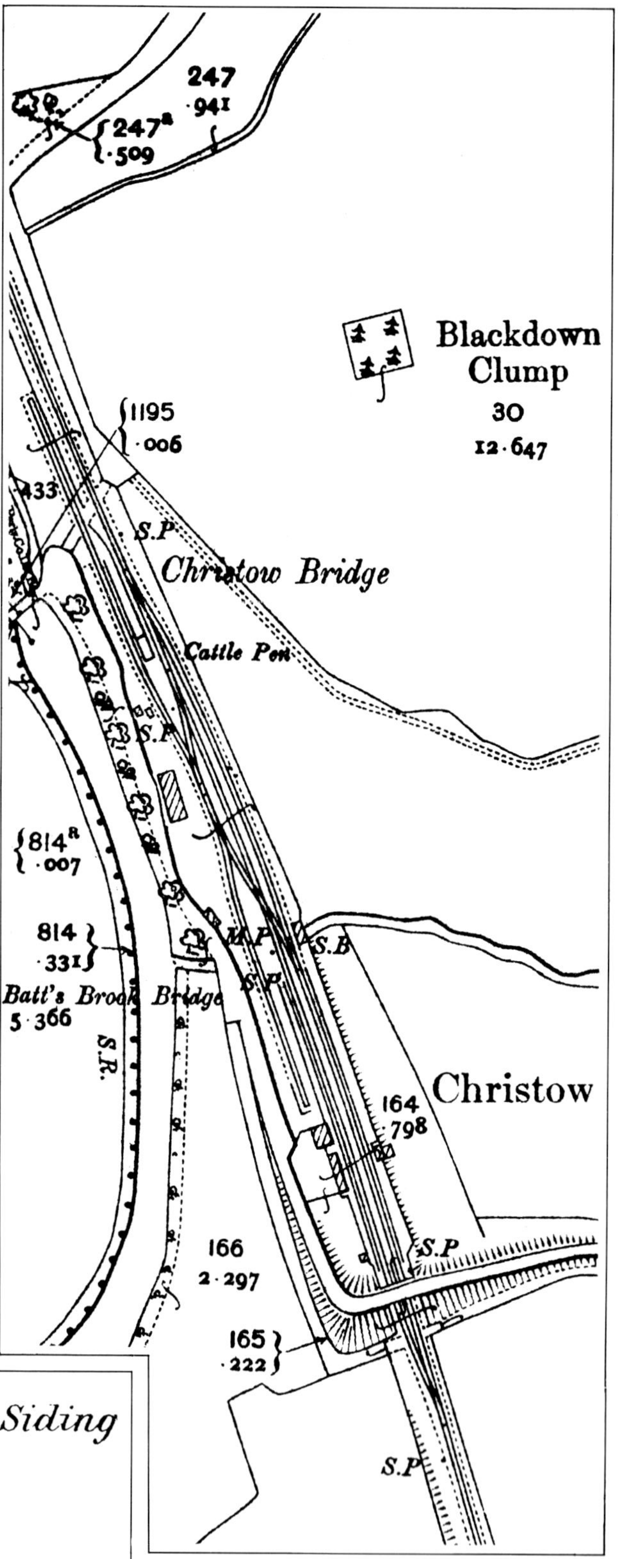

247
·941

{ 247ᵃ
  ·509

Blackdown
Clump
30
12·647

1195
·006

433

S.P.

Christow Bridge

Cattle Pen

S.P.

Christow Bridge

Stone

814
·338

Batt's Brook Bridge

165
·811

164
1·027

163
3·632

{ 814ᴿ
  ·007

814 }
·331 }

Batt's Brook Bridge
5·366

S.R.

M.P.   S.B.
S.P.

164
·798

Christow

166
2·297

Teignhouse Siding

166
2·297

165 }
·222 }

Crane

87
6·307

River Teign

S.P.

60

S.P.

822
·304

86

25in Ordnance Survey for 1904.

CHRISTOW

Christow station in its original form was illustrated and described at page 115. In contrast, this summer 1921 view shows the station with the Scatter Rock traffic at its height. Note the pine trees at the north end of the platforms, which grew considerably over the years and became a feature of the station scene. Views of the 1905-30 period (e.g. pages 104, 129) show a sizeable stocking ground and hut complex on the up side at the far north end of the yard by the Devon Basalt & Granite Company's siding, no doubt in connection with that company's activities. *L & GRP*

Teign House siding, opened 1882 and closed as from 1st July 1903, was discussed in Chapter 12. The O.S. maps here show its exact location in relation to the later Christow station.

As the only passing place on the line 1903–1911, and the only passing place for passenger trains until 1943, Christow was always the most important location on the line in operating terms after 1903. Its greatest days were between c1911 and c1933 when the stone traffic was at its height; it also had the largest passenger traffic on the line between the collapse of Chudleigh in 1920 and its own decline (following the start of bus services) in 1947–50. With the stone traffic all gone and few passengers left, Christow was a shadow of its former self after 1950.

The bulk traffics handled at Christow, stone from the Devon Basalt & Granite Co. and Scatter Rock quarry, and barytes from the Bridford Barytes Mine, are discussed in detail in the sections that follow.

The major changes in the layout at Christow (see diagram p. 229) were:

1910 — Addition of the Devon Basalt & Granite Co's private railway and alteration of the up siding to join it.
1914 — Addition of the Scatter Rock private sidings on the down side.

1924 — Provision of an Up Refuge Siding/Weighbridge Siding, partly for dealing with the stone traffic and partly to enable longer trains to be crossed under diversionary working.
1930/1 — Removal of the Devon Basalt & Granite Co's railway and restoration of the up siding back to its original position.
1943 — Extension of the loop at the north end to 1100ft.
1957 — Removal of the Scatter Rock sidings.

Christow was provided with a full range of goods facilities in 1903, including a loading bank with a 5 ton crane, cattle pens, and a weighbridge for road vehicles. Having said that, the general goods traffic here was never particularly great, although the quarries did bring extra traffic in machinery and parts. The crane was also used for loading outwards timber from time to time. The cattle traffic was mainly to Newton Abbot on Wednesdays; in the interwar years a truck was regularly attached to the rear of the first down train (the motors were able to haul a cattle truck). There was never a large coal traffic at Christow as Howards delivered to the village from Ashton station, but W.S. Elphinstone-Stone, and later Fred Clarke the local road haulier, did act as coal merchants and bring coal into Christow in small quantities.

Collett 0—4—2T No. 4808 arriving at Christow with the 2.57 p.m. Heathfield—Exeter on 9th September 1933. Exeter shed received six of these locos new in 1932/3 to replace the '517s', but their duties on the Teign Valley line were comparatively limited until the motors were withdrawn in 1935. This auto-train may itself have been deputising for a failed motor. The 45XX class 2—6—2T seen waiting in the 1924 up refuge/weighbridge siding with the 4.55 p.m. Christow—Exeter goods, still had 1½ hours to go before its booked departure time. The train seems to have finished its work at Christow and the crew were sitting in the sunshine. With the stone traffic falling off, this must have been a regular luxury by this date. The 45XXs first came to Exeter in 1922 and had replaced 0—6—0 pannier tanks on the Teign Valley goods workings by the 1930s.

G. N. Southerden

The 11.24 a.m. Exeter to Heathfield auto starting away from Christow in September 1924. The trailers were Nos. 42 and 44 whilst the loco is believed to have been 831. The extension of the station building to join up with the goods shed had been done only a few weeks before this and stands out clearly, as does the new entrance gate and screen by the Gents provided in consequence. Note at upper left the 1916 road bridge over the Teign on the direct road to the Teign House. *G. N. Southerden*

The original (1903) staffing was station master, signal porter, goods porter, and lad porter (no signalmen as such being employed). Staffing then had to increase to meet the demands of the stone traffic and the paperwork it generated, and at the station's height in the 1920s there were station master, two signalmen, and three porters, one of whom was on a middle turn and did most of the clerical work. The number of porters was cut to two in 1933 and so it stayed until 1958. In 1929–32 the Christow station master took over control of Chudleigh, Trusham, and Ashton stations also, as well as supervising Dunsford Halt from 1928.

SIGNALLING

Christow signal box was a Block Post from 1903 to 1958. The major signalling alterations were in 1914, when the original 21-lever frame was replaced by a 30-lever frame in connection with the installation of the Scatter Rock sidings, and in 1943 for the extension of the Loop. Full details are given in the alterations table here.

The station master's house at Christow was not built until 1932, being authorised by the GWR Traffic Committee on 8th October 1931 at an estimate of £678, Messrs. Heath Bros. being the contractors. It was located in Foxhole Hill, the road up to Christow village, a quarter of a mile away from the station, and became known as 'Woodlands'. A large garden was provided. Station Master Channing, the first occupant, was tubercular, and Alf Haywood asked him how he was going to manage the garden. "Wide paths and plenty of them" was Channing's reply! The photograph was taken c.1955 during the Yandells' residence. *Cty. Freda Yandell*

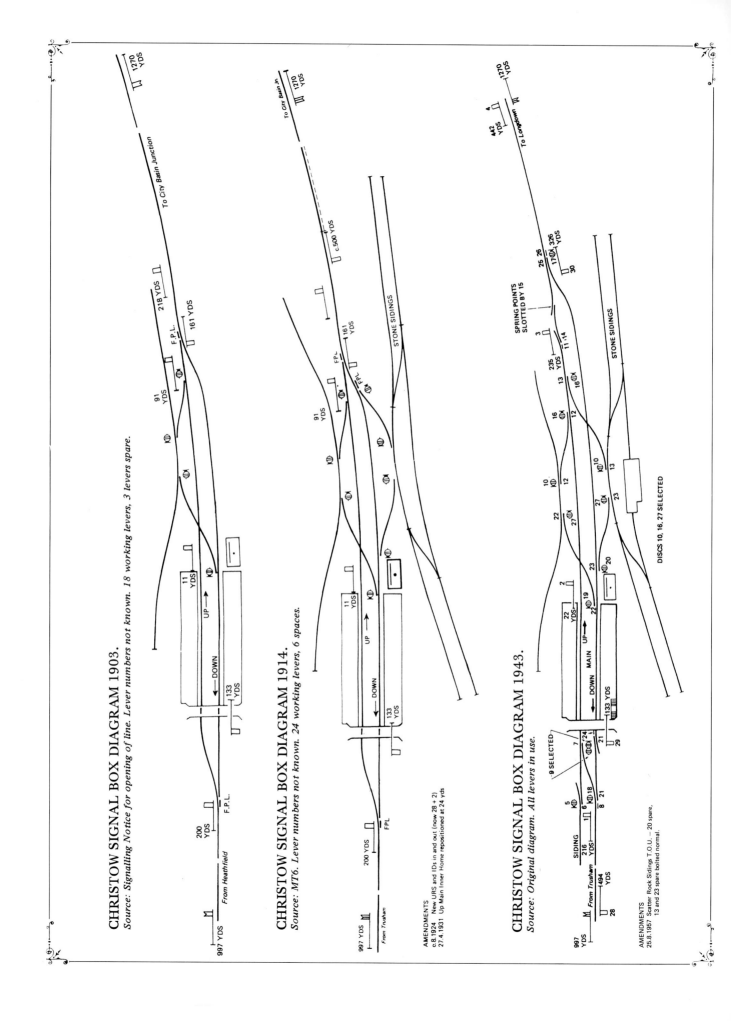

CHRISTOW SIGNAL BOX DIAGRAM 1903.
Source: Signalling Notice for opening of line. Lever numbers not known. 18 working levers, 3 levers spare.

CHRISTOW SIGNAL BOX DIAGRAM 1914.
Source: MT6. Lever numbers not known. 24 working levers, 6 spaces.

AMENDMENTS
c.8.1924   New URS and IDs in and out (now 28 + 2)
27.4.1931   Up Main Inner Home repositioned at 24 yds

CHRISTOW SIGNAL BOX DIAGRAM 1943.
Source: Original diagram. All levers in use.

AMENDMENTS
25.8.1957   Scatter Rock Sidings T.O.U. — 20 spare,
            13 and 23 spare bolted normal.

DISCS 10, 16, 27 SELECTED

CHRISTOW
SIGNALLING ALTERATIONS 1903–1961

26.6.1903	Signal Box brought into use with layout as shown in 1903 diagram.
7.1904	New Down Main Outer Home signal added at *c.* 500yds, in connection with the increased train service introduced at this date, to enable down trains to be accepted from City Basin Jn whilst the previous train was still at Christow.
date nk	Up Main Advanced Starting renewed at 300yds.*
1911	Track Circuit provided in rear of Down Main Outer Home signal
4.1914	Scatter Rock sidings, and 4 IDs in and out, b.i.u. New frame in box.
c. 8.1924	New Up Refuge Siding and IDs in and out, b.i.u.
27.4.1931	Up Main Inner Home repositioned at 24yds.
16–21.5.1943	Loop extended to 1,100ft at north end, with spring slotted catch point.
	Alterations to loop connections at south end.
	New Down Main Home, Down Main Advanced Starting, Up Main Starting, Up Main Advanced Starting signals.
	Up Main Home re-erected at 216yds.
	(Old Down Main Starting retained.)
	Old Down Main Home† (and TC in rear), Down Main Inner Home, Up Main Inner Home, Up Main

Starting, and Up Main Advanced Starting signals recovered.

New IDs for moves both ways over south end loop connections, and from single line to Up Main at north end.

Disc 16 repositioned.

19.9.1943	New Up Main Inner Home signal at 22yds.
9.6.1958	Signal Box reduced to ground frame. Line closed beyond 7m61ch.
	All signals and discs removed.
	6, 7, 14, 22 points spiked and padlocked.
	All levers except 8, 12, 21, 24, 25, 26 now spare bolted normal.
	12, 21, 25 points clipped and padlocked, key of padlocks attached to train staff.
	(The connections taken out of use were left in situ clipped.)
1.5.1961	Ground frame (former S.B.) taken out of use on closure of line.

* So shown in 1912 plan in Scatter Rock P.S.A. This states that it is to be shifted back again in connection with the construction of the sidings, but it is not clear that this was done (the 1914 MT6 shows it as an old signal).

† Formerly known as Down Main Outer Home (see 1904/1911 entries above).

LOCKING TABLE CHRISTOW 1943

	Released by	Locks in Normal Position	Locks in Either Position	Releases
1 Up Main Home	7. 8	9. 12. 13. 15. 22. 28		
2 Up Main Inner Home	11	9. 12. 13. 15. 22	6. 7. (8 when 7R)	
3 Up Main Starting	11. 14. (15 when 4N)	9. 16. 17	12. 13 (22 when 13N)	
4 Up Main Advanced Starting		15. 30	14. 25. 26 (11 when 14R)	
5 Disc for 6	6	9. 17. 12. 13		
6 Weighbridge Siding Safety		7. 22		5. (9). (17)
7 Up Main from Weighbridge Siding		6. 21		1. (9)
8 FPL for 21		21		1
9 Discs at 7 (selected)	(6 or 7)	1. 2. 3. 5. 12. 13. 22	11. 14. 15 (8 when 7R)	
10 Discs for 12 and 13 (selected)	11. (12 or 13)	16		
11 FPL for 14			14	2. 3. 10
12 Up Main		1. 2. 5. 9. 13. 22		(10). (16)
13 Up Main		1. 2. 5. 9. 12. 23. 25		(10). (16)
14 Up Main Safety Facing		25		3. 15
15 Spring Points in Up Main (Slotted)	14	1. 2. 4. (22 when 13N)		(3). 17
16 Discs for 13 and 12 (selected)	(12 or 13)	3. 10	11. 14. 15	(17)
17 Disc at 25	15 (6 when 7. 12. 13N) (16 when 12 or 13R)	3. 5	11	
18 Disc for 21	21 (19 when 22R) (20 when 23R) (25 when 22. 23N)	28. 29. 30	24. 26	
19 Disc for 22	22	27. 29	21. 24	(18)
20 Disc for 23	23	27. 29	21. 24	(18)
21 Up & Down Main Facings		7. 8		18. 29
22 Down Main		1. 2. 6. 9. 12. 23. 25 (15 when 13N)		19. (27)
23 Down Main		13. 22. 25		20. (27)
24 FPL for 21			21	27. 29. 30
25 Down Main Facing		13. 14. 22. 23		(18) 26
26 FPL for 25	25			30
27 Discs for 23 and 22 (selected)	24 (22 or 23)	19. 20		
28 Down Main Advanced Starting		1. 18	7. 8. 21. (24 when 21R)	
29 Down Main Starting	21. 24	18. 19. 20	22. 23. (13 when 22N) 25. 26	
30 Down Main Home	24. 26	4. 18		

Dated 23.6.1943

Taken c.1929, this view shows the much-enlarged Scatter Rock plant of the 1920s (for which see page 229). The 45XX loco had probably stopped to take water at the crane installed in 1928. The water tank and cranes at Christow were authorised in December 1927 at an estimate of £3,535, to replace the supply at Ashton. The tank is seen in the view at page 241.

Chapman collection, cty. Steven Court

Wilf Cox was Christow's longest-serving signalman. Born in Christow in 1900, he worked at Crowcombe and Kingskerswell before a signal porter's job came up at Ashburton, where the station master was a Mr. Box and people made jokes about 'Box and Cox'! The vacancy at Christow box, which gave him his first signalman's post and brought him back to his home village at the same time, came in 1922. He then stayed at Christow for 30 years. He had two brothers, Stanley and Clifford, in the Christow permanent way gang. *Left:* Christow box c.1923 with Wilf in the box and Mrs. Cox and baby sitting on the steps. *Right:* Wilf with an unidentified colleague outside the box in the late 1930s.

Cty. Frank & Cynthia Edworthy

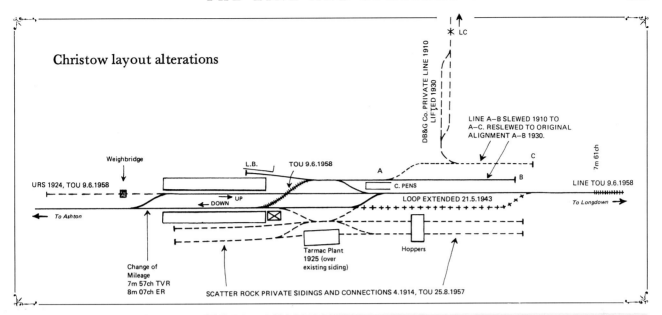

Christow layout alterations

Looking north from the end of the up platform on the evening of 19th August 1933, with a good view of the Scatter Rock sidings and the enlarged Scatter Rock facilities of 1923, plus the tarmacadam plant of c.1925 (the double-gabled structure immediately left of the signal box). The method of working the siding was as follows. The empties would arrive on the morning Exeter–Newton Abbot goods and be pushed by the locomotive, over the connection from the down line seen here, into the far end of the two loading hopper sidings. The brakes were put on as these sidings were (purposely) built on a gradient. During the course of the day, the wagons would be gravitated down, one by one, into position under the hoppers for loading, and, after loading, into the sidings behind the down platform to await collection. This was all done by the Scatter Rock employees, who would run beside the trucks manipulating the brakes to ensure that they did not crash too hard into the trucks already in the sidings. The loaded trucks would be taken away by the afternoon and evening trains (after first being taken to the weighbridge for weighing). It was usual to clear the sidings each day rather than leave loaded trucks there overnight. Wagons for loading under the tarmacadam plant were dealt with in the same way. The down auto-train here was being propelled by 4819 which had come to Exeter shed new in April 1933.   *G. N. Southerden*

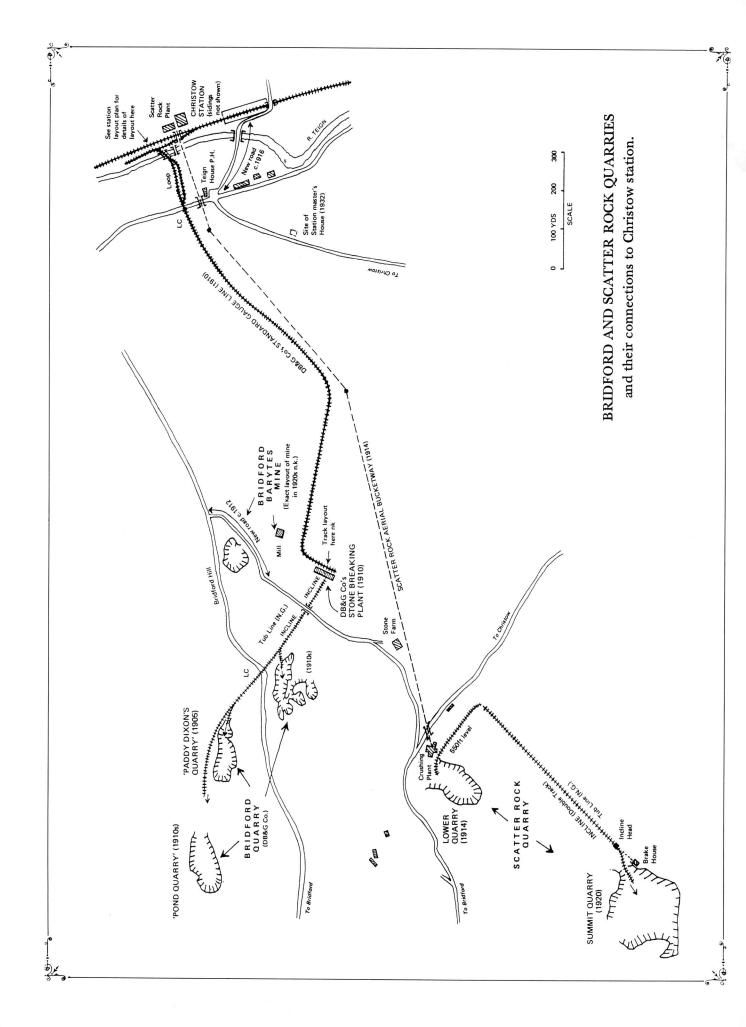

BRIDFORD AND SCATTER ROCK QUARRIES
and their connections to Christow station.

SCALE

0   100 YDS   200   300

See station layout plan for details of layout here

Scatter Rock Plant

CHRISTOW STATION (sidings not shown)

Loop

LC

Teign House P.H.

New road c.1916

R. TEIGN

To Christow

Site of Station master's House (1932)

DB&G Co's STANDARD GAUGE LINE (1910)

BRIDFORD BARYTES MINE
(Exact layout of mine in 1920s n.k.)

New road c.1912

Bridford Hill

Mill

Track layout here n.k.

INCLINE

DB&G Co's STONE BREAKING PLANT (1910)

SCATTER ROCK AERIAL BUCKETWAY (1914)

Tub Line (N.G.)

INCLINE

Stone Farm

To Christow

LC

(1910s)

'PADDY DIXON'S QUARRY' (1905)

'POND QUARRY' (1910s)

BRIDFORD QUARRY (DB&G Co.)

To Bridford

Crushing Plant

550ft level

LOWER QUARRY (1914)

To Bridford

SCATTER ROCK QUARRY

INCLINE (Double Track)

Tub Line (N.G.)

Incline Head

Brake House

SUMMIT QUARRY (1920)

BRIDFORD QUARRY

We have already referred to J.H. Dickson's quarry at Trusham and his formation of the Devon Basalt & Granite Co. Ltd in 1909. Dickson's other quarry at Bridford, known variously as Bridford Quarry, Christow Quarry, Great Hill Quarry, or 'Paddy Dixon's Quarry', was opened in October 1905. The 1905 quarry was north of the Bridford road (see map) but two further quarries were later opened either side of it and regarded as part of the same operation. At first the stone was taken by road unbroken to Christow station (and broken at the station) but this cost 9d per ton, and in 1908, with output increasing, Dickson decided that improved transport facilities were needed. The need to raise capital for this was a prime motive in setting up the limited company. In 1909/10 a stone breaking plant was built on a site immediately south of the Bridford Barytes Mine, linked to the quarry by a narrow gauge tub line (including an incline section), and in the other direction connected to Christow station by a ¾ mile standard gauge railway line. Dickson had great difficulty in persuading the Exeter Railway to come to terms over the necessary agreement for connecting this line to the sidings at Christow, largely because the ER were at this time also involved in planning for the proposed Scatter Rock sidings at Christow which might have required the same land. Relationships became strained as the ER were manifestly showing favour to the Scatter Rock plans, in which the ER Directors were themselves involved, even though the DB&G Co was to date by far the ER's best customer. The Scatter Rock plans had to be put on the back-burner in 1909, and, as it was necessary to provide some facility for the DB&G Co, it was decided to adopt the cheapest option and alter the existing cattle pen sidings on the up side, on land that had originally been bought for the Chagford branch, to join up with the DB&G Co's new line. A Private Siding Agreement on this basis was signed on 3rd June 1910 and the new railway came into use shortly after this.

The ER's favouritism towards their own Directors' Scatter Rock scheme soon re-emerged. In September 1911, only a year after the new line had come into use and at a time when the DB&G Co were forwarding over 20,000 tons annually, the ER gave formal notice to 'determine' the DB&G Co's lease of their lands at Christow station (i.e. the land on which the final few yards of their railway were built) in order that new sidings for the rival quarry could be laid there. Gloyens, the DB&G Co's Secretary, responded 'I am certainly surprised at your intention to take such strong measures for the purpose of favouring another Company which has not yet put any stone on the market, and I must say I consider your treatment of my company most unfair, if not illegal'. (It must of course be borne in mind that there were family matters at stake in all this as John

Dickson, the ER Director and promoter of the Scatter Rock scheme, was J.H. Dickson's uncle.) The DB&G Co demanded £2,750 compensation to recompense them for the cost of the railway which would now become useless, and this was a major factor in persuading the Scatter Rock promoters to adopt instead an aerial ropeway system which would enable the DB&G Co's siding to be left (see next section). February 1912 saw Gloyens writing again: 'I must ask you to let me have a definite answer as to how the Exeter Railway Co. intend to deal with my company, their best customer, within a week without fail, and if they decide to stand by the notice they have given me, kindly forward me a cheque for £2,750 at the same time.' This letter did the trick; with the plans for an aerial ropeway now definite, the ER replied on 26th February withdrawing the notice of termination! After this the DB&G Co were left undisturbed.

The growth of the traffic from the quarry in the early years, and subsequent collapse when the rival Scatter Rock quarry eventually opened in 1914, are shown in the table here. Bridford quarry's period of prosperity was, it will be seen, shortlived. The figures for 1916 and later do not amount to more than a couple of trucks a day on average. In 1923 Martin, the Scatter Rock manager, was able to dismiss the DB&G Co as 'nothing serious, they are very small, practically negligible'. By this date the DB&G Co was running at a loss, and the Bridford quarry appears to have closed in or about 1927. The standard gauge railway between the Stone Breaking Plant and Christow was sold off to the Bridford Barytes Mine in 1930, and they lifted the rails and converted most of it to a road (see later). Following the winding up of the DB&G Co Ltd in 1931, the Private Siding Agreement at Christow was terminated,

---

STONE DESPATCHED FROM CHRISTOW STATION BY DEVON BASALT & GRANITE CO.

1905	c.2,000	1914	c.22,000
1906	c.4,000	1915	c.9,000
1907	c.8,000	1916	6,870
1908	c.10,000	1917	4,500
1909	c.14,000	1918	4,033
1910	c.21,000	1919	5,326
1911	c.27,000	1920	9,129
1912	c.25,000	1921	6,428
1913	c.30,000	1922	9,193

Sources:
1905–1907 based on quoted figures of quarry output for financial years.
1908–1915 based on the total Goods Out traffic at Christow station less an estimate for the amount of other (general) goods and (in the case of 1914 and 1915) less the Scatter Rock traffic which is known.
1916–1922 Exact figures for DB&G Co traffic despatched by rail, quoted in RAIL 253/747.

No figures known for post-1922 period.

this taking effect retrospectively as from 31st December 1930. The narrow gauge tub lines west of the plant were also taken up soon after closure, except that the rails across the road at the Bridford Hill level crossing remained for many years.

Two locomotives are recorded as having worked on the standard gauge line: Manning Wardle 0-4-0 ST No. 1420 of 1899, acquired in 1911 from R.T. Relf & Son Contractors of Fareham; and Lilleshall Co. Ltd of Oakengates 0-4-0 ST, No. 3 *Alderman*.

The main features of the line were the gated level crossing over the Teign Valley road near the Teign House public house, and the bridge over the River Teign at Christow station. There was a loop in the line between these two points. Nothing has survived to tell us exactly how the line was worked, but, given the falling gradient towards Christow, one might surmise that the loco was run at the Christow end of the train in both directions. The track layout at the Stone Breaking Depot is also unknown.

There is no information available as to the working of the narrow gauge tub lines.

SCATTER ROCK QUARRY

Ideas of quarrying at Scatter Rock were initiated in 1907 by the Exeter Railway Directors John Dickson, V.W. Yorke, and Joseph Tiplady, with Dickson taking the most active role. Inspiration had probably been provided by the apparent success of J.H. Dickson's operations at the nearby Bridford quarry. However, it was to take some years, in the event, to get Scatter Rock off the ground. In 1908 Dickson and Tiplady bought the necessary land at Scatter Rock itself, and the ER bought a large area of land on the west side of the line immedi-

ately south of Christow station with the intention that they would lay sidings there for the quarry traffic. Approaches were made to the GWR during 1908, but it was found that the GWR was reluctant to accept such an arrangement, firstly because the siding points would have joined the TVR line and not the ER section, and secondly because the GWR considered that this was a private siding that should be paid for by the quarry company and not by the ER. After a meeting at Paddington in October 1908 the ER decided to aban-

These four photographs were taken on 30th September 1921 for use in a publicity booklet, 'Particulars of Basalt Quarries worked by Scatter Rock Macadams Ltd, proprietors of the Toughest Stone on Record'. This view of the then newly-opened Summit Quarry shows tubs of the usual type being loaded by hand at the quarry face. Horses were used on these lines in the Summit Quarry, to haul the tubs to the top of the incline. The lines in the quarry were taken up about 1940 and dumper trucks introduced to carry the stone to the incline top.

Collection Dick Lystor

The crushing plant from the north. The ledge in the hillside carrying the line at the 550ft level from the incline foot (out of picture to the left) to the top of the plant, is clearly seen here. Part of the lower quarry is visible at this level at top right. The large timber staging at bottom left, where the aerial ropeway crosses the Christow—Bridford road, was there to protect the road in case of material falling out of buckets etc. (a similar staging was erected over the Teign Valley road near the Teign House, and another over the railway at Christow station as seen in several of the views here). The ropeway terminated in the base of the plant. *Collection Dick Lystor*

don these original plans for the sidings, and the land that had been acquired was never used for railway purposes.

After this, alternative ideas were mooted, all confused by the Devon Basalt & Granite Co's seeking sidings at the same time. From mid-1909 the whole Scatter Rock idea went very dead for a couple of years (one imagines because the promoters could not find financial backing) and, as noted above, the DB&G Co siding was opened at this stage. Eventually, on 27th June 1911, the new limited company to work the quarry, Scatter Rock Macadams Ltd, was registered. The company had a nominal capital of £25,000 of which £11,500 was taken up at the time of incorporation. The backers were mostly Yorkshire contacts of Tiplady and the usual City interests, plus a large number of small local shareholders. William H. Tinney, a mining engineer of Newton Abbot who had taken a £1,000 holding, was appointed Managing Director (but resigned in 1913 before operations began). It was originally arranged that the company would lease the quarry land from Dickson and Tiplady, but in the event it was purchased in 1914.

With the company organisation sorted out, thoughts turned again to the need to have sidings built some-where at Christow station. In the autumn of 1911 came the ill-conceived attempts to throw out the DB&G Co so that Scatter Rock sidings could be built north of the station on the up side (as related in the previous section). Then, around December 1911, came the decision to install an aerial ropeway system from the quarry to Christow station, one result of which was that it was now possible to lay the sidings on the down side of the line (previously unfavoured because there was no road access on the down side). In December 1912 the Scatter Rock company agreed to pay the GWR £1,153 for the cost of laying in the siding connections (Dickson and Tiplady having given up their attempts to get the ER company to pay for their private sidings!), and a Private Siding Agreement was made on 31st December 1912. The quarry opened in April 1914 and the sidings were brought into use at the same date.

In return for the County Council giving permission for the ropeway to cross over several public roads, the Scatter Rock company were obliged to agree to construct a new road from the Teign House Inn to Christow station. This was done around 1916 and was a benefit to all station users as it shortened the distance and avoided the old Christow bridge which was very narrow.

This view appears to have been taken from the west end of the staging over the road at Teign House, looking westwards towards the quarry (the crushing plant can be seen on the hillside in the distance). The aerial ropeway, built by the German firm Blieghert, was just over one mile in length and had a capacity of 350-400 tons per 8 hour shift. It had two 'Angle stations' where it changed direction slightly, and a further 8 ordinary standards, the highest of which was 70ft. These were all built of timber originally but were changed over to steelwork in the 1940s. It was a dangerous job maintaining the ropeway; the fitter Jimmy Treen used to have to ride in the buckets which were the only means of access. This picture also provides a glimpse of the Devon Basalt & Granite Co's railway (bottom right) which is very elusive in photographs. It seems very weedy, as one might expect. The level crossing over the valley road was just off picture to the right.

Collection Dick Lystor

The new quarry quickly got into full stride. Production figures in the early years were as follows:

	Total output of quarry (tons)	Amount despatched by rail (tons)
1914	27,853	nk
1915	36,202	nk
1916	31,381	26,877
1917	32,021	31,349
1918	32,169	32,073
1919	42,373	38,216
1920	52,028	48,780
1921	nk	42,472
1922	nk	53,752

The postwar boom saw an 8% dividend for the shareholders in 1919, and 10% in 1920. A report by Prof.C. Gilbert Cullis in 1922 estimated that there were 1,451,600 tons of stone available on the company's property.

There were in fact two quarries at Scatter Rock. The Summit Quarry, not opened until 1920 but latterly the more important, was situated 860ft above sea level on the higher part of Christow Common, and a 462-yard self-acting incline brought the tubs from Summit Quarry down to the 550ft level, a short distance to the east of the crushing plant. The tubs were hauled by horses over this distance and the stone was then tipped directly into the top of the crushing plant. The Lower Quarry (the original quarry of 1914) was located at the 550ft level immediately west of the crushing plant. The rockbreakers and screens of the plant deposited the stone in different bins according to size; these had doors through which the stone was dropped directly into the buckets of the aerial ropeway.

The plant at Christow station was much expanded over the years. Originally there was only a granulating plant and bins for the various sizes of chippings, with overhead hoppers for loading trucks in the sidings. In 1923 the plant was much enlarged to a capacity of 90,000 tons per annum (more than was ever required).

Around 1925 a tarmacadam plant was built and around 1929 a concrete plant for the manufacture of concrete kerbs, slabs etc.

The main sales were to Local Authorities for roadstone, in the Devon, Dorset, Somerset, Wilts, Hants, and South West London areas. The GWR took some stone as ballast but considered the Scatter Rock stone to be of unnecessarily high quality (and high price) as a rule. John Dickson discovered on one visit to Christow that the stone taken by the GWR was all invoiced to Newton Abbot only, even though much was actually for more distant destinations; the station staff could only say that this was done under instructions from above (it was of course a ploy by the GWR to reduce the 'rebates' payable to the ER).

Output declined from the 1920s, particularly in the early 1930s, and, with road competition for local hauls, the rail traffic was down to very low levels by the late '30s. Changes in the specification for roadstone had gone against the Scatter Rock stone; although it was extremely hard, it had a tendency to polish excessively with heavy traffic. The quarry's fortunes improved in 1939–45, however, as competition from seaborne stone declined.

The Scatter Rock company continued to be an independent concern until 1938. John Dickson resigned as a Director around 1923 in view of his age, and died shortly after this. Tiplady also died around 1929. The Chairman in later years was General Ralphe M. Yorke, the brother of V.W. Yorke, the former Exeter Railway Chairman. In 1938 the company was taken over by Roads Reconstruction (1934) Ltd and the Board replaced by their nominees.

The quarry closed in 1950 and the plant was dismantled over the next few years. The company was retained in existence until 1977 although it was only for paper purposes latterly. The Private Siding Agreement at Christow was not terminated until 1957, as the sidings were used by the Bridford Barytes Mine's traffic in the 1952–57 period (see next section).

A close view of the granulating plant and loading hoppers at the station in their original form (the hoppers were the timber structure immediately to the right of the signal post). The train being shunted here was on the Down Main and the Scatter Rock sidings are hidden behind. The use of the 'Toughest Stone on Record' slogan on the company's private owner wagons once brought complaints about advertising! The slogan was true enough — tests on the Scatter Rock stone had proved it the hardest in the country — but the hardness of the stone was really a handicap to the quarry's operations, as it meant excessive costs in crushing it. *Collection Dick Lystor*

This August 1949 view of the mine was taken to show the new 200-ton 'ore bin' installed that year in the middle of the conveyor system from the shaft (out of picture, immediately to the right of the 'screening tower' at the far end of the conveyor). Phil Tonkin, the mine manager, can be seen standing (with cap) in the bottom left of the picture. The tubways in the centre of the picture were used for tipping waste material from the shaft. The Christow station master's house is visible in the distance above the ore bin.

Cty. Leroy George

THE BRIDFORD BARYTES MINE

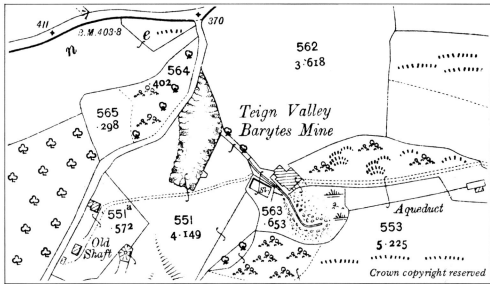

The mine in 1904. The opencast site was extended much further west after this date and was still used to some extent after 1930 to provide 'fill' for the underground workings. The road past the opencast site was declared unsafe by the County Surveyor in 1911 and the mine was obliged to pay for a road diversion, as shown in the map on page 230. The pre-1930 cart track to Teign House runs off to the right.

Barytes (Barium Sulphate, BaSo4) is a heavy whitish-grey to brown mineral found in association with lead and zinc lodes. It it used primarily in paints, as a 'filler' in paper manufacture, and to produce a high-density mud used in drilling for oil.

The first attempts at mining on the site later known as the Bridford Barytes Mine were in 1847–55.[4] The prospectors were looking for lead. They found very little lead but much barytes. At this date there was little demand from industry for barytes, so operations ceased until March 1870 when a new company, The Teign Valley Lead & Barytes Mining Co. Ltd, was formed to reopen the mine. There were small sales in 1870–72 but after that three years of inactivity until 1875 when mining began, on a larger scale, for barytes only. From this date the name 'Bridford Barytes Mine' was used. National demand for barytes was now increasing (total national production went up from 9,000 tons per annum in the 1870s to 25,000 tons in the 1890s and 37,000 tons in the 1900s).

The Secretary of the new company was John Oak Harris of Exeter, and Edward Ellis, the Exeter-based surveyor, was also much involved. As we saw in Chapter 8, they were both prime proponents of a railway link between Teign House and Exeter, Harris being the Secretary of the Provisional Committee of the ETV&CR in 1882/3. Matthew J. Dunsford became the Manager of the mine, with day-to-day running in the hands of Samuel Rundle (succeeded in 1893 by his son Joseph Rundle). Although a shaft had been sunk in 1852, the workings in the 1875–1927 period were all opencast (see 1904 25in map). There was a mill at the mine, but final processing to get the barytes to the purest possible colour (which was the determinant of price)

was carried on at a mill in Commercial Road, Exeter, near Exeter Quay, to which the entire output had to be carted, originally by road, at a cost of 8s–10s per ton. This cost cut the company out of many markets and Ellis estimated in 1878 that sales could be increased five-fold if a direct rail link could be provided to Exeter. After the Teign Valley Railway opened in 1882, it was used instead of road transport despite the fact that the rail journey from Teign House to Exeter was 32 miles; the rail rate was 2s 6d per ton although there was still a one-mile road journey from the mine to Teign House Siding to be added to the costs, plus another one-mile road journey from St David's to the Exeter mill. When the Exeter Railway eventually opened in 1903, reducing the rail journey to 8 miles, Dunsford was annoyed to find that the GWR would only reduce the rate to 1s 10d per ton — but the previous rate had, of course, been exceptionally favourable. Alphington Road station was now used instead of St David's as it was much closer to the mill. Despite the reduction in transport costs since the 1870s, they were still high by comparison with those of rival mines elsewhere, and were a factor in keeping production at Bridford down to the low figure of 1,000 tons per annum or so until the 1900s. In the 1914–18 war production was increased to 3,000 tons per annum as much barytes had been imported from Germany previously. To raise extra capital a new company, The Devonshire Baryta Company Ltd, was formed in 1917, and this name was used for trading purposes thereafter.

Demand became much more uncertain in the 1920s and the company found itself in difficulties and decided to seek a merger with a larger barytes company. In February 1927 approaches were made to the Malehurst Barytes Co. Ltd who were large producers in Shropshire

(Derbyshire and the North Pennines were the other main barytes areas). Malehurst had a consultants' report prepared and in September 1927 they took over the entire shareholding of the Devonshire Baryta Co. for £4,500. This resulted in drastic changes at Bridford where production and marketing methods had fallen behind the times. Lt. Col. J.V. Ramsden (1876–1952) was brought in as Manager from Shropshire, and P.J. Tonkin (also from Shropshire) replaced Rundle as 'Mine Manager' in day-to-day control. However, the name 'Devonshire Baryta Co.' was retained for trading purposes until 1950.

The Exeter mills, which were both antiquated and a prime cause of the company's excessive transport costs, were given up and a new processing plant provided at the mine itself (the old mill at the mine being removed and entirely new buildings erected). New land leases were taken to enable underground workings to begin on a large scale, the previous opencast workings having reached a depth of 90ft which was near the practical limit. A new shaft was sunk in 1929/30 and from this time all mining was underground. The original level was at 80ft, but 180ft, 280ft, and 380ft levels were introduced in the 1930s. By 1943 there were six miles of underground drives, in which hand-powered tub lines were used.

Sales shot up after 1927, thanks to the new owners' improved marketing and the gaining of large contracts including 160 tons per week to Bernard Laporte & Co. Ltd (paint manufacturers) of Luton from 1929, and 2,000 tons over two years to the Silicate Paint Co. of Charlton. The 1930s and 1940s were therefore a period of unprecedented success for the mine. The increased output required improved transport facilities, and in June 1930 the old railway line of the Devon Basalt & Granite Co. was purchased, the rails lifted, and the section between the mine and the main road at the Teign House Inn converted to a road, to replace the old cart track down to the main road, and enable more efficient lorry transport to Christow station. The road opened in October. The great majority of the output was still sent out from Christow by rail, now of course direct to the customer instead of to Exeter. Indeed from 1934, thanks to the collapse of the stone traffic, the barytes (which had been insignificant compared to the stone traffic up to 1930) was the Teign Valley branch's most important goods traffic in most years.

In 1948 another period of development began. The now aged Ramsden was replaced as Manager by Messrs John Taylor & Sons, a mining consultancy organisation. They began new drives to search for barytes at 500ft and 600ft levels, as the good sales of previous years had exhausted a large part of the available barytes at the existing levels.

In October 1950 the Malehurst Barytes Co. became a subsidiary of Laportes, and the Bridford mine traded under the Laporte name from this date. Another new Manager, Mr Stewart, was appointed, but he was killed by a rockfall in the mine in June 1954, an event which drew attention to the condition of the mine. C.F. Lloyd-Jones was appointed in Stewart's place. The positive thoughts of 1948–50 had now given way to a realisation

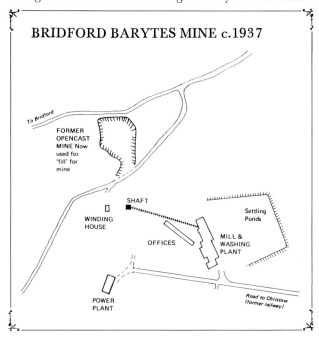

BRIDFORD BARYTES MINE c.1937

To Bridford

FORMER OPENCAST MINE Now used for 'fill' for mine

SHAFT

WINDING HOUSE

OFFICES

Settling Ponds

MILL & WASHING PLANT

POWER PLANT

Road to Christow (former railway)

SALES OF BRIDFORD BARYTES MINE
Tons per Annum 1928–47

Year	Tons
1928	1123
9	4921
1930	9680
1	12458
2	13175
3	15338
4	16988
5	16367
6	20128
7	18433
8	22267
9	21310
1940	23159
1	17083
2	14791
3	12601
4	12828
5	12511
6	12373
1947	11325

Source: Information from Devonshire Baryta Co. Ltd notes in Devon C.R.O. 4634M/B1–8.

The figures for barytes despatched by rail are not known exactly, but the great majority of the output was despatched by rail.

that barytes mining at Bridford was not likely to last much longer. Factors in this were:

1. the poor condition of the shaft and mine workings
2. the high sulphide content of the barytes in the 500ft and 600ft levels
3. the lack of any known large-scale reserves of good-quality barytes at Bridford
4. a recession in the demand for barytes
5. Laportes had other barytes mines elsewhere in the country which were better suited for development.

There were ideas of keeping Bridford open as a lead mine, but this never came to anything. The final decision to close was made in June 1958 and the last shift was on 31st July 1958. Forty men were made redundant (between 40 and 100 had been employed in the postwar years). This, of course, was just after the railway passenger service had been withdrawn and the Employment Exchange noted that there would be difficulties in finding alternative jobs because 'Bridford and Christow are so isolated'! The mine equipment was dismantled and the mine flooded. The site was sold off in 1966. Today the 'Catch Pits' (slurry ponds) are still to be seen, a conspicuous reminder of the valley's industrial past and now looking curiously out of place.

The barytes came out of the mine as a crumbly lumpy stone, with much lead mixed in with it. The lead, which was lighter than the barytes, was washed off at the 'washing tables' and ran down into the catch pits. As transported by rail, the barytes was a lumpy greyish sand. It was carried latterly in coal trucks and 2ft 3in of barytes in the bottom of the truck weighed a full 16 tons (a measuring-rod was used in practice, instead of weighing the trucks as ought to have been done). The loading bank by the up siding was used originally, but from 1952 to 1957 the Scatter Rock sidings on the down side were used. Then the loading bank was heightened with a ramp for lorries to drive up and tip directly into the wagons, and this served for the last year.

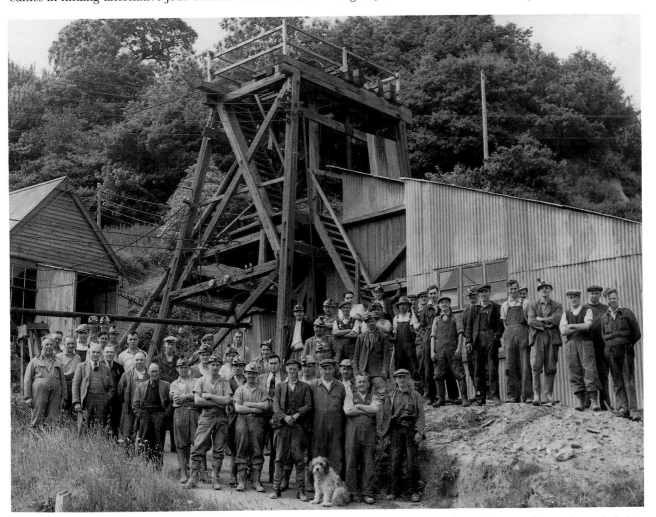

The mine's workforce photographed by the shaft, c.1950. Twenty-one of the 52 men were miners, the rest surface workers. The hoist house on the left powered the shaft lifting gear.   *Cty. Leroy George*

ALF HAYWOOD

Alf Haywood* was Wilf Cox's colleague as signalman at Christow from 1928 to 1936. Born in 1900, Alf joined the GWR on 25th May 1914 as a lad in the Receiving Office at Bridge Street, Exeter. After service in the Navy he came back as Parcels Porter at Teignmouth in 1919, and then went to Chard as Porter-Signalman in 1924. He came to the Teign Valley as signalman at Longdown in 1925, expecting a quick stay before finding promotion to a main line box. Alas, life was a little harder on the promotion front in the 1920s than it had been in the 1900s, and Alf found that all the vacancies were going to redundant men from the Welsh valleys with many years seniority. He had to stay at Longdown until 1928, cycling every day along the hilly road from Exeter. Christow was not a main line box with overtime, but it was a more sociable and interesting job than Longdown, and Alf was also able to get a cottage at Christow, just vacated by his predecessor A.W. Wonnacott who had got promotion to Exminster box.

Under Station master Cuddeford at Christow, Horace Baker was the middle-turn porter and Charlie Pullen and Jack Moorcraft the early/late porters. The late-turn porter finished at 7pm so the late-turn signalman had to go to the Booking Office to book any passengers there might be for the last trains. Other non-signalling functions which the Christow signalmen had to carry out were the balancing of the goods accounts at the end of the month (done in the box in the evenings), and working the Pump House by the Water Tank after the installation of the loco water facilities. This job was done at lunch time when there was an overlap in the signalmen's shifts; the little paraffin engine would be run for a while until enough water had been pumped to last the next 24 hours.

One of the highlights of Alf's time at Christow was the day he put the Up 'Cornish Riviera' in the Refuge Siding (before the 1943 lengthening of the loop, there was no other way of crossing such a train here). An Inspector from Swindon was in the box and was annoyed that he had not got a camera with him to photograph this event, as he said they would never believe him when he got back to Swindon and told them!

Eventually in 1936 Alf got a job at Bishopsteignton box. He moved on to Hackney around 1940, and then on to the Newton Abbot relief staff around 1945, in which capacity he worked every box from Cotfield to Kingswear. He retired in 1965.

* No relation of George Alfred Haywood, the first Christow Station master.

The overbridge at the south end of the platforms, built in 1896. Around 1932 (after the view at page 131, but before that at page 229 where there is a notice at the north end of the platforms prohibiting passengers crossing) these steps were provided as the passenger route to and from the down platform, in lieu of the flat crossing at the north end. Note the stop board for down goods trains to pick up brakes, and the 1943 layout of the loop points which, as at Trusham, enabled trains from opposite directions to run into the station simultaneously. The 1943 works at Christow are further illustrated at page 151. The 1924 up refuge siding and weighbridge (seen when new in the photograph at page ix) can be seen beyond the bridge.   *J. H. Moss*

Christow in the mid-1950s, before the former Scatter Rock sidings were taken out. Shortly before Scatter Rock Quarry closed in 1950, the company had altered the original 1914 loading hoppers to the form seen here, and demolished the 1925 tarmacadam plant.

J. H. Moss

CHRISTOW STATION MASTERS

July 1903	George Alfred Haywood
c. 1912	Albert William C. Boon
c. 1915	George F.D. Cuddeford (to Cullompton 1930)
1931	F.J. Channing (from Stoke Canon)
1933	H.A. Payne (from Dunster, to Watchet)
1934	C.J. Webber
1936	E.J. (Jack) Tucker (from Bampton)
c. 1950	Charlie Eugster
1954	Bernard Yandell (to Tiverton Jn 1958)

Bernard Yandell was Christow's last station master. His father had been Fred Court's mate in Watchet signal box c.1925, and, after Fred moved to Trusham, Bernard had, as a child, often been to stay with the Courts at Exmouth Cottages. He joined the railway himself as a junior clerk at Barnstaple in 1937, and then, after war service in North Africa and Italy, returned as a relief clerk and then (1950) as a clerk at Penzance. When the Christow SM's post came up, he put in for it because of his affection for the Valley, and he and his wife Freda had a very happy time here and were sad to have to leave in 1958. Subsequently, he was station master at Tiverton Junction, then moving to Plymouth where he was Area Manager from 1966 until his death in service in 1977.   *Cty. Freda Yandell*

DUNSFORD HALT

On leaving Christow, the character of the line changed noticeably. The climb to Longdown began immediately. The line said farewell to the River Teign at Leigh Cross and turned north to follow the Sowton Brook valley for a mile to Dunsford Halt, running alongside the Leigh Cross–Farrants Corner road, in many places on embankment shrouded in later years by trees.

Dunsford Halt was authorised by the GWR Traffic Committee on 27th October 1927 under the more honest name 'Farrants Corner Halt'. It was over 1½ miles from Dunsford village and was never likely to win back the Dunsford people, who had in years past had to walk even further to Longdown station to find public transport but who now had a good bus service passing through the village. The Halt opened on 16th January 1928 and consisted of a 100ft platform with sleeper facing and earth filling, a 12ft × 8ft lean-to shelter with corrugated iron walling and roof, two oil lamps (tended daily by a porter from Christow) and a concrete-post nameboard. It was reached by a fenced footpath across the corner of the field south of the line.

In postwar days the platform was reconstructed in blocks and the oil lamps removed, hurricane lamps brought on the trains daily being used instead.

Dunsford Halt is seen here in as-new condition on 4th April 1928, looking towards Exeter.

G. N. Southerden

The Halt on 9th November 1957, showing the later concrete blocks platform and the closure notice posted on the shelter. The 1 in 64 rising gradient is very evident.

P. W. Gray

The west end of the siding on 11th April 1927, with motor 77 approaching on an up service. The West Ground Frame was hidden behind the LMS truck. The stop board for down goods trains to stop to pin down brakes can just be made out to the right of the motor.

G. N. Southerden

LONGDOWN

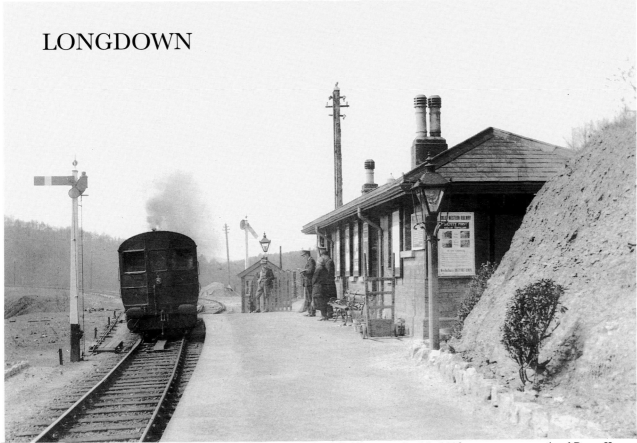

Motor No. 81 arriving from Christow in April 1924. The 1906 signal (left) was retained in 1916, now as a conventional Down Home. The earth bank behind the platform had clearly been sloped back, and this probably accounts for the newly-tipped soil evident at left. See page 106 for an earlier view.   *G. N. Southerden*

From Dunsford Halt the train ran through farmland for half a mile, before entering woodland on the approach to Culver tunnel. Longdown station itself was surrounded by woods. It was always the quietest station on the line, and even in the 'good' period before Longdown and Dunsford villages deserted the railway for the new buses in the mid-1920s, there would never be more than half-a-dozen people boarding a train. The 'busiest' day was Friday when the farmers or their wives would go into Exeter market. After 1930 the station was left only with those living in the immediate vicinity, and by the 1950s the passenger traffic was down to less than one ticket per day. Coal for Culver House had been the only regular goods traffic handled in the siding, although the Culver estate had sent out timber by rail in some years; the goods train was called upon to shunt at Longdown two or three times a week in the 1920s. At one time there was also a little 'smalls' traffic in the form of goods for the local farmers. But by the 1950s there was in practice no goods or parcels traffic of any kind (notwithstanding which, the station remained open for goods in theory until the end).

The original staffing was station master and porter. C. Kemp was the first station master but it would be unprofitable to relate the names of all subsequent holders of the post as the station was of such low grade that many of them only stayed a few months.[5] The station master's post was abolished in 1931 and the station put under the control of the St Thomas station master; thereafter two signalmen were employed (the station having become a Block Post in 1916, as described below). Longdown was a very lonely place to work; in later years the signalman was unlikely to see anybody except the ganger once a day and the train crews.

SIGNALLING

1903–1916: Longdown was not originally a Block Post. The connections to the siding were worked by two 2-lever open ground frames released by a key on the Electric Train Staffs. There were no signals. However, in March 1906 a down signal was added at Longdown, worked by a third lever added to the East Ground Frame. The instructions regarding this signal (1909 Appendix) were: 'When a Down Passenger train is

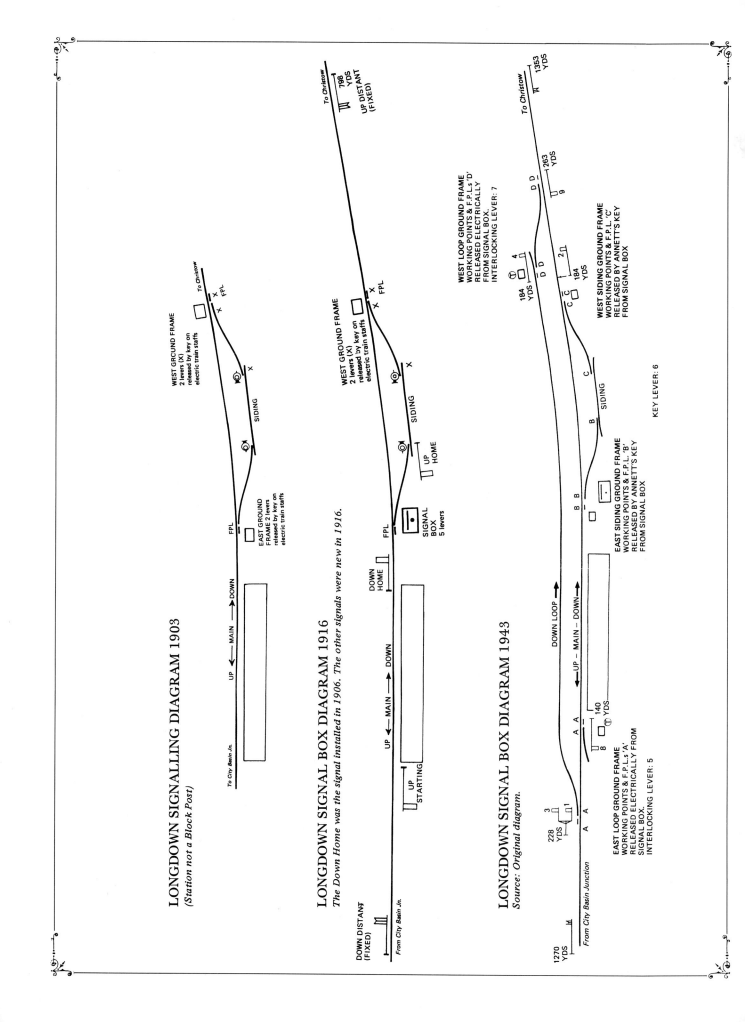

LONGDOWN SIGNALLING DIAGRAM 1903
(Station not a Block Post)

WEST GROUND FRAME
2 levers (X)
released by key on
electric train staffs

FPL

X
X
FPL

To Christow

SIDING

X

EAST GROUND
FRAME 2 levers
released by key on
electric train staffs

FPL

UP ← MAIN → DOWN

To City Basin Jn.

LONGDOWN SIGNAL BOX DIAGRAM 1916
The Down Home was the signal installed in 1906. The other signals were new in 1916.

WEST GROUND FRAME
2 levers (X)
released by key on
electric train staffs

X
X
FPL

To Christow

798
YDS
UP DISTANT
(FIXED)

SIDING

X

UP
HOME

FPL

SIGNAL
BOX
5 levers

DOWN
HOME

UP ← MAIN → DOWN

UP
STARTING

DOWN DISTANT
(FIXED)

1270
YDS

From City Basin Jn.

LONGDOWN SIGNAL BOX DIAGRAM 1943
Source: Original diagram.

1353
YDS

To Christow

D D
263
YDS
9

WEST LOOP GROUND FRAME
WORKING POINTS & F.P.Ls 'D'
RELEASED ELECTRICALLY
FROM SIGNAL BOX.
INTERLOCKING LEVER: 7

4
184
YDS
D D

2
184
YDS
C C

WEST SIDING GROUND FRAME
WORKING POINTS & F.P.L 'C'
RELEASED BY ANNETT'S KEY
FROM SIGNAL BOX

C

SIDING

B

DOWN LOOP

← UP – MAIN – DOWN →

B B

EAST SIDING GROUND FRAME
WORKING POINTS & F.P.L 'B'
RELEASED BY ANNETT'S KEY
FROM SIGNAL BOX

KEY LEVER: 6

A A
140
YDS

A A
3
228
YDS
1

EAST LOOP GROUND FRAME
WORKING POINTS & F.P.Ls 'A'
RELEASED ELECTRICALLY FROM
SIGNAL BOX.
INTERLOCKING LEVER: 5

8

1270
YDS

From City Basin Junction

approaching Longdown, the stop signal fixed at the Christow end of the platform must be placed at Danger. Before the train is allowed to depart, the Station Master or person in charge at Longdown must ask Christow on the telephone if the line is clear, and on receiving an assurance that the line is clear as far as the loop line facing points at Christow, the stop signal may be placed at All Right and the train allowed to proceed.' As a stop signal half-way through an ETS section, this signal contravened all known principles of block signalling — so one wonders if it was installed after some 'incident'? (Note the reference to the telephone, which if correct, means that a purely local telephone communication between these two stations must have been put in in 1906.)

1916–1943: In March 1914 a plan was approved to make Longdown station a Block Post, in order to increase the capacity of the line and to enable banking engines to return from here to Christow or Exeter instead of having to run through pointlessly to the other end of the line. Thanks to the war, this scheme was delayed, and not implemented until 1916.[6] A small

(Type 21) signal box was provided, but the Electric Train Staff instruments were installed in the Booking Office which remained the centre of the station's activities, the staff only going to the signal box when necessary to pull off the signals. The East Ground Frame was abolished, the points at this end of the siding now being worked directly from the signal box, but the West Ground Frame was unaffected.

1943–1954: As part of the 1943 schemes for upgrading the line as a diversionary route, Longdown was provided with a loop, brought into use on 19th September 1943. The 1916 signal box was retained (with a new frame) but the new loop was not worked from the box in any conventional way. Instead, ground frames were provided at each end of the loop, electrically released from the signal box. This was done to reduce the costs of the scheme but naturally resulted in a somewhat convoluted method of working which was not looked upon highly by the local signalmen. The loop was not used in normal service, all trains running via the platform line as before, except that one crossing a week was timetabled at Longdown for some years, in order to keep the equip-

Looking east from the signal box in April 1924. In its original form as seen in the view at page 106, the Longdown station building was a mirror image of Christow's, the rooms from this end being Station Master's Office, Booking Office, Booking Hall, Ladies, and Gents at the far end. However, probably in 1916 when the ETS instruments were put in, the Station Master's Office and Booking Office were (as was done at Christow also at this period) made into a single room and the nearer chimney moved to the end wall as seen here. These two rooms had been accessed by the same door on the platform side anyway.   *G. N. Southerden*

ment in order and the signalmen in practice. For this the whole work was done by the regular signalman, but when there were diversions over the line a relief signalman was sent to Longdown to work the ground frames and speed up operations.

All the signals, except the Up Starting, were replaced under the 1943 alterations. Additionally, two new ground frames were provided to work the East and West Siding connections, released by Annett's Key, the original West Ground Frame being abolished.

1954–1958: Occasional use during diversions could not really justify the retention of the loop in the postwar situation, and it was taken out of use on 20th July 1954 (and removed on 8th August). After this, Longdown had to 'Block Back' to Christow when a train was offered from City Basin Jn (and vice versa), a standard procedure for Electric Train Staff Block Posts with no loop (to avoid trains being absent-mindedly accepted from both directions at the same time!).

On 18th November 1956 the goods siding and its two ground frames were taken out of use, leaving only the plain single line and Nos 1, 2, 8 and 9 signals. There was no longer any need for Longdown to be a Block Post at all but, with line closure already in mind, it was not considered worthwhile to undertake the expense of abolishing it as such, and its two signalmen therefore continued in their post until 7th June 1958.

All goods trains stopped at Longdown station to put down brakes. In the line's heyday it was regularly necessary to bank up goods trains from Christow to Longdown. Originally this required a special engine to

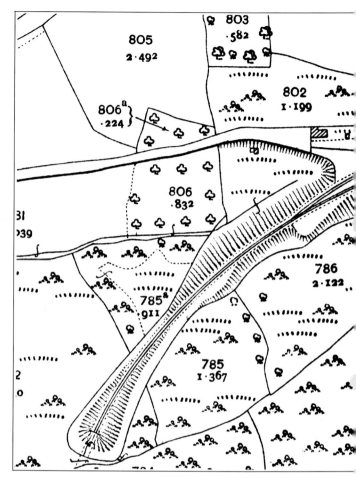

Views taken during the lifetime of the loop are very rare. The date here is 14th October 1950 and the loco 1440.   *W. A. Camwell*

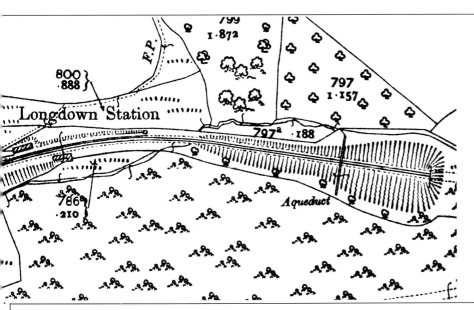

25-inch Ordnance Survey for 1904. The siding, as shown here and existing latterly, was actually laid-in in 1899 to serve as a 'loop' for construction trains. This is confirmed by exact chainage references given in contemporary material. It is not known what the large buildings (a) at the end of the approach road (b) on the down side opposite the platform, as shown on this map, were. They did not last long and one wonders if they were temporary structures left by the Dicksons. The only other structure latterly was the lamp hut at the Exeter end of the platform, which also appears on this map.

The signalman exchanging staffs with the driver of the 4.35 p.m. Exeter–Heathfield on 28th May 1958. The loco was No. 5536. The disused 1943 East Siding G.F. can be seen to the right of the signal box. Note that the track of the siding remained in situ after it had been disconnected in 1956. The last signalmen at Longdown were Dave Bright and Peter Davies (the latter actually a relief signalman, but he was at Longdown all the last seven months as the vacancy was not filled with closure pending). *Ronald A. Lumber*

The signal box was originally an all-timber structure; the brick base was added in 1943, and only rested on timbers. After closure, the box was bought by Teignmouth S&T Inspector, E. E. Dudman, and for some years served as a greenhouse at his home in Coombe Vale Road, Teignmouth. The 1943 works at Longdown are illustrated at pages 152/3, and other views of the signalling here will be found at pages 166 and 171.   *P. W. Gray*

Looking down from the end of the field footpath which provided the station's quickest link to the road to Longdown village (see 6in maps, page 280).

R. A. Lumber

Longdown village in 1959. The Lamb Inn was the calling point for the Devon General bus services, and the usual bus-stop-cum-timetable board can be seen on the pub wall. There were 15 buses a day to Exeter in the 1950s so it is no surprise that none of the inhabitants of Longdown ever travelled by train from their remotely-situated station.

Chapman collection, cty. Devon C.R.O.

be sent out from Exeter (cf. the 1908 Notice in Chapter 14), but in the 1920s and early '30s when the Exeter–Christow goods was running, this train was timetabled so that its loco was available at Christow to bank the Newton Abbot–Exeter goods to Longdown (cf. the 1931 Timetable in Chapter 14). With Longdown now a Block Post, it could return from there to Christow. The Trusham–Exeter evening goods was also often banked; this was done by the same loco, returning light to Christow after it had taken its own train back to Exeter. The Appendices provided that a banking engine might run through to City Basin Jn to act as extra braking power on the down grade, but in practice the banker of the Trusham train always came off at Longdown and waited there until the train cleared City Basin Jn. It was not necessary in normal service to bank down goods trains from City Basin Jn to Longdown, as the nature of the traffic was such that down trains consisted primarily of empties. However, when diversions were in force, banking might be needed in either direction. Frank Edworthy, signalman at Longdown in the 1940s, remembers one occasion during diversionary working when a down train got stuck in the wet Perridge Tunnel and could not be restarted even with the assistance of the loco of an up train; it took a third loco brought in as banker at the Exeter end before the train could be moved. Diverted passenger trains were normally double-headed rather than banked.

The forlorn-looking station in November 1957. In these last years the vegetation seemed to be closing in.   *P. W. Gray*

FRANK EDWORTHY

Frank Edworthy was signalman at Longdown 1944–49. He lived in Exeter and had been in a clerical job at St. David's until, at the age of 17, he was (like many young railway clerks at this date) offered a transfer to the operating side as an alternative to being called up. Like Alf Haywood before him, he had to cycle out to Longdown every day up the hilly road. The other signalmen at 1944 were Sid Pike, who had come back from retirement, and Reg Squires, three men being needed because of the line's 24hr wartime opening. On night shifts there was nothing to do, so one simply slept the night in the station office instead of at home! On one occasion one of the men made the mistake of going to sleep with the oil lamp still on, and found everything black when he woke up in the morning.

The station was comparatively busy (if one can use that word!) in 1944/5. There were a number of schoolchildren going in to Exeter. Col. Eden from Culver still used the trains and on one occasion asked for two 1st class returns to London; it was so many years since the station had sold a 1st class ticket that the first tickets in the rack were found to be covered in the dirt of time! Mr Emmett, the St. Thomas station master, used to pay a weekly visit to this remote part of his empire, and when diversions were on, Exeter District Inspector Vickery chose Longdown as the centre for 'exerting his authority'. Roses were still grown along the platform — at one time the Longdown signalmen had offered flowers for sale to passing passengers — but Frank spent most of his time reading 'to finish off my education'.

From Longdown Frank went to Exeter Yard box and then to St. Thomas where he had his father-in-law Wilf Cox as his mate. He left the area in 1956 for a job at Paddington Control Office.

Years after the station master was dispensed with, the Booking Office door at Longdown continued to bear this sign. In later years the few passengers would walk into the Booking Office itself to buy tickets (the minimal takings meant that there was no security problem!) and sit down in there to wait in inclement weather; the far end of the building was turned over to timber storage.   *P. W. Gray*

Ide station in 1921, looking west, the view emphasising the unnecessarily lengthy platform. The station staff would have had plenty of time to engage in horticultural operations, and the station had a well-cared-for look at this date. A new concrete 'Ide Halt' nameboard was provided in 1923.

L & GRP

IDE

After leaving Perridge tunnel, the trains ran through the woods of the Perridge Estate for a mile, before entering into a landscape of farmland and fields which characterised the majority of the last three miles of the line.

Ide station never produced the traffic that had been hoped of it, largely because the trains were too infre-

quent and the stations in Exeter too inconveniently sited. It was one of the stations which the GWR selected for closure in the darkest days of the First World War (closed 1st January 1917–5th May 1919). The original staff was a station master and one porter, but when an all-motor service was introduced in 1923, it was decid-

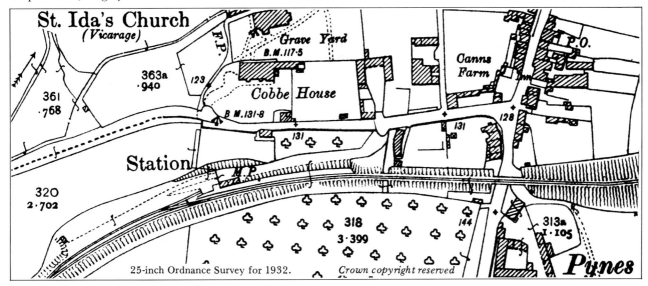

25-inch Ordnance Survey for 1932.   *Crown copyright reserved*

Steam railmotor No. 81 calling at Ide on the way to Heathfield in 1924. The station building was arranged the same way around as Christow's, i.e. with the Booking Office at the near end in this view.   *G. N. Southerden*

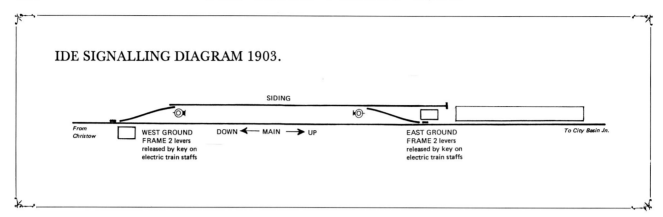

IDE SIGNALLING DIAGRAM 1903.

SIDING

From Christow

WEST GROUND
FRAME 2 levers
released by key on
electric train staffs

DOWN ← MAIN → UP

EAST GROUND
FRAME 2 levers
released by key on
electric train staffs

To City Basin Jn.

ed that Ide need not be staffed all day. As from 1st October 1923 the station master was abolished and the staffing reduced to the porter on early turn; the station was renamed 'Ide Halt' on this date.

A camping coach was introduced at Ide in 1935,[7] but did not reappear after 1939.

The always-modest goods traffic had fallen to very low levels by BR days, and with the passenger traffic down to about 10 per day, the station was destaffed as from 7th March 1955 and closed to goods traffic on the same date. The notice for this announced that 'Ide

Station will be reduced to an unstaffed Halt', apparently oblivious to the fact that it had been 'Ide Halt' for 32 years! The sidings were lifted shortly after this (the exact date of removal is unknown). The station was now lit by hurricane lamps brought in daily by train.

SIGNALLING
Ide was not a Block Post and there were no signals. The siding connections were worked by two 2-lever open ground frames released by a key on the Electric Train Staffs. The arrangements were never altered.

Long-serving Ide porter Bert Beer (he was known as 'Station Master Beer' in the village) with three ladies staying in the camping coach. 2nd July 1938.

Cty. Mrs. M. Piller

Steam railmotor No. 74 approaching Polehouse Lane bridge, east of Ide, on the 10.55 a.m. Exeter to Heathfield on 8th April 1925. The Exeter Railway's canyon-like cuttings are evident.

G. N. Southerden

Alphington Halt was but sixteen days old when this view was taken on 18th April 1928. Motor 76 (and trailer) was approaching on an up service but there were no passengers waiting. The signal was the City Basin Junction Distant. The oil lamps here were later replaced by hurricane lamps brought in on the trains daily, but (unlike the other halts on the line) Alphington Halt retained its timber-built platform until closure.

G. N. Southerden

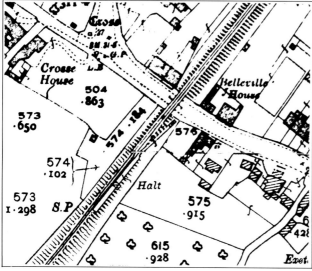

25-inch Ordnance Survey for 1932.   *Crown copyright reserved*

ALPHINGTON HALT

Alphington Halt, situated on the Exeter–Alphington main road on the outskirts of Alphington Village, was authorised by the GWR Traffic Committee on 16th February 1928 at an estimate of £210, and opened on 2nd April 1928. It was similar to the recently-opened Dunsford Halt, with a 100ft timber platform and a 12ft by 8ft lean-to shelter with corrugated iron walling and roof.

ALPHINGTON ROAD and CITY BASIN JUNCTION

Steam railmotor No. 82 on a down service and an up Teign Valley train at City Basin Junction on 10th September 1927.

G. N. Southerden

It is not intended here to give a full account of changes at City Basin Junction or of the traffics handled at Alphington Road Goods Depot in later years (both of which subjects belong more properly to a book on the history of the railways of Exeter) but only to note those aspects of the situation which affected the Teign Valley branch trains.

The origins of City Basin Jn signal box were discussed in Chapter 17, and the Ordnance Survey map of 1904 reproduced here shows the 1903 layout. Unfortunately, no signalling diagram survives from this period.

Picking Up and Setting Down posts for the Electric Train Staffs were provided by the Down and Up Branch lines, a necessity at this busy main line box. The first stretch of the branch was double line to enable a down branch train to wait clear of the main line if an up train was running late in the section from Christow/ Longdown, or to cross an up branch train that was being held here awaiting a path on the main line. In the former case the guard would have to go to the signal box after the train came to a stand at No. 8 signal, and wait there until the up train arrived and the staff was restored to the instrument and then taken out again for the down train, upon which he would take it to his driver and the train could proceed.

For many years the last train of the day (on most days) on the branch was the up Trusham Exeter goods, and an instruction in the Sectional Appendices provided that if this train was held at City Basin Jn awaiting a path on the main line, the guard was to take the Staff to the signal box himself (rather than the driver leaving it on the post). This was in order that Longdown box could close for the night.

Up to 1939, the connections to the Alphington Road Branch and the Exeter Railway Canal Branch were worked by a 4-lever ground frame released by a key on the Electric Train Staffs, not by the signal box direct. This was an inconvenient arrangement which had been installed by the GWR on the assumption that there

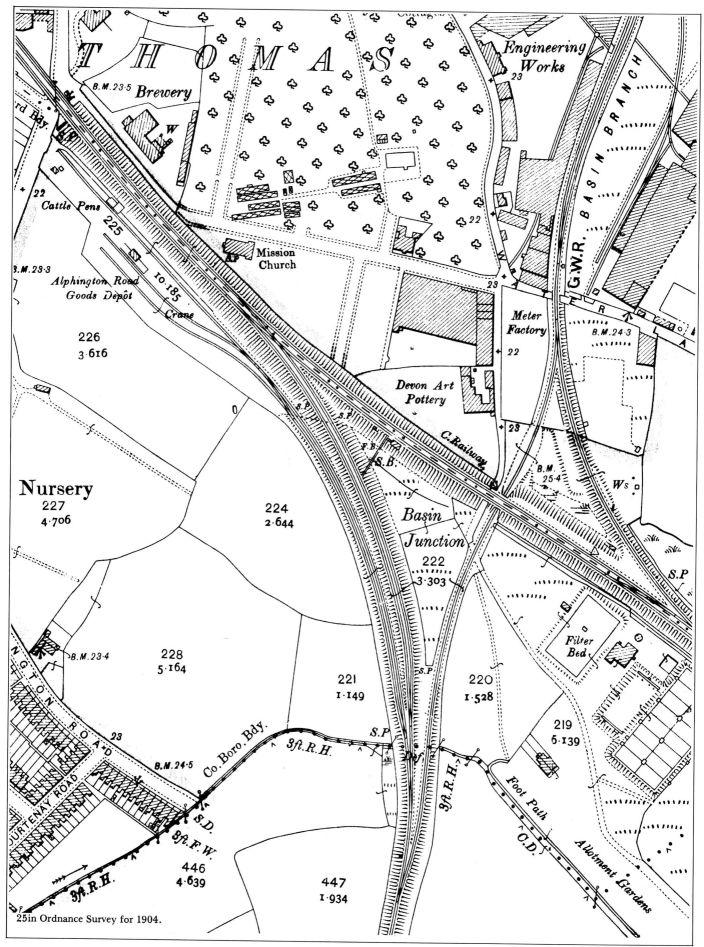

THOMAS

B.M.23.5 Brewery

Engineering
Works

23

G.W.R. BASIN BRANCH

rd Bdy.

22

Cattle Pens

225

B.M.23.3

Alphington Road
Goods Depôt

Io.185

Crane

226
3.616

Mission
Church

22

Meter
Factory

22

B.M.24.3

R

L

A

23

Devon Art
Pottery

C.Railway

S.P.

S.P.

23

B.M.
25.4

Ws

Nursery
227
4.706

224
2.644

F.B.

S.B.

Basin

Junction

222
3.303

S.P.

Filter
Bed

NGTON ROAD

B.M.23.4

228
5.164

23

221
1.149

S.P.

220
1.528

219
6.139

B.M.24.5

Co. Boro. Bdy.

3ft.R.H.

S.P.

S.P.

3ft.R.H.

S.D.

Foot Path

C.D.

COURTENAY ROAD

3ft.F.W.

446
4.639

447
1.934

Allotment Gardens

3ft.R.H.

25in Ordnance Survey for 1904.

would not be much traffic on these branches. When a train was booked to spend a lengthy period at Alphington Road and be crossed or passed by other branch trains whilst there, it was necessary for the guard to take the staff to the signal box when the train arrived (after he had set the points back to the normal position) so that the other train(s) could obtain a staff. Similarly, the guard would have to return to the signal box to obtain a staff again before the train could leave Alphington Road. The timetabling demanded some fast movement in this respect, for example the 1906 timetable shows an up goods booked to arrive in Alphington Road at 6.18pm and a down branch passenger leaving St Thomas at 6.20pm! The Exeter–Alphington Road–Exeter short workings run after 1919 still had to obtain the staff for the Longdown–City Basin Jn section in order to get into Alphington Rd. As noted in Chapter 14, a Sunday train was run from Exeter to Alphington Road for some years in the 1930s and to enable this to be done without having to open up

Photographs of City Basin Junction and Alphington Road are few and far between, and this 1903 view is the only one known of the 1903-39 City Basin Junction Ground Frame. The view was taken towards the junction with the Canal Branch on the right and the Alphington Road branch points by the City Basin Junction box Home signal. Immediately behind the photographer was the stop board at which all up branch goods trains had to stop to pick up brakes after the descent from Longdown.

An up goods, perhaps off the Teign Valley, about to pass over Alphington Road bridge in the 1920s. The City Basin Junction Down Home signals are seen behind the train, and there is a tantalising glimpse of Alphington Road goods yard behind its closed entrance gate.
G. N. Southerden

CITY BASIN JUNCTION SIGNAL BOX DIAGRAM, undated but showing the 1939 layout.

The sidings within Alphington Road yard are not shown in full. Trap points 16 and backing signal 14 were installed in 1921 to enable the Down Branch line to be used for refuging Down Main line goods trains.

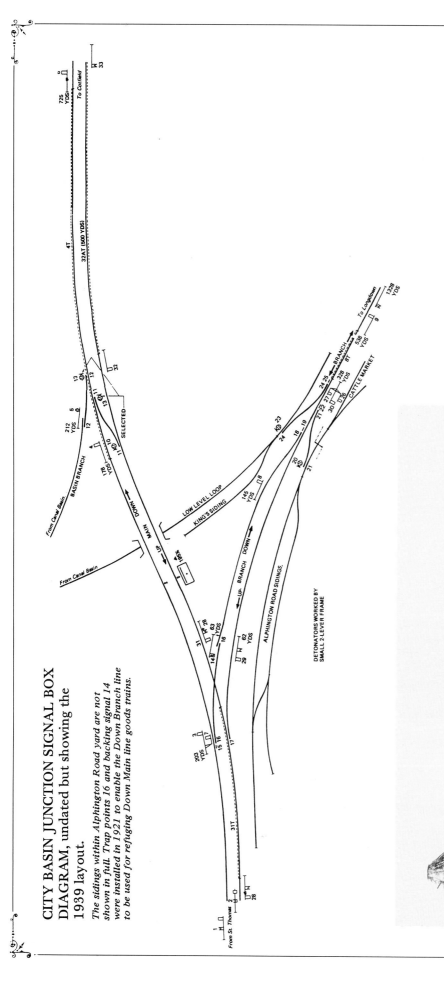

DETONATORS WORKED BY
SMALL 2-LEVER FRAME

City Basin Junction in transition in August 1962. This is the only known view of the 1902 signal box (right). The new BR box in the centre replaced it on 9th December 1962. The 'bridge' between the 1902 box and the branch, carried rodding and wires across the gap between the embankments, and enabled the signalman to walk to the staff posts. The large new warehouse of 1960 can be seen in the goods yard.   *Michael Hale*

We leave the branch at City Basin, and this view shows the fireman leaning out to deposit the staff on the 'cow's horn'. The lamp in the foreground lit the horn at night; the notice read 'Speed Not to Exceed 15 miles per hour'. The train was the 12.40 p.m. Newton Abbot–Exeter of 18th January 1958, when the branch was already under sentence of death. This is the only view of Alphington Road Goods Depot that has come to light. The leftmost and rightmost of the five sidings were added at a date unknown post-1904. In later decades the depot did have a significant coal traffic, as seen here, as the Exeter Railway's promoters had originally hoped for but been deprived of pre-1923 by GWR antipathy. *P. W. Gray*

Longdown box, the staff was always taken out at City Basin Jn on Saturday nights.

Alphington Road was a busy depot by the 1920s, and traffic increased further after 1923 when it became GWR-owned and the GWR no longer had an interest in discouraging its use. Further traffic at this location came from the opening of King's Asphalt Siding, on the previously hardly-used Canal Branch, in 1928. In 1939 yet another source of traffic was introduced when a new Cattle Market was opened by Exeter Corporation at Marsh Barton, with rail sidings accessed off the Alphington Road branch. It was therefore decided to abolish the ground frame and work the Alphington Road and Canal Branch points direct from City Basin Jn signal box, so that it would no longer be necessary for trains working these sidings to carry a staff. This was done on 19th October 1939 and the diagram shows the revised signalling brought into use at that time.

After 1939 there were no changes of significance until 9th December 1962 (4½ years after the closure of the branch beyond 0m 56ch), when the 1902 signal box was replaced by a new BR (WR) Type 37 box, the Teign Valley branch being reduced to siding status and the Alphington Road and Canal Branch connections converted to hand points. Subsequent changes are outside the scope of this book.

---

1. In fact, the Bay platform line had to be shortened a little at the stops end in 1927 to enable the Goods Shed to be moved back. In this shortened form there would certainly have been insufficient room for a motor to run round, had not the arrangements been altered.

2. Referred to as 'Granite Siding' in the 1905 Appendix, but the name 'Crockham Siding' was soon officially adopted.

3. 'Work done' report dated 29.11.56 for removal of Middle GF and connection, indicated that the job was done a few days earlier. The connection was removed (photographs confirm) but the ground frame was left disused *in situ*. The outer siding is still there in a summer 1957 photograph, but R.P. Walford in notes in the *Railway Observer* July 1958 refers to its removal 'in 1957'. Information (wrongly, however, stating 'sidings' removed) given to R.A. Cooke quotes a 1.9.57 date for removal. A BR plan updated to 1958 shows only one siding.

4. For further information on the history of the mine see C.J. Schmitz, *The Early Growth of the Devon Barytes Industry 1835–75*, Transactions of the Devon Association for the Advancement of Science Vol. 106 pp 59–76; and *The Development and Decline of the Devon Barytes Industry 1875–1958*, idem Vol. 109 pp 117–133.

5. Most of the holders of the post in the 1922-31 period will be found in the Table at page 142.

6. The exact date is not known. The frame for the signal box was sent out from Reading works on 13th May 1915, but the station does not appear as a Block Post in the Working Timetable until July 1916.

7. It was also planned to put a coach at Longdown at this date, but this was not done.

P. W. Gray

No. 5536 leaving Dunsford Halt with the 10.43 a.m. Heathfield on what should have been the line's last day, 1st March 1958.

CHAPTER NINETEEN
CLOSURE

No. 4553 departing from Ide on a down service in the last winter. Two-coach sets were used in this last timetable.　　*L. W. Folkard*

WHEN the Western Region began to consider seriously a passenger closure programme, the Teign Valley line was inevitably going to be near the head of the list. In the event it was preceded in Devon only by the Princetown branch (which closed in 1956).

The brief for the Transport Users' Consultative Committee was drawn up in May 1957 and given to the Parish Councils and the press at the same time. It was stated by BR that 193 journeys were made per average day (16 per train) and that an expenditure of £30,000 would be needed on bridge reconstruction and permanent way renewals if the line were to stay open (the line had been allowed to deteriorate between Exeter and Christow since the goods trains had ceased, and some sections were now restricted to 10–15mph — although there had also been some recent relaying).

'Careful consideration had been given to the possibility of making the passenger service remunerative by the introduction of lightweight diesel units', but this was not considered achievable, and no DMU ever appeared on the line.

The application was ill-timed insofar as post-Suez petrol rationing was still in force, followed by the long 1957 bus strike which saw Chudleigh and Longdown's annual takings doubled in the course of a few days. But these were temporary distractions and there was little doubt in anybody's mind that the closure proposal would be proceeded with. Debate concentrated on the replacement bus services required for Ashton and Trusham; initially it was proposed to run buses only between Leigh Cross and Chudleigh, connecting with existing services there, which St Thomas RDC regarded as inadequate. It was also claimed that some of the roads were too narrow for buses.

In January 1958 it was announced that the passenger service would cease as from 3rd March, and closure

263

Reverting for the moment to the summer 1957 timetable, a deserted (as usual) Chudleigh station with No. 5536 calling on the 10.45 a.m. Heathfield–Alphington Halt on Saturday, 22nd June 1957. The coaches, ex-Laira suburban auto-trailers, only had a short spell on the Teign Valley. The goods traffic at Chudleigh was also much reduced by early BR days and this enabled the introduction of a camping coach (although Chudleigh had also had one for a couple of summers before the war). *P. W. Gray*

Heathfield junction on 15th February 1958, with the 10.5 a.m. Paignton–Moretonhampstead departing behind No. 1466, and No. 5536 waiting in the Bay with the 10.43 a.m. to Exeter. *P. W. Gray*

notices were posted. However, due to continued opposition to the proposed replacement bus services, led by Christow Parish Council, BR was obliged in mid-February to announce a postponement of the closure so that the matter could be considered again by the TUCC at its next meeting on 14th March.

Finally, on 12th May 1958 it was announced that closure was to be as from Monday 9th June, and this time it was not to be evaded. The last trains therefore ran on Saturday 7th June, with the usual crowded scenes as the day wore on. The last train, the 9.30pm from St David's, left 18 minutes late after 'Auld Lang Syne' had been

With less than two weeks to go before closure, No. 3606 is seen here at Newton on the 4.35 p.m. up on Tuesday, 27th May 1958. No. 4980 was on an up Cardiff train.
Ronald A. Lumber

The branch's last passenger timetable, from 16th September 1957 to 7th June 1958 WR timetable (the branch closed on the same date as the Summer 1958 timetable began). It will be noted that the prospective passenger is not actually able to tell from the book that the service has been improved with more of the trains now through to/from Newton Abbot (the 7.30 a.m., 12.45 p.m., 5.58 p.m. and 9.30 p.m. down, and the 7.30 a.m., 12.40 p.m., 4.35 p.m. and 6.15 p.m. up, all ran through). However, a 'use-it-or-lose-it' campaign was actually run at the start of this timetable, and succeeded in boosting loadings for a few weeks before the locals reverted to their normal habits. As the decision to withdraw the passenger service had been taken already, the campaign was somewhat pointless anyway!

All trains in this timetable were ordinary trains. Through workings to the Exe Valley, as booked in the WTT, were:

DOWN
9.25 a.m. is 8.10 a.m. Dulverton
5.58 p.m. is 5.20 p.m. Tiverton (to Newton Abbot)

UP
10.43 a.m. is through to Dulverton
12.40 p.m. is through (Newton Abbot) to Bampton
4.35 p.m. is through (Newton Abbot) to Dulverton

Being unadvertised, these could, of course, be altered if necessary.

Eric Youlden travelled regularly on the 5.58 p.m. in this last winter and confirms it arriving from Tiverton in Platform 3 at St. David's. He recalls: "The 'rush' amounted to about 10 passengers and all except myself had detrained by the time we left Christow. From here the guard, having notified the driver, would lean out at the stations and, on seeing no awaiting passengers, would flag the train off without stopping, the driver having slowed to about 10 mph – unofficial request stops!"

Table 88 **EXETER, CHRISTOW and HEATHFIELD**

WEEK DAYS ONLY (Second class only)

Miles		am	am	pm	pm	pm	pm S
	Exeter (St. David's) .. dep	**7 30**	**9 25**	**12 45**	**4 35**	**5 58**	**9 30**
¾	" (St. Thomas)	**7 33**	**9 28**	**12 48**	**4 38**	**6 1**	**9 33**
2	Alphington Halt	7 38	9 33	12 53	4 43	6 6	9 38
3¼	Ide Halt	7 43	9 38	12 58	4 48	6 11	9 43
6	Longdown	7 51	9 47	1 6	4 56	6 19	9 52
7¼	Dunsford Halt........	7 55	9 51	1 10	5 0	6 23	9 56
9¼	Christow	8 3	9 58	1 17	5 7	6 38	10 1
10¾	Ashton	8 8	10 4	1 23	5 12	6 44	10 6
12¾	Trusham	8 14	10 10	1 29	5 18	6 50	1012
14¾	Chudleigh........	8 19	10 15	1 34	5 23	6 55	1017
16	Chudleigh Knighton Halt..	8 23	10 19	1 38	5 27	6 59	1021
17	**Heathfield** .... arr	**8 28**	**10 24**	**1 43**	**5 32**	**7 4**	**1026**
20¾	**90** Newton Abbot .. arr	8 38	10 50	1 55	5 42	7 14	1035

Miles		am	am	pm	pm	pm	pm S
	90 Newton Abbot .. dep	7 30	10 30	12 40	4 35	6 5	8 0
—	**Heathfield** .... dep	**7 40**	**10 43**	**12 49**	**4 44**	**6 15**	**8 9**
1	Chudleigh Knighton Halt..	7 44	10 47	12 53	4 48	6 19	8 13
2¼	Chudleigh........	7 48	10 51	12 57	4 52	6 23	8 17
4¼	Trusham	7 53	10 56	1 2	4 57	6 28	8 22
6¼	Ashton	7 58	11 1	1 7	5 2	6 33	8 27
7¾	Christow	8 4	11 8	1 16	5 8	6 40	8 32
9¾	Dunsford Halt........	8 10	11 14	1 23	5 15	6 45	8 40
11	Longdown	8 15	11 19	1 28	5 20	6 50	8 45
13¾	Ide Halt	8 22	11 26	1 35	5 27	6 57	8 52
15	Alphington Halt	8 26	11 30	1 39	5 31	7 1	8 56
16¼	**Exeter** (St. Thomas)	**8 31**	**11 35**	**1 44**	**5 36**	**7 6**	**9 1**
17	" (St. David's).. arr	**8 35**	**11 41**	**1 48**	**5 40**	**7 10**	**9 5**

S Saturdays only

For OTHER TRAINS between Exeter (St. David's) and Exeter (St. Thomas), see Table 81

The usual last-day mixture of locals and railway enthusiasts at Heathfield. No. 5536 on the left had arrived with the 4.35 p.m. Exeter–Heathfield whilst No. 1427 (right) can be seen propelling the connecting 5.10 p.m. Moreton-hampstead–Newton Abbot out of the station.   *P. W. Gray*

TRAIN WORKINGS 7TH JUNE 1958
(The arrangements on this day were special)

UP

7.30am Newton Abbot–Exeter	5533	BSK 5239, SK 5034, LMS SO 8172 (3)
10.43am Heathfield–Dulverton	5536	BSK 5239, SK 5034, LMS SO 8172 (3)
12.40pm Newton Abbot–Bampton	1451	SK 5712, BSK 4758, SK 5165 (3)
4.35pm Newton Abbot–Exeter	5530	BSK 5985, SK 4862, LMS BCK 6668, LMS SK 2151, LMS CK 3708(5)
6.15pm Heathfield–Exeter	5536	SK 5712, BSK 4758, SK 5165 (3)
8.00pm Newton Abbot–Exeter	5533	SK 5077, BSK 5231, BSK 2196, CK 6214, SK 5713, BSK 2159 (6)

DOWN

7.30am Exeter–Newton Abbot	1451	SK 5712, BSK 4758, SK 5165 (3)
9.25am Exeter–Heathfield	5536	BSK 5239, SK 5034, LMS SO 8172 (3)
12.45pm Exeter–Newton Abbot	5530	BSK 5985, SK 4862, LMS BCK 6668, LMS SK 2151, LMS CK 3708 (5)
4.35pm Exeter (ex Bampton)– Heathfield	5536	SK 5712, BSK 4758, SK 5165 (3)
5.58pm Exeter–Newton Abbot	5533	SK 5077, BSK 5231 (2)
9.30pm Exeter–Newton Abbot	5533	SK 5077, BSK 5231, BSK 2196, CK 6214, SK 5713, BSK 2159 (6)

1451 with strengthened Exeter trainset worked 7.30am down, 12.40pm up to Bampton and back to Exeter St. David's, where 1451 replaced by 5536 on same train to work 4.35pm to Heathfield and 6.15pm return.

5530 with another Exeter trainset, strengthened with three LMS coaches, worked 12.45pm Exeter and 4.35pm Newton Abbot.

5533 with Newton Abbot trainset, strengthened with one LMS coach, worked 7.30am Newton Abbot to Exeter, where replaced by 5536 on same train to work 9.25am to Heathfield and 10.43am return.

5533 with a different trainset worked 5.58pm from Exeter. At Newton Abbot four coaches added for last trip, 8.0pm from Newton Abbot/9.30pm from Exeter.

Source: notes by R.P. Walford ■ *Railway Observer* July 1958.

sung by children and station staff on the platform and a wreath placed on the engine (5533). Driver George Russell and Fireman John Thompson, with two guards including W. Collecutt, who had been 44 years on the line, were in charge of the six-coach train and its 500 passengers. The stations and halts were unwontedly crowded with onlookers and the long train had to stop twice, to the accompaniment of singing and cheering. The longest stop was at Christow where the loco took water. A bugler provided music and the guards had great difficulty persuading people to rejoin the train. Eventually it left, to the explosion of fog signals, but Newton Abbot was not reached until 11.35pm, an hour late.

As from 9th June 1958, therefore, the line between Alphington (0m 56ch) and Christow (7m 61ch Exeter Railway mileage) was closed completely, and Alphington Halt, Ide, Longdown, and Dunsford Halt closed for all traffic. The section between City Basin Junction and 0m 56ch was retained to serve Alphington Road Goods depot and a new branch opened on 7th July 1958 to serve the Marsh Barton Industrial Estate. The subsequent history of this section will not be covered in this book; suffice it to say that Alphington Road Goods closed to public traffic in 1967 but part of the Marsh Barton line serving Pearce's scrapyard is still in use.

The line between Heathfield and Christow was retained for goods traffic. The existing pattern of the goods service was retained, i.e. one Newton Abbot–Christow train TThSO. The signal boxes at Trusham and Christow were abolished as block posts but retained as ground frames to work such points as remained in use (much of the layout at both stations was spiked out of use). The line was now worked on a 'One Engine In Steam' basis with the ground frames released by a key on the OEIS Heathfield–Christow train staff. The loop at Trusham was spiked out of use so that the train had to run to Christow every time to run round. At the time this decision was made, it was not unreasonable since the substantial barytes traffic at Christow was likely to make it necessary to run to Christow on every trip for traffic purposes. As it turned out, though, the barytes traffic ended altogether in summer 1958 with the closure of the Bridford Barytes Mine, leaving very little traffic at Christow, so that the train's need to run to Christow and back soon became seen as an act of folly. Had BR known that the barytes traffic was to end, one doubts if the Trusham–Christow section would have been retained at all in 1958.

One porter was retained at each of Chudleigh, Trusham, Ashton, and Christow stations to deal with goods and parcels (the parcels arriving by BR lorry). In fact there was very little for them to do, especially at Ashton and Christow. The Christow station master was

TIMETABLE JUNE–SEPTEMBER 1959		
	9.0am	10.55am
	Newton Abbot SO	Newton Abbot TThO
	K	K
Heathfield	9.10/9.20	11.27/1.0
Chudleigh	9.28/9.38	1.8/1.15
Trusham	R	R
Ashton	R	R
Christow	9.58	1.38
	SO	TThO
	K	K
Christow	10.30	2.05
Ashton	10.46	2.20
Trusham	10.54/11.20	2.28/3.10
Chudleigh	11.27/11.37	3.17/3.27
Heathfield	11.47/12.30	3.33/4.40
	to Newton Abbot	to Newton Abbot

abolished in June 1958 and the line put under the Heathfield station master (until January 1966, when the Newton Abbot Area Manager scheme was implemented).

Although the loss of the barytes traffic was a blow to the line, the stone traffic at Crockham was at better levels in the 1950s than it had been in the 1930s, and this gave the 'stump' a satisfactory traffic. 1959 Goods figures (statistics survive for this one year only) were:

	IN (Tons)	OUT (Tons)
Chudleigh	984	1,344
Trusham	3,650	14,882
Ashton	424	0
Christow	305	0

CLOSURE OF THE TRUSHAM–CHRISTOW SECTION (1961)

On 30th September and 1st October 1960, Devon was subjected to widespread flooding which damaged rail lines in a number of places. The line was cut between Ashton and Christow by the washing away of the embankment and, in view of the low traffic north of Trusham, it was decided not to repair it. After 1st October no train ran beyond Trusham and such goods traffic as there was for Ashton and Christow was taken by road. On 1st May 1961 these stations were officially closed to all traffic.

After the floods, stops were erected at 4m 29ch north of Trusham station, and the loop at Trusham returned to use with hand points (the ground frame, ex-signal box, being abolished). However, when the track was lifted on the Trusham–Christow section in summer 1963, the loop at Trusham was shortened and new stops erected at 4m 20ch half-way along the platform.

CLOSURE OF TRUSHAM STATION (1965)

Trusham station was, latterly, really only being used to run round trains, there being no run-round facility at Crockham Siding.

It was decided in 1965 that trains could be propelled from Heathfield, and on 10th February 1965 stops were erected at 3m 76ch immediately north of Crockham

The person-in-charge at Heathfield, Ossie Biddiscombe came to South Devon from Pontypridd where his father had been a Taff Vale man. After spells at Heathfield, Bovey and Teignbridge – where he was nearly drowned in the 1960 floods and only rescued by a passing tractor – he came back to Heathfield in the mid-'60s to run on his own the station where he had previously had a station master and several colleagues. In addition to the office work for the local goods traffic and assisting with shunting at Heathfield itself, the person-in-charge went with the train to Crockham and Bovey to open the crossing gates and generally assist the travelling shunter.   *cty. O. Biddiscombe*

Siding G.F., and the line beyond to 4m 20ch was taken out of use. It was officially closed on 5th April 1965 when Trusham station was officially closed to goods traffic. The track beyond 3m 76ch was lifted immediately.

On 14th June 1965 the Newton Abbot Freight Concentration Scheme came into operation. This meant the official withdrawal of the general goods facilities at Chudleigh, but as arrangements were made for the main traffic (gas oil tanks) to continue, it had little impact. Coal traffic also continued at Chudleigh.

CHANGES IN WORKING

After 1963 the train no longer appeared in the Working Timetable but ran untimetabled from Newton Abbot each morning to whichever locations on the Bovey or Trusham lines had traffic, often serving both lines on the same trip. On some days an additional trip was made in the afternoon, on a few days no train ran at all. Trains now ran without a guard, with a travelling shunter.

Heathfield signal box had been retained after the closure of the Moretonhampstead branch to passenger traffic in

The only known view of Chudleigh station's exterior is this June 1965 shot from the station yard entrance.   *J. P. Alsop*

Chudleigh (after the removal of the canopy) with oil tanks and coal trucks in the yard. The notice posted on the station building almost certainly announced the introduction of the Newton Abbot Freight Concentration Scheme in this same month.   *J. P. Alsop*

1959, with Absolute Block working retained between Newton Abbot East and Heathfield. However, on 12th October 1965 Heathfield box was abolished and the layout at Heathfield all turned over to hand points. The Newton Abbot East–Heathfield section was converted to Telephone Working under the control of the Newton Abbot East signalman, and the Heathfield–Crockham section to 'C2' working under the control of the person-in-charge at Heathfield, without train staff.

FINAL CLOSURE (1968)

The stone traffic at Crockham had still been substantial in the early 1960s. However, by 1966 it had largely gone over to road transport, and the train only rarely ventured beyond Chudleigh for the occasional load from the concrete works. Roads Reconstruction Ltd, the quarry owners, did not necessarily see this as a permanent drift away from the railway, but two circumstances conspired to put an end to the railway link at Crockham before this might have been expected.

Firstly, the sidings at Crockham had got into poor condition. In October 1966 there was a site meeting between Roads Reconstruction Ltd and the BR Engineers to try to agree estimates for restoring them, but BR failed to ever produce the estimates as promised. Nothing then happened until November 1967 when the Newton Abbot Permanent Way Supervisor put a stop on the further use of the sidings due to their condition. (In fact, at least one further train did run to Crockham after this date, to collect a bridge for BR from the Concrete Works). The initial reaction of Roads Reconstruction Ltd was still to seek to restore the sidings. But the second factor then came into play. This was the plan evolved by Devon County Council (as agents to the MoT) for an A38 Chudleigh Bypass using the railway trackbed for much of the way. It was claimed by the County that extra costs of £100,000 would be incurred if the railway line could not be closed (although it is difficult to see in retrospect why the new road could not have been built alongside the railway line throughout). The pressure from the County to release the trackbed put negative thoughts in the minds of BR management who convinced themselves that an alternative loading point might be established for the Crockham stone traffic somewhere else in the area. BR then put pressure on Roads Reconstruction Ltd during the November 1967 discussions, and made them 'tentatively accept' that the volume of traffic did not in all the circumstances justify a railway link at Crockham.

Meanwhile, 4th December 1967 had seen the end of the coal traffic at Chudleigh under the Exmouth Junction Coal Concentration Depot scheme, and, with the oil tanks also now ceased, this was the end of regular traffic on the line.

In February 1968 the County Council put further pressure on BR to come to a definite decision, and BR 'advised them to progress their planning on the basis that the line will be closed'. BR advised Roads Reconstruction Ltd of this decision on 7th February, promising 'all possible assistance' in providing alternative loading facilities in the area. The Private Siding Agreement was terminated as from 31st March 1968. No alternative loading facilities were ever provided.

The official closure date of the line between 0m 21ch and 3m 76ch was 1st July 1968. The track was lifted in 1969/70 and work on the new road begun. It opened on 27th June 1973.

The last section of line at Heathfield, to 0m 21ch, was left as headshunt for the Banana Siding established in 1961. This siding closed in 1975 but the remaining section of the branch was only lifted c1983.

Life went on, for a while, at Chudleigh Knighton Crossing house after 1958. Mrs. Edwards had retired in the early '50s and the job then passed officially to her daughter Eva. Mrs. Edwards died shortly after this and Eva and her newly acquired husband Alex (Sandy) Joiner took over the house. Here is Eva proudly displaying baby in 1960, with relatives from Leeds visiting. The keeper's job disappeared after the passenger closure, but Eva and Sandy bought the house from the railway and remained there until they were forced out around 1970 by the building of the new A38, which demolished the house and turned this formerly pleasant spot into concrete and noise. Nothing of the crossing cottage now remains, and few now realise that this was a place where people once lived at all. *Collection Cecil Edwards*

APPENDICES

A SUMMARY OF TEIGN VALLEY PASSENGER STOCK WORKING IN THE GWR PERIOD

by JOHN COPSEY

At the time of the opening of the line between Heathfield and Ashton and Teign House Siding, on 9th October 1882, 132 of the '517' class 0−4−2T engines were already in service, and it is likely that the engines operated the line from the outset, no doubt with the four- or six-wheel passenger stock that had been supplied. Certainly, by the mid-1890s, the class were working from Ashton shed, with No. 1468 recorded on the 5.35 p.m. Heathfield to Ashton on 28th October 1896, No. 524 on the 7.5 a.m. Ashton to Heathfield on 24th August 1897, and No. 1468 again on the 8.30 a.m. Heathfield to Ashton on 28th January 1898.

Allocation records show that the branch engine at Ashton throughout 1901 was '517' class No. 540, with Nos. 1468 from January to April 1902, and 1472 from April onwards. Although the class dominated services over the branch, they did not hold a monopoly, as '850' class 0−6−0ST No. 859 (a Cornish engine) was shown at Ashton during November 1902 whilst No. 1472 paid a brief visit to Newton. Nevertheless, the Branch Line Statement of that year indicates the sole use of '517s', with maximum goods loadings shown as 9 coal, 15 goods, 17 mixed (goods and empties) or 18 empties, though the number of vehicles 'normally run per train' is shown as just 6.

On 1st July 1903, the Exeter Railway's connection with the Teign Valley at Christow brought about new operating arrangements; once again, the '517s' were regularly utilised, and examples of workings in this period include No. 535 on the 1.12 p.m. Exeter to Heathfield on 2nd October 1905, and No. 520 on the 6.35 a.m. Exeter to Heathfield on 17th September 1907.

The local coach working programme for the summer of 1911 shows a variety of 4- and 6-wheel sets operating over the branch. As discussed in Chapter 14, three trains ran from Exeter to Christow daily in addition to the Heathfield trips. The arrangements, as taken from the coach programme and supplemental information, were as follows:

Engine & Van Third, Compo, Van Third (plus Third WFSO) — No. 1
Teign Valley Set
6.35 Exeter−Heathfield
8.33 Heathfield−Exeter
9.45 Exeter−Heathfield
12.22 Heathfield−Exeter
3/12 Exeter−Heathfield
6/20 Heathfield−Exeter

Engine & Van Third, Compo, Compo, Van Third — No. 2 Exe Valley
Set
7.40 Exeter−Christow
8.22 Christow−Dulverton
6/12 Exeter−Heathfield
9/20 Heathfield−Exeter

Engine & Brake Compo (8-wheel)
11.7 Exeter−Christow
11.50 Christow−Exeter

Engine & Van Third, Compo, Van Third — No. 2 Teign Valley Set
1/12 Exeter−Heathfield
3/18 Heathfield−Exeter

Engine & Van, Compo, Third — 'C' Set
7/20 Exeter−Christow
8/5 Christow−Exeter

NOTE: Times − 0.00 denotes a.m., 0/00 p.m.

The No. 2 Teign Valley and the No. 2 Exe Valley sets also ran to and from Dulverton, whilst the 'C' set (4- or 6-wheel) was rostered for an Exeter & Kingswear return trip before working the evening train to Christow.

In the early 1920s, recovery was under way from the war, with an Exeter steam railmotor operating on the line alongside the branch passenger sets, which were now formed of five 4-wheel vehicles daily. The two sets worked the majority of trains, including through working to and from the Exe Valley line. The operating arrangement for the summer of 1922 was:

Engine & Van Third, Third, Compo, Compo, Van Third − Teign
Valley Set
7.0 Exeter−Heathfield
8.30 Heathfield−Exeter
5/45 Exeter−Heathfield
7/20 Heathfield−Exeter
9/0 Exeter−Heathfield (SO)
10/10 Heathfield−Exeter (SO)

Engine & Van Third, Third, Compo, Compo, Van Third − Exe
Valley Set
9.5 Dulverton−Heathfield
12/57 Heathfield−Exeter

EXE SRM (with Third SO)
12/50 Exeter−Heathfield
3/40 Heathfield−Christow
4/12 Christow−Heathfield
5/45 Heathfield−Exeter

Once more, the Teign and Exe Valley sets worked through onto the other lines to afford the best utilisation of stock. Steam Railmotors Nos. 72 and 86 were allocated to Exeter during 1922, as were '517' class 0−4−2Ts Nos. 559, 832, 1431, 1433, 1439 and 1481. '1076' class 0−6−0Ts Nos. 737, 1148, 1244 and 1286 were available for goods services.

A considerable expansion in services took place during the 1920s, and the line became largely the preserve of steam railmotors, though with a gradual expansion of autocars. In this period, the line saw, each day, the greatest variety of passenger train types in its existence; the working arrangements for the winter of 1929/30 illustrate this:

EXE SRM [A]
7.0 Exeter−Heathfield (+ Trailer MWFO)
8.23 Heathfield−Exeter (+ Trailer MWFO)
10.55 Exeter−Heathfield (+ Trailer FSO)
1/0 Heathfield−Exeter (+ Trailer FSO)
2/45 Exeter−Chudleigh (+ Trailer)
3/52 Chudleigh−Christow (Empty + Trailer)
4/11 Christow−Heathfield (+ Trailer)
5/10 Heathfield−Exeter (+ Trailer)

EXE SRM [B]
9.25 Exeter−Heathfield (+ Trailer WFSO)
11.0 Heathfield−Exeter (+ Trailer WFSO)
12/55 Exeter−Heathfield (+ Trailer)
2/40 Heathfield−Newton Abbot (WSO)
3/0 Newton Abbot−Heathfield (WSO)
3/26 Heathfield−Exeter (+ Trailer)

EXE Auto [A] − 2 Trailers
9/40 Exeter−Heathfield*
10/44 Heathfield−Newton Abbot*
10/55 Newton Abbot−Exeter (via Dawlish)*

*Daily to 26th October 1929 and from 31st March 1930,
Saturdays only, 2nd November 1929 to 29th March 1930.

EXE Auto [B] − 2 Trailers
6/15 Exeter−Heathfield
7/40 Heathfield−Exeter

Engine & Trailer
7.20 Exeter−Christow
8.0 Christow−Exeter

Engine, Brake Third & Compo
4/18 Exeter−Christow
7/0 Christow−Exeter

NOTES
[ ]   Author's designation of unit only
MWFSO Designation of days operated (Mondays, Wednesdays,
         Fridays and Saturdays Only)

In all instances, the SRMs and auto-trains were involved with other services, mainly on the Tiverton and Dulverton lines. At this time, railmotors Nos. 72 and 97 were at Exeter, as were '517s' Nos. 205, 831, 847, 1162, 1164, 1165, 1431, 1433 and 1487.

During the autumn of 1932, Exeter shed received four of the new Collett '48XX' class 0—4—2Ts, eventually acquiring seven for its five daily auto turns upon the withdrawal of the SRMs.

In the winter of 1937/8, three of these auto units operated the six daily return trips from Exeter, and were joined on Thursdays and Saturdays by the Tiverton auto for a late-night run to Trusham and back:

EXE Auto & Trailer No. 158
7.0 Exeter—Heathfield
8.23 Heathfield—Exeter
10.55 Exeter—Heathfield
12/55 Heathfield—Exeter
2/45 Exeter—Trusham
3/45 Trusham—Chudleigh
3/53 Chudleigh—Christow (Empty)
4/12 Christow—Heathfield
5/15 Heathfield—Exeter

EXE Auto & Trailer No. 156
9.25 Exeter—Heathfield
11.0 Heathfield—Exeter
12/50 Exeter—Heathfield
2/25 Heathfield—Chudleigh (WSO)
2/35 Chudleigh—Heathfield (WSO)
2/40 Heathfield—Newton Abbot (WSO)
3/0 Newton Abbot—Heathfield (WSO)
3/26 Heathfield—Exeter

EXE Auto & Two Trailers
6/15 Exeter—Heathfield
8/5 Heathfield—Exeter

Tiverton Auto & Two Trailers
9/47 Exeter—Trusham (ThSO)
10/35 Trusham—Exeter (ThSO)

In January 1938, '48XX' class 0—4—2T Nos. 4805, 4819, 4827, 4835, 4851, 4868 and 4869 were allocated to Exeter.

In 1947, the '48XX' ('14XX') class engines were still dominant, although the 6.30 a.m. trip from Exeter to Trusham and back occasionally ran as non-auto; for example, the train was hauled by '45XX' class No. 4530 on Monday, 11th November 1946, and by '57XX' class 0—6—0PT No. 9646 on Friday, 26th September 1947. '14XX' class engines at Exeter in January 1947 and beyond were Nos. 1405, 1429 (Tiverton), 1435, 1440, 1449 and 1468 (Tiverton).

No. 4807, seen here at Exeter St. David's on 1st October 1932, had just been transferred from Swindon Works, one of a batch of five (Nos. 4805-09) to be allocated to Exeter and Tiverton Junction sheds in the autumn of that year. During 1935, No. 4807 was moved to Reading. Like the '517s' before them, Exeter's 48XXs saw service daily on the Teign Valley line, on the Exe Valley branch to Tiverton, onwards over the North Devon branch to Dulverton, between Tiverton and Tiverton Junction, and on main line turns as far north as Sampford-Peverell. In the late 1930s, seven engines of the class were allocated to Exeter shed to cover the five daily auto duties, though this allocation was reduced to six during the war years. The 48XXs remained on passenger services over the Teign Valley line to the end.
G. N. Southerden

SUMMARY OF ACTS
Also showing failed Bills (in italics)

Name of Act	Number	Date of Royal Assent	Main provisions
DEVON CENTRAL RAILWAYS			
Devon Central Railways Bill 1861	–	–	
TEIGN VALLEY RAILWAY			
Teign Valley Railway Act 1863	clix	13th July 1863	Authorisation of line Jews Bridge–Teign House, powers to July 1868, to be broad gauge.
Teign Valley Railway Bill 1864	–	–	
Teign Valley Railway Act 1865	cliv	29th June 1865	Additional capital. Agreements with SDR.
Teign Valley Railway Bill 1866	–	–	
Teign Valley Railway Act 1868	xcix	13th July 1868	Deviation in Chudleigh area. Extension of time to July 1870.
Teign Valley Railway Act 1870	cliii	1st August 1870	Extension of time to July 1871. Agreements re station at Jews Bridge.
Teign Valley Railway Act 1872	cxcv	10th August 1872	Extension of time to February 1874. Additional capital. Building of line to standard gauge if desired. Mineral Branches at Trusham.
Teign Valley Railway Bill 1873	–	–	
Teign Valley Railway Act 1874	lvi	30th June 1874	Extension of time to August 1877 (including mineral branches).
Teign Valley Railway (Extension) Act 1875	clxxxiii	2nd August 1875	Teign House–Crediton line (powers to August 1880) and additional capital for same. Agreements with SDR or LSWR.
Teign Valley Railway Act 1878	ccxix	8th August 1878	Extensions of time for Jews Bridge–Teign House section (including mineral branches) to December 1878, for Crediton line to August 1883 — Authorisation of Ashton level crossing.
Teign Valley Railway Bill 1879	–	–	
Teign Valley Railway Act 1880	cc	26th August 1880	Additional capital. Abandonment of Dunsford–Crediton section (and repeal of capital powers for same). Agreements with GWR.
Teign Valley Railway Act 1881	ccii	11th August 1881	Reconstruction of capital.
Teign Valley Railway Act 1882	xx	19th May 1882	Abandonment of Teign House–Dunsford section.
Teign Valley Railway Act 1884	cliii	14th July 1884	Additional debentures. Retrospective authorisation of Bovey Lane and Chudleigh Knighton level crossings.
EXETER & CHAGFORD RAILWAY			
Exeter & Chagford Railway Bill 1878	–	–	
EXETER, TEIGN VALLEY & CHAGFORD RAILWAY			
Exeter, Teign Valley & Chagford Railway Act 1883	ccv	20th August 1883	Authorisation of lines Teign House–Exeter, Alphington Road branch, Canal branch, Chagford branch & Lea Cross curve, powers to August 1888. Agreement with GWR.
Exeter, Teign Valley & Chagford Railway (Extension of Time) Act 1886	xxiii	25th Sept. 1886	Extension of time to August 1891.
Exeter, Teign Valley & Chagford Railway (Abandonment) Bill 1891	–	–	
Exeter, Teign Valley & Chagford Railway (Extension of Time) Act 1891	cxc	5th August 1891	Extension of time to August 1894. Additional capital.
Exeter, Teign Valley & Chagford Railway (Extension of Time) Act 1894	cxc	17th August 1894	Extension of time to August 1897.
Exeter Railway Act 1898	ccxix	12th August 1898	Abandonment of Chagford branch and Lea Cross curve. Extension of time for other lines to August 1901. Reduction of capital. Deviations at Culver and west of Ide. Change of company's name.
Exeter Railway Act 1903	xv	30th June 1903	Extension of time to August 1904. Additional debentures.

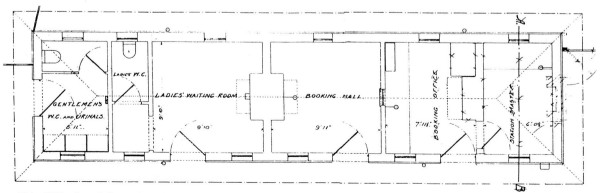

This GWR plan of the main building at Christow shows the original form, but with the alterations for the merging of the Booking Office and Station Master's Office added in pencil. The roof line is shown dashed, highlighting the considerable overhang of the roof on all sides.

A NOTE ON RESEARCH SOURCES

The number of original documents that need to be consulted in researching a book of this kind is so large that it becomes quite impracticable to follow the (theoretically very admirable) academic practice of annotated references citing a source for every statement made. Had this been done, an already large book would have had to be made many pages longer and could not have been produced at a viable price; in any case, the majority of readers would merely have been annoyed by a torrent of reference numbers on every page of the text. In many cases sources are referred to naturally in the text itself; in a few cases where doubt exists (and there are not, in fact, many significant 'problems' with this line) the situation is discussed in the text or a footnote. The major archive source documents are listed below, but many other documents of lesser importance were of course consulted. Any reader wishing for more information on a particular point is welcome to communicate with the author.

In this listing 'ER' is used throughout to save cumbrous references to 'ETV&CR/ER'.

PUBLIC RECORD OFFICE

RAIL 688/1–5	TVR Board Minutes, Cash Book, etc.
RAIL 203/1–7	ER Board and Committee Minutes.
Also GWR (RAIL 250ff), LSWR (RAIL 411), M&SDR (RAIL 501) and SDR (RAIL 631) Minutes as appropriate.	
RAIL 253/72	Press cuttings re M&SDR.
RAIL 253/515	GWR staffing 1934.
RAIL 253/399	GWR track layout diagrams.
RAIL 253/747 and 762	GWR papers re Absorption of ER and TVR companies 1923.
RAIL 264/422	GWR staff records.
RAIL 266/52	GWR station traffic figures.
RAIL 282/410–415, 420	GWR/BR (WR) signal box records.
RAIL 937	GWR Working Timetables, *passim*.
RAIL 1014/1	Memorial from Christow & District re train services 1904.
RAIL 1014/2	ER Prospectus 1898.
RAIL 1057/156	ER Solicitors' papers re 1898 Act.
RAIL 1057/157	ER Underwriting contracts 1894.
RAIL 1057/158	ER Correspondence with Ecclesiastical Commissioners.
RAIL 1057/159	ER Correspondence with GWR re sleepers.
RAIL 1057/160	ER, Gidley court case 1898–1904.
RAIL 1057/163	ER, St. Thomas RDC, roads.
RAIL 1057/164	ER complaints against GWR and court action.
RAIL 1057/165	ER complaint, published proceedings between GWR and ER.
RAIL 1057/166	ER correspondence with the Dicksons.
RAIL 1057/167	ER contract with the Dicksons 1893.
RAIL 1057/168	ER Engineer's Certificates 1894–1903.
RAIL 1057/169	ER Engineer's Reports 1896–1903.
RAIL 1057/170	ER v. GWR Court case 1903–5.
RAIL 1057/171	ER returns to Board of Trade 1904–22.
RAIL 1057/172	ER summary of traffic receipts 1903–24.
RAIL 1057/173	ER 1907 Scheme, creditors.
RAIL 1057/174	ER, proposed Fingle Glen Motor Track 1907.
RAIL 1057/175	ER, correspondence re bridge at Christow 1908–12.
RAIL 1057/177	ER, correspondence of R.J. Jenkins.
RAIL 1057/178	ER, miscellaneous correspondence.
RAIL 1057/181	ER, list of shareholders.
RAIL 1057/182	ER, correspondence re DB&G Co sidings at Christow 1908–9.
RAIL 1057/185	ER, agreement re Rev. Sheepshanks' advancing of money.
RAIL 1057/189–191	ER, correspondence re absorption 1920–24.
RAIL 1057/193–207	TVR, papers re Acts and Bills 1863–1882.
RAIL 1057/208	TVR, reports on line 1870–82.
RAIL 1057/209	TVR, share certificates etc. 1866–82.
RAIL 1057/212	TVR, arrears of shareholders.
RAIL 1057/215	TVR, Schemes 1867/1879.
RAIL 1057/217	TVR, parliamentary papers re Exeter & Chagford 1878.
RAIL 1057/219	TVR, correspondence re absorption 1920–23.
RAIL 1057/220	TVR, land at Chudleigh 1906–21.
RAIL 1057/222	TVR, Lord Haldon's mortgage 1880–2.
RAIL 1057/224	TVR, Ellis' court action 1879–84.
RAIL 1057/225	TVR, Toogood's court action 1866–81.
RAIL 1057/227	TVR, SDR correspondence 1866–9 re junction at Jews Bridge.
RAIL 1057/229	TVR, Receipts 1882–1906.
RAIL 1057/230	TVR, Traffic returns 1893–1914.
RAIL 1057/233	TVR, Teign House Siding traffic 1903.
RAIL 1057/239	TVR, Reports 1862, Walker's contract 1881, and miscellaneous.
RAIL 1057/240	TVR, Walker's contract 1877 and W.J. Browne's reports.
RAIL 1057/246	TVR, Cash Book.
RAIL 1110/133, 134	ER half-yearly reports.
RAIL 1110/456, 457	TVR half-yearly reports.
BT31 1480/4327	The Tram-Rail Co. of Great Britain Ltd.
BT31 18733/101702	The Devon Basalt & Granite Co. Ltd.
BT31 12956/105537	The Teign Valley Concrete Works Ltd. (also file at Companies House — 116520 Scatter Rock Macadams Ltd).
BT31 5647/39383	The Railway and Industrial Syndicate Ltd.
MT6 121/6, 352/3, 458/5, 982/2, 1169/9, 1192/2, 1317/13, 1377/5, 1897/12, 2009/10, 2298/3, 2462/8; also MT29 80, 82, 84, 87, 95	
	Board of Trade Inspection Reports.
Bradshaw's Manual (*passim*).	

DEVON COUNTY RECORD OFFICE

48/14/150/1–18	TVR legal papers 1863–82.
D3/Box 5/369	TVR papers 1864.
1259M/B1–92	TVR legal papers 1877–81.
1508M/Transport/Alphington Railway 1–3	ER/Earl of Devon land papers.
32502	Brent Ashburton & Heathfield Railway Book of Reference 1897.
4634M/B1–8	Records of the Devon Baryta Co. Ltd.
1896B/South 5/11	Papers re Crockham and Whetcombe quarries 1929/30.
1177 Z/Z1–4	Scatter Rock Macadams brochure and photographs.

Lt. Col. Ramsden's papers (re Bridford Barytes Mine).

Newspapers

Exeter Flying Post, all indexed items relevant.
Torquay Directory, Western Morning News, Western Times, Mid Devon Advertiser, Mid Devon Times, Devon Evening Express, and others (*passim*).

Ordnance Survey Maps

All relevant 25in plans 1st edition, 2nd edition, and later editions as available.

Parliamentary material

Bills, Acts, Deposited Plans, and (where existing) Parliamentary Committee evidence, for all the Acts/failed Bills listed in the Appendix here. (Devon County Record Office/House of Lords Record Office.)

GWR and BR(WR) original documents still held by the railway or in private collections

GWR Private Siding Agreements with Teign Valley Granite Co, Devon Basalt & Granite Co, Scatter Rock Macadams Ltd, Stoneycombe Basalt Ltd, J. & J. Dickson.
GWR Signal Alterations Notices.
GWR Exeter Division, Notice Shewing Arrangements for the Diversion of Through Trains to Alternative Routes in cases of Emergency, May 1941.
GWR Exeter Division, Emergency Arrangements for Opening the Teign Valley Branch Line for Diversion purposes, November 1945.
GWR Exeter Division, various notices re Diversions, January 1930.
Newton Abbot station master's office record book 1906–1974.
GWR 2-chain survey.
GWR/BR Engineer's bridge records.
GWR Sectional Appendices 1905, 1909, 1934, 1947.

The main articles in contemporary journals are:
Railway Magazine August 1903, 'The Exeter Railway'.
Contractors' Chronicle 29th June 1903, 'The Exeter Railway'.
Railway Magazine June 1929, 'The Teign Valley Branch of the GWR', G.N. Southerden.
Railway Observer July 1958 p190, Notes by R.P. Walford.

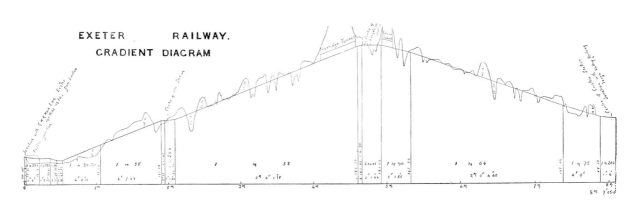

EXETER RAILWAY. GRADIENT DIAGRAM

Gradients on the Heathfield–Christow section were not of any great significance, but the Exeter Railway section was a very different kettle of fish, with the summit at Longdown approached by a four-mile climb at 1 in 56/1 in 58 from City Basin Junction (with only a brief respite of 1 in 200 through Ide station), and a three-mile climb at 1 in 75/1 in 64/1 in 90 from Christow. This heavily limited the loadings of goods trains (see the tabulation at page 170). The worse climb from the Exeter end explains why the maxima for down trains were less than those for up trains. For banking arrangement see page 251.

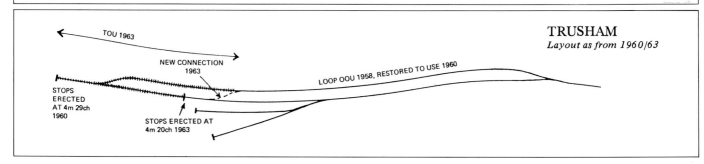

TRUSHAM
Layout as from 1960/63

TOU 1963

NEW CONNECTION 1963

LOOP OOU 1958, RESTORED TO USE 1960

STOPS ERECTED AT 4m 29ch 1960

STOPS ERECTED AT 4m 20ch 1963

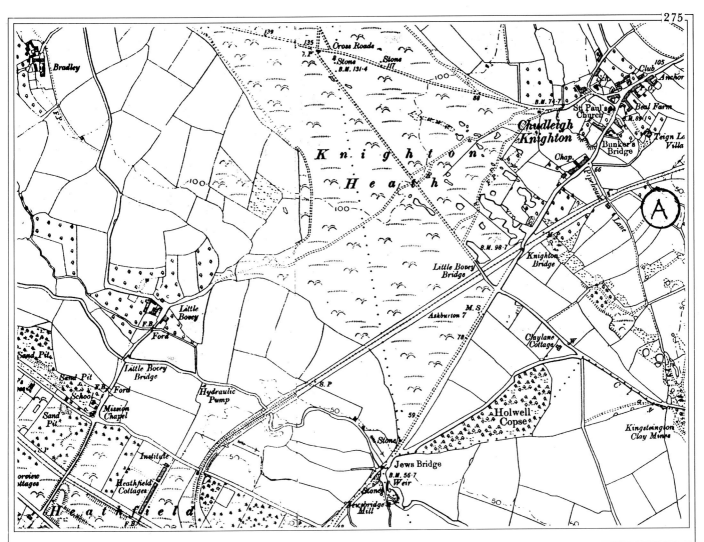

MAP OF THE TEIGN VALLEY LINE

Taken from Ordnance Survey for 1904.
Crown copyright reserved

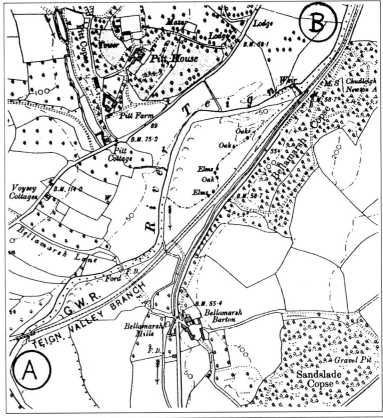

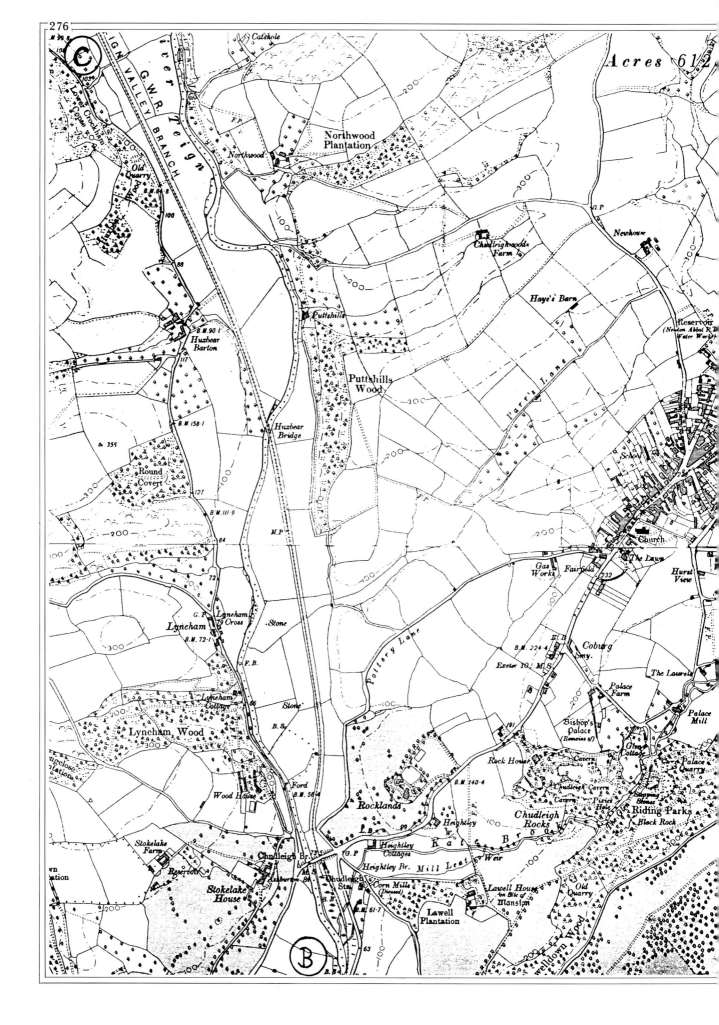

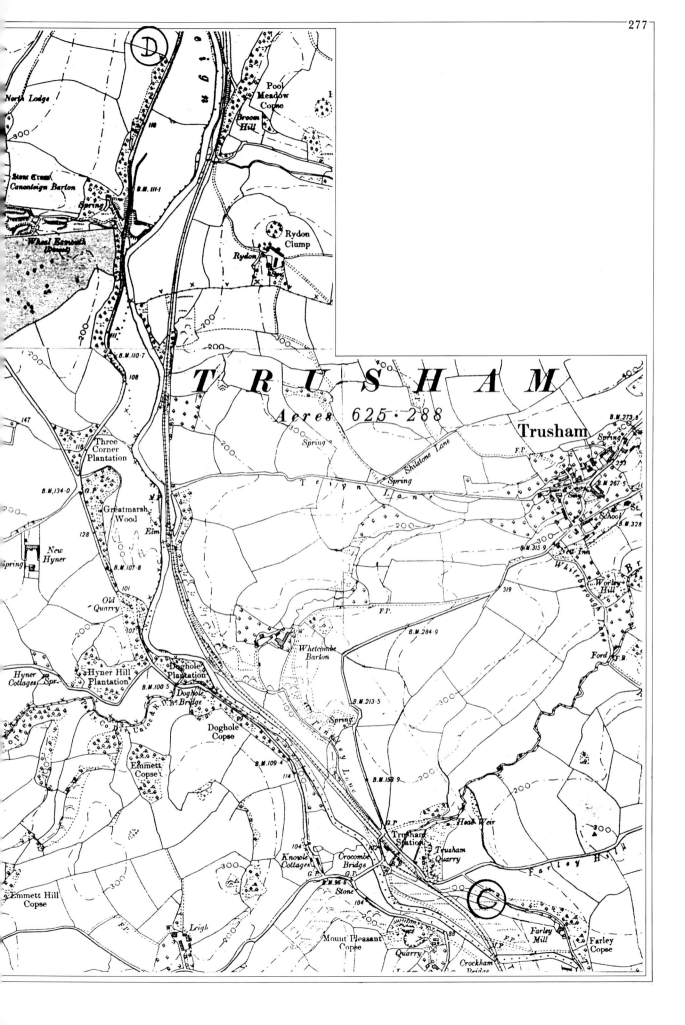

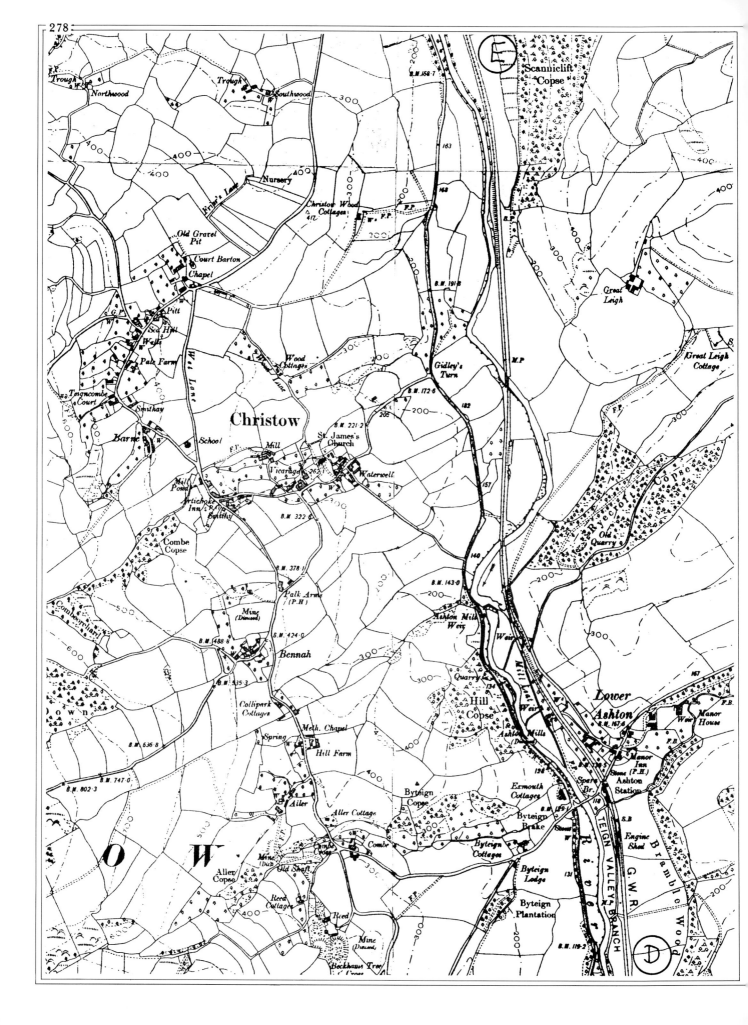

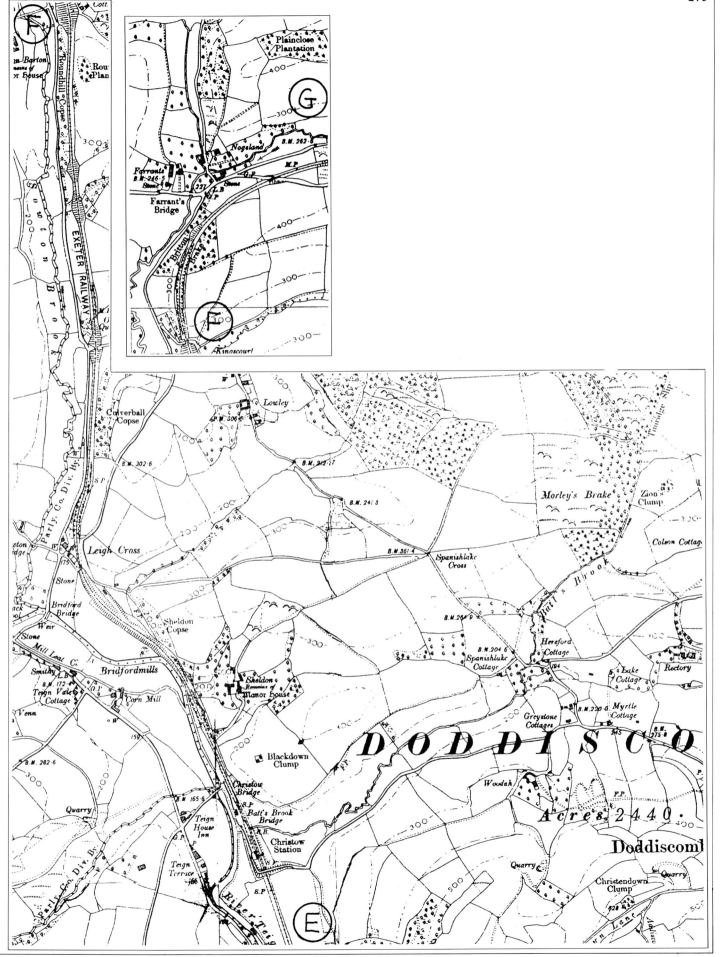

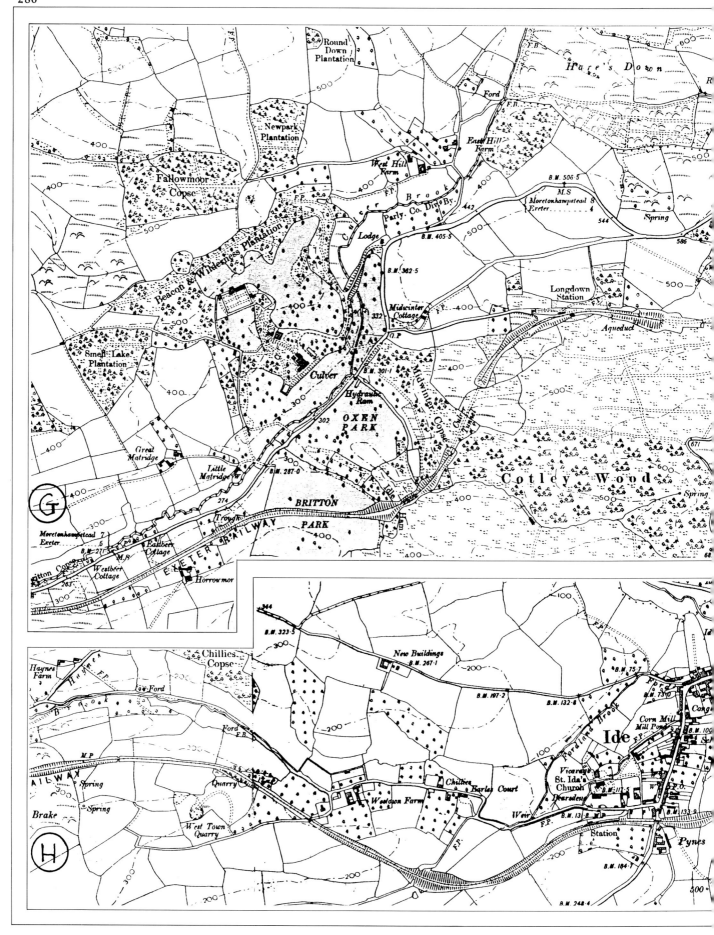

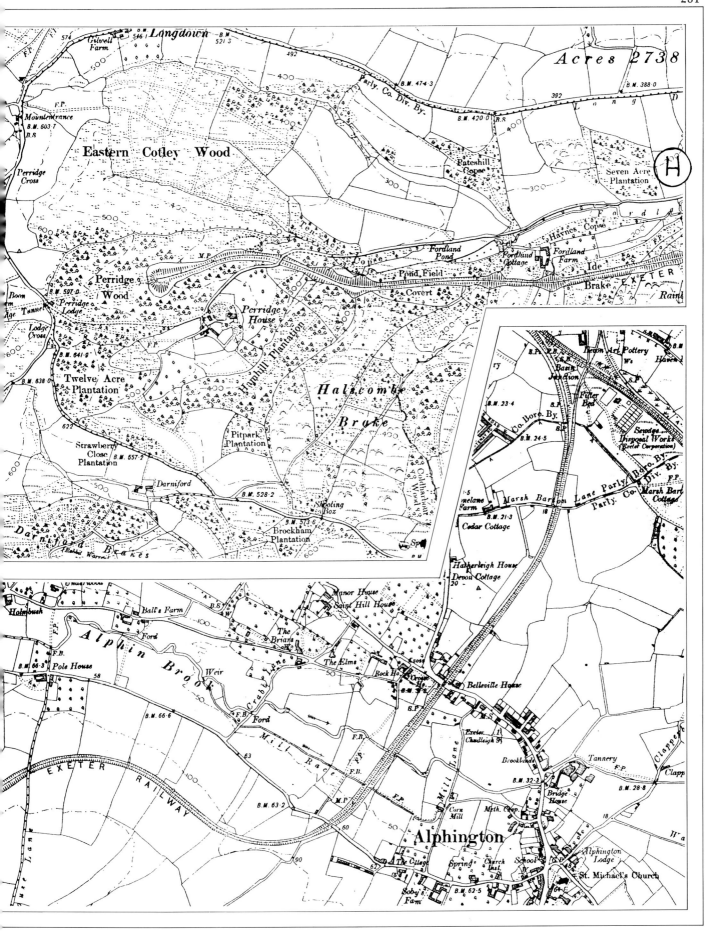

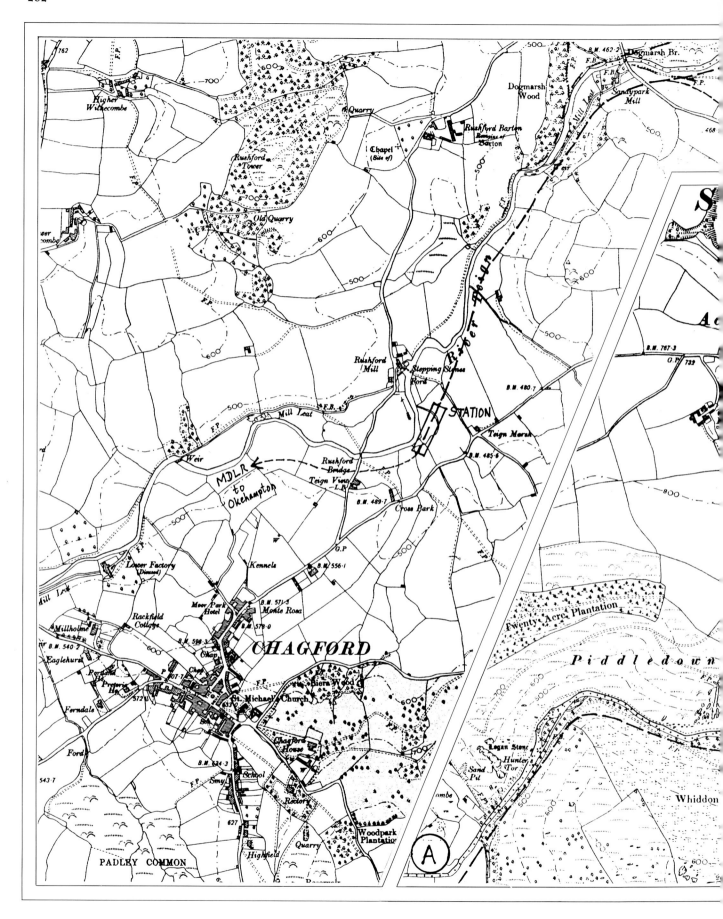

PROPOSED ROUTE OF THE
CHAGFORD BRANCH

*Taken from Ordnance Survey for 1904.
Crown copyright reserved*

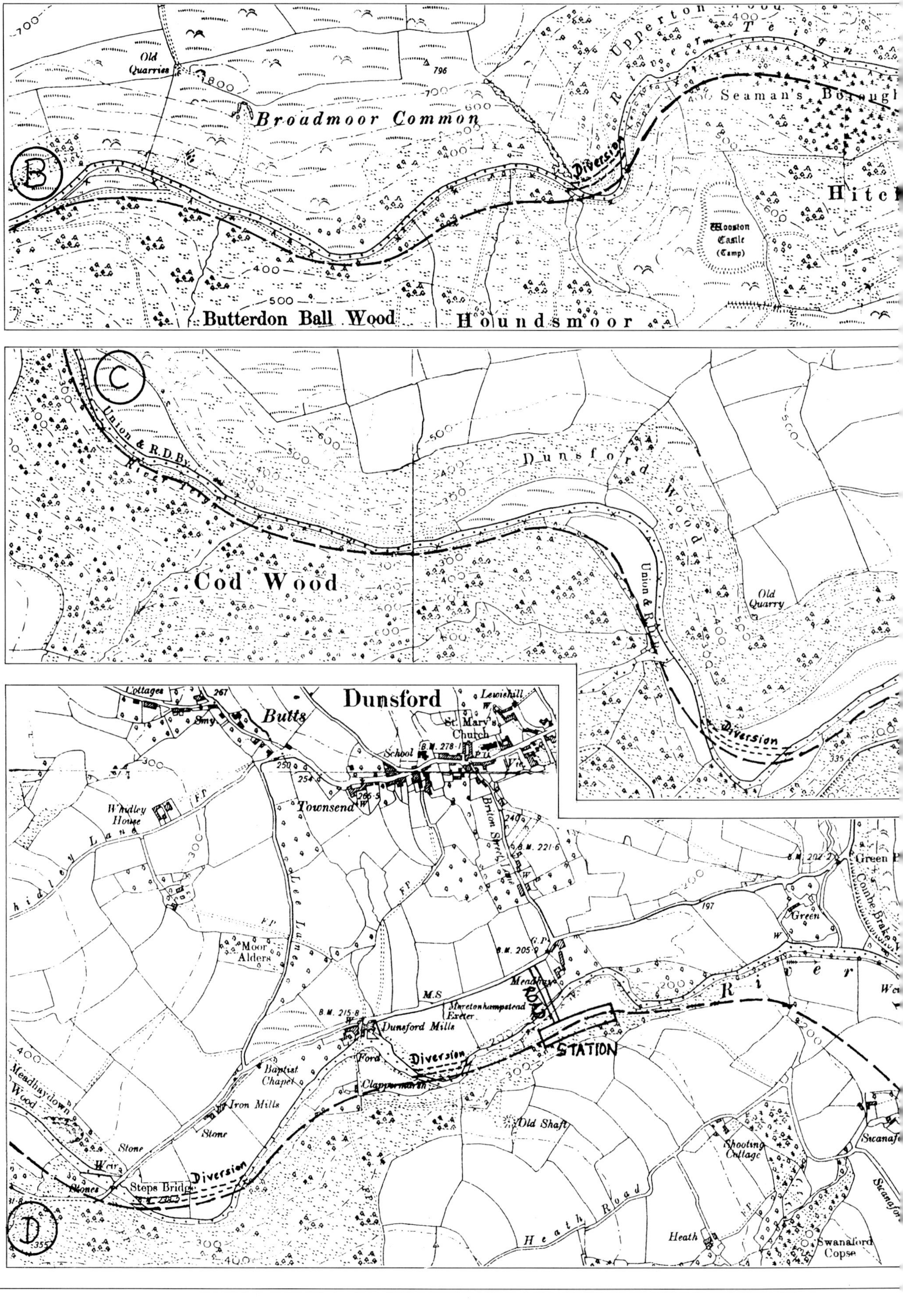

B

Broadmoor Common

Old Quarries

Upperton Wood

River Teign

Seaman's Borough

Diversion

Wooston Castle (Camp)

Hitch

Butterdon Ball Wood   **Houndsmoor**

C

Union & R.D.By

River Teign

Dunsford Wood

Cod Wood

Union & R

Old Quarry

Diversion

Dunsford

Cottages   267   Butts   Lewishill

Smy   St. Mary's Church

School   B.M. 278·1

Townsend   266·5   240

Whidley House   300   254

B.M. 221·6

FP

Brixton Shreys Lane

Lee Lane

B.M. 202·7   Green

Green   197

Combe Brake

Moor Alders   FP   B.M. 205·7

G.P

M.S.   Moretonhampstead   B.M. 205   Meadhay

B.M. 215·8   Exeter

Dunsford Mills   **STATION**   River   We

Ford   Diversion

Baptist Chapel   Clappermarsh

Meadhaydown Wood   Iron Mills   Old Shaft

Stone   Shooting Cottage   Swanafe

Stone   Stone   War

Stones   Steps Bridge   Diversion

D   Heath Road   Heath   Swanaford Copse

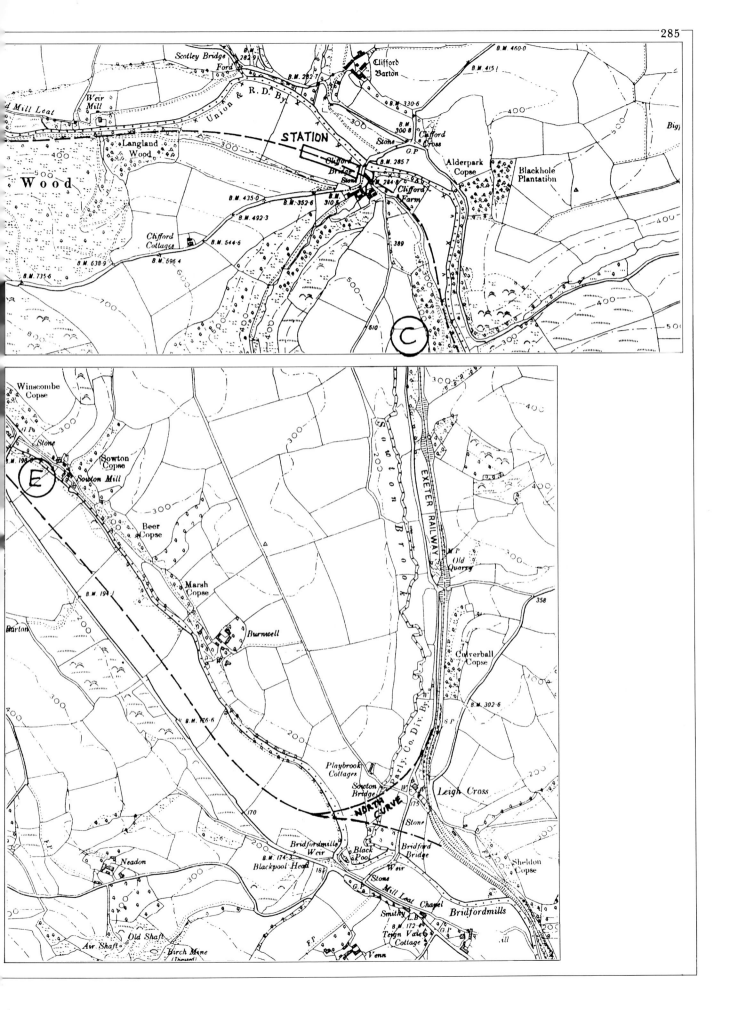

INDEX

From June 1957, auto working was restricted to the 12.50 p.m. Exeter and return on Saturdays, and the 4.25 p.m. Exeter and return daily. In this view, 1435 is shown leaving Perridge Tunnel with the 12.50 p.m. down on 22nd June 1957. The photograph was taken from Longdown Down Home signal post. Comparison with the picture on page 80 shows what an enormous growth of foliage there had been since the 1920s.

P. W. Gray